THE COMPLETE GUIDE
TO USING
Color
IN YOUR
GARDEN

THE COMPLETE GUIDE
TO USING
Color
IN YOUR
GARDEN

DAVID SQUIRE

Rodale Press, Emmaus, Pennsylvania

© Salamander Books Ltd., 1991
129-137 York Way,
London N7 9LG,
United Kingdom

This 1991 edition published by Rodale Press Inc., 33 East Minor Street, Emmaus, PA18098.

Distributed in the book trade by St. Martin's Press

2 4 6 8 10 9 7 5 3 1 hardcover

If you have any questions or comments concerning this book, please write to:

Rodale Press
Book Reader Service
33 East Minor Street
Emmaus, PA 18098

ISBN 0-87857-968-0

Library of Congress Cataloging-in-Publication Data

Squire, David, 1938–
The complete guide to using color in your garden: how to combine perennials, annuals, trees, and shrubs for a more beautiful landscape/David Squire.
p. cm
Includes bibliographical references and index.
ISBN 0-87857-968-0 hardcover
1. Color in gardening. I. Title.
SB454.3.C64S68   1991
712 — dc20   90-29086 CIP

CREDITS

Project Editor: Veronica Ross

Editor in Chief: William Gottlieb

Senior Managing Editor: Margaret Lydic Balitas

Senior Editor: Barbara W. Ellis

Editor: Sarah Price

Associate Editor: Paula Bakule

Assistant Editor: Nancy Ondra

Research Associate: Heidi Stonehill

Book design by Barry Savage and Rachael Stone

Cover design by Denise Mirabello
The majority of the photographs in this book were supplied by Eric Crichton and David Squire
(Photo credits are given at the back of the book.)
Illustrations by Nicky Kemball and Jane Pickering

Typeset by Barbican Print & Marketing Services Ltd.

Color separation by Melbourne Graphics Ltd. and P & W Graphics, Pte. Ltd.

Printed in Belgium by Proost International Book Production, Turnhout, Belgium

CONTENTS

Introduction

HOW TO USE THIS BOOK

Gardeners are like painters, but with a fresh canvas available to them only once a year. Borders are planned, plant and seed catalogs avidly searched and gleaned for more vibrant and long-lasting colors, and fellow gardeners consulted. But should you or your family have a predilection for certain colors, perhaps those that contrast with established plants in your garden or blend happily against certain painted walls, then you need practical and visual help at your elbow. A reliable book which clearly portrays the range of garden plants within a particular part of the color spectrum will be invaluable, and that is the purpose of this lavishly illustrated all-color book. *The Complete Guide to Using Color in Your Garden* comprises five chapters: *The Flower Border, Rock and Naturalized Gardens, Container Gardening, Walls and Trellises* and *Trees and Shrubs*. Within each of these chapters plants are grouped into several ranges of color. These are *Reds and Pinks, Blues and Purples, Golds and Yellows, Greens and Variegated* and *Whites, Grays and Silvers*. Green and variegated plants are superb as features on their own or as backgrounds for other plants, perhaps creating exciting color contrasts. This information enables single-color theme gardens to be created, as well as providing the 'know-how' to mix-and-match plants.

The introductory pages explain the nature of light and color, and how different colors are measured and defined, according to their hue, value and intensity. There is useful information on the use of color in the garden, why some colors are dominant and the effects of bright sunlight and the shadows of evening. Planning color with the aid of a *color-circle* is explained, and the concept of complementary and harmonizing colors is discussed.

The Complete Guide to Using Color in Your Garden reveals a wealth of plants for all parts of the garden: filling annual and herbaceous borders, adorning rock and naturalized gardens, bringing color to windowboxes, hanging baskets, tubs and other containers on patios and terraces, climbing walls and trellises or serving as a harmonious framework to knit together the various elements within a garden. Each plant is illustrated in full color and clearly described, including its botanical and common names, height and spread (in imperial and metric units), cultivation and propagation. Within each color range the plants are listed alphabetically according to their botanical names. At the base of each page there are valuable tips on using combinations of plants to create color-contrasts, subtle harmonies, focal points and interesting shapes and patterns. Detailed all-color border plans, showing how to arrange plants, enable everyone to create a colorful garden.

At the end of this book there are two comprehensive indexes. The first lists all common names, the second index is of botanical names, including synonyms (alternative names). The inclusion of the latter helps in the identification of plants botanists have recently re-classified and given new names, but which are frequently sold under their old, better-known names. This book is a valuable and informative addition to your gardening bookshelf, offering information which colorfully provides the 'know-how' that enables your garden to be transformed into a bright and colorful leisure area for the whole family.

Above: Cercis siliquastrum *This tree bears lovely rose-pink flowers during early summer. It is related to* Cercis canadensis, *which is native to North America.*

Above: Camassia quamash *This dramatic purple or blue flowered bulbous plant from North America brings color to a border during mid-summer.*

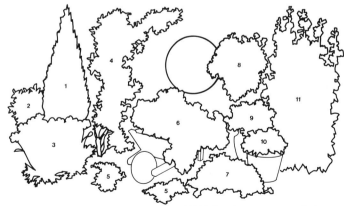

1 *Juniperus chinensis* 'Pyramidalis'
2 *Philadelphus coronarius* 'Aureus'
3 *Papaver orientale*
4 *Clematis* 'Nelly Moser'
5 *Thymus praecox arcticus*
6 *Lobelia erinus, Pelargonium x hortorum, Petunia x hybrida, Tagetes patula,* and *Tropaeolum majus.*

7 *Helianthemum nummularium* 'Cerise Queen'
8 *Lobelia erinus, Pelargonium x hortorum, Petunia x hybrida, Tagetes patula,* and *Tropaeolum majus.*
9 *Pelargoium x hortorum*
10 *Petunia x hybrida*
11 *Alcea rosea*

Introduction

SCIENCE OF COLOR

What are light and color?

The vast range of colors we see in our gardens and homes, with their near infinite subtleties of quality, shades of light as well as intensity, can be accurately measured. But what exactly are light and color? To state coldly and scientifically that they are forms of electromagnetic radiation clearly disregards their beauty, but, technically speaking, that is their nature.

Electromagnetic radiation comes from the sun, and its range is wide, from gamma rays to low-frequency radio waves. But only a very small part of this extensive spectrum is in the form of visible light, from wavelengths at around 0.0004mm when the color is deep violet, through blue, green, yellow, orange and red to deep red, with a wavelength of 0.0007mm.
See Diagram 1, below.

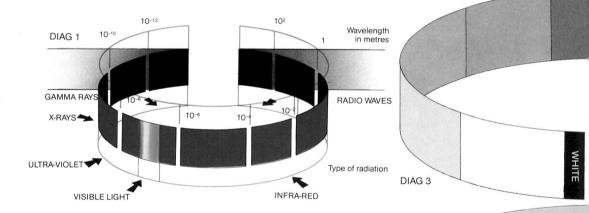

Defining color

Colors can be conceived as having three dimensions - hue, value and intensity.

Hue

This first dimension is the quality by which colors are basically distinguished from each other, such as yellow from red, green, blue or purple. For convenience, the colors so defined are those that are easily recognized, such as red, yellow, green, blue and violet. However, the Munsell System defines the principal hues as red, yellow, green, blue and purple, with intermediate ones as yellow-red, green-yellow, blue-green, purple-blue and red-purple. In reality these names do no more than define points in a continuous range of hues that form a transitional and continuous band of color. They are best conceived as a circle of pure color, containing no white, gray or black.

If a strip of paper with ten equal divisions is marked and colored with the five principal and five intermediate hues of the Munsell System and held in a circle the continuous range of hues and their relationship to each other can be seen.
See Diagram 2, top right.

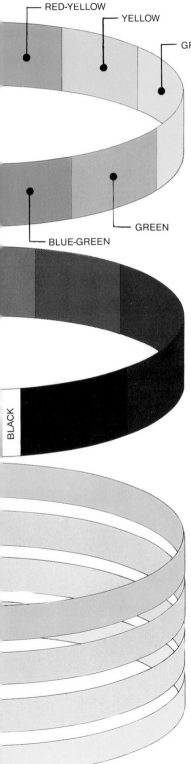

RED-YELLOW

YELLOW

GREEN-YELLOW

GREEN

BLUE-GREEN

BLACK

Value

This second dimension defines the quality by which a light color is distinguished from a dark one. This is most easily depicted on a scale using black and white as the extremes. When defining the lightness or darkness within a color, those with dark colors are called *shades,* while those that are light are *tints.*
See Diagram 3, center left.

Intensity

This third dimension is also known as *saturation purity* or *chroma.* It defines the strength or weakness of a color - its brightness or grayness. For instance, yellow can be highly saturated with color, or the pigments slowly decreased to a point when it becomes light gray. Other light colors will produce similar results, but dark hues such as red will become gray, and purple will become dark gray.
See Diagram 4, bottom left.

Color absorption

When sunlight falls upon colored surfaces a few of the colors present in the white light – which contains a mixture of all wavelengths of the visible spectrum – may be absorbed by the surface and not reflected. This process is known as *color absorption* and tends to make primary hues such as red, blue and yellow more dominant.

When white light falls on a white surface, most of the rays are reflected and the subject appears white. This, however, does not apply to other surfaces. Yellow surfaces absorb the blues, indigos and violets in white light, reflecting mainly yellow as well as some green, orange and red.

Reds, the most color saturated of all hues, absorb green and blue light but reflect red, while blue surfaces absorb red, orange and yellow rays, and scatter blue, together with green, indigo and violet.

This intensification of reds, blues and yellows tends to make them dominant. Fully saturated hues reflect no more than two of the primary colors, whereas pink, which is a desaturated red - a pastel shade - reflects all three of the primary colors but a greater amount of red.
See Diagram 5, below.

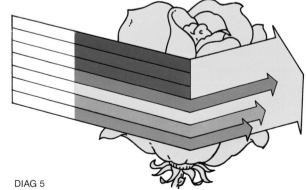

DIAG 5

Introduction

COLOR IN THE GARDEN

Color wheels

Color wheels are frequently used to aid color planning in the garden. When the great English scientist Sir Isaac Newton investigated light in the late 1600s, he made a wheel formed of seven colors (red, orange, yellow, green, blue, indigo and violet). During the late 1800s the American scientist A.H. Munsell researched color assessment based on equal changes in the visual spectrum. He created a color wheel formed of five principal colors (red, yellow, green, blue and purple, with intermediate ones between them). Other wheels have been created using four colors (red, yellow, green and blue). However, the easiest color circle to use is formed of three basic hues (red, yellow and blue) with three secondary ones (orange, green and violet). The secondary colors are created by overlapping the basic hues.

These color circles indicate complementary colors (those diametrically opposite) and those that harmonize with each other (those in adjacent segments). Complementary hues are those with no common pigments, while harmonizing ones share the same pigments. Therefore, it can be seen that yellow and violet, blue and orange, red and green are complementary colors, while yellow harmonizes with green and orange, blue with green and violet, and red with orange and violet.

This color-circle is formed by mixing colored paints, by the process known as *subtractive color mixing*. The other method of creating color is by projecting three separate colored lights (red green and blue) onto a white surface. This process is known as *additive color mixing* and creates colors with a different bias. *See Diagram 6, of a subtractive color circle, below.*

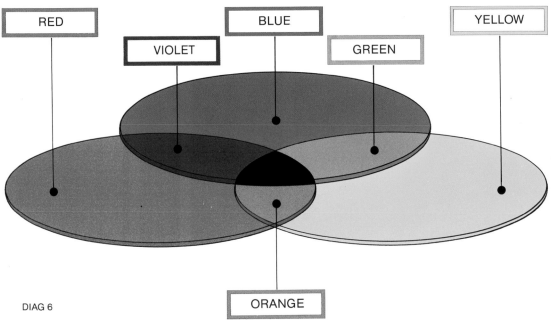

RED BLUE YELLOW VIOLET GREEN ORANGE

Shiny and matt surfaces

The surface texture of a leaf, flower or stem influences the reflected light and its effect on the eye. A smooth surface reflects light at the same angle at which the light hits it. This makes the light purer in color than the same light reflected from a matt surface. There, the irregularities of the surface scatter the reflected light and create an impression of dullness. Another effect of different surface texture is that smooth surfaces appear darker and matt ones lighter. In Nature, however, few plant surfaces are as smooth as glass, and the scattering of reflected light occurs from most of them. *See Diagram 7, below*

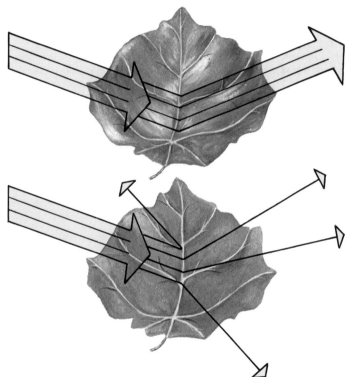

DIAG 7

The evening factor

The well-known delight of shepherds to have red sky at night, indicating a fine tomorrow, results from a clear sky as the sun's rays penetrate atmospheric particles and the air molecules themselves. Even though the sky appears blue, the rays become redder, because blue light is not created but scattered out of white light. This change to the violet end of the spectrum makes dark colors even darker. Blues and especially purples are made darker, while whites and yellows are not so dramatically affected. Conversely, bright sunshine glaring down at midday highlights light colors more than dark ones.

Above: Heliotropum x hybridum *This half-hardy perennial is usually grown as a half-hardy annual. Its flowers have a beautiful fragrance, said to resemble that of a cherry pie.*

Introduction

HARMONIES AND CONTRASTS

All colors have their own personalities: some are dominant, perhaps overpowering when *en masse*, others are demure and reserved, with a gentle and soft quality. Creating a balance of harmonies and contrasts throughout the garden, as well as in one particular area, is very important if it is to be a pleasing area for outdoor living.

White, gray and silver borders reveal a sense of space, coolness and serenity that no other color can achieve. Consider the impression of unending space created by a snow-covered field, the coolness revealed in summer by silver and gray-leaved plants, and the serenity and tranquillity of a white-flowered climber trailing over an old white-washed brick wall. Areas of the garden totally devoted to white, gray and silver plants are fascinating and unusual, but do not plant all of your garden in this way. Use them in an area which is not immediately apparent, so that on turning a corner a display of relaxing colors comes as a surprise. Green foliaged plants harmonize with white and silver plants, offering a background that does not vie for attention or become dominant, yet one that reveals its own qualities of calm and a sense of continuation from season to season.

Reds are the most dominant of all colors in a garden and in a totally color-saturated form are exceptionally strong and powerful, often overpowering to the eye. Strong reds need to be used with care, especially in large groupings. When seen against a mid-green background, densely-red flowers, such as poppies, have a three-dimensional effect and appear to stand out from the foliage and stems. Most red flowers however, are not totally color saturated and appear as shades. Pinks, for example, are desaturated reds, which means that they contain only a small proportion of red pigments.

Golds and yellows are the brightest colors in a garden. Yellow flowers bring life and brightness, especially in spring and early summer. However, these colors have a vibrancy that can soon overpower and subdue demure and light colors, and therefore need to be used carefully. Soft yellows, however, happily blend with whites, silvers and grays, provided that the total area given to yellow is less than that allocated to the white.

Blues and purples have a range that extends from soft and gentle blues to strong and dominant purples. Indeed, such is the color range that the spire-like heads of delphiniums when packed with deep purple flowers are even highlighted by blue sky. Shades at the pastel end of this range blend with the less dominant shades of yellow, but do not create a mixture of strong reds, purples and yellows - unless you have strong sunglasses!

Throughout this all-color book we have both described individual plants as well as suggesting those which form pleasing color and shape combinations with them.

Above: Rudbeckia 'Autumn Leaves' *This beautiful annual creates a distinctive splash of color (center) in a mixed border.*

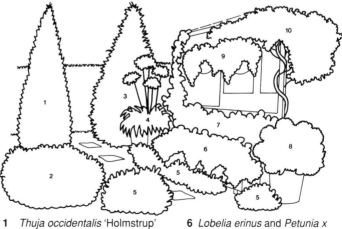

Above: Aster thompsonii nanus
This lovely 8in (20cm) high rock garden plant produces masses of star-like lavender blue flowers set off by gray-green leaves.

1 *Thuja occidentalis* 'Holmstrup'
2 *Euonymus fortunei* 'Emerald and Gold'
3 *Juniperus chinensis* 'Aurea'
4 *Agapanthus campanulatus*
5 *Thymus vulgaris*

6 *Lobelia erinus* and *Petunia x hybrida*
7 *Ipomoea tricolor* 'Heavenly Blue'
8 *Hydrangea macrophylla*
9 *Lobelia erinus* and *Pelargonium x hortorum*
10 *Clematis montana* var. *rubens*

CHAPTER ONE

THE FLOWER BORDER

F lower borders are invariably a medley of different types of plants. Early in the year many borders are packed with spring-flowering bedding plants and bulbs, such as pansies forget-me-nots, daffodils and tulips, while in summer they are awash with summer-flowering bedding plants. Additionally, some borders are a mixture of shrubs and herbaceous perennials, as well as quick-growing and colorful space fillers such as annuals and summer-flowering bulbs. These 'mixed' borders are usually a potpourri of different colors, with shrubs providing a framework of color from year to year, while annuals create attractive splashes of color which can be changed each year.

As well as mixed-color borders, single-color theme ones are also possible. These are devoted to plants within a certain color range, such as *whites, grays and silvers, pinks and reds, blues and mauves,* and *golds and yellows.* Additionally, *green foliaged plants* can be used to create borders with soft and gentle tones, as well as provide backgrounds for more vividly-colored plants. Some plants have *variegated foliage*, and as well as being visually dramatic on their own, they can be attractively harmonized with plainer-leaved types.

Within this chapter, plants are arranged according to their flower or leaf colors, enabling a paintbox of colors to be readily seen. Single color-theme borders have immediate impact, thanks to their originality and eye-catching qualities, but they can often be further enhanced with small patches of harmonizing colors. For instance, blue borders are enhanced with patches of demure white or delicate pale lemon-yellow (but not blinding bright yellow, which commands too much attention in full sunlight and suppresses the beauty of pastel-blue tints). White and silvery borders, with their cool and spacious influence, can be given a slightly warm glow by introducing patches of pink or light blue flowers. Avoid strong colors, as these soon dominate and spoil a white-theme border.

Left: Summer-bedding schemes *need to create a mixture of colors, heights and textures, yet also be symmetrical and attractive.*

Acanthus mollis

Common Bear's Breeches

Acanthus plants are easily recognizable by their long, upright spires of tubular, rather foxglove-like flowers and handsome leaves. The attractive bold foliage makes the plant useful as a groundcover or in contrast with other plants. The most commonly grown species is *Acanthus mollis*, with white and purple flowers borne during mid- to late summer in 1½ft (45cm) long spires. Others include *Acanthus spinosus*, the spiny bear's breeches, and *Acanthus balcanicus*, the long-leaved acanthus.

Height: 3ft (90cm)
Spread: 2½ft (75cm)
Hardiness: Zones 5-10
Cultivation: Deeply cultivated well-drained soil and a sunny position suit this plant. It can be left to form large clumps; in spring, cut last year's foliage down to soil-level.
Propagation: Although seeds can be sown in spring in loam-based potting soil in pots placed in a cold frame, it is easier for the home gardener to propagate by lifting and dividing overgrown clumps in spring.

Left: **Acanthus mollis** *This dramatic herbaceous perennial displays purple and white flowers in long spires from mid- to late summer. In small gardens just one plant is often enough, as the roots can be invasive.*

Achillea millefolium

Common Yarrow

This is a well-known hardy creeping herbaceous perennial; the original species is often seen as a wildflower in meadows and open woodlands. Several attractive forms are now available and will enhance any mixed or herbaceous border. The deep green leaves provide a perfect foil for the 4in (10cm) wide flattened flower heads from mid- to

Acanthus plants have had a marked influence on architecture. The leaves of *Acanthus mollis*, common bear's breeches, are said to have been the model for decorations in the Corinthian style of architecture.

late summer. The form 'Cerise Queen' displays cherry-red flowers. Other cultivars include 'Fire King' (crimson), and 'Rosea' (soft pink).
Height: 2-2¹/₂ft (60-75cm)
Spread: 1¹/₂ft (45cm)
Hardiness: Zones 3-9
Cultivation: Any well-drained garden soil and a position in full sun suits this tolerant plant. In autumn cut down the stems to soil level. Supporting the plants with twiggy sticks is necessary only in exposed areas. Remember to stake the plants early so that they grow up and through the supports.
Propagation: The easiest way to increase this plant is by lifting and dividing established plants in early spring .

Below: **Achillea millefolium** '**Cerise Queen**' *This beautiful cherry-red form of the common yarrow brings color and deep green foliage to a mixed border.*

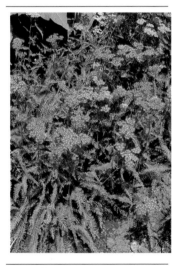

Right: Alcea rosea
This showy plant, often better known as Althaea rosea, *can be grown as an annual or a biennial. It looks especially effective when planted against a wall, and is splendid for bringing summer color to a garden. It grows higher when cultivated as a biennial.*

Alcea rosea

(*Althaea rosea*)
Hollyhock

This well-known biennial is appropriate for the back of a border or against a wall. Its funnel-shaped single or double flowers, to 4in (10cm) wide, are borne on short stalks from mid- to late summer and even into early autumn. The light-green leaves have hairy surfaces. Flowers range in color from soft pink to deep burgundy, and also come in white, yellow, and near black. There is an annual variety, 'Summer Carnival' that has double flowers. Biennials include 'Chaters Double' a double-flowered form available in separate or mixed colors; 'Single Mixed' an old-fashioned single bloom sold in mixed colors; and 'Silver Puffs', with double, silver-pink flowers.
Height: 7-9ft (2.1-2.7m)
Spread: 2ft (60cm)
Hardiness: Zones 2-10

Cultivation: Hollyhocks like fertile, well-drained soil and a sheltered position. They usually require staking but the supports should be unobtrusive – green bamboo stakes are ideal. In humid climates they are susceptible to rust, creating unsightly foliage but not affecting the bloom.
Propagation: To grow as an annual, sow seeds in late winter ¹/₄in (6mm) deep in loam-based potting soil and keep at 50°F (10°C). When the seedlings are large enough to handle prick them off into pots and leave them in a cold frame to harden off. Plant out into the garden when all risk of frost has passed. To grow as a biennial, sow seeds ¹/₂in (12mm) deep in the open garden in mid-summer. When the seedlings are large enough to handle – usually in late summer or early autumn – thin them out or transplant the young plants to 1¹/₂-2ft (45-60cm) apart. During spring of the following year set them in the garden.

Achillea millefolium is a delightful plant for the flower border with a medicinal past. Old English herbalists called it nose-bleed because its leaves promoted bleeding when applied to the nose.

Alcea rosea, with its large flowers on long spires, blends with many summer flowering plants. It is attractive in cottage gardens, perennial borders, or on its own against a wall.

THE FLOWER BORDER

Amaryllis belladonna

Belladonna Lily · Cape Belladonna · Naked-lady Lily

A bulbous, tender plant with mid-green strap-like leaves from late winter to mid-summer. In late summer, these die down and the fragrant trumpet-shaped satiny pale-pink 4-5in (10-13cm) wide flowers appear on bare stems, usually in clusters of three or four, sometimes up to twelve.

Height: 2-2½ft (60-75cm)
Spread: 12-15in (30-38cm)
Hardiness: Zones 9-10, usually grown as a potted plant.
Cultivation: Well-drained soil in a sunny and sheltered position is best. A site at the base of a south or west-facing wall is ideal. Late frosts will damage the early foliage. Set the bulbs in the soil in early summer, with 6-8in (15-20cm) of soil covering them. Remove dead flowers as they fade; as well as the leaves and stems when they die down.
Propagation: Clumps that become too large can be lifted in summer as soon as the leaves turn yellow. Divide and replant immediately.

Alstroemeria aurantiaca

Peruvian Lily

A fleshy, tuberous-rooted Chilean herbaceous perennial, the hardiest and most vigorous of all alstroemerias. The trumpet-shaped 1½-2in (4-5cm) wide flowers, borne from mid- to late summer, boast a range of colors, from rich orange to orange-scarlet. The long, lance-shaped leaves are glaucous (blue-gray) beneath. Alstroemeria makes a long-lasting cut-flower.
Height: 3ft (90cm)
Spread: 15-18in (38-45cm)
Hardiness: Zones 7-10
Cultivation: Alstroemerias prefer fertile, well-drained, light soil and a sunny or partially shaded position. Set new plants (preferably pot-grown) in position during spring, 4-6in (10-15cm) deep. To encourage the development of further flowers,

Above: Alstroemeria aurantiaca
This richly-colored tuberous-rooted herbaceous perennial is ideal for mixed borders, where it creates colour during mid- to late summer. The flowers are ideal as cut flowers; they last a long time in water.

remove the blossoms as they fade, and in autumn cut the plants down to soil level.
Propagation: New plants can be raised from seed sown in loam-based potting soil in spring and placed in a cold frame, but it is easier for the home gardener to lift and divide overgrown clumps in spring. Take care not to damage the roots. To produce a large number of plants lift and divide established clumps in midspring and pot up small individual pieces. Place in a cold frame.

Alstroemeria aurantiaca, with its vivid colors, needs a strong contrast from a large, spectacularly colored shrub, such as the purple-leaved *Cotinus coggygria* 'Royal Purple'.

Amaryllis belladonna gained its common name belladonna lily in Italy from the fancied resemblance of its blend of red and white flowers to the complexion of a beautiful woman *(bella donna).*

Aster novi-belgii

Michaelmas Daisy
New York Aster

A beautiful and well-known herbaceous perennial. The original type came from North America and when introduced into Britain gained one of its common names because it flowers on Michaelmas (September 29), a significant feast day in the agricultural calendar. The plant has deep green, stem-clasping, slender-pointed leaves and 2in (5cm) wide flowers borne in dense clusters during late summer and early autumn. Many pink and red forms are available, including 'Ernest Ballard' (semi-double, redddish-pink), 'Patricia Ballard' (semi-double, pink), 'Winston S. Churchill' (double, glowing ruby-red), 'Crimson Brocade' (double, vivid crimson),

'Fellowship' (semi-double, pink) and 'The Cardinal' (single, deep rose-red). There is also a range of dwarf forms, 1-1½ft (30-45cm) high. These include, 'Jenny' (red), 'Alert' (deep crimson), and 'Alice Haslam' (double, rose pink).

Height: 3-4ft (90cm-1.2m)
Spread: 1½-2ft (45-60cm)
Hardiness: Zones 4-8
Cultivation: Fertile, well-drained but moisture-retentive soil (especially in late summer) is essential, as is a position in full sun. Most of the tall varieties will need staking with twiggy sticks. Do this early so that the plants grow up through the sticks and eventually hide them. In the spring, cut the plants down to soil level. The clumps are best divided every three years to prevent the quality of the flowers from deteriorating. For stockier plants, cut back by half in mid-July.

Propagation: This is easily done by lifting and dividing clumps in early spring, every three years. To produce large numbers of plants *Aster novi-belgii* is best increased by lifting and dividing healthy clumps in midspring every spring and separating the healthy outside parts into small pieces. These can be planted in a nursery bed if very small or planted into the border. Because they are small they will have to be planted close together.

Below: **Aster novi-belgii**
'Fellowship' *This richly coloured semi-double pink variety of Michaelmas Daisy brings life and colour to borders in late summer and into autumn. Fertile, well-drained but moisture-retentive soil is essential, and a sunny position.*

Below: **Amaryllis belladonna**
This exotic-looking bulbous border plant is useful for providing late summer colour in mild areas of the country. In areas colder than zone 9 it is grown as a winter-blooming pot plant.

Aster novi-belgii and **Aster novae-angliae** are superb for late colour. They are ideal for mixed and herbaceous borders, while the dwarf forms of *Aster novi-belgii* are ideal for small courtyard gardens.

THE FLOWER BORDER

Right: **Canna x generalis** *When planted in a group in a summer-bedding scheme, cannas are ideal for bringing height and color to the picture.*

Canna x generalis

(*Canna x hybrida*)
Garden Canna

An erect, large-leaved rhizomatous perennial, frequently used in summer bedding schemes. The leaves reach 2ft (60cm) long and 1ft (30cm) wide. There are many hybrids available, some with purple or brown leaves and others with green ones. The 2-3in (5-7.5cm) gladioli-like flowers are borne at the tops of the stems during summer. Outstanding cultivars include 'City of Portland' (green leaves, deep pink flowers). 'Red King Humbert' (bronze leaves, scarlet flowers) and 'President' (green leaves, vivid scarlet flowers).
Height: 3-3½ft (90cm-1m)
Spread: 15-18in (38-45cm)
Hardiness: Zones 8-10. North of Zone 8 lift and treat as dahlias.
Cultivation: During early spring, plant the rhizomes in trays or large pots of rich loam-based potting soil and keep at 61°F (16°C). Before planting them, give the rhizomes a thorough soaking with water. They will soon send up shoots; if more than one shoot appears, split them up and pot them. When they are well established, pot them up into a rich potting soil, and subsequently into containers or beds where they are to flower. Make sure you do not do this until all risk of frost has passed. In autumn, dig up the plants or move them into a greenhouse before the onset of frosts. May be overwintered in ground in Zone 8 and milder areas.
Propagation: Divide the rhizomes in early spring. Cannas can also be increased from seed, although the progeny will not resemble the parents. Nick the seed coats with a knife or soak in water for a day or so before sowing.

Celosia cristata plumosa

Feathered Cockscomb · Feathered Amaranth · Plumed Celosia

A distinctive half-hardy annual useful for annual borders and summer-bedding displays. Striking, feathery, 3-6in (7.5-15cm) high flower plumes appear during late summer in a range of colors. Good cultivars include 'Apricot Brandy' (orange-red), and 'Fire Dragon' (crimson). Others have mixed colours – red, pink, yellow and orange – as in 'Century Mix' and 'Fancy Plumes'. Crested cockscomb (*Celosia cristata cristata*) is widely grown for arrangements and dried flowers.

'Fireglow' (orange-scarler) and 'Treasure Chest' (mixed colors) are two varieties.
Height: 15-24in (38-60cm)
Spread: 10-12in (25-30cm)
Cultivation: Fertile well-drained soil and a sunny and sheltered position are essential. They do best in warm weather.
Propagation: During mid-spring, sow seeds ⅛in (3mm) deep in loam-based potting soil kept at 68°F (20°C). When they are large enough to handle, prick off the seedlings into flats or small pots and slowly harden them off, without sudden drops in temperature. Plant them out into the garden when all risk of frost has passed.

Cannas with bronze foliage can be used to create an interesting summer bedding scheme with an edging of light blue lobelias and a carpet of scarlet-flowered *Begonia semperflorens*.

Crocosmia masonorum

Montbretia

A hardy corm-producing border plant with strap-like leaves, patterned pleats and ribs. The flame-orange flowers are borne from mid- to late summer at the tips of the arching stems. A similar plant is *Crocosmia x crocosmiiflora (Montbretia crocosmiiflora)*. These are beautiful plants with 1½in (4cm) long trumpet-shaped flowers from mid- to late summer. There are many exciting varieties, such as 'Firebird' (orange-red) and 'Spitfire' (orange-red).

Height: 2½ft (75cm)
Spread: 8-10in (20-25cm)
Hardiness: Zones 5-9
Cultivation: Light, well-drained and fertile soil is best, but do not let the soil dry out during summer. Crocosmias appreciate a sunny position. Set the corms in position in early spring, 2-3in (5-7.5cm) deep and 6in (15cm) apart. In warm areas the plants can be left in the soil to form large clumps, but in exceptionally cold areas lift the plants in late autumn, dry off the corms and store them over winter. When storing the corms keep them neither too dry, or they will shrivel, nor too damp, or they will rot.
Propagation: Large clumps left in the soil can be lifted and divided just after flowering, or you can wait until spring.

Above: **Crocosmia masonorum**
This spectacular plant for summer color provides a strong upright form. The flowers can be cut for house decoration. In mild areas it can be left in the ground to form large clumps.

Left: **Celosia argentea plumosa 'Aprlcot Brandy'** *This distinctive half-hardy annual needs a warm and sheltered position. The plume-like flowers last for many weeks in summer and contrast well with the light green foliage.*

Celosia cristata plumosa is often used in formal bedding schemes, but it can also look effective planted as a filler in mixed borders or with hardy annuals. Take care not to overwater plants.

Crocosmia x crocosmiiflora forms a stately display in mixed borders. Several varieties are available, including 'A.E. Amos' (orange-red flowers) and 'Emily McKenzie' (brilliant orange).

Left: **Cuphea miniata 'Firefly'**
This highly branched annual bears masses of bright scarlet flowers during summer. It is best planted in the center of the annual border as it does not require staking.

Dahlia

These reliable and well-known garden flowers can be divided into two main groups: the compact bedding dahlias, which can be used in beds and containers; and the taller border dahlias, which are best grown in mixed borders, mingling with herbaceous plants and flowering shrubs.

BEDDING DAHLIAS

These half-hardy perennials from Mexico are grown as half-hardy annuals, displaying 2-3in (5-7.5cm) wide single, double or semi-double flowers from midsummer to autumn. There are many varieties in a wide colour range, in mixed and self-colors.

Height: 12-20in (30-50cm)
Spread: 15-24in (38-45cm)
Cultivation: Well-cultivated, fertile, compost or manure-enriched soil and a sunny position suits bedding dahlias. If the soil is too rich, however, the plants produce excessive foliage at the expense of flowers. There is no need to stake them – unlike the large border types. Removal of dead flowers encourages the plants to produce further blooms. Water the plants during dry spells.
Propagation: During late winter and early spring, sow seeds ¼in (6mm) deep in a loam-based seed-starting mix at 61°F (16°C). When they are large enough to handle, prick off the seedlings into flats or small pots of loam-based potting soil and slowly harden them off in a cold frame. Set them out in the garden as soon as all risk of frost has passed.

BORDER DAHLIAS

These are half-hardy tuberous plants, easily damaged by frost, that quickly bring colour to the garden. There are several classifications and many varieties.

Cuphea miniata

Cigar Flower

A spectacular Mexican half-hardy annual. Cupheas bear slender-pointed mid-green leaves covered with white hairs. During mid-summer and into autumn, they produce a fine display of bright-red 1½in (4cm) long tubular flowers. Often grown as a pot plant for a cool greenhouse or conservatory, they can also be used as summer annuals. The variety 'Firefly' has brilliant scarlet flowers.
Height: 1½-2ft (45-60cm)
Spread: 15-18in (38-45cm)
Cultivation: Any ordinary garden soil suits cupheas, and they can be grown in full sun or light shade.
Propagation: During spring, sow seeds ¼in (6mm) deep in loam-based seed-starting mix at 59°F (15°C). When they are large enough to handle, prick the seedlings off into loam-based potting and harden them off in a cold frame. After all risk of frost is over, set the plants out in the garden. Alternatively, the seedlings can be pricked off into small pots of loam-based potting soil, and potted up into larger pots as the plants grow. In the fall, take cuttings for growing indoors.

Cuphea also does well as a pot plant for the home or greenhouse. Sow seeds in spring and prick out the seedlings into small pots of loam-based potting soil. Pot up into larger pots when the roots become pot-bound.

Anemone-flowered
(2-3½ft/60cm-1m): These have double flowers with flat outer petals and short, tubular inner ones. Flowering is from midsummer to the frosts of autumn.

Ball-type (3-4ft/90cm-1.2m): As the name implies, these have ball-shaped flowers, with tubular, blunt-ended petals. There are *Small Ball* types with blooms 4-6in (10-15cm) wide, and *Miniature Ball* forms with flowers up to 4in (10cm) wide.

Cactus and Semi-cactus
(3-5ft/90cm-1.5m): These are sub-divided into five groups, *Miniature* (blooms up to 4in/10cm wide); *Small* (blooms 4-6in/10-15cm wide); *Medium* (blooms 6-8in/15-20cm); *Large* (blooms 8-10in/20-25cm wide); and *Giant* (blooms 10in/25cm or more wide). Cactus types have petals rolled back or quilled for more than half their length. Semi-cactus types have similar petals, but quilled or rolled back for less than half their length.

Collarettes (2½-4ft/75cm-1.2m): These have blooms with a single outer ring of flat ray florets, with a ring of small florets in the center, forming a disc.

Decoratives: These have double flowers without central discs. They are formed of broad, flat ray florets. This group is further divided into: *Miniature* (3-4ft/90cm-1.2m): These have flowers up to 4in (10cm) wide. *Small* (3½-4ft/1-1.2m): Flowers 4-6in (10-15cm) wide. *Medium* (3½-4ft/1-1.2m): Flowers 6-8in (15-20cm) wide. *Large* (3½-5ft/1-1.5m): Flowers 8-10in (20-25cm) wide. *Giant* (4-5ft/1.2-1.5m): Flowers 10in (25cm) or more wide.

Peony-flowered (up to 3ft/90cm): The flowers are formed of two or more rings of flat ray flowers, with a central disc.

Pompon (3-4ft/90cm-1.2m): The flowers closely resemble those of *Ball* types, but are more globular and are no more than 2in (5cm) wide. The florets curl inwards for their entire length.

Single-flowered
(1½-2½ft/45-75cm): These display flowers up to 4in (10cm) wide, with

a single row of petals arranged around a central disc.

Cultivation: Well-drained soil, with plenty of moisture-retentive compost or well-decomposed manure added, is required. Include a sprinkling of bonemeal before setting the tubers in the ground during mid- to late spring at 4in (10cm) deep. If sprouted tubers are used, take care that they are not planted too early, or frost will damage them. The young plants will need staking for support. Pinch out the growing tips of all shoots to encourage sideshoots to develop, and if you want large flowers, remove sideshoots and buds from around the developing flowers. The removal of dead flowers helps the development of further flowers.
In autumn, carefully dig up the

Above: Dahlia 'Bishop of Llandaff' *This is a peony-flowered type with rings of flat crimson petals surrounding a central core of stamens. Its foliage is dark and although it is a dahlia used in bedding schemes, at 2½ft (75cm) high it grows taller than most varieties used for bedding.*

tubers about a week after the foliage has been blackened by frost. Remove soil from the tubers and store them upside down for a few weeks to encourage them to dry out. Then place them in boxes of peat in a dry, frost-proof position until the following year.

Propagation: The easiest way for the home gardener to do this is to divide the tubers in spring.

Formal planting schemes for bedding dahlias are easy to create. One example is as a carpet of salmon-pink and cherry-red plants, with an edging of pale blue lobelia.

Ball types to look for include 'Boxo's Boy' (red), 'Bright Ball' (red), 'Camano Candy' (pink), 'Red Admiral' (miniature, red) and 'Valerie Buller' (miniature, plum red).

THE FLOWER BORDER

Above: Dahlia 'Alva's Doris'
A beautiful bright crimson small cactus dahlia, 4-6in (10-15cm) wide. It rises to 3 ½-4ft (1-1.2m) high with a spread of 2 ½ft (75cm) wide.

Left: Dahlia 'Geerling's Elite'
A brilliantly-colored free-flowering collarette variety, this has orient-red petals tipped buff, and a buff collar. It rises to 3 ½ft (1m) and is ideal for setting towards the front of a mixed border.

Decorative types to look for include 'Hamari Girl' (giant dec., pink), 'Jo's Choice' (miniature dec., red), 'Liz B' (small dec., red) and 'Paul Harris' (medium dec., red).

Top right: Dahlia 'Scarlet Comet'
An anemone-flowered variety with brilliantly-colored flowers formed of an inner ring of petals that surround the center like a halo. It is ideal for bringing an intense splash of color to a border.

Right: Dahlia 'Salmon Keene'
This cactus-type displays the rolled or 'quilled' petals distinctive of this group. It produces attractively spiked flowers that will enhance a border.

Cactus types to look for include 'Athalie' (semi-cactus, pink blends), 'Camana Coho' (Large cactus, pink), 'Doc Van Horn' (large semi-cactus, pink) and 'San Francisco Sunset' (miniature semi-cactus, flame blends).

Euphorbia griffithii 'Fireglow'

Griffith's Spurge

An attractive perennial with lance-shaped, midgreen leaves and orange-red bracts at the top of the stems during early summer.
Height: 2-2½ft (60-75cm)
Spread: 2-2½ft (60-75cm)
Hardiness: Zones 4-8
Cultivation: Fertile, well-drained soil and a position in full sun suit euphorbias.
Propagation: The plants are easily increased by lifting and dividing large clumps in spring or autumn.

Dicentra spectabilis

Bleeding Heart

This widely grown Japanese herbaceous perennial has long been known as bleeding heart. Its gray-green, finely-divided and rather fern-like leaves are a perfect foil for the 1in (2.5cm) long, pendulous, rose red, heart-shaped flowers, borne on arching stems during early to midsummer. It does best in partial shade and cool climates. When the soil is allowed to dry out, the foliage will yellow and the plant will go dormant in mid- to late summer. Our Eastern native bleeding heart, *Dicentra eximia,* is smaller [9-18in (23-45cm)] and less showy, but the foliage doesn't go dormant in mid-season. Many varieties are available including 'Alba' (white), 'Boothman's Variety' (soft pink), and 'Silversmith' (white flowers flushed with pink).
Height: 1½-2½ft (45-75cm)
Spread: 1½ft (45cm)
Hardiness: Zones 2-9
Cultivation: Rich, well-cultivated fertile soil and a sheltered, sunny or partially shaded position suit this plant. The roots are somewhat brittle, so the plants are best left undisturbed once established.
Propagation: It is easily increased by carefully lifting and dividing established clumps in spring or autumn.

Above: **Dicentra spectabilis**
This well-known and distinctive hardy herbaceous perennial with dainty flowers needs well-cultivated fertile soil in full sun or partial shade. The flowers appear from early to midsummer.

Below: Euphorbia griffithii
'Fireglow'*This unusual perennial creates a mound of green foliage topped by bright orange-red bracts in mid-summer. When the bracts fade the foliage remains attractive, providing a shrub-like mound.*

Dicentra cucullaria, or Dutchman's breeches, is native to North America and was once commonly found wild in New York State. It has white blooms and is less showy than bleeding heart.

Freesia x hybrida

This well-known South African tender, corm-bearing plant produces sweetly-scented 1-2in (2.5-5cm) long fragrant blooms often sold as cut flowers. These hybrids have narrow mid-green leaves and, when planted outside in spring, produce flowers during late summer. They are not hardy enough to be left outside all year in most climates. Many varieties are available, in a wide color range and in both single and double flowers. 'Oberon' has a strawberry-red, yellow centered single blossom.
Height: 1½-2ft (45-60cm)
Spread: 5-8in (13-20cm)
Hardiness: Zones 9 and 10
Cultivation: Fertile, light, sandy soil and a sheltered sunny position suit freesias. During spring, plant the corms about 2in (5cm) deep. Use small twiggy sticks to support the foliage, and in autumn, when the foliage has turned yellow, lift the plants and corms. Dry off the corms and remove the offsets. In very mild areas and in well-drained light and sandy soils it is possible to leave the corms outside all winter. Corms planted in late summer to early autumn will flower in late spring. Although freesias can be induced to flower in a greenhouse or cool room, a temperature of 45°F (5°C) is needed. Plant the corms in boxes or pots of loam-based potting soil in late summer and early autumn to bring about flowering from mid winter to spring. Be sure you maintain the right temperature.
Propagation: Although seeds can be sown in late winter and spring, it is easier for home gardeners to remove the corms and offsets and to replant these in spring.

Euphorbia griffithii provides a mound of leaves from soil level to the orange-red bracts at the tops of shoots. Partial shade is best for this euphorbia, although it will tolerate full sun in cool climates.

Above: Galega x hartlandii
These plants have a sprawling habit, but create a superb patch of color, with their small pea-shaped flowers borne on branching stems with attractive, narrow leaves.

Galega hartlandii

Goat's Rue

A bushy and sprawling hardy herbaceous perennial with light green, short-stalked, compound leaves formed of many leaflets. During mid-summer it produces dense clusters of pale lilac, mauve or white flowers in short spires. Varieties include 'Her Majesty' (lilac blooms) and 'Lady Wilson' (white and mauve pink).
Height: 3½-5ft (1-1.5m)
Spread: 2½ft (75cm)
Hardiness: Zones 3-7
Cultivation: Any well-drained garden soil and a position in full sun or light shade are suitable. It usually needs staking. After flowering, cut the stems down to soil level because the foliage becomes unattractive.
Propagation: Although it can be increased by sowing seeds in spring in a nursery bed, it is much easier to increase by lifting and dividing large clumps in spring or autumn.

Galega officinalis, one of the parents of **Galega x hartlandii**, has pale blue flowers. Like the hybrid, it is best used in the back of the border.

Large-flowered gladioli are ideal for mixed, newly planted borders, where they create bright color while shrubs and perennials are becoming established. They may also be included in a cutting garden.

Gladiolus: Large flowered Hybrids

These are the well-known, large-flowered, tender corm-bearing plants that create such spectacular displays from mid to late summer. The erect spikes of flowers are often 20in (50cm) long, formed of florets 4-7in (10-18cm) wide in a wide color range, with many lovely reds and pinks. These include 'First Kiss' (rosy-pink, 1989 All-American winner), 'Fond Memory' (shades of pink, rose and salmon), 'Intrepid' (ruffled scarlet), 'Notre Dame' (pink), 'Rose Garden' (Pink with rose throat), and 'St. Peter's ' (rich red).

Height: 2¹/₂-3¹/₂ft (75cm-1m)
Spread: 8-10in (20-25cm)
Cultivation: Ordinary well-drained garden soil and a position in full sun assure success for this reliable favourite. Plant the corms in mid-spring, 4in (10cm) deep in heavy soil but 6in (15cm) in light soils. Plant 6in (15cm) apart for a display; in a cutting garden rows should be 2ft (60cm) apart. Anchored at these depths, the plants will not require staking in sheltered areas. In exposed positions, support the stems with small canes. While in growth , don't allow to dry out; water every 3 days during dry weather. After flowering, when the foliage turns yellow, carefully dig up the plants and allow them to dry for a week or so. Cut off the stems ¹/₂in (12mm) above the corms if they have not already broken off, and remove all soil. Then store them in shallow boxes in a cool, dry and vermin-proof position.
Propagation: In autumn, when the corms are lifted and dried for storage, remove the cormlets from around them. During spring, plant these in drills 2in (5cm) deep in a nursery bed.

Left: Gladiolus *These beautiful large-flowered gladiolus hybrids give reliable garden display. The colour range is wide and includes many red and pink.*

Above: **Godetia grandiflora 'Dwarf Vivid'** *This beautiful, unusual, hardy annual grows well in most soils. Avoid excessively rich ones that encourage leaf growth at the expense of flowers.*

Godetia amoena

(Clarkia amoena)

This beautiful, compact, hardy annual from western North America has light green, lance-shaped leaves that present a superb foil for the 2in (5cm) wide rose-purple, funnel-shaped flowers during mid-summer and into late summer. The most widely available varieties are the 'Grace' hybrids in red, rose pink, and shell pink. Most godetias prefer cool weather but the Grace series will tolerate heat.

Height: 1¹/₂-2¹/₂ft (45-75cm)
Spread: 1-2ft (30-60cm)
Cultivation: Light and moist soil and a position in full sun suit it best. Avoid excessively rich soils that encourage lush foliage at the expense of flowers.
Propagation: In late spring, sow seeds ¹/₄in (6mm) deep where they are to flower. When they are large enough to handle, thin out the seedlings to 6in (15cm) apart.

Above: Godetia Grace
This is a beautiful hardy annual that produces a mass of single rose-pink and white flowers from mid- to late summer. It creates delicately-colored mounds.

Godetia can also be grown as a houseplant. Sow seeds thinly in pots or boxes of loam-based potting soil in late summer. Pot up the seedlings and grow them on in a cool greenhouse.

THE FLOWER BORDER

Hemerocallis x hybrida

Daylily

A superb hardy herbaceous perennial with stiff, arching, bright green sword-like leaves and lily-like flowers, 5-7in (13-21cm) wide. Daylilies are available in a full range of colors. The number of varieties including reds and pinks is virtually limitless. You will find early, mid and late season varieties; plain and ruffled; striped; bi-colored; and even fragrant ones.

Height: 1-4ft (30-120cm)
Spread: 1-3ft (30-90cm)
Hardiness: Zones 3-10
Cultivation: Good garden soil that does not dry out during summer and a position in full sun or light shade are best for daylilies. Once planted, they can be left in the same position for many years. In autumn cut the plants down to soil-level. Daylilies should be deadheaded to encourage foliage and root growth.
Propagation: Increase plants by lifting and dividing overcrowded clumps in spring or autumn. Replant immediately.

Heuchera sanguinea

Coral Bells

This bright and cheerful hardy perennial from New Mexico, Arizona and Mexico has attractive, evergreen, round or heart-shaped, dark green leaves. The small, bell-shaped, bright red flowers are borne in loose heads on long and wiry stems from midsummer to autumn. Several superb forms are available, including 'Bressingham Blaze' (salmon-scarlet), 'Chatterbox' (pink) and 'Mt St. Helens' (brick-red).

Left: **Heuchera sanguinea** Coral Bells have bright red flowers borne on slender stems from late spring to midsummer. Light soil is needed: do not plant in a heavy acid soil. Full sun to partial shade.

Hemerocallis are admirable for setting in a mixed or herbaceous border, to which they contribute both height and color. Also, their stiff, upright form means they look good alongside paths.

Heuchera sanguinea is a delight at the edge of a border or woodland garden. It combines well with many perennials, including geranium 'Wargrave Pink' and daylilies.

Kniphofia

Red Hot Poker · Torch Lily

These hardy herbaceous perennials produce distinctive poker-like heads from midsummer to autumn. The flowering spike is often described as two-tone, because flowers on the bottom open first showing a different color than the upper buds. It has thick sword-shaped leaves. There are many hybrids as well as true species. In color they range from yellow and orange to red, and include 'Pfitzeri' (deep orange), 'Wayside Flame' (orange-red), 'Rosea Superba' (rose-red), 'Royal Standard' (scarlet buds opening to yellow) and *Kniphofia uvaria* (red orange and yellow).

Cultivation: Kniphofias like well-drained, fertile soil in full sun. It is essential that the soil does not remain wet during winter. Give the plants a mulch of well-rotted manure or compost in spring.

Propagation: The easiest way to increase the plants is by lifting and dividing large clumps in late spring. True species breed true from seeds, sow them ½in (12mm) deep in seedbeds in spring. They have a thick fibrous root system and resent being moved.

Height: 1-1½ft (30-45cm)
Spread: 15-18in (38-45cm)
Hardiness: Zones 3-8
Cultivation: Well-drained soil in full sun or light shade in the South suits heucheras. They will not tolerate heavy, acidic soil. Set out new plants in spring or autumn. After flowering, cut down the flower stems.
Propagation: Heucheras are easily increased by lifting and dividing old plants in spring. This usually needs to be done every three or four years, particularly when the crowns appear to rise out of the ground. Heucheras can also be raised by sowing seeds in early spring in boxes of loam-based potting soil placed in a cold frame. When large enough to handle, plant out seedlings into a nursery bed. Plants will be ready for the garden in autumn.

Above: **Hemerocallis** *Daylilies come in many eye-catching colors, this variety, 'Pink Damask' boasts warm pink flowers with yellow throats. Hemerocallis are ideal for planting and leaving in one position for a long time. Each flower lasts for only a day, but is quickly replenished by further flowers. Plant varieties, that bloom at different times for color all summer long.*

Right: **Kniphofia praecox**
This beautiful tall herbaceous perennial has stiff stems bearing torch-like brilliant scarlet flowers in late summer and into early autumn. They look best when planted in a large stand with the bright torch-like heads silhouetted against blue sky, and are ideal for use in island beds where the plants are grown without supports.

Kniphofias, with their upright bursts, of color, are superb in perennial beds, combined with shrubs, or grown in cutting gardens. They have a thick, fibrous root system and resent moving.

Lilium 'Enchantment'

This distinctive and widely-grown hardy Asiatic lily, bears heads of up to sixteen cup-shaped, nasturtium-red flowers up to 6in (15cm) wide in midsummer. Another superb lily from the same group is 'Cover Girl', with stunningly attractive, demure-pink flowers.

Height: 3-4ft (90cm-1.2m)
Spread: 8-12in (20-30cm)
Hardiness: Zones 3-8
Cultivation: Fertile, well-drained soil in full sun or light shade assures success. Set the bulbs in position, 4-6in (10-15cm) deep, in late autumn. Although it must be well-drained, the soil should also retain moisture, so during spring and summer keep the surface well mulched with peat or compost. Ensure the soil is moist before adding this moisture-retentive material. In sheltered gardens the lilies do not need staking, but on windswept sites – which really should be avoided – support from thin bamboo canes may be necessary.
Propagation: Every three or four years, lift and divide the congested clumps during late autumn or early spring.

Lavatera trimestris

Mallow

This is one of the most beautiful of all hardy annuals, with a bushy habit and pale green, smooth, roughly heart-shaped, lobed leaves. The 4in (10cm) wide, glowing pink flowers are borne profusely from mid- to late summer. Several varieties are available, including 'Silver Cup' (silver-pink) and 'Mont Rose' (rose-pink).

Height: 2-3ft (60-90cm)
Spread: 18-20in (45-50cm)
Cultivation: Moderately rich garden soil and a sheltered but sunny site are best. They do not like high heat and humidity.
Propagation: During mid- and late spring, sow seeds where the plants are to flower, setting them 1/2in (12mm) deep. When the seedlings are large enough to handle, thin them to 20-24in (50-60cm) apart.

Above: Lavatera trimestris **'Silver Cup'** *This beautiful hardy annual is a gem in any garden, and is also ideal as a cut flower for home decoration. Avoid sowing the seeds in very rich soil, which encourages lush leaf growth at the expense of flowers.*

Below: Lavatera trimestris *A superb setting for this hardy annual is to contrast it with the woolly gray-leaved hardy perennial Ballota pseudodictamnus.*

Lavatera trimestris, like many delicate pink flowers, needs careful positioning if it is not to be dominated by other colors. Mix it with gray foliage plants, such as *Ballota pseudodictamnus* or artemisias.

Lilium 'Enchantment' is ideal among rhododendrons and azaleas beneath a light canopy of tall pines. Lilies are useful for extending color in a group of azaleas, which often look bleak in midseason.

Linum grandiflorum 'Rubrum'

Scarlet Flax

This hardy annual with 1½in (4cm) wide, single, saucer-shaped scarlet flowers comes from Algeria. The flowers are borne from mid- to late summer on wispy stems above a mat of narrow, pale green, pointed leaves. So wispy are the stems, even the slightest breeze sets them moving. White and pink varieties are also available.

Height: 15-18in (38-45cm)
Spread: 8-10in (20-25cm)
Cultivation: Any good well-drained soil in full sun suits flaxes.
Propagation: During spring or early summer, sow seeds ¼in (6mm) deep where the plants are to flower. When they are large enough to handle, thin the seedlings to 5in (13cm) apart.

Below: **Linum grandiflorum 'Rubrum'** *This spectacular hardy annual has bright scarlet flowers from mid- to late summer. A sunny position is essential for the rich coloring of the flowers.*

Below: **Lilium 'Enchantment'**
This really spectacular Asiatic lily, has clustered heads of cup-shaped flowers up to 6in (15cm) wide. It delights in a sunny position.

Above: **Lilium 'Cover Girl'**
An appealing Asiatic lily, this variety has large, wide open flowers that provide color in a border in sun or light shade.

Lilies need moist soil and by setting them amid low, large-leaved plants, such as peonies, the ground will stay cool and damp. After blooming, cut off seedheads but allow foliage to remain until it yellows.

Linum grandiflorum can also be grown as a pot plant for spring colour. Sow seeds thinly in late summer; thin to six seedlings per pot when large enough to handle and grow in a cold greenhouse.

Lobelia cardinalis

Cardinal Flower

A stunningly impressive though short-lived North American hardy herbaceous perennial with erect stems bearing oblong, lance-shaped, midgreen or reddish leaves and brilliant scarlet, 1in (2.5cm) wide, five-lobed flowers during mid- to late summer. Varieties include 'Arabella's Vision' (briliant red) and 'Twilight Zone' (shell pink). There are also hybrids between *Lobelia cardinalis* and *L. fulgens*, but these are less hardy than the native species.
Height: 2¹/₂-3ft (75-90cm)
Spread: 12-15in (30-39cm)
Hardiness: Zones 2-9
Cultivation: Rich, fertile, moist soil and a partially shaded position suit this plant. Fork in generous amounts of peat or well-rotted manure when preparing the soil. Set the plants in position in spring.
Propagation: In spring, separate the rosettes and re-plant in the garden. The species also may be propagated from seed.

Left: **Lobelia x hybrida**
These hybrids between Lobelia cardinalis *and* Lobelia fulgens, *produe brilliant scarlet flowers in late summer on stems up to 4ft (1.2m) high. They are less hardy than the species.*

Lychnis coronaria

Rose Campion · Mullein Pink

This beautiful perennial is short-lived but self-sows with abandon. It has silvery, woolly-textured, lance-shaped, leathery leaves and ¹/₂in (12mm) wide, rich magenta, rather bell-shaped flowers, borne in loose round heads from mid- to late summer. The variety 'Abbotswood Rose' boasts sprays of intense rose pink, 'Atrosanguinea' has strong red flowers and 'Alba' has white bloom.
Height: 1¹/₂-2ft (45-60cm)
Spread: 12-15in (30-38cm)
Hardiness: Zones 4-8

Lobelias are named in honour of the Belgian botanist Matthias de Lobel (1538-1616). He went to England in 1584, and became physician to James I of England (James II of Scotland).

Lychnis coronaria will bloom through the fall if deadheaded. At the end of the season allow it to go to seed. White short-lived it self-seeds abundantly.

Cultivation: Any well-drained garden soil in full sun or light shade suits lychnis. In exposed areas it requires support from twiggy sticks, and removing dead flowerheads prevents the formation of seeds.

Propagation: Because it is only short-lived as a perennial, it is best to start new plants. Sow seeds in late winter in loam-based seed starting mix at 55°F (13°C). When they are large enough to handle, prick out the seedlings into flats of loam-based potting soil and slowly harden them off, eventually in a cold frame. Plant them out into the garden during late spring at 9-12in (23-30cm) apart. Alternatively, sow the seeds in midsummer where the plants are to flower the following year. Thin the seedlings when they appear to 9-12in (23-30cm) apart.

Lythrum virgatum 'Mordens Pink'

Purple Loosestrife

A beautiful, resilient, and reliable hardy herbaceous perennial with lance-shaped, midgreen leaves and handsome, pinkish-purple flowers, borne in spires 9-12in (23-30cm) long during midsummer and into early autumn. 'Mordens Pink' does not produce viable seed. Grow only sterile cultivars, as the species is invasive in wetlands and meadows.

Height: 2-3ft (60-90cm)
Spread: 2ft (60cm)
Hardiness: Zones 3-9
Cultivation: Moisture-retentive soil in a sunny position suits it best, although it does quite well in ordinary garden soil. After flowering, cut back flowerstalks for a second bloom.

Propagation: The roots can be divided in spring or autumn, but often old clumps become very woody and difficult to divide. Instead, take cuttings 3in (7.5cm) long from the base of the plant during spring and insert them in pots placed in a cold frame.

Above: Lychnis coronaria **'Abbotswood Rose'** *This short-lived perennial displays loose heads of intense rose-pink flowers from mid- to late summer. The silvery foliage is an attractive bonus with this border brightener.*

Below: Lythrum salicaria **'Firecandle'** *This popular and reliable herbaceous perennial displays intense rosy-red flowers from mid-summer through to early autumn. It is another sterile Lythrum.*

Lythrum salicaria is an invasive loosestrife that overruns wetlands and meadows throughout the North and Northeast. Most cultivated varieties are sterile (without viable seeds) and are safe to grow.

THE FLOWER BORDER

Nerine bowdenii

This tender pretty South African bulbous plant from Cape Province is grown in pots North of Zone 7. It has narrow, strap-like, midgreen leaves which develop after the flowers appear from late summer to early winter. The distinctive rose or deep pink flowers are each formed of six strap-like petals usually twisted at their ends. They are borne in heads of up to eight flowers, at the end of stiff stems up to 2ft (60cm) long.
Height: 20-24in (50-60cm)
Spread: 6-8in (15-20cm)
Hardiness: Zones 7-10
Cultivation: Any good well-drained soil and a sunny position against a south or west-facing wall are suitable. Once established, the plants can be left in position to produce a spectacular display. However, when they are too cramped and congested, the number of flower stems decreases. In the North, grow in pots, similar to amaryllis
Propagation: Every four or five years, lift and divide overcrowded clumps. The plant can also be increased by sowing the soft, fleshy seeds in loam-based potting soil during late spring.

Macleaya microcarpa

(*Bocconia microcarpa*)
Plume Poppy

A large, graceful, hardy herbaceous perennial from Northern China, with large heart-shaped leaves and feathery pink plumes, from mid- to late summer. They are best positioned at the back of a border or woodland edge, where they can be given plenty of room. The plume-like heads flower above other plants and create a very attractive background. These plants spread rapidly by invasive underground suckers. Despite its height, it rarely needs staking. *Macleaya cordata* is white blooming and somewhat less invasive.

Height: 5-8ft (1.5-2.4m)
Spread: 3-3½ft (90cm-1m)
Hardiness: Zones 3-8
Cultivation: Rich, fertile relatively light soil suits the plume poppy. Give it a site sheltered enough to prevent its tall stems being blown and battered by strong wind. In autumn, cut them down to soil level.
Propagation: The invasive roots can be lifted and divided in spring or autumn, and for the home gardener this is the easiest method. Alternatively, 2-3in (5-7.5cm) long cuttings from basal shoots can be taken in early summer and inserted in pots containing equal parts of peat and sharp sand, placed in a cold frame. Pot up the plants when they are well rooted.

Above: Macleaya microcarpa
A beautiful herbaceous perennial with feathery plumes. It is an invasive plant and because of this it is not very well suited to small gardens.

Top right: Nerine bowdenii
An eye-catching bulbous plant for autumn flowers or growing as a pot plant. It is unusual, in that the leaves appear after the flowers.

Right: Paeonia officinalis
'Rubra Plena' *A beautiful large-flowered herbaceous perennial sometimes called the old double crimson peony, with crimson-red flowers in early to midsummer. Once established it is best to leave peonies undisturbed.*

Macleaya microcarpa is ideal for filling a large corner position against a wall. Its tall flower plumes are ideal for breaking up the often imposing nature of a large brick wall.

Nerine bowdenii, a mild climate plant, is best given a relatively narrow border against a warm wall all to itself. Its late flowering makes it a tricky plant to combine effectively with others.

Paeonia officinalis

Common Peony

A distinctive and well-known herbaceous perennial, more popular in the past than today, but still deserving a position in a mixed border. The large, deeply incised midgreen leaves are a perfect foil for the 5in (13cm) wide, single crimson flowers that appear on stiff stems in early to midsummer. The species, however, is rarely seen and it is the varieties such as 'Rubra Plena' (crimson-red), 'Rosea Plena' (deep pink) and 'Alba Plena' (pink at first, fading to white) that are mainly grown. *Paeonia lactiflora,* also known as *P. albiflora,* is another herbaceous perennial and rises to about 2ft (60cm) high. The true species bears 3-4in (7.5-10cm) wide single, white and scented flowers in early summer. However, there are many varieties in pink and red, which can be up to 7in (18cm) wide. These include 'Alice Harding' with double, light pink flowers; 'Cytherea' with scented, semi-double deep cherry blooms; 'Dinner Plate' displaying double, pink blossoms, 'Felix Crousse' with double, clear red blooms;'Phillipe Rivoire' with fragrant,double rosy-red flowers; 'Pink Parfait' displaying double bloom of strong, pink with a silvery edge; 'Kansas' a double, bright red blossom; 'Raspberry Ice' double displaying silver highlights on raspberry petals and the well-known 'Sarah Bernhardt' with scented, double, pink flowers. These are plants with dramatic flowers that soon create interest in the garden.

Height: 2¹/₂-3ft (75-90cm)
Spread: 3ft (90cm)
Hardiness: Zones 3-8
Cultivation: Paeonies thrive in a rich, well-drained but moisture-retentive soil in full sun or light shade. When preparing the soil, dig in plenty of well-rotted manure or compost.
Propagation: During early spring or autumn, lift and divide large clumps.

Paeonia officinalis is originally a native of Southern Europe, from France to Albania. The true species is difficult to obtain, though there are several excellent hybrid varieties.

THE FLOWER BORDER

Papaver orientale

Oriental Poppy

This hardy and stunningly attractive herbaceous perennial with rough, bristly, hairy stems and leaves is a wonderful scene-setter. The mid- to deep green leaves are deeply incised, with the 3½-4in (9-10cm) wide scarlet flowers with black centers appearing during early to midsummer. Poppies go dormant in mid- to late summer so plant next to full-growing perennials such as *Gypsophila* or *Perovskia*; or plan to fill the with summer-blooming annuals. They make a good cut flower, after searing ends with a flame.

Height: 2-3ft (60-90cm)
Spread: 2-2½ft (60-75cm)
Hardiness: Zones 2-7
Cultivation: Any good well-drained garden soil and a position in good light suit Oriental poppies. Remove all dead flowers.
Propagation: The easiest way to increase Oriental poppies is by lifting and dividing overgrown plants during spring. Alternatively, sow seeds thinly during summer, ¼ in (6mm) deep, in a well-prepared seedbed outdoors. When the seedlings are large enough to handle, thin them to 6in (15cm) apart. In autumn or spring, transfer them to their flowering positions.

Phlox paniculata

Phlox Garden

A well-known and reliable herbaceous perennial for borders, which produces abundant displays of dense 4-6in (10-15cm) heads of 1in (2.5cm) wide flowers from mid- to late summer above midgreen, lance-shaped leaves. The range of colors is wide, from white to purple, and red and pink forms, including 'Bright Eyes' (pale pink with deeper eye – not susceptible to mildew), 'Starfire' (deep red), 'Fairy's Petticoat' (shell-pink), and 'Pinafore Pink' (bright pink).

Height: Range of varieties from 2-4ft (60cm to 1.2m)
Spread: Range of varieties from 1½-2ft (45 to 60cm)
Cultivation: A fertile, well-drained but moisture-retentive soil in full sun or light shade assures success. Give the plants a mulch of well-decomposed compost or manure in spring to help reduce the loss of moisture from the soil. During dry summers, water the soil. Good air circulation is essential to reduce chances of powdery mildew in hot, humid summers. Thinning out stems in spring will allow better air circulation. New research indicates anti-transpirants help reduce mildew where plants are susceptible. Choosing mildew

resistant varieties is the best defense. In exposed areas, it is advisable to support the plants with twiggy sticks, and in autumn cut down the plants to soil level to tidy them up.

Propagation: Plants can be increased easily by lifting and dividing overgrown clumps in spring or autumn and replanting the young outside parts. They may also be propagated by taking root cuttings in winter or early spring. Cut the thicker roots into ½in (12mm) pieces and place in loam-based potting soil at 55°F (13°C). Cover the compost lightly. When shoots from these roots are 2½in (6.5cm) high, move the flats to a cold frame to harden off. Plant out into nursery rows in late spring and leave for a couple of years before transplanting to the permanent site. Herbaceous phloxes can be grown from seeds, but named forms will not breed true. However, if you like to experiment when raising plants, phloxes can be easily grown by sowing seeds in loam-based seed starting mix during late spring. Place the sown flats in a cold frame. Prick off the seedlings into further flats when large enough to handle, and when growing strongly plant out into a well-prepared nursery bed. Set out in the garden during the autumn of the following year.

Left: **Papaver orientale**
Few herbaceous perennials capture as many early to mid-summer glances as this Oriental poppy. There are several varieties available, in a wide colour range.

Right: **Phlox paniculata** This old-fashioned perennial is a favorite for borders. There are a wide-range of varieties in pinks, purples, reds and white to choose from.

Far right: **Polygonum amplexicaule 'Atrosanguinea'**
This herbaceous perennial gives a ground-covering of deep green leaves with spires of red flowers.

Papaver orientale needs a rustic, cottage garden setting to show off its charms – it never looks as good in a formal setting. When allowed to splay outwards over an old brick path, it is a delight.

Polygonum amplexicaule 'Atrosanguinea'

Mountain Fleece

A beautiful Himalayan herbaceous perennial with deep green, heart-shaped, long and tapering, pointed leaves. This variety displays 6in (15cm) long spikes of red flowers during midsummer and early autumn. The variety 'Firetail' creates attractive bright crimson-scarlet spikes. The polygonums are difficult to find in catalogs or nurseries, but well worth the search. *Polyghonum bistorta* 'Superbum' is hardier (Zones 3-8), lower growing (18-30in/45-75cm), and more common in cultivation than *P.* 'Atrosanguinea'; it is a superb pink-flowering perennial; ideal for a small garden.

Height: 3-4ft (90cm-1.2m)
Spread: 2-2¹/₂ft (60-75cm)
Hardiness: Zones 6-9
Cultivation: Fertile, moist soil in full sun or partial shade is needed. After flowering, cut down the stems to soil level.
Propagation: Increase by lifting and dividing the overgrown clumps in autumn or spring.

Polygonum bistorta, the snakeweed is another widely-grown species. It is a mat-forming plant with light green leaves and spikes of pink flowers.

THE FLOWER BORDER

Potentilla atrosanguinea

Himalayan Cinquefoil

A delightful Himalayan herbaceous perennial; the original form is little grown itself but it has given rise to a wide range of hybrids. They have gray-green, somewhat strawberry-like leaves, with the flowers borne in loose sprays of single or double flowers in heads up to 1½ft (45cm) wide, from mid- to late summer. Varieties to look for include 'Firedance' (small, single salmon orange flowers), 'Gibson's Scarlet' (single, brilliant-red) and 'William Rollinson' (semi-double, flame orange).

Height: 1½-2ft (45-60cm)
Spread: 15-18in (38-45cm)
Hardiness: Zones 5-8
Cultivation: Potentillas will do well in a fertile, well-drained soil in full sun. Each spring, mulch them with well-rotted manure or compost, and in dry weather water the plants thoroughly.
Propagation: The easiest way for a home gardener to increase them is by lifting and dividing large clumps in spring or autumn.

Above: Potentilla atrosanguinea 'Gibson's Scarlet' *The single brilliant-red flowers of this distinctive herbaceous perennial are a joy from mid- to late summer. The strawberry-like leaves supply an ideal foil for the flowers.*

Left: **Sedum 'Autumn Joy'** *A hybrid between S.spectabile and S. telephium, it is one of the best garden plants, never failing to create interest through its autumn heads of salmon-pink flowers.*

Sedum spectabile

Stonecrop

This is one of the most reliable and attractive of all border perennials. The blue-gray, succulent foliage is attractive throughout the season. During late summer and autumn, it bears dense 3-6in (7.5-15cm) wide

---

Potentilla nepalensis has also produced some superb herbaceous perennials, like 'Roxana' (pink brown-red and orange flowers) and 'Miss Willmott' (cherry pink). Both are 2ft (60cm) high.

Sedum spectabile mixes well with several blue plants, such as rose-purple colchicums and the stiff, upright spires of the violet bead-like flowers borne by *Lirope muscari,* the lily turf.

heads of pink flowers flushed with a mauve tinge. Several superb varieties are available; perhaps the best known is the hybrid 'Autumn Joy' with flowers that change from pale rose to a beautiful salmon-pink. 'Meteor' has deep carmine-red heads and 'Brilliant' deep rose ones. As a bonus, the seed heads are attractive in winter.

Height: 1-1½ft (30-45cm)
Spread: 1½ft (45cm)
Hardiness: Zones 4-10
Cultivation: Any ordinary well drained soil and a position in full sun are suitable. Set new plants in position during spring or autumn. In spring, remove the dead flower heads.
Propagation: The easiest way for a home gardener to increase sedums is by lifting and dividing established clumps in spring or autumn. Alternatively, take stem cuttings 1-3in (2.5-7.5cm) long in late spring and insert them in pots of sandy compost in a cold frame.

Schizostylis coccinea

Crimson Flag · Kaffir Lily

A well-known South African rhizomatous-rooted herbaceous perennial with midgreen, sword-like leaves and long stems bearing star-shaped 1½in (4cm) wide rich crimson flowers in late summer and early autumn. The flowers are arranged in spikes about 6in (15cm) long. The form 'Major' displays extra-large red flowers on strong stems, 'Sunrise' has salmon pink flowers, 'Viscountess Byng' bears pale pink blooms, and 'Mrs. Hegarty' pale pink flowers.

Height: 2-3ft (60-90cm)
Spread: 12-15in (30-38cm)
Hardiness: Zones 6-10
Cultivation: Moist, fertile soil and a position in full sun are essential. It is vital that the soil is kept moist, so each spring give it a mulch of compost or peat. In autumn, cut the plants down to soil level.
Propagation: During spring, lift the plants and divide them into pieces, each containing five or six shoots. Replant these pieces before their roots become dry.

Above: **Schizostylis coccinea 'Major'** *This vivid-red South African plant needs moist, fertile soil. As well as providing late season flowers for the garden it is ideal for use as a cut-flower.*

Schizostylis coccinea is in flower at the same time as the Michaelmas daisy *Aster novi-belgii*. Soft blue asters blend well with schizostylis, and with silver-leaved *Santolina chamaecyparissus*.

THE FLOWER BORDER

Sidalcea malviflora

Checkerbloom · Mallow

An erect, slender, rather twiggy-stemmed hardy herbaceous perennial native to the West Coast. The midgreen lower leaves are roundish, with five to nine shallow lobes. The funnel-shaped, 2in (5cm) wide, mallow-like pink flowers appear in clustered spires towards the tops of the stems from mid- to late summer. Several forms are available including 'Loveliness' (shell-pink), 'Oberon' (clear pink), 'Rose Queen' (rose-pink) and 'William Smith' (warm salmon-pink).

Height: 2½-4ft (75cm-1.2m)
Spread: 45-60cm (1½-2ft)
Hardiness: Zones 5-10
Cultivation: Ordinary garden soil suits this plant, but it must not be in full sun or strong shade. A position with light speckled shade in soil that does not dry out during summer is ideal. It grows best in cool, dry climates and does poorly in heat and humidity.
Propagation: It is easily increased by lifting and dividing overgrown clumps in mid-spring, replanting only the pieces from around the outside. It can be increased from seeds sown in spring in a cold frame, but named forms do not come true in this way.

Above: Tigridia pavonia *The beautiful plant is only half-hardy and requires a warm position. It produces a succession of vividly colored flowers, each lasting only a day but followed by others to give color over a long period. The strange markings and spots on the flowers amply justify the plant's common name tiger flower.*

Left: Sidalcea malviflora *The mallow-like pink flowers of this herbaceous perennial are borne on tall stems. After the delicately colored flowers have faded, cut down the stems to 9in (23cm) of soil level to encourage the development of lateral shoots.*

Tigridia pavonia

Tiger Flower · Shell Flower · One-day Lily

This is one of the brightest and most eye-catching of all summer flowering bulbous plants. *Tigridig* is Latin for "Tiger" and refers to the markings on the flower. Originating from Mexico and Peru, it is only half-hardy and should be treated similiar to gladiolus where it is not hardy. The long sword-like midgreen pleated leaves grow up to 2ft (60cm) high. From midsummer to autumn, it produces 4in (10cm) wide yellow flowers spotted with crimson-brown. These are formed of three large petals and three small ones. Each of these flowers lasts for one day, but fortunately each stem

Sidalcea malviflora, with its delicate pink flowers, needs careful positioning in a border if it is not to be dominated by strong colors. An old brick wall provides an attractive background.

Tigridia pavonia does not look good with other plants: its color and shape are dramatic and can all too easily overwhelm other plants. It is best grown against a warm wall and given a spot to itself.

Tulipa

The range of these much-loved spring bulbs is extensive. They can be used in bedding schemes during spring, or in mixed borders, rock gardens, containers, as well as indoors during winter and early spring. There is a wide range of species, and in addition botanists have classified those that have been created by bulb experts. There are many different divisions encompassing the wide range of flower sizes, shapes and heights. These are:

Division 1: Single Early (6-15in/15-38cm): The single flowers appear in spring when grown outdoors, or during winter indoors. Each flower is 3-5in (7.5-13cm) wide and sometimes opens flat when in direct and full sun. Many varieties are available, including some fine red and pink ones, as well as white, yellow, orange and purple.

Division 2: Double Early (12-15in/30-38cm): The double flowers appear in spring when grown out-of-doors in bedding schemes, or earlier when forced indoors. Each flower is 4in (10cm) wide and rather like a double peony. The color range is wide, including pink and red.

bears up to eight flowers. Several varieties are available in red or scarlet. *Tigridia pavonia* is only one of a genus formed of about twelve species, all coming chiefly from Mexico but some also from Guatemala. Except for the tiger flower, which is descriptively known as the jockey cap in New Zealand, they are rarely grown in the U.S. and really need the benefit of a frost-proof greenhouse, although they can be planted outdoors in spring and lifted for storage in a frost-proof place during autumn.
Height: 1½-2ft (45-60cm)
Spread: 8-10in (20-25cm)
Hardiness: Zones 7-10

Cultivation: Rich, well-drained soil and a warm, sunny position are best. Treat *Tigridia* like *Gladiolus*, planting the bulbs 3in (7.5cm) deep in spring, and after flowering lifting and storing them in a frost-free and vermin-proof place during winter. Only in exceptionally warm areas and when grown against a west or south-facing wall can the bulbs be left in position during winter.
Propagation: When the plants are lifted and divided in autumn, detach the young offsets from around the sides of the mother bulbs and re-plant them separately into the garden during the warmer spring weather.

Blue, pink and lavender mixtures can be created by an underplanting of a pale blue forget-me-not *(Myosotis)* and the tulips 'Dreaming Maid' and 'Cum Laude'.

THE FLOWER BORDER

Above: **Tulip 'Aladdin'**
*A lily-flowered tulip from Division 7
with a typical waisted appearance
and pointed petals. 'Other lily-
flowered tulips are 'Red Shine' (fire
engine red) and 'Queen of Sheba'
(red, with orange edges).*

Division 3: Mendel
(15-20in/38-50cm): These flower
later than the previous types, with
rounded, 4-5in (10-13cm) wide
flowers on quite slender stems.
Colors include white and red, as
well as yellow. They look like a
cross between single early types
and Darwins.

Division 4: Triumph (up to 20in/
50cm): These bear angular-
shaped, 4-5in (10-13cm) wide
flowers on strong stems in midspring. Colors include yellow, gold
and lilac, as well as pink and red.

Division 5: Darwin Hybrids
(2-2½ft/60-75cm): These are
among the most large flowered and
brilliant of all tulips, with flowers up
to 7in (18cm) during mid-
spring. There are multi-colored
forms, as well as orange purple,
yellow and red varieties.

Division 6: Darwin
(2-2½ft/60-75cm): These are
widely used in bedding schemes,
producing rounded flowers up to

5in (13cm) wide in late spring.
Varieties are available in white,
yellow and purple, as well as multi-
colours and pink and red.

Division 7: Lily-flowered
(1½-2ft/45-60cm): These are
characterized by the narrow waists
of the flowers, also the pointed
petals that curl outwards, reaching
8in (20cm) wide during midspring.
They look distinctive when massed
in a bedding scheme. Colors
include white, orange, yellow and
multi-colored forms, as well as
shades of red.

Division 8: Cottage (up to 3ft/
90cm): This old grouping has oval

or rounded flowers 4-5in (10-13cm)
wide in midspring. The petals
sometimes have a hint of fringing
at their tips, and are looser than in
other forms. Flower colors include
white, pink, yellow, lilac and green,
as well as red.

Division 9: Rembrandt
(2½ft/75cm): These are tulips with
"broken" colors. The rounded, 5in
(13cm) wide flowers have vivid
splashes of color on the petals
during midspring. Base colors
include white, orange, yellow, pink,
violet and brown, as well as red,
with eye-catching broken colors
superimposed.

For a **yellow, pink and blue mixture** try a
deep blue forget-me-not *(Myosotis),* salmon pink
'Queen of the Bartigons' and the yellow 'Mrs. John T.
Scheepers'. Both of these tulips are in Division 8.

pointed flowers that open nearly flat, giving the appearance of a water-lily. They open in spring on sturdy stems, and are ideal for fronts of borders, rock gardens and containers. Most have two-colored flowers.

Division 13: Fosteriana varieties
(1½ft/45cm): These are derived from *Tulipa fosteriana* and produce large blunt-ended flowers in red and yellow in mid-spring.

Division 14: Greigii varieties
(10in/25cm): These are mainly derived from *Tulipa greigii,* bearing brilliant, long-lasting red, yellow and near-white flowers in midspring. The petals reach 3in/7.5cm long when the flowers are fully open.

Cultivation: When grown in the garden, select well-drained soil, preferably facing south and in a sheltered position. Set the bulbs 6in (15cm) deep during early winter. Space them 4-6in (10-15cm) apart. Remove dead flowers and allow foliage to remain until it yellows. Tulips will re-bloom in following years; however, the blooms will be smaller. For strong displays plant new bulbs each year.

Division 10: Parrot
(1½-2ft/45-60cm): These have flowers up to 8in (20cm) wide, easily recognizable by their feather-like and heavily-fringed petals, appearing in mid-spring. The color range includes brilliant white, orange, yellow and purple, as well as red and pink.

Division 11: Double Late
(1½-2ft/45-60cm): These have very large and showy double flowers, somewhat resembling peonies and up to 8in (20cm) wide. They remain in flower for a long period during mid-spring. Colors include white, orange, yellow and violet, as well

as pink and red. Also, some are multi-colored, with stripes and edgings.

Division 12: Kaufmanniana varieties
(4-10in/10-15cm): These have been developed from *Tulipa kaufmanniana,* and have fine-

---

For a **blue and red spring-bedding mixture,** perhaps at the top of a dry stone wall, try blue *Aubrieta deltoidea* and the early-blooming tulip 'Red Emperor', a tulip derived from *Tulipa fosteriana*.

THE FLOWER BORDER

Propagation: The easiest way is to remove off-set bulbs clustered at the bases of the bulbs. These can be planted in a nursery bed to develop into flowering-sized bulbs.

Right: **Tulip 'Allegretto'**
This double late tulip from Division 11 is flamboyant, with long-lasting flowers during spring. Others are 'Angelique' (soft rose-pink) and 'Maywonder' (rich deep pink).

Below right: **Tulip 'Flaming Parrot'** *An exciting Division 10 tulip with a yellow and white background vividly striped red. Many parrot tulips are bicoloured, and when fully open may measure up to 8in (20cm) wide.*

Below: **Tulipa greigii** *A superb species tulip with gray-green lance-shaped and distinctively veined leaves. The blunt-pointed orange-scarlet flowers appear in mid-spring. It is the parent of many hybrids in Division 14, and itself is well worthy of a prominent position in a rock garden.*

For an **orange-red and yellow display** try a mixture of the orange-red 'Dillenburg', yellow and red 'Play of Flames' and the yellow 'Mrs. John T. Scheepers'.

Above: Tulip 'Greenland'
A demure tulip from Division 8 that reveals green stripes on a pink background. Other outstandingly attractive pink cottage tulips include 'Palestrina' (salmon-pink) and 'Mirella' (deep salmon-pink).

Further plants to consider

Anemone x hybrida
Japanese Anemone
Height: 2-3ft (60-90cm)   Spread 1-1¹/₂ft (30-45cm)
Hardiness: Zones 4-8
A hardy herbaceous perennial with several pink forms, including 'September Charm' (clear pink), 'Queen Charlotte' (semi-double and pink) and 'Max Vogel' (pink).

Bergenia cordifolia
Heart-leaf Bergenia
Height: 1ft (30cm)   Spread: 12-15in (30-38cm)
A hardy herbaceous perennial with large, mid-green, leathery leaves and lilac-rose flowers in dome-shaped heads during spring. The hybrid 'Ballawley' bears large red flowers.

Malcomia maritima
Virginia Stock
Height: 8in (20cm)   Spread: 2-4in (5-10cm)
A fast growing erect annual that bears small fragrant red, pink, lavender, or white flowers. A succession of sowings will produce flowers from spring to fall.

Matthiola incana
Stock
Height: 1-2¹/₂ft (30-75cm)   Spread: 1ft (30cm)
Stocks are available in awide range of annual and biennial strains and cultivars. They bear white, red, pink, or lavender flowers that are highly fragrant. *Matthiola longipetala,* night-scented stock, has grayish lilac flowers that open in the evening to release their sweet scent.

Monarda didyma
Oswego Tea · Bee Balm · Sweet Bergamot
Height: 2-3ft (60-90cm)   Spread: 1¹/₂ft (45cm)
Hardiness: Zones 4-9
A hardy herbaceous perennial with beautiful whorled heads of flowers from midsummer to early autumn. Pink and red forms include 'Cambridge Scarlet' (bright scarlet), 'Croftway Pink' (rose pink) and 'Mahogany' (dark red).

Primula x polyantha
Polyantha Primrose
Height: 8-10in (20-25cm)   Spread: 8-10in (20-25cm)
Hardiness: Zones 3-8
Polyantha primroses are available in a number of strains and hybrids. They are sold in single or bicolor shades. These primroses are also popular as potted plants.

If you like a **yellow and scarlet and gold mixture** try the stunning combination of a planting of a yellow viola and the scarlet and gold 'Keizerskroon'. The latter is a single early tulip from Division 1.

Above: Agapanthus praecox
This half-hardy evergreen creates dense 2-3in (5-7.5cm) wide heads of pale blue flowers during mid to late summer.

Agapanthus x 'Headbourne Hybrids'

African Lily

This popular hybrid is hardier than most other species. Like its relatives, it has long, strap-like midgreen leaves, with stunningly attractive deep violet-blue to pale blue flowers held in large heads like upturned umbrellas during mid-to late summer.
Height: 2-2¹/₂ft (60-75cm)
Spread: 1¹/₂-2ft (45-60cm)
Hardiness: Zones 8-10, in colder climates may be over-wintered indoors.
Cultivation: Fertile, well-drained soil and a sheltered position are needed. The foliage dies down in autumn, with fresh leaves appearing in spring. Ensure that the soil is not waterlogged during winter.
Propagation: The easiest way to increase it is by lifting and dividing established clumps in late spring, just as the new growth makes an appearance.

Right: Agapanthus x 'Headbourne Hybrids' *A beautiful plant in the amaryllis family, often grown in containers for summer display.*

Aconitum carmichaelii wilsonii

Wolf's Bane ·
Aconite · Monkshood

This erect hardy herbaceous plant has deeply divided dark green leaves and 2in (5cm) amethyst-blue hooded flowers during late summer and into early autumn. Several varieties are available including 'Kelmscott Variety' (lavender-blue) and 'Barker's Variety' (deep blue).
Height: 4-6ft (1.2-1.8m)
Spread: 1¹/₂-2ft (45-60cm)
Hardiness: Zones 2-8
Cultivation: Deep, fertile, moisture-retentive soil in slight

Above: Aconitum carmichaelii wilsonii *A stately and erect herbaceous perennial, displaying amethyst-blue hooded flowers . It gets one of its common names, wolf's bane, from its poisonous roots, leaves, and stems.*

shade suits it best. Do not allow the soil to dry out. Cut the plants to soil level in autumn.
Propagation: It is easily increased by lifting and dividing established clumps in spring or autumn. Seeds can be sown in flats of sterile potting soil in spring and placed in a cold frame, but this method takes two years to produce plants for a strong display.

Aconitum napellus is another monkshood, with deep-blue flowers during midsummer. It blends well with a background of the smoke tree, *Cotinus coggygria* 'Royal Purple'.

Agapanthus blends well with yellow-flowered and silver-foliaged plants. For silver foliage choose *Stachys byzantina*, while *Achillea* x 'Coronation Gold' with its flat flower heads provides an ample splash of yellow.

Ageratum houstonianum

Ageratum · Flossflower

A half-hardy annual with midgreen, hairy, heart-shaped leaves and 3-4in (7.5-10cm) wide clusters of powdery bluish-mauve flowers from early to late summer. Several superb forms are grown, including 'Blue Blazer' and 'Blue Danube'.

Height: 5-12in (13-30cm)

Spread: 8-12in (20-30cm)

Cultivation: Moisture-retentive soil is best, and a position in full sun or partial shade. Do not set the plants in heavy shade. Removing the dead flower heads helps to extend the flowering season. This is important where the plants are being grown in containers on a patio.

Propagation: During late winter and early spring, sow seeds thinly ⅛in (3mm) deep in pots of sterile potting soil kept at 50°F (10°C). When the seedlings are large enough to handle, prick them off into flats and harden them off in a cold frame. Plant them out when all risk of frost has passed.

Below: **Ageratum houstonianum 'Adriatic Blue'** *A well-known half-hardy annual for summer-bedding schemes. It is especially eye-catching as a border edging and looks good alongside gravel paths.*

Ageratum houstonianum is a long-blooming summer annual. It looks good in combination with snapdragons, nicotiana and portulaca.

Anchusa azurea

Alkanet · Italian Bugloss

A brightly colored hardy herbaceous perennial with lance-shaped midgreen leaves, rough and hairy stems, and large bright blue flowers similar to forget-me-nots displayed in large heads during midsummer. There are several superb varieties, including 'Opal' (soft blue), 'Royal Blue' (rich royal blue), 'Loddon Royalist' (gentian-blue) and 'Little John' (half the height of others – deep blue).
Height: 3-5ft (90cm-1.5m)
Spread: 1½-2ft (45-60cm)
Hardiness: Zones 3-9
Cultivation: Deep, fertile, well-drained soil in a sunny position is best. Anchusas need support from twiggy sticks; in autumn cut down the stems to soil-level.
Propagation: It is easily increased from root-cuttings. These are best taken in winter, cutting the roots into 2in (5cm) long pieces. At the stem end of each cutting make a flat cut at right-angles to the stem, while at the root end form a slanting cut. This helps to sort out the cuttings if they become mixed up. Insert them flat end upwards in pots or flats of potting soil, and put them in a cold frame.

Aster amellus

Italian Aster

This well-known herbaceous perennial from Italy displays rough-surfaced gray-green leaves and 2-2½in (5-6.5cm) wide daisy-like flowers with golden-yellow centers during late summer and into autumn. Several superb varieties are available including 'King George' (soft blue-violet), 'Nocturne' (lavender-pink), 'Sonia' (large and pink) and 'Violet Queen' (compact and dwarf).
Height: 1½-2ft (45-60cm)
Spread: 15-18in (38-45cm)
Hardiness: Zones 5-8
Cultivation: Well-drained but moisture-retentive soil and a sunny position suit it best. It dislikes excessive water during autumn and winter. In late autumn, cut down the stems to soil level.
Propagation: Dividing established clumps in spring is the easiest method of increasing this plant. Alternatively, take basal cuttings.

Below: **Aster amellus 'King George'** *This variety has remained popular since it was first bred in 1914. It displays soft blue-violet flowers with dramatically contrasting golden-yellow centers.*

Above: **Anchusa azurea** *The beautiful blue flowers appear during midsummer, creating a strong color impact. The plants need support from twiggy sticks inserted at an early stage so that they can grow up through them.*

Anchusa azurea looks spectacular when grown against a background of yellow foliage, such as that of the golden privet *(Ligustrum ovalifolium* 'Aureum'). Lady's mantle *(Alchemilla mollis)* is small enough to be set around the front of the anchusa.

Asters are among the brightest flowering plants in our gardens, and suit bold plantings in a herbaceous or mixed border. A few asters are small enough to be planted in a rock garden setting, such as *Aster alpinus* which is only 6in (15cm) tall.

Above: **Aster amellus 'Nocturne'**
This an especially good form that has a compact and bushy habit with semi-double lavender-pink flowers. Free-draining soil is essential for this late summer and autumn-flowering plant to produce a good display. Unfortunately, in areas of high rainfall the flowers tend to become sodden with water and to be weighed down. This can be prevented by covering the flower heads with plastic sheeting.

Aster x frikartii

This brightly-colored hybrid aster between *A. amellus* and *A. thomsonii* reveals 2in (5cm) wide blue daisy-like flowers with orange centers during late summer and well into autumn. The variety 'Mönch' produces masses of clear lavender-blue flowers with yellow rayed centers. 'Wonder of Staffa' has lighter blue flowers and is slightly taller.

Above: **Aster x frikartii 'Mönch'**
A superb hybrid aster bearing lavender-blue flowers during late summer and into autumn, it is useful for providing color earlier than Aster amellus *varieties.*

Height: 2½ft (75cm)
Spread: 15-18in (38-45cm)
Hardiness: Zones 5-8
Cultivation: Fertile, well-drained soil and a sunny position suit this flower. Dry soil in late summer spells doom, but at the same time excessive wetness from heavy soils is also detrimental. Despite its height it does not need staking. If planted in the front of the border it will gracefully flop forward. In spring, cut the flowered stems down to soil-level. *Aster x frikartii* blends well with late-flowering plants. For a really stunning arrangement, use a mixture of *Anemone x hybrida* 'September Charm' with clear pink flowers, *Aster x frikartii* 'Mönch' and the pink phlox 'Bright Eyes'. *Aster x frikartii* also looks lovely with the white *Anemone x hybrida* 'Honorine Jobert'.
Propagation: The plants will not come true from seed. Dividing established clumps in spring is the easiest method of increasing this plant, or take basal cuttings in spring and put them in a frame.

Aster x frikartii is useful in herbaceous or mixed borders, and can be grown with many other plants such as *Anemone x hybrida, Acanthus mollis, Boltonia asteroides, Stachys byzantina* and *Sedum* 'Ruby Glow'.

THE FLOWER BORDER

Borago officinalis

Borage

This is a hardy annual, well-known as a culinary herb, with leaves used when young and fresh to flavour salads and fruit cups. They have a flavour reminiscent of cucumber and are large, oval, green and covered with hairs. The five-petalled, blue, $3/4$-1in (18-25mm) wide flowers appear in pendulous clusters from midsummer onwards. White and purple forms are also available.
Height: $1^{1}/_{2}$-3ft (45-90cm)
Spread: 12-15in (30-38cm)
Cultivation: Although this plant will grow in most soils, it does better in well-drained ground in a sunny position. It is well suited to a sunny bank or for a warm mixed border.
Propagation: During spring, sow seeds in shallow drills where the plants are to flower. When they are large enough to handle, thin the seedlings to 10-12in (25-30cm).

Campanula lactiflora

Milky Bellflower

This beautiful hardy herbaceous perennial has stems smothered in small light green leaves. The miniature bell-like light lavender-blue flowers appear during mid-summer. There is a wide range of varieties including 'Prichard's Variety' at 3ft (90cm) with lavender-blue flowers, 'Loddon Anna' at $3^{1}/_{2}$-4ft (1-1.2m) with flesh-pink flowers, and 'Pouffe' at 10in (25cm) with light lavender-blue flowers.
Height: 3-5ft (90cm-1.5m)
Spread: 2-3ft (45-90cm)
Hardiness: Zones 4-8
Cultivation: Fertile deeply-cultivated and well-drained soil in full sun or slight shade suits it. But ensure that the soil does not dry out during summer. The tall-growing varieties

Borago officinalis, like many other seed-raised culinary and medicinal herbs, can be used in mixed borders or in odd corners, especially when a separate herb garden cannot be given entirely to them.

Below: **Campanula lactiflora 'Pouffe'** *A beautiful dwarf and hummockforming campanula with light lavender-blue flowers during mid-summer.*

need support in exposed areas.
Propagation: The easiest way to increase it is by division of large clumps during spring or autumn. Alternatively, take 1½-2in (4-5cm) long cuttings in spring, inserting them in pots of equal parts peat and sharp sand and placing these in a cold frame. When the plants are well grown, set them into their permanent positions in the garden. Alternatively, grow on the plants in a nursery bed before final planting.

Campanula medium

Canterbury Bell

Most gardeners know this lovely old hardy biennial, with an upright stance and 1-1½in (2.5-4cm) long bell-shaped blue, pink, white or purple flowers from late spring to mid-summer. The best known form is the so-called cup-and-saucer variety, 'Calycanthema'. 'Bells of Holland', 15in (38cm) high and with a conical growth habit, has a mixture of single flowers in shades of blue, mauve, rose and white. Another form, 15-20in (38-50cm) high, is 'Dwarf Musical Bells' with multi-colored bell-like flowers smothering the plants in blue, white and pink.
Height: 1½-3ft (45-90cm)

Above: **Campanula medium**
This reliable old favorite hardy biennial should find a place in any garden. It is ideal for filling bare areas in mixed borders, or as a high edging to paths.

Spread: 15-18in (38-45cm)
Cultivation: Moderately rich, well-drained soil in a sunny position suits this lovely plant.
Propagation: From spring to early summer, sow seeds ¼in (6mm) deep in a prepared seedbed. After germination and when large enough to handle, thin the seedlings to 9in (23cm) apart. During autumn, plant them into their flowering positions when the soil is in a workable condition.

White or yellow-flowered plants look superb with *Campanula lactiflora*. The tall-growing varieties blend well with *Lilium regale* and the Madonna lily, *Lilium candidum*. They can also join shape-contrasting, but similarly-colored, plants to create blue textures.

Campanula medium is ideal grown as bold clumps in a mixed border, where it will bring color while perennial plants are developing, perhaps blending with other annual plants such as love-in-a-mist *Nigella damascena* and candytuft *Iberis umbellata*.

Above: Centaurea moschata **'Dobies Giant'** *A less commonly grown annual* Centaurea, *with large fragrant flowers in pastel tints from early summer to autumn.*

Centaurea cyanus

Bachelor's Button · Cornflower

This beautiful plant, native to Europe and the Near East, is grown as a hardy annual. From early summer to autumn it displays sweetly-scented cornflower-like flowers in shades of blue, pink, white or red. The flowers, up to 1½in (3.5cm) wide, are borne above the narrow gray-green leaves. Bachelor's buttons are a very showy garden flower and make a long-lasting cut flower for arrangements.
Height: 1-2ft (30-60cm)
Spread: 10-12in (25-30cm)
Cultivation: Fertile well-drained garden soil and full sun suit it. They prefer cool growing conditions. Removing dead flower heads helps to prolong the lives of the plants. In exposed areas they will need support from twiggy sticks.
Propagation: During spring, sow seeds where they are to flower. Set them in shallow drills, thinning the seedlings to 9in (23cm) apart when they are large enough to handle.

Ceratostigma plumbaginoides

Leadwort

This hardy perennial has wide lance-shaped midgreen leaves that become bronze-red during autumn. The terminal clusters of blue flowers appear from late summer onwards. It brings late color to mixed borders.
Height: 10-12in (25-30cm)
Spread: 12-15in (30-38cm)
Hardiness: Zones 5-9
Cultivation: Light soil and a sunny site suit this attractive plant.
Propagation: It is easily increased by lifting and dividing clumps in spring, just before shoots appear.

Above: Centaurea cyanus *This hardy annual is very reliable and seldom fails to create a dominant display with its striking flowers in shades of blue, red, pink and white from early summer to autumn. It rises to about 2ft (60cm) high if the soil is kept moist, slightly less than this in dry conditions. It often naturalizes along roadsides where it provides a cheerful display. A good plant for meadows.*

Below: Ceratostigma **plumbaginoides** *A pretty perennial, ideal for late blue color in a rock garden. Its foliage is a delight in autumn, when it turns bronze-red, and looks superb at the base of a wall.*

Centaurea cyanus is a delight in an annual border where its flowers can be used alongside many other hardy annuals without any fear of its color dominating its neighbors. It is good for cut flowers, so plant it within arm's length of scissors.

Ceratostigma willmottianum is a half-hardy deciduous shrub (Zones 8-10) with diamond-shaped stalkless leaves. It bears terminal clusters of small rich blue flowers during midsummer, and is ideal in a mixed border.

Left: **Chelone obliqua** *An attractive herbaceous perennial with snapdragon-like flowers during late summer. This Southeastern native plant can often be invasive in the garden.*

Chelone obliqua

Rose · Turtle-head

This interesting, rather curious looking, hardy herbaceous perennial has 1in (2.5cm) long deep rose snapdragon-like flowers during late summer. These are borne on stiff, erect stems, from joints also bearing dark green lance-shaped leaves with serrated edges. *Chelone lyonii*, a hardier (zones 3-8) Southeastern native has terminal clusters of 1in (2.5cm) long pink flowers from mid-summer to early autumn. The plant eventually rises to about 2½-3ft (75-90cm) high.

Height: 2-2½ft (60-75cm)
Spread: 12-15in (30-38cm)
Hardiness: Zones 6-9
Cultivation: Fertile, well-drained but moist soil is needed, with a position in full sun or light shade. In windy sites it may require support from twiggy sticks. In autumn cut down the stems to soil level. *Chelone lyonii*, native to mountains rather than wetlands, will tolerate drier sites.
Propagation: It is easily increased by division of the roots during spring or autumn, replanting only the young parts from around the outside of the clump. Alternatively, seeds can be sown under glass in 59°F (15°C) in early spring. Using this method takes two years to produce flowering-sized plants.

Left: Ceratostigma willmottianum *This hardy deciduous shrub is quite similar to* Ceratostigma plumbaginoides *(far left). However* C. willmottianum *has lance-shaped leaves. The small, rich blue flowers are borne in terminal clusters from midsummer to autumn, and the leaves turn red in autumn. In spring, cut out old, dead or damaged shoots to soil level. You can trim the entire plant to make this job easier.*

Chelone obliqua is best planted in a mixed or herbaceous border, alongside color-contrasting and vigorous herbaceous plants such as the shasta daisy, *Chrysanthemum maximum*.

THE FLOWER BORDER

Above: **Cactus-form Dahlia** *There are many bedding dahlias in a variety of forms for summer displays. They come in a wide color range including many bi-colors.*

Dahlia

These fast-growing garden favorites can be divided into two main groups: those grown as half-hardy annuals for use in bedding schemes; and those that are best in mixed borders, mingled with herbaceous plants.

BEDDING DAHLIAS

These half-hardy perennials from Mexico are grown as half-hardy annuals, displaying 2-3in (5-7.5cm) wide single, double or semi-double flowers from midsummer to autumn. There are many varieties in a wide color range, in mixed or self-colors.

Height: 12-20in (30-50cm)
Spread: 15-24in (38-45cm)
Cultivation: Well-cultivated, fertile, compost or manure-enriched soil and a sunny position suit bedding dahlias. Soil too rich, however, will create excessive foliage at the expense of flowers. There is no need to stake them, unlike the larger border types. The removal of dead flowers assists in

the development of further blooms. Water the plants during dry periods.
Propagation: During the late winter and early summer sow seeds ¼in (6mm) deep in a sterile potting soil at 61°F (16°C). When they are large enough to handle, prick off the seedlings into flats or small pots of potting soil and slowly harden them off in a cold frame. Set the plants out in the garden as soon as all risk of frost has passed.

Above: **Ball-type Dahlia** *Ball type dahlias have very neat and compact blooms that look equally good in the garden or cut and displayed in a vase indoors. Dahlias thrive in rich soil and need a sunny position. The globular flowers are produced on stiff stems that carry the flowers above the foliage. To encourage rapid growth the soil must be carefully enriched before planting with the addition of well-rotted compost or manure.*

Bedding dahlias are available in every color of the rainbow except blue. They grow quickly from seed, are useful in providing color throughout the summer, and make attractive cut flowers.

Left: Semi-cactus-type Dahlia
A distinctive semi-cactus, not as quilled or tubular as the cactus types. The flowers have flatter petals.

BORDER DAHLIAS

These half-hardy tuberous plants, though easily damaged by frost, are unsurpassed for bringing color to a garden quickly. They come in rich colors of almost every hue. There are several classifications and many varieties. Indeed, each year hundreds of new varieties are introduced by dahlia specialists, while others are no longer marketed. When the dahlia was first grown as an exhibition flower in the early 1800s it consisted solely of ball types. At first no classification was recognized for the ball types, or for various other types of dahlia that were produced. However, catalogs were soon issued by traders in dahlias and these contained a rough classification. Currently dahlias are grouped into categories depending on flower size and form. The American Dahlia Society recognizes 12 distinct categories and catalogs new varieties.

Anemone-flowered (2-3½ft/60cm-1m): These have double flowers with flat outer petals and short, tubular inner ones. Flowering is from mid-summer to the frosts of autumn.

Ball-type (3ft/90cm): As implied, these have ball-shaped flowers, with tubular petals displaying blunt ends. There are *Small Ball* types with blooms 4-6in (10-15cm) wide, and *Miniature Ball* forms with flowers up to 4in (10cm) wide.

Cactus and Semi-cactus (3-5ft/90cm-1.5m): These are divided into five groupings – *Miniature* (blooms up to 4in/10cm wide); *Small* (blooms 4-6in/10-15cm wide); *Medium* (blooms 6-8in/15-20cm wide); *Large* (blooms 8-10in/20-25cm wide); and *Giant* (blooms 10in/25cm or more wide). Cactus types have petals rolled back or quilled for more than half their length. Semi-cactus types have similar petals, but quilled or rolled back for less than half of their total length.

Dwarf dahlias are thought to have been developed from low-growing forms found in 1750 on the lower slopes of the Sierra del Ajusca mountains in Mexico. The plants were said to be about 15-18in (38-45cm) high.

THE FLOWER BORDER

Collarette (2½-4ft/75cm-1m): These have blooms with a single outer ring of flat ray florets and a ring of small florets in the center, forming a disc.
Decorative: These have double flowers without central discs. They are formed of broad, flat ray florets. This grouping is subdivided into:
Miniature (3-4ft/90cm-1.2m): these have flowers up to 4in (10cm) wide.
Small (3½-4ft/1-1.2m): flowers 4-6in (10-15cm) wide.
Medium (3-4ft/1-1.2m): flowers 6-8in (15-20cm) wide.
Large (3½-5ft/1-1.5m): flowers 8-10in (20-25cm) wide.
Giant (4-5ft/1.2-1.5m): flowers 10in (25cm) or more wide.
Peony-flowered (up to 3ft/90cm): flowers formed of two or more rings of flat ray florets, with a central disc.
Pompon (3-4ft/90cm-1.2m): flowers closely resemble those of *Ball* types, but are more globular and do not exceed 2in (5cm) wide. The florets curl inwards for their entire length.
Single-flowered (1½-2½ft/45-75cm): flowers up to 4in (10cm) wide, with a single row of petals arranged round a central disc.
Cultivation: Well-drained soil, with plenty of moisture-retentive compost

or well-decomposed manure added, is required. Add a sprinkling of bonemeal before setting the tubers 4in (10cm) deep in the soil during mid to late spring. If you are planting sprouted tubers, take care that you do not plant them too early, as frost will damage them. The plants will need staking. Pinch out the growing tips of all shoots to encourage sideshoots to develop. If you want large flowers, remove sideshoots and buds from around the developing flowers. Removing dead flowers helps in the development of further blooms. In autumn gently dig up the tubers about a week after the foliage has been blackened by frost. Remove soil from the tubers and store them upside down for a few

Left: Dahlia 'Scaur Princess'
A beautifully-colored type which brings distinction to any garden.

Dahlias are superb for filling large blank areas in mixed borders, where they create spectacular colorful displays during late summer and into early autumn until frosts damage them.

weeks to dry them out. Then place them in flats of peat in a dry, frost-proof position until the following year.

Propagation: The easiest way for the home gardener to do this is to divide the tubers in spring.

Dahlias in floral art: As well as creating color in the garden the flowers of dahlias are ideal for decorating the home. The art of presenting dahlias for room decoration is not difficult, and part of the skill in using them relies on the choice of colors. Blue flowers, whatever their tone, need to be carefully used as the color tends to fade in artificial light. Purples and mauves, however, can be used subtly, especially where they echo the same tones in the room. When used with white-flowered dahlias, which both lighten and dramatize the arrangement, the effect can be quite different. In contrast, other colors such as yellow and orange are much warmer and radiate a strong feeling of cheerfulness. Those flowers rich in scarlet, however, can create the effect of warmth in rooms facing east and north and not subjected to strong summer sunshine. Rooms facing north or east generally benefit from warm colors, such as orange, scarlet, yellow and amber, whereas cool colors such as pale mauve, lilac-pink, purple shades and lavender are better in south and west-facing rooms. If strong colored blooms are used they can be given even greater impact by mixing them with pastel-colored flowers.

Collarette type dahlias originated in the municipal gardens of the Parc de la Tete d'Or at Lyons, France, during the last years of the last century. They are often bi-colors, with the outer ring (or collar) of a different color.

Left: **Echinacea purpurea** *This stately herbaceous perennial is justifiably famous for its richly colored flowers, from midsummer to autumn. The cone-like orange centers to the flowers are a particularly attractive feature.*

Echinacea purpurea

Purple Cone Flower

A well-known hardy herbaceous perennial, formerly called *Rudbeckia purpurea*. Its upright stems bear purple-crimson daisy-like flowers 4in (10cm) wide, at their tops from mid- to late summer. The lance-shaped, dark green leaves are slightly toothed and rough to the

Echinacea purpurea is a dominant flower, with the erect stems often holding the flowers high above neighboring plants, like islands of color. Surrounding plants should have subdued colors.

touch. Several varieties are available, including 'Robert Bloom', (carmine-purple), 'The King' (crimson-purple) and 'White Lustre' (white petalled with deep orange centers).

Height: 3-4ft (90cm-1.2m)
Spread: 2-2½ft (60-75cm)
Hardiness: Zones 3-8
Cultivation: Well-drained fertile soil and a sunny position are essential for success. In autumn cut stems down to soil-level.
Propagation: Although it can be increased from seeds sown in spring at 55°F (13°C), division of established clumps during spring or autumn is a much easier method. Use only the young parts from around the outside of the clump for replanting in the border.

Above: **Echinops ritro**
This hardy herbaceous perennial is highly cherished by flower arrangers. The globular flower heads appear during midsummer and last a long time after cutting.

Left: **Echium plantagineum 'Monarch Dwarf Hybrids'**
A hardy dwarf mixture, up to 1ft (30cm) high these hybrids produce flowers in many pastel tints. When grown in a sunny position, they seldom fail to attract bees.

Echinops ritro

Globe Thistle

This hardy herbaceous perennial has deep green, thistle-like leaves and round, 1½-2in (4-5cm) wide, steel-blue flowers held on stiff stems during midsummer. Bees find the flowers especially attractive.
Height: 3-4ft (90cm-1.2m)
Spread: 2-2½ft (60-75cm)
Hardiness: Zones 3-8
Cultivation: Most soils are suitable, but they should be well-drained and in full sun. This is a plant that is self-supporting and therefore ideal for island beds. During autumn, cut the plant down to soil-level.
Propagation: It can be increased from root-cuttings taken in late autumn, inserted in sandy potting soil and placed in a cold frame

before planting out in the garden. But the division of established clumps in spring or autumn is a much easier and quicker method.

Echium plantagineum

(*Echium lycopsis*)
Viper's Bugloss

This distinctive hardy annual from Europe has midgreen leaves and upturned blue or pale purple bell-shaped flowers from midsummer onwards. Although it normally grows up to 3ft (90cm), several lower-growing forms at 1ft (30cm) are available, including 'Blue Bedder' and 'Monarch Dwarf Hybrids' with blue, pink, lavender and white flowers. Several other species of echium can be grown in the garden, including the bushy, tender perennial (Zones 9-10) *Echium fastuosum*. From early to midsummer it displays 1ft (30cm) long, spikes of brilliant blue flowers. Another species, *Echium vulgare*, the common viper's bugloss, is a hardy biennial, but is invariably grown as an annual. It is relatively short (2ft/60cm high) bushy and compact and bears tubular, ½in (12mm) long, purple-budded, violet flowers from mid- to late summer. *Echium vulgare* and *Echium plantagineum* are both natives of the British Isles. *E. vulgare* is found in grassy places near the coast, while *E. plantagineum* grows in sandy areas near the sea, in the South-west.
Height: 2½-3ft (75-90cm)
Spread: 1½ ft (45cm)
Cultivation: Light, dry soil and a sunny position are needed, although partial shade also suits it.
Propagation: During spring, sow seeds ¼in (6mm) deep in their flowering positions, thinning the seedlings to 6in (15cm) apart. Seeds can also be sown in autumn, but wait until spring before thinning them. For earlier flowers, sow seeds in sterile potting soil in late winter or early spring at 55°F (13°C). Prick out the seedings into flats when they are large enough to handle, and harden them off before planting them out.

Echinops ritro is best planted in large clumps, where its dominant flower heads blend with a background grouping of *Campanula lactiflora* with small bell-shaped light lavender-blue flowers.

Echium plantagineum in one of its dwarf forms is more useful in a garden than taller types. An unusual annual, it is ideally suited for borders, and also for bringing height and shape contrast to small ornamental grasses.

THE FLOWER BORDER

Eryngium bourgatii

Sea Holly

This hardy herbaceous perennial has stiff, upright and branching bluish stems bearing spiny, holly-like leaves and silver-blue, thistle-shaped flower heads during mid- to late summer.

Height: 15-18in (38-45cm)
Spread: 12-15in (30-38cm)
Hardiness: Zones 5-8
Cultivation: It grows best in fertile well-drained soil in a sunny spot. Only in exposed areas will it need support from twiggy sticks. In autumn, cut it down to soil level.
Propagation: It can be increased by taking root cuttings in autumn and inserting them in pots of equal parts peat and sharp sand. Place them in a cold frame during winter and set the plants out into their permanent sites in the garden when they are well-grown.

Right: Eryngium bourgatii
This hardy herbaceous perennial displays strikingly attractive foliage and flower heads, much cherished by flower arrangers.

Below right: Eupatorium purpureum 'Atropurpureum'
This exciting hardy and reliable herbaceous perennial with purplish foliage and rosy-lilac flowers is admirable for mixed or herbaceous borders, as well as wild gardens.

Eupatorium purpureum

Joe-pye Weed

This handsome upright hardy herbaceous perennial native to Northeastern meadows has purplish stems bearing slender and pointed midgreen leaves. Fluffy, branching, 4-5in (10-13cm) wide heads of rose-purple flowers are borne from mid- to late summer. The form 'Atropurpureum' bears rosy-lilac flowers and purplish leaves. A clump of this dramatic perennial is a highlight of the fall garden. It deserves more use in American gardens.

There are several other superb **Sea Hollies,** including *Eryngium alpinum,* with frilled collars around the bases of its steel-blue flower heads, and *E. x oliverianum* which is graced with deep blue heads.

Eupatorium purpureum is a dramatic plant, often standing above its neighbors. In a mixed border, its height and color create a pleasing combination with the blue *Hydrangea macrophylla.*

Height: 4-6ft (1.2-1.8m)
Spread: 2½-3ft (75-90cm)
Hardiness: Zones 4-9
Cultivation: Any good moisture-retentive and fertile soil suits it, in full sun or light shade. The seedheads are dramatic through the winter to the spring. It benefits from a mulch with well-rotted manure or compost every spring.
Propagation: It is easily increased by lifting and dividing established clumps in autumn or spring.

Left: **Festuca ovina 'Glauca'**
This densely-tufted perennial grass is ideal for the front of a border. To create an impressive clump, use three or five plants, each 8in (20cm) apart.

Festuca ovina 'Glauca'

Blue Fescue

This hardy perennial grass forms a striking clump of bristle-like blue-gray leaves. It is ideal for planting at the edge of a border, where it can be used to soften harsh edges, and blends well with gravel paths. It is also a useful groundcover and can be grown in combination with dwarf evergreens. During summer it is adorned with oval, purple spikelets of flowers.
Height: 8-10in (20-25cm)
Spread: 6-8in (15-20cm)
Hardiness: Zones 4-9
Cultivation: Well-drained light soil and a sunny position are best.
Propagation: Lift and divide every two to three years in spring or autumn.

Filipendula purpurea

Japanese Meadowsweet

A handsome though dominating hardy herbaceous perennial with large lobed leaves held on crimson stems and surmounted by large flat heads of small carmine-rose flowers during midsummer.
Height: 2½-4ft (75cm-1.2m)
Spread: 2½-3ft (75-90cm) and more
Hardiness: Zones 3-8
Cultivation: An ideal plant for rich, fertile, moisture-retentive soil in partial shade, perhaps in a wild garden or at the side of an informal garden pond. If allowed to dry out the leaves will brown and drop.
Propagation: It is easily increased by lifting and dividing large clumps in autumn or spring.

Left: **Filipendula purpurea**
An impressive herbaceous perennial for a fertile moist, cool position in slight shade. Its carmine-rose flower heads form a dramatic display during midsummer.

Festuca ovina 'Glauca' is superb for a color contrast with yellow-flowered plants, such as golden garlic *Allium moly*, yellow-leaved hostas and Orange coneflower (*Rudbeckia fulgida* 'Goldsturm').

Filipendula rubra is another attractive filipendula, with large pinkish flower heads up to 11in (28cm) across. It is widely grown in the variety 'Venusta' with deep pink flowers. It loves moist soil and slight shade.

Gladiolus byzantinus

Byzantine Gladiolus

This hardy species gladiolus has 10-15in (25-38cm) long flower spikes loosely packed with up to twenty plum-colored 1-3in (2.5-7.5cm) long blooms during mid-summer. The narrow, sword-like and upright ribbed leaves with pointed tops rise to 2ft (60cm). They provide long-lasting cut flowers.
Height: 2ft (60cm)
Spread: 5-7in (13-18cm)
Hardiness: Zones 7-10
Cultivation: Rich, fertile, well-drained but moisture-retentive soil and full sun suit it best. The corms can be left in the soil from year to year in mild climates. In harsher climates remove the corms from the ground after a frost. Dry and store in a cool location for spring planting. Remove dead flower stems after flowering and cut down the yellowed foliage to soil-level in autumn – but not too early or it will not have transferred its food content to the corms, which act as storage organs for the winter.
Propagation: Every four or five years lift the plants in autumn and remove the little cormlets attached to the corm. Dry them and replant them in spring in sand-lined drills in a nursery bed.

Above: **Gladiolus byzantinus** *This small-flowered gladiolus flowers much earlier than its large-flowered relatives. Well-drained soil and a position in full sun assure success.*

Hosta

Plantain Lily

These hardy perennials with beautiful leaves, variegated in some varieties, were once known as *Funkias*. Hostas are mainly grown for their decorative foliage. The neat, clump-forming habit makes hostas a good choice for a shady spot. Blue, purple, lavender or white flowers appear in summer or fall. Many species of hosta are available, including *H. ventricosa*, with blue to violet flowers, and *H. tardiflora*, with deep purple flowers. Blue-leaved hosta cultivars also add color to the shade garden. Among these are 'Krossal Regal', 'Blue Moon', and 'Blue Boy'.
Height: 3½-4½ft (1-1.3m)
Spread: 2½-3ft (75-90cm)
Hardiness: Zones 3-8
Cultivation: Plant in well-drained but moisture-retentive soil enriched with leaf mold and in a lightly shaded position. During dry summers it will be necessary to water the soil.
Propagation: In spring, lift and divide large clumps. Many hostas can also be raised from seed.

Hostas are among the most attractive of flowers for naturalized or woodland settings. There are over 400 different hostas to choose among including many foliage colors and variegations.

Left: **Hosta rectifolia 'Tall Boy'**
This beautiful violet-mauve-flowered plant is ideal for a wild garden, where the soil does not become dry during summer. Even when not in flower, the foliage forms a strong display, especially in early summer.

Right: **Hosta 'Halcyon'**
This attractively-flowered hosta creates a dominant display in a slightly-raised border, where the leaves can spread safely without being trodden upon or splashed with soil during heavy rainfall. Here it is planted against the grass Hakonechloa macra 'Albo-aurea' with narrow bronze-tinted, variegated green and buff leaves. This grass has a cascading growth habit and looks good positioned at a corner.

Iberis umbellata

Globe Candytuft · Annual Candytuft

This well-known highly-fragrant hardy annual from Southern Europe has midgreen, pointed, narrow leaves. The 2in (5cm) wide clustered heads of purple, white and rose-red flowers appear from early summer to autumn from successive sowings. It is an annual that blooms best during cool weather. It soon germinates and forms an edging for the side of a path. Alternatively, set it in bold drifts towards the front of a border.
Height: 6-15in (15-38cm)
Spread: 9in (23cm)
Cultivation: Well-drained, even poor soil in full sun suits it. Remove dead flower heads to extend the flowering season.
Propagation: From late spring to early summer, sow seeds in shallow drills where the plants are to flower. The seeds take ten to fourteen days to germinate. When the seedlings are large enough to handle, thin them to 8-9in (20-23cm) apart.

Right: **Iberis umbellata** *This easily-grown and highly fragrant hardy annual flowers over a long period from successive sowings. It is superb for planting in poor soils.*

Iberis umbellata is a very amenable plant and associates with many others, such as Canterbury bells (*Campanula medium*), sweet alyssum (*Lobularia maritima*) and Virginian stock (*Malcolmia maritima*).

Incarvillea mairei

(*Incarvillea grandiflora brevipes*)
Hardy Gloxinia

This herbaceous perennial has attractive, deep green, pinnate leaves and bears rich pinkish-purple flowers with long tubular yellow throats during early to mid-summer. It should be more widely grown in the United States. The fleshy taproot is often available from bulb catalogs.

Height: 1ft (30cm)
Spread: 8-10in (20-25cm)
Hardiness: Zones 5-7
Cultivation: Fertile, well-drained light soil in full sun assures success. During spring, plant the fleshy roots 3in (7.5cm) deep, and in cold areas protect the young and newly-emerging shoots and leaves with a layer of straw. In particularly cold places they may require protection throughout winter. Often the new shoots are slow to emerge from the soil in spring, so take care not to damage them with early spring cultivations.
Propagation: Although the crowns can be lifted and divided in spring, they are sometimes tough and difficult to split. Instead, sow seeds in a prepared seedbed in spring, transplanting them the following spring to their permanent positions.

Right: Incarvillea mairei *This beautiful herbaceous perennial has yellow-throated pinkish-purple flowers in early to midsummer.*

Right: Iris douglasiana
This beautiful Californian iris needs alkaline soil and forms a large clump of color in early summer.

Iris douglasiana

Pacific Coast Iris

This beardless hardy iris from California has slender, coarse, deep green leaves that are normally evergreen and spread out to a width of 2ft (60cm). The 3in (7.5cm) wide flowers are borne in fours or fives on branched stems. They are in shades

Incarvillea delavayi is another well-known species, rising to 2ft (60cm) and displaying 2-3in (5-7.5cm) long rose-pink flowers during early summer. This species is taller than *Incarvillea mairei*.

Iris douglasiana is ideal for setting around rhododendrons, where it helps to produce ground cover and to create color when some of the rhododendrons have finished flowering.

of blue-purple and lavender, with distinctive veining on the 'falls' (the three outer petals), and appear from early to midsummer.

Height: 1-1¹/₂ft (30-45cm)
Spread: 2-2¹/₂ft (60-75cm)
Hardiness: Zones 8-9
Cultivation: This iris tolerates a little lime in the soil, and needs full sun or partial shade. However, it also grows well in neutral or slightly acid soil.
Propagation: It tends to be short-lived, but fortunately it is easily increased from seed sown during autumn in flats of sterile potting soil kept at 50°F (10°C). Alternatively, lift and divide the rhizomes in autumn, but take care that they do not dry out.

Iris sibirica

Siberian Iris

This versatile iris is suitable for a herbaceous border as well as the margins of an informal pond. The slender, sword-like, midgreen leaves die down in winter. The flowers are about 2¹/₂in (6.5cm) wide and are borne during mid-summer. In the original species, they are in various shades of blue, with white veining on the 'falls' (the three outer petals). Because the original species hybridizes freely, usually only hybrids are available. Good ones are 'Heavenly Blue' (rich azure blue), 'Sky Wings' (pale blue), 'White Swirl' (clear white) and 'Perry's Blue' (deep blue).

Height: 2¹/₂-3¹/₂ft (75cm-1m)
Spread: 1¹/₂-2ft (45-60cm)
Hardiness: Zones 3-9
Cultivation: It grows best in moist soil, but will also perform well in a herbaceous border, where it does not usually grow so high. Plant the rhizomes 1in (2.5cm) deep in the soil during autumn or spring.
Propagation: It is easily increased by lifting and dividing congested clumps in late autumn or spring. Replant the divided rhizomes 1in (2.5cm) deep. Large clumps tend to become hollow and bare at their centers, and are best lifted and divided every four or five years to keep them healthy.

Above: **Iris sibirica 'Heavenly Blue'** *This is a hardy iris for a border or the moist margin of a pond. Its rich blue flowers are borne two or three to a stem above the grassy sword-like leaves.*

Iris sibirica, planted in a moist area, mixes well with yellow-flowered candelabra primrose, *Primula japonica* and ferns. It also looks good against an old wall or edging a path.

Liatris spicata

Spike Gayfeather · Blazing Star

This hardy, tuberous-rooted, herbaceous perennial has small, strap-like, narrow, midgreen leaves. It bears dense, 6-12in (15-30cm) long, paintbrush-like spikes of pinkish-purple flowers during late summer and early autumn on stiff, leafy stems. It is native to the Northeast and is often seen in roadside meadows. The variety 'Kobold' is even more attractive, with frothy bright carmine flower spikes, often up to 1ft (30cm) long. It grows well even on poor soil. When planted in a small grouping, it creates a superb splash of midsummer color. This attractive variety has the advantage of growing to only 2ft (60cm) high, whereas the species, Liatris spicata, rises to 3ft (90cm) and requires much more room. Other varieties include 'August Glory' (purple-blue flowers), 'Floristan White' (creamy-white flowers) and 'Silver Tip' (lavender flowers). During late summer and into early autumn it produces lavender flowers borne in 1in (2.5cm) heads, in late summer. A native of the Central Plains it grows 4-6ft (1.2-1.8cm) tall and is hardy from Zones 3-9. The variety 'White Spires' has white blooms.

Height: 2-3ft (60-90cm)
Spread: 15-18in (38-45cm)
Hardiness: Zones 3-9
Cultivation: Ordinary garden soil – not too heavy – and a position in full sun suit the Blazing Star.
Propagation: During spring lift and divide established clumps. To ensure the clumps are readily identified, mark them in autumn. Alternatively, wait until late spring before dividing them, when the young shoots will be apparent.

Left: Liatris spicata 'Kobold' *The frothy flowers of this tuberous-rooted herbaceous perennial are a delight during midsummer to early autumn.*

Liatris spicata is ideal for the middle of a mixed or herbaceous border. Suitable companions include red hot pokers (*Kniphofia),* cone flower (*Rudbeckia*) and the oregon grape *Mahonia aquifolium.*

Linum narbonense

Flax

This well-known hardy perennial has narrow, lance-shaped, gray-green leaves and graceful, arching stems that usually die back in winter in colder climates but may persist throughout winter in milder regions. The 1-1¼in (2.5-3cm) wide rich blue flowers with a white eye, borne at the tops of the stems, appear throughout the summer months. *Linum perenne* is another perennial flax, slightly hardier (to Zone 4), rising to 1-1½ft (30-45cm). It has narrow lance-shaped grayish-green leaves and 1in (2.5cm) more open sky-blue flowers during mid- to late summer. Like *Linum narbonense* it is also short-lived, but can be easily raised from seed. *Linum usitatissimum*, the common flax or linseed, is a pale-blue-flowered hardy annual. It rises to about 2ft (60cm), with slender stems

Above: **Linum narbonense** *A feathery perennial that combines well with irises. The flowers, borne at the ends of long stems, appear throughout summer.*

bearing ½in (12mm) wide, saucer-shaped flowers during midsummer.
Height: 1-2ft (30-60cm)
Spread: 12-15in (30-38cm)
Hardiness: Zones 5-9
Cultivation: Ordinary well-drained garden soil and a sunny position suit flax best.
Propagation: During early summer, sow seeds ¼in (6mm) deep in a prepared seed bed. When the seedlings are large enough to handle, thin them to 8-9in (20-23cm) apart. In autumn, transfer them to their flowering positions. The plants are quite short-lived, so it is best to buy fresh plants every three or four years and replace old ones.

Liriope muscari

Lilyturf

This hardy, compact and clump-forming evergreen perennial has dark green grass-like leaves and upright stems, which bear 3-5in (7.5-13cm) long spikes of bell-shaped, lilac-mauve flowers from late summer through to autumn. The plant is often used as a groundcover, and will even tolerate deep shade. The species *Liriope spicata* is quite similar, but with more erect and narrower leaves.
Height: 12-15in (30-38cm)
Spread: 15-18in (38-45cm)
Hardiness: Zones 5-10
Cultivation: Well-drained light and fertile soil in full sun or shade. Remove the flower heads when they fade. The plant can be mowed or cut to the ground in the spring when fresh foliage will appear.
Propagation: During spring, lift and divide congested clumps.

Linum narbonense, with its cottage-garden appeal, is at home by the side of an old-looking flight of steps, against a weathered wall or as a perfect foil for gray-leaved plants.

Liriope muscari is ideal for the edge of a border or alongside a path. It harmonizes well with the autumn crocus (*Colchicum autumnale*), lungwort (*Pulmonaria saccharata*) or *Sedum* x 'Autumn Joy'.

THE FLOWER BORDER

Lupinus polyphyllus 'Russell Hybrids'

Lupine

These hardy herbaceous perennials are familiar to most gardeners. Their slender, upright spires of many colors including intense blues are borne above mid-green leaves formed of a circle of ten to seventeen leaflets. They bloom late spring to summer. Varieties available include: 'The Governor' (blue and purple), 'Minarette' (dwarf mixed colors) and 'Gallery Hybrids' (mixed blue, pink, red and white).

Height: 3-5ft (90cm-1.5m)
Spread: 2-3ft (60-90cm)
Hardiness: Zones 4-9
Cultivation: Well-drained moderately fertile soils are best, in full sun or light shade. Set the plants in position in autumn or spring, and cut them down to soil-level in autumn. They won't tolerate hot, humid summers.
Propagation: Increase named forms from 3-4in (7.5-10cm) long basal cuttings in spring. Otherwise, easily grown from seed, which should be scarified (notched) to ease germination.

Right: Lupinus polyphyllus 'Russell Hybrids' *These hardy herbaceous perennials are popular short-lived plants, providing a mass of color.*

Left: Nemophila menziesii *This hardy annual has a spreading growth habit and bears sky-blue buttercup-like flowers from early summer onwards. It is ideal for edging an annual border or even a mixed border. It prefers cool weather and does well in Northern gardens.*

Nemophila menziesii

Baby Blue Eyes

This bright-eyed hardy annual from California has light green deeply-cut feathery foliage and 1¼in (3cm) wide, sky-blue flowers with white centers from early to late summer.

Lupinus polyphyllus 'Russell Hybrids' mixes with a wide range of herbaceous plants. Highlight the flowers by planting it against a dark green hedge, or use its own foliage as a background for lower-growing plants.

Nemophila menziesii has flowers that are not strongly colored, so it can be mixed with plants such as the poached egg plant (*Limnanthes douglasii,*) with its yellow-centered white flowers.

Nicandra physaloides

Shoo-fly Plant · Apple of Peru

This hardy annual from Peru is vigorous and strong growing, its spreading shoots bearing oval, mid-green leaves with finely-toothed, wavy edges. The pale-blue, bell-shaped, 1½in (4cm) wide flowers have white throats, and appear from mid- to late summer. These are followed by non-edible apple-shaped green fruits that can be dried for home decoration. It is said to gain the name *physaloides* from the resemblance of the fruits to those of *Physalis alkekengi*, commonly called Chinese lantern or bladder cherry.

Height: 2½-3ft (75-90cm)
Spread: 15-18in (38-45cm)
Cultivation: Rich, moist soil and a sunny position are the keys to success. When preparing the site, fork in plenty of well-rotted compost. A native to the Tropics, it prefers warm weather.
Propagation: During late winter or early spring, sow seeds ⅛in (3mm) deep in flats of sterile potting soil kept at 50°F (10°C). When the seedlings are large enough to handle, prick them off into seedflats and put them in a cold frame to harden them off. Set the plants in the garden during late spring. Alternatively, sow seeds in late spring where the plants are to flower, ¼in (6mm) deep. Subsequently, thin the seedlings to 10-12in (25-30cm) apart.

Height: 7-9in (18-23cm)
Spread: 6-8in (15-20cm)
Cultivation: Although this annual grows in ordinary garden soil, it does even better in fertile, moisture-retentive soil in full sun or slight shade. It requires cool summer weather.
Propagation: During spring and early summer, sow seeds ¼in (6mm) deep in their flowering positions. When the seedlings are large enough to handle, thin them to 6in (15cm) apart. As well as being suitable for sowing in the garden, this annual can also be grown for flowering in pots in a cold greenhouse. To grow such plants sow seeds thinly in 5in (13cm) wide pots of sterile potting soil in a cold frame during late spring or early summer. When they are large enough to handle, thin the seedlings to three in a pot. Ensure the greenhouse is not too hot.

Right: **Nicandra physaloides**
This tall, vigorous, branching hardy annual needs space in which to develop properly. The pale-blue, bell-shaped flowers are borne over many weeks during summer.

Nicandra physaloides gains one of its common names, shoo-fly plant, from its ability to repel flies. It makes a lovely choice for the back of a border, with its attractive bell-shaped flowers.

Polemonium foliosissimum

Leafy Polemonium

A hardy herbaceous perennial native to the Western U.S., leafy polemonium has stiff, upright stems bearing leaves formed of narrow dark green leaflets. From early to late summer, it bears ½in (12mm) wide mauve-blue flowers in clustered heads. The handsome flowers are highlighted by orange-yellow stamens. The better known *Polemonium caeruleum*, Jacob's ladder, is a short-lived, less dramatic species.

Height: 2½-3ft (75-90cm)
Spread: 1½-2ft (45-60cm)
Hardiness: Zones 2-8
Cultivation: Rich, deep, loamy soil in partial shade, does not tolerate heat and humidity. These plants soon exhaust the soil, which will need annual mulching or feeding with fertilizer.
Propagation: The easiest way to increase this plant is by lifting and dividing established clumps in autumn or spring.

Below: Polemonium foliosissimum
This herbaceous perennial is ideal for borders and flowers over a long period of time. It needs rich soil, because the roots quickly exhaust the supply of nutrients.

Physostegia virginiana

Obedient Plant · False Dragonhead Virginia Lion's Heart

This distinctive hardy herbaceous perennial bears long spires of mid-summer tubular pink-mauve flowers above large, glossy, dark green, coarsely-toothed leaves. The plant gets its common name from its flowers, which have hinged stalks and can be moved from side to side, remaining as positioned. It is suitable for the border or meadow garden. Several varieties are available, including 'Rose Bouquet' (pink-mauve), 'Summer Snow' (pure white) and 'Vivid' (deep pink).

Height: 1½-3½ft (45cm-1m)
Spread: 1½-2ft (45-60cm)
Hardiness: Zones 2-9

Above: Physostegia virginiana 'Rose Bouquet' *A native of the Northeast, this popular hardy herbaceous perennial bears spires of mauve-pink, tubular flowers which resemble small snapdragons.*

Cultivation: This plant needs ordinary fertile garden soil that does not dry out during summer. Site it in a location where it has room to roam, as it spreads by underground runners. Plants will need pea-staking to avoid flopping, especially in rich soils. During autumn, cut it down to soil-level.
Propagation: It is easily increased by lifting and dividing plants in autumn or spring. Clumps will need dividing every 2 to 3 years.

Physostegia virginiana is a reliable plant for a mixed or herbaceous border. The deep pink-mauve variety 'Rose Bouquet' needs non-conflicting colors set around it at a lower level.

Polemoniums come mostly from Western America and Europe, and tend to be short-lived in Eastern climates. Plant in partial shade, excellent for woodland gardens.

Above: **Salvia x superba** *This hardy eye-catching herbaceous perennial forms a dramatic splash of color in any border.*

Above: **Salvia viridis** *is a beautiful hardy annual with pale pink or purple flowers which feature especially striking colored bracts at the tops of the stems. It is raised as a half-hardy or a hardy annual, and it delights in a sunny and well-drained position in the garden.*

Salvia x superba

Hybrid Sage

A planting of this superb hardy herbaceous perennial will immediately attract attention. Its erect stems bear abundant, rich violet-purple flower spires in mid-summer, so set it at the edge of a border. Dwarf forms rise to less than half the height of the plant, and include 'Lubeca' (violet-blue, 2¹/₂ft/75cm high) and 'East Friesland' (violet-purple, 1¹/₂ft/45cm high).

Height: 1¹/₂-3ft (45-90cm)
Spread: 1¹/₂-2ft (45-60cm)
Hardiness: Zones 4-7
Cultivation: Rich, well-drained but moisture-retentive soil in full sun. Dry soils are not suitable. If plants are dead-headed, they will re-bloom in late summer. Staking with twiggy pea-sticks is necessary for tall-growing forms in exposed areas. Cut down old stems to soil-level in late autumn.
Propagation: It is easily increased by lifting and dividing plants during autumn or spring.

Salvia viridis

(*Salvia horminum*)

This hardy annual from Southern Europe bears (¹/₂in/12mm) long pale pink or purple flowers from mid- to late summer. It is better known, however, for its 1¹/₂in (4cm) long brightly colored terminal bracts (modified leaves), which can be dried with the stems for home decoration. There are several fine varieties, with a range of colored bracts, such as 'Blue Bouquet' (rich purple-blue bracts) and 'Rose Bouquet' (rose-carmine bracts).

Height: 15-18in (38-45cm)
Spread: 9-12in (23-30cm)
Cultivation: Ordinary well-drained soil in full sun suits it. To encourage well-branched plants, pinch out the growing tips when the plants are only a few inches high.
Propagation: During late spring or early summer, sow seeds ¹/₄in (6mm) deep where the plants are to flower. When the seedlings are large enough to handle, thin them out to 9in (23cm) apart. You can raise earlier-flowering plants by sowing seeds thinly in trays of sterile potting soil at 64°F (18°C) during late winter or early spring. When the seedlings are large enough to handle, prick them off into pots of potting soil and place them in a cold frame to harden off.

Salvia x **superba** demands space to be at its best. Plant it at the front of the border, with tall light blue delphiniums at the back and a sandwich of yellow achillea between them.

Salvia viridis, also known as *Salvia horminum*, is grown for its colored bracts rather than for its flowers. For best displays, start salvias indoors in late winter. They do best in warm weather.

THE FLOWER BORDER

Above: Trachymene caerulea
*The delicate heads of small
lavender-blue flowers appear from
mid-summer to autumn. This is a
useful plant for bringing delicate
blue shades to flower arrangements.*

**Above: Tradescantia x andersoniana
'Isis'** *This well-known spiderwort has
striking purple-blue flowers during
most of summer. Well-drained but
moisture-retentive soil ensures
success with this reliable plant.*

Right: Tulip 'Lilac Time' *This
beautiful tulip from Division 7 is
distinctive, with its mauve, lily-like
flowers. Flowers in this division are
usually 6-8in (15-20cm) wide and
appear in midspring.*

Trachymene caerulea

(*Didiscus caeruleus*)
Blue Lace Flower

This is one of the most delicate and
pretty of all half-hardy annuals. The
delicate flowers are a blue version
of the wildflower, Queen Anne's-
lace. It forms a bushy plant with light
green, deeply-divided foliage. The
small dainty, lavender-blue flowers
are displayed in heads 1-2in (2.5-
5cm) wide and appear from
midsummer to autumn. They are
suitable for cutting for home
decoration, but the leaves and
stems are sticky to touch.
Height: 1½ft (45cm)
Spread: 10-12in (25-30cm)
Cultivation: Ordinary well-cultivated
garden soil and a sunny, sheltered
position suit it.
Propagation: During late winter
and early spring, sow seeds ⅛in
(3mm) deep in flats of sterile potting
soil at 61°F (16°C). When the
seedlings are large enough to
handle, prick them out into small
pots or flats of potting soil. Plant the
young plants out into the garden as
soon as all risk of frost has passed.

Tradescantia x andersoniana

Spiderwort

This hardy herbaceous perennial
with smooth, glossy, strap-like,
dull-green leaves and long lasting,
1-1½in (2.5-4cm) wide, three-petalled
flowers, is a delight throughout
summer and into autumn. The garden
cultivars are from hybrids with T.
virginiana, T. *ohiensis* and T.
subaspera. Spiderworts are usually
blue or purple, but pink, white and
red varieties also exist. The
resulting plants are superb and
include 'Carmine Glow' (carmine),
'Isis' (purple-blue), 'Iris Pritchard'
(white, stained azure blue)
and 'Purewell Giant' (carmine-purple).
Height: 1½-2ft (45-60cm)
Spread: 1½ft (45cm)
Hardiness: Zones 4-9
Cultivation: Ordinary garden
soil, well-drained but also
moisture-retentive, is best. In
late autumn, cut the plants down
to soil level.
Propagation: Lift and divide
congested clumps in spring.

Tulips

The range of form and color of
these well-known hardy bulbs is as
wide as their possible uses in the
garden. They can be used in
bedding schemes during spring, in
mixed borders or rock gardens, and
in containers for brightening up a
patio in spring. There is a wide
range of species, and in addition
botanists have classified those that
have been created by bulb experts
into fifteen divisions, encompassing
the wide range of flower sizes,
shapes and heights. These are:
Division 1 – Single Early (6-15in/
15-38cm): The single flowers
appear in spring when grown out-of-
doors, or during winter indoors.
Each flower is 3-5in (7.5-13cm)
wide and sometimes opens flat
when in direct and full sun. Many
purple varieties are available, as
well as ones with white, pink, red,
orange and yellow flowers.
Division 2 – Double Early (12-
15in/30-38cm): The double flowers
appear in spring when grown out-of-
doors in bedding schemes, or
earlier when forced indoors.

Trachymene caerulea from Australia soon attracts
attention when grown in a drift among hardy
annuals or in a mixed border. It can also be grown in
pots in an unheated greenhouse for summer color.

Tradescantia x **andersoniana** is ideal for a mixed or
herbaceous border. Many plants combine well with
them it, including border geraniums and *Campanula
lactiflora* 'Pritchard's Blue'.

Division 10 – Parrot (1½-2ft/45-60cm): These bear flowers up to (8in) 20cm wide in midspring, easily recognizable by their feather-like, heavily-fringed petals. The color range includes brilliant white, pink, orange and yellow, as well as some lovely purples.

Division 11 – Double Late (1½-2ft/45-60cm): These have very large and showy double flowers, similar to peonies and up to 8in (20cm) wide. They remain in flower for a long period during midspring. There are some stunning violet varieties, as well as white, orange, pink, red and yellow ones. There are also multi-colored forms.

Division 12 – Kaufmanniana varieties (4-10in/10-25cm): These have been developed from *Tulipa kaufmanniana*, and have fine-pointed flowers that open nearly flat, giving the appearance of water-lilies. They appear in spring on sturdy stems and are ideal for fronts of borders, rock gardens and containers.

Division 13 – Fosteriana varieties (1½ft/45cm): These are derived from *Tulipa fosteriana* and display large blunt-ended flowers in reds and yellows in midspring.

Division 14 – Greigii varieties (10in/25cm): These are mainly derived from *Tulipa greigii*, and produce brilliant red, yellow and near-white long-lasting flowers during midspring.

Cultivation: When growing tulips in the garden, select well-drained soil, preferably facing south and in a sheltered position. Plant the bulbs 6in (15cm) deep during early winter, spacing them 4-6in (10-15cm) apart. Remove dead flowers after blooming. Bulbs will rebloom for several years. If the bed is needed for another planting, dig up the bulbs as soon as flowering is over and heel them into a trench until the foliage has died.

Propagation: The easiest way is to remove the bulb offsets clustered at the bases of the bulbs. Plant these in a nursery bed and leave them to develop into flowering-sized bulbs.

Each flower is 4in (10cm) wide and rather like a double peony. The color range is wide, including good purple varieties, as well as red, violet, pink and yellow ones.

Division 3 – Mendel (15-20in/38-50cm): These flower later than the previous types, with rounded 4-5in (10-13cm) wide blooms on somewhat slender stems. Colors include white and red. They look like a cross between single early types and Darwins.

Division 4 – Triumph (up to 20in/50cm): In midspring these bear angular-looking 4-5in (10-13cm) wide flowers on strong stems. There are lovely lilac-flowered varieties, as well as red and pink ones.

Division 5 – Darwin Hybrids (2-2½ft/60-75cm): These have some of the largest and most brilliant flowers, up to 7in (18cm) wide; they appear during mid-spring. There are multi-colored varieties, as well as purple, red, orange and yellow varieties.

Division 6 – Darwin (2-2½ft/60-75cm): These are extensively used in bedding schemes, producing rounded flowers up to 5in (13cm) wide in late spring. There are some excellent purple varieties, also yellow, white, pink and red ones.

Division 7 – Lily-flowered (1½-2ft/45-60cm): These are characterized by the narrow waists of their flowers, also by the pointed petals that curl outwards as much as 8in (20cm) during midspring. They look especially attractive when massed in bedding schemes. Colors include white, orange, red, yellow and multi-colors.

Division 8 – Cottage (up to 3ft/90cm): This old grouping has oval or rounded flowers 4-5in (10-13cm) wide in midspring. The petals sometimes have a hint of fringing, and are looser than those of other varieties. As well as lilac, flower colors include green, white, pink, red and yellow.

Division 9 – Rembrandt (2½ft/75cm): These tulips all have 'broken' colors. The rounded 5in (13cm) wide flowers display vivid splashes of color on the petals during midspring. Base colors include violet, as well as brown, white, orange, red, yellow and pink.

For a **violet and yellow display**, try the deep violet Darwin tulip (Division 6) 'The Bishop' with the golden blooms of the popular Darwin 'Golden Apeldoorn'.

For a **mixture of creamy-white and blue,** try planting a bed with the mauve-blue parrot tulip (Division 10) 'Blue Parrot', dark purple Darwin tulip, (Division 6) 'Queen of Night' and the white 'White Parrot'.

Right: **Veronica prostrata** *This beautiful ground-covering veronica produces masses of small deep blue flowers from early to midsummer*

Veronica prostrata

(*Veronica rupestris · V teucrium prostrata*)
Harebell Speedwell

A hardy mat-forming alpine veronica. It is useful as a ground cover plant, displaying toothed mid-green leaves and 2-3in (5-7.5cm) long spikes of deep blue flowers from early to midsummer. Several reliable forms are available, including 'Spode Blue' (clear pale blue), 'Heavenly Blue' (sapphire-blue), 'Blue Sheen' (wisteria-blue) and Mrs. Holt' (bright pink).
Height: 4-8in (10-20cm)
Spread: 15-18in (38-45cm)
Hardiness: Zones 5-8
Cultivation: Any well-drained garden soil and a sunny position suit it.
Propagation: During midsummer, take 2in (5cm) long cuttings and insert them in pots of equal parts peat and sharp sand. Place the pots in a cold frame and when the cuttings are rooted, pot them up singly into potting soil. During the following spring, plant them out into the garden.

Veronica spicata

Spiked Speedwell

An upright slim-flowered hardy herbaceous perennial, this veronica is well-suited to the front of a border. It displays long, toothed, lance-shaped, midgreen leaves. The narrow, 3-6in (7.5-15cm) long spires of small blue flowers are borne throughout mid-summer. Several superb forms are worth growing, including 'Blue Fox' (ultramarine blue), 'Blue Charm' (deep blue) and 'Barcarolle' (rose-pink). *Veronica longifolia* (hardy in Zones 4-8) is another purple-blue-flowered border plant. It rises up to 4ft (1.2m) and bears 6in (15cm) long

terminal spires of flowers from early to late summer. To create a dramatic clump, set the individual plants about 1½ft (45cm) apart.
Height: 1-1½ft (30-45cm)
Spread: 12-15in (30-38cm)
Hardiness: Zones 3-8
Cultivation: Well-drained but moisture-retentive friable soil in full sun or slight shade assures success. In late autumn, cut the stems down to soil level.
Propagation: During spring, lift and divide overgrown clumps – you can usually do this every three or four years. This ensures healthy plants.

Top right: Veronica spicata
This is a reliable hardy herbaceous perennial for the front of a border, where it can display its spires of small blue flowers to advantage during mid-summer. There are several excellent varieties from which to choose.

Right: Catananche caerulea
This beautiful short-lived perennial brings a wealth of color to a border. It is also excellent as a cut-flower, and can be dried for winter decoration in the home. The flowers appear during summer. For details see under **Further plants to consider** *on the opposite page.*

Veronica prostrata blends well in a rock garden with yellow-flowered plants such as *Linum flavum*, with 1in (2.5cm) wide midsummer flowers, and the ever-reliable *Hypericum olympicum*, with golden-yellow flowers.

Further plants to consider

Ajuga reptans
Common Bugleweed
Height: 4-10in (10-25cm)   Spread: 12-20in (30-50cm)
Hardiness: Zones 3-9
A well-known, groundcover, hardy herbaceous perennial, with whorls of blue flowers borne on upright stems during midsummer. The form 'Atropurpurea' is distinctive, with purple leaves.

Campanula persicifolia 'Telham Beauty'
Peach-leaved Campanula
Height: 2-3ft (60-90cm)   Spread: 12-15in (30-38cm)
Hardiness: Zones 3-8
A delightful perennial, with an evergreen basal rosette. The rich blue, 1in (2.5cm) wide, saucer-shaped flowers appear during midsummer.

Catananche caerulea
Cupid's Dart
Height: 1½-2½ft (45-75cm)   Spread: 1½-2ft (45-60cm)
Hardiness: Zones 3-9
A short-lived herbaceous perennial with narrow, lance-shaped leaves and lavender-blue flowers during summer.

Delphinium x elatum
Larkspur
Height: 3-5ft (90cm-1.5m)   Spread: 1½-2ft (45-60cm)
Hardiness: Zones 2-7
A short-lived perennial with tall, dense spikes of blooms. The range of blue-flowered varieties is wide, including 'Blue Tit' (indigo-blue), 'Bonita' (gentian-blue) 'Black Knight' (dark purple) and 'Betty Hayes' (pale blue).

Geranium x magnificum
Height: 1½-2ft (45-60cm)   Spread: 18-20in (45-50cm)
Hardiness: Zones 3-8
An eye-catching hybrid geranium, with violet-blue (1in) 2.5cm wide flowers during mid- to late summer.

Geranium 'Johnson's Blue'
Height: 15in (38cm)   Spread: 15-18in (38-45cm)
Hardiness: Zones 4-8
A well-known light-blue midsummer flowering hardy herbaceous perennial.

Limonium latifolium
Sea Lavender
Height: 2ft (60cm)   Spread: 1½-2ft (45-60cm)
Hardiness: Zones 3-9
A distinctive hardy perennial, formerly classified as *Statice*. From mid- to late summer, it displays lavender-blue flowers in large, loose heads.

Veronica spicata gains its second name from the spike-like arrangement of its flowers. It will provide a second bloom if the spent flower spikes are removed.

large enough to handle. In autumn, plant out the established plants in their flowering positions. In cold areas, wait until spring to do this.

Left: **Achillea 'Coronation Gold'**
The eye-catching deep yellow saucer-like flower heads of this hardy herbaceous perennial are superb when the sun sets their bright color alight. The flowers are excellent for floral arrangements, especially those that are dried for winter decoration.

Top right: **Alchemilla mollis**
This beautiful herbaceous plant is ideal for setting alongside a paved garden path where it helps to soften the edge, merging the border with the path. It blends well with other plants.

Alchemilla mollis

Lady's Mantle

This hardy herbaceous perennial is grown primarily for its light-green shallowly lobed foliage. Frothy sprays of sulphur-yellow star-shaped flowers 1/8in (3mm) wide, are borne from early to midsummer.
Height: 1-1½ft (30-45cm)
Spread: 1-1½ft (30-45cm)
Hardiness: Zones 4-7
Cultivation: Well-drained but moisture-retentive soil in full sun or light shade is needed. If spent flower heads are removed, *Alchemilla* will rebloom. Tired summer foliage may be cut to the ground for fresh regrowth.
Propagation: Seeds can be sown in flats of seed starting mix in early spring and placed in a cold frame. When they are large enough to handle, prick out the seedlings into flats of potting soil, later setting the plants in nursery rows. In autumn, or spring in cold areas, set the plants in the garden. Large clumps can be lifted, divided and replanted in autumn or spring. However, do not lift and divide them during wet or cold weather.

Achillea X 'Coronation Gold'

Coronation Gold Yarrow

This hardy herbaceous perennial displays 4-6in (10-15cm) wide, plate-like, deep-yellow heads at the tops of upright, stiff stems from mid- to late summer. The gray-green, deeply indented, feathery leaves provide attractive foliage throughout the season. Another excellent hybrid is x 'Moonshine' with pale yellow slightly smaller, 2-3in (5-8cm) wide, flower heads.
Height: 3-4ft (90cm-1.2m)
Spread: 2½-3ft (75-90cm)

Hardiness: Zones 3-9
Cultivation: Well-drained or even dry soil suits it, and a position in full sun. During early winter, cut back dead stems to soil level.
Propagation: Propagate yarrow by lifting and dividing the overgrown clumps in spring. Replant only the young parts from around the outside. Select pieces with four or five shoots.

Alternatively, seeds of the species can be sown ¼in (6mm) deep in a prepared seedbed during late spring and early summer, thinning the seedlings to 10-12in (25-30cm) apart when they are

---

Achillea contrasts well with plain backgrounds and differently-shaped plants. For instance, the achillea's flowers are highlighted by a Japanese holly or yew hedge. They are also attractive when set with tall variegated grasses.

Alchemilla mollis is a useful plant which blends with many other plants, such as *Centranthus ruber* 'Albus' and roses, red-hot Pokers (*Kniphofia*), and *Hosta*.

Right: **Argemone mexicana**
This annual is excellent for hot and dry places. Its beautiful, prickly, silvery-green leaves are able to roll up slightly to conserve moisture. The large lemon-yellow flowers appear during summer.

Argemone mexicana

Mexican Poppy

Few plants are as distinctive as this hardy annual. Its prickly silvery-green glaucous leaves are borne on sprawling stems, with the saucer-shaped flowers appearing from early summer onwards. They are lemon-yellow, scented and poppy-like, 3½in (9cm) wide.
Height: 2ft (60cm)
Spread: 1-1¼ft (30-39cm)
Cultivation: Well-drained, light, relatively dry soil and full sun assure success. They do best in hot weather. Remove dead flower heads to encourage others to develop.
Propagation: During spring, sow seeds in the border where the plants are to flower. Thin the seedlings to 1ft (30cm) apart when they are large enough to handle. Alternatively, sow seeds in flats of a sterile potting mix during early spring, keeping them at 64°F (18°C). When large enough to handle, prick out the seedlings into flats of potting soil and harden them off in a cold frame. Plant them in spring.

Above: *The delicate sulphur-yellow flowers of* **Alchemilla mollis** *stand above the light green hairy leaves and form a pleasing combination with the rich royal-purple flowers of* **Tradescantia 'Isis'**. *The dull green strap-like leaves of the tradescantia complete the picture.*

Argemone mexicana is best grown with other plants in an annual border. Do not let other plants crowd and hide the attractive leaves. It survives hot, dry, inhospitable places.

Right: Calendula officinalis 'Lemon Gem' *This hardy annual bears double yellow flowers above compact foliage during summer. It is a very reliable plant, ideal for poor soils in sunny areas. It can also be grown in tubs and window-boxes.*

Calendula officinalis

Pot Marigold

This is one of the most reliable hardy annuals, with light green, pungent, lance-shaped leaves. The daisy-like, pastel-colored flowers in yellow or orange, up to 4in (10cm) wide, appear from early summer to autumn. There are many varieties, including 'Lemon Gem' with yellow flowers, 'Bon Bon' available in bright or soft yellow, orange and apricot, 'Pacific Beauty' in mixed colors and good for cutting, and 'Dwarf Gem' also in mixed yellows, but only 1ft (30cm) tall. The dwarf types do well in containers such as tubs and windowboxes. The taller ones are best in a border.
Height: 1-2ft (30-60cm)
Spread: 1-1½ft (30-45cm)
Cultivation: Like many other annuals, pot marigolds grow well in poor, free-draining soils. But in a medium-rich, well-drained soil in full sun they do even better. They can even become a problem, creating masses of self-sown seedlings, but this can be dealt with by removing dead flowers, which also encourages repeat blooms. Pinching out the growing tips of young plants encourages the development of side-shoots.
Propagation: During spring, sow seeds ½in (12mm) deep where the plants are to flower. When the seedlings are large enough to handle, thin them out to 1ft (30cm) apart. To raise plants for containers, pot up seedlings in small pots before setting them in containers. If you would like to raise plants for very early spring flowering, you should sow seed in the border during late summer and early autumn.

Centaurea macrocephala

Globe Centaurea

A handsome, hardy herbaceous perennial with 3-4in (7.5-10cm) wide, yellow, thistle-like flower heads at the top of upright, stiff stems during midsummer. The rough-surfaced, stiff, elongated lance-shaped leaves clasp the stems right up to the flower heads. When cut, the flowers last well in water. Bees find the flowers very attractive.
Height: 3-5ft (90cm-1.5m)
Spread: 1½-2½ft (45-75cm)
Hardiness: Zones 3-7
Cultivation: Light, fertile, well-drained soil and a sunny position are essential. On exposed sites, you will need to support the plants with twiggy sticks. Centaureas benefit from being lifted and divided in early spring every four years or so.
Propagation: Seeds can be sown in spring in flats of sterile potting soil and placed in a cold frame. When they are large enough to handle, prick off the seedlings into flats of potting soil. When they are well grown, plant them out into a nursery bed to remain for the rest of the summer. Set the plants out in the garden in autumn. Alternatively, divide established clumps in spring.

Calendula officinalis has long been grown amid old-style borders packed with annuals and border plants. It gains its common name, pot marigold, from being grown in earlier times in pots for use in the kitchen.

Centaurea macrocephala does well when filling bare areas between roses. The stiff stems of the centaureas allow the handsome flowers to appear between the rose blooms.

Above: Cladanthus arabicus
This delightful hardy annual has orange buds opening to golden-yellow, fragrant flowers in succession throughout summer. A light soil and plenty of sunshine are essential. Remove dead flower heads to encourage the development of further blooms.

Left: Centaurea macrocephala
Favored by nectar-seeking bees the thistle-like yellow flower heads are often 3-4in (7.5-10cm) wide. They are borne on stiff stems, and are ideal as cut flowers, lasting a long time in water. The leaves form an attractive foil for the brightly-colored flowers.

Cladanthus arabicus

(*Anthemis arabica*)

A bright hardy annual from Spain, with daisy-like, 2in (5cm) wide, fragrant, single flowers from early to late summer, and light green feather-like foliage.
Height: 2½ft (75cm)
Spread: 1-1¼ft (30-38cm)
Cultivation: Light, well-cultivated slightly acid soil in full sun is best. Rich soils tend to encourage foliage at the expense of flowers. Seeds are difficult to obtain.
Propagation: During spring, sow seeds where the plants are to flower. Sow the seeds in drills, thinning to 1ft (30cm) apart.

Cladanthus arabicus is an ideal plant to choose for the center or rear of an annual border, because it displays an overall mound shape. It tends to sprawl at its sides, quickly merging with neighboring plants.

Above: Coreopsis verticillata
The finely-divided deep green leaves are very distinctive and from early summer to early autumn, star shaped yellow flowers are borne on stiff stems. It is ideal for use in floral arrangements.

Coreopsis verticillata

Thread-leaf Coreopsis

An attractive, long-lived, hardy herbaceous perennial native to the northeast, with distinctive, deep green, finely-divided leaves. The bright yellow, star-like flowers 1¹/₂in (4cm) wide, appear from early summer to early autumn.
Height: 1¹/₂-2ft (45-60cm)
Spread: 1¹/₄-1¹/₂ft (38-45cm)
Hardiness: Zones 3-9
Cultivation: Well-drained fertile soil in a sunny position suits coreopsis. Fortunately, it does not require staking in any but the most exposed sites. Cutting flowered stems back to soil level encourages the development of further shoots.
Propagation: It is easily increased by lifting and dividing established and overgrown clumps in spring. Be sure each new piece has several strong healthy shoots. Do not let the roots dry out.

Above: Anemone-flowered dahlia
This is an example of an anemone-flowered dahlia. These have double flowers with flat outer petals and short tubular inner ones. They are popular cut flowers.

Below: Decorative dahlias
These double dahlias are among the most popular. Decorative dahlias have a range of flower sizes, from 4in (10cm) in Miniatures, to 10in (25cm) or more in Giants.

Coreopsis verticillata is ideal in a mixed border producing a long-lasting display of color. 'Moonbeam' is a popular cultivar. It has pale yellow flowers and is especially long-blooming.

New dahlia varieties are introduced every year, and many of the less good ones are abandoned. To be sure you buy up-to-date, reliable varieties send for a catalog from one of the major dahlia growers.

Dahlias

These bright flowers can be divided into two main groups: those which can be grown as half-hardy annuals for use in bedding schemes, and those which are best in mixed borders, mingled with herbaceous plants and flowering shrubs.

BEDDING DAHLIAS

These half-hardy perennials from Mexico are grown as half-hardy annuals, displaying 2-3in (5-7.5cm) wide single, double or semi-double flowers from midsummer to autumn. There are many varieties in a wide color range.

Height: 1-1³/₄ft (30-53cm)

Spread: 1¹/₄-2ft (38-45cm)

Cultivation: Bedding dahlias need well-cultivated, fertile, compost or manure-enriched soil in a sunny position. Soil too rich, however, will create excessive foliage at the expense of flowers. There is no need to stake them – unlike the large border types. Removing dead flowers helps the development of further blooms. Water the plants during dry periods.

Propagation: During late winter and early spring, sow seeds ¹/₄in (6mm) deep in a sterile seed starting mix at 61°F (16°C). When they are large enough to handle, prick off the seedlings into flats or small pots of a potting soil and harden them off in a cold frame. Set the plants out in the garden after risk of frost has passed.

BORDER DAHLIAS

These are half-hardy tuberous plants, easily damaged by frost, which quickly bring color to the garden. There are several classifications and many varieties.

Hardiness: Zones 7-10, elsewhere lift and grow as annuals.

Anemone-flowered (2-3¹/₂ft/60cm-1m): These have double flowers with flat outer petals and short, tubular inner ones. Flowering is from midsummer to the frosts of autumn.

Ball-type (3-4ft/90cm-1.2m): As

their name implies, these have ball-shaped flowers, with tubular, blunt-ended petals. There are *Small Ball* types with blooms 4-6in (10-15cm) wide, and *Miniature Ball* forms with flowers up to 4in (10cm) wide.

Cactus and Semi-cactus (3-5ft/90cm-1.5m): These are divided into five groupings, *Miniature* (blooms up to 4in/10cm wide); *Small* (blooms 4-6in/10-15cm wide); *Medium* (blooms 6-8in/15-20cm wide); *Large* (blooms 8-10in/20-25cm wide); *Giant* (blooms 10in/25cm or more wide).

Collarettes (2¹/₂-4ft/75cm-1.2m): These have blooms with a single outer ring of flat ray florets, with a ring of small florets in the center, forming a disc.

Decoratives: These have double flowers without central discs. They are formed of broad, flat ray florets. This grouping is further divided into:

Miniature (3-4ft/90cm-1.2m): These have flowers up to 4in (10cm) wide.

Small (3¹/₂-4ft/1-1.2m): Flowers 4-6in (10-15cm) wide.

Medium (3¹/₂-4ft/1-1.2m): Flowers 6-8in (15-20cm) wide.

Large (3¹/₂-5ft/1-1.5m): Flowers 8-10in (20-25cm) wide.

Giant (4-5ft/1.2-1.5m): Flowers 10in (25cm) or more wide.

Peony-flowered (up to 3ft/90cm): The flowers are formed of two or more rings of flat ray florets, with a central disc.

Pompon (3-4ft/90cm-1.2m): The flowers very much resemble those of *Ball* types, but are more globular

Above: Semi-cactus dahlia *This exotic-looking type has beautiful flowers. All dahlias are useful for the color they bring to the garden, right up to the frosts of autumn.*

and are no more than 2in (5cm) wide. The florets curl inwards for their entire length.

Single-flowered (1¹/₂-2¹/₂ft/45-75cm): These display flowers up to 4in (10cm) wide, with a single row of petals arranged around a central disc.

Cultivation: Well-drained soil, with plenty of moisture-retentive compost or well-decomposed manure added, is required. Include a sprinkling of bonemeal before setting the tubers 4in (10cm) deep in the ground during mid- to late spring. If sprouted tubers are used, take care that they are not planted too early, or frost will damage them. The young plants will need staking. Pinch out the growing tips of all shoots to encourage sideshoots to develop, and if you want large flowers, remove sideshoots and buds from around the developing flowers. The removal of dead flowers helps the development of further flowers. In autumn, dig up the tubers carefully about a week after the foliage has been blackened by frost. Remove soil from the tubers and store them upside down for a few weeks to encourage them to dry out. Then place them in a frost-proof place.

Propagation: The easiest way for the home gardener to do this is to divide the tubers in spring.

Dahlias are natives of Mexico, where they grow in sandy meadows at about 5000ft (1525m) above sea-level. Since their introduction to Europe in the late 1700s, hundreds of cultivars have been developed.

Doronicum caucasicum

Leopard's Bane

This is one of the earliest-flowering hardy herbaceous perennials, revealing heart-shaped, bright green, shallowly-toothed leaves surmounted by single, golden-yellow, daisy-like flowers, 2½in (6.5cm) wide, during late spring and into early summer. Several superb cultivars are available, including 'Magnificum' (taller and larger flowering) 'Spring Beauty' (deep yellow and double) and the hybrid 'Miss Mason' (bright yellow flowers).

Height: 1½-2ft (45-60cm)
Spread: 1¼-1½ft (38-45cm)
Hardiness: Zones 4-7
Cultivation: Leopard's bane appreciates fertile, moisture-retentive, deeply-cultivated soil in full sun or light shade. The plant often goes dormant in the summer, especially in hot climates. Don't allow to dry out, even when dormant.
Propagation: The easiest way to increase them is by lifting and dividing plants during autumn or early spring. Replant young pieces from around the edges of the old clump.

Above: Doronicums *The cheerful yellow flowers bloom after early daffodils are over.*

Above: Doronicum 'Miss Mason' *The yellow, daisy-like flowers of this early-flowering herbaceous perennial are a welcome sight in spring. They are excellent as cut-flowers.*

Doronicum 'Miss Mason' is ideal for
harmonizing with spring-flowering bulbs such as tulips.
These will hold their heads above the
doronicums, giving added height and interest.

Eschscholzia californica

Californian Poppy

This delicate, highly attractive perennial from California is commonly grown as a hardy annual. It has attractive, finely-cut, fern-like, blue-green leaves, and from early summer to autumn has saucer-shaped, bright orange-yellow flowers with silky petals, 3in (7.5cm) wide. An added attraction is the crop of blue-green seedpods, each 3-4in (7.5-10cm) long. Several varieties are available, including some lovely clear yellow and orange flowered forms.
Height: 1-1¼ft (30-38cm)
Spread: 9-12in (23-30cm)
Cultivation: Light, sandy, poor soil and a sunny site are needed. Prefers cool weather.
Propagation: From early spring to early summer, sow seeds ¼in (6mm) deep where the plants are to flower. When they are large enough to handle, thin the seedlings to 6-9in (15-23cm) apart.

Below: Eschscholzia californica
The original Californian poppy has been developed into a range of colors. Dry, light, poor soil and plenty of sunshine assure success. It often produces self-sown seedlings in subsequent years.

Above: Helianthus annuus 'Sungold' *This low-growing sunflower, with double golden-yellow flowers up to 6in (15cm) wide, grows only 2ft (60cm) high. Many other varieties grow up to 10ft (3m). Sunflowers seldom fail to capture the attention of children, and are an ideal introduction to gardening. Tall-growing varieties are excellent for creating a short-lived screen in the garden. Place the plants in groups rather than in rows for the best effect. Make sure you give them firm support with stout stakes and secure ties.*

Helianthus annuus

Common Sunflower

Popular in children's drawings and gardens the world over, this hardy native annual bears gigantic, daisy-like flowers, 1ft (30cm) or more wide, singly at the tops of stems up to 10ft (3m) high. Flowering is from mid- to late summer. There are many varieties, such as 'Autumn Beauty' (6ft/1.8m), with sulphur-yellow flowers stained copper-bronze, 'Sungold' (2ft/60cm), with double golden-yellow flowers up to 6in (15cm) wide, and 'Russian Giant' (8-10ft/2.4-3m), yellow-flowered.
Height: 3-10ft (90cm-3m)
Spread: 1½-2ft (45-60cm)
Cultivation: Well-drained soil in full sun suits the sunflower best. Support the plants with stout stakes. The dried seeds make a popular snack and handy bird food.
Propagation: During early spring and into early summer, sow seeds ½in (12mm) deep. Thin the seedlings to 1-1½ft (30-45cm) apart when they are large enough to handle. Perennial species of sunflowers are best increased by dividing the plants during autumn or early spring, but they can also be propagated in the same manner as for the annual types.

Eschscholzia caespitosa is another species, with finely-cut blue-green leaves and yellow flowers, 1in (2.5cm) wide. A dwarf, only 5in (13cm) high, it is ideal for bare patches in a rock garden, or as a border edging.

Helianthus annuus, the sunflower, is often grown on its own in a sunny corner of a garden. But some varieties are superb at the back or center of an annual border, mixing well with color contrasting annuals such as *Celosia argentea plumosa.*

THE FLOWER BORDER

Left: **Limonium sinuatum 'Gold Crest'** *A yellow-flowered form of statice. It is available in many cultivars and colors and is generally grown for drying. However, its unusually shaped and brightly colored flowers make it an interesting choice for a border.*

Right: **Narcissus 'Rembrandt'** *This is a large daffodil from* **Division 1,** *with rich yellow flowers and frilled trumpets. It is superb for setting in mixed borders, or naturalizing in grass. One flower is produced on each stem. It looks best when planted in sweeps, rather than singly over a large area.*

Limonium sinuatum 'Gold Coast'

Statice

This hardy perennial, usually grown as a half-hardy annual, has bright yellow flowers in 4in (10cm) long clusters on erect stems from mid- to late summer. It is one of the everlasting flowers, dried and used for home decoration in winter. For this purpose, cut the flower stems just before the flowers are fully open and, holding them upside down, tie them in bundles. Hang these up in a dry, airy shed until all moisture has gone. There are many other varieties, with flower colors including pink, lavender, white and dark blue, as well as various shades of yellow.
Height: 15-18in (38-45cm)
Spread: 12-15in (30-38cm)
Cultivation: Statice likes light, well-drained soil in full sun.
Propagation: Sow seeds ½in (6mm) deep during late winter and early spring, in a seed starting mix at 61°F (16°C). When they are large enough to handle, prick off the seedlings into flats of potting soil and harden them off in a cold frame. Plant them out in the garden in late spring. Alternatively, direct seed in spring, but flowering will be later.

Limonium sinuatum is only one of the everlasting flowers. Others include *Helichrysum bracteatum, Helipterum roseum* and *Xeranthemum annuum,* with purple flowers.

Narcissus

Daffodils

Much-loved heralds of spring, these are all bright-faced flowers with central trumpets, in various sizes. There are many different species, from 3-18in (7.5-45cm) high. In addition, there are the many garden types, again in a range of shapes and sizes, which have various classifications. Flower size ranges from 1-4in (2.5-10cm) wide, with one or several flowers on each stem, blooming from late winter to late spring.

Below: Narcissus 'Fortune' *A large-cupped daffodil from* **Division 2.** *This well-known daffodil with yellow petals and trumpets in shades from orange to red is ideal for mixed borders and naturalizing in grass. One flower is produced on each stem.*

DIVISION 1 – TRUMPET DAFFODILS (15-18in/38-45cm):
These are of garden origin and produce just one flower on each stem. The trumpet is as long as the petals. They have been further divided into subsections: those with all-yellow trumpets, bicolors, white-trumpeted, and reversed bicolor trumpets.

DIVISION 2 – LARGE-CUPPED DAFFODILS (15-22in/38-55cm):
These are large-cupped, with one flower on each stem and with the trumpet more than one-third the length of the petals. These are further divided into yellow large-cupped, colored cups, bicolored large-cupped, bicolored red-cupped, and white large-cupped.

DIVISION 3 – SHORT-CUPPED DAFFODILS (14-18in/36-45cm):
These have just one flower on each stem, with the cup part less than one-third of the length of the petals. Again, they are sub-divided, into colored small-cupped, bicolored small-cupped and white small-cupped.

DIVISION 4 – DOUBLE DAFFODILS (12-18in/30-45cm):
These have double flowers, with one or more blooms on each stem.

DIVISION 5 – TRIANDRUS DAFFODILS (up to 12in/30cm):
These are derived from *Narcissus triandrus,* distinguished by swept-back petals, and with two or three flowers on each stem.

DIVISION 6 – CYCLAMINEUS NARCISSI (8-15in/20-38cm):
These are known for their long trumpets and swept-back petals, and are subdivided into those flowers where the trumpets are more than two-thirds the petal length, and those which are less.

DIVISION 7 – JONQUILLA NARCISSI (11-17in/28-43cm):
These are of garden origin and developed from *Narcissus jonquilla.* They have two to four

Daffodils are universally admired. Spring has truly arrived when banks and beds glow with these beautiful flowers, many in shades of yellow. Forsythia blends well with daffodils.

Daffodils harmonize with many small-flowered and low-growing bulbs, such as the blue-flowered *Chionodoxa luciliae.* To create further interest, plant with spring-blooming perennials, such as *Dicentra spectabilis* (bleeding heart) and *Mertensia virginica* (Virginia bluebells).

flowers on each stem. The flowers are highly scented and up to 2in (5cm) wide.

DIVISION 8 – TAZETTA NARCISSI (15-17in/38-43cm): These are descended from *Narcissus tazetta*, with its characteristic bunched appearance. They are highly scented, and divided into two main types: those resembling *N. tazetta* and those developed from crossing *N. tazetta* and *N. poeticus*. These latter ones are known as poetaz narcissi.

DIVISION 9 – POETICUS NARCISSI (14-17in/35-43cm): These are of garden origin and are characterized by white petals and frilled bright red cups. They are delightfully scented.

DIVISION 10 – WILD FORMS AND HYBRIDS (3-18in/7.5-45cm): Within this section are the species narcissi, encompassing all the wild forms, wild hybrids, and all the miniature types. Many are superb in a rock garden or naturalized in a woodland.

Cultivation: They can be grown in many ways – for instance, in rock gardens, in meadows, filling gaps in borders, or naturalized in woodland. The bulbs grow best in rich, well-drained soils in light shade.

Below: Narcissus 'Irene Copeland' *A double narcissus from **Division 4**, with camellia-like yellow and white flowers. Its form is attractive and contrasts well with the trumpet types. Another good variety is 'Mary Copeland' which has orange and white flowers.*

Above: Narcissus 'Grand Soleil d'Or' *A bunch-flowered narcissus, known as a paper-white, from **Division 8**. It develops several flowers at the top of each flower stem, and makes a dominant display. It is tender and therefore best grown in pots in the house.*

Sprinkle a general fertilizer over the soil before planting them during late summer and early autumn. Set the bulbs in holes three times their depth. (For example, it is best to set a 2in (5cm) deep bulb in a hole 6in (15cm) deep, covered with 4in (10cm) of soil.) You should set large-flowered types 4-8in (10-20cm) apart, and the smaller species types 2-3in (5-7.5cm) apart. Most daffodils should be left where they are planted for several years. If you are growing the bulbs in shrub borders, rather than in grass, plant them slightly deeper to ensure they are not damaged by hoeing during summer. After flowering, leave the foliage to die down naturally. The best-sized flowers are produced from bulbs in their second year after planting.

Narcissus poeticus 'Actaea', the poet's narcissus, is highly fragrant, and superb when set in large drifts in a wild garden. Bulbs are ideal for bringing splashes of color to informal areas during spring.

However, to prevent the bulbs forming large and overgrown clumps in borders, lift and divide them every four years. Lift them as the foliage turns yellow. If they are left in the soil to be lifted later, mark the position, because otherwise they will be difficult to find.

Propagation: Lift and divide overgrown clumps after flowering, when the foliage has turned yellow.

Below: **Daffodils** *and* **forsythia** *are the epitome of spring to many gardeners. They are easy to establish and grow in a garden and seldom fail to create spring color. Plant the daffodils in front of the forsythia in clumps rather than rows to achieve a natural effect.*

Above: **Narcissus 'Bartley'** *This highly distinctive small narcissus from **Division 6** has Narcissus cyclamineus as a parent. The petals sweep back from the trumpet. Set near the front of the border.*

Narcissus cyclamineus, with petals that curl back sharply on themselves, brings life to rock gardens and protected corners during spring. In warm and mild areas, it may appear as early as the end of winter. *N. cyclamineus* 'February Gold' mixes well with small crocuses.

Phlomis russeliana

This distinctive hardy herbaceous perennial has large, wrinkled mid-green leaves and hooded tubular flowers, each 1-1¹/₂in (2.5-4cm) long, borne in circular tiers up the stems during midsummer. They resemble the flowers of Jerusalem sage (*Phlomis fruticosa*).
Height: 2¹/₂-4ft (75cm-1.2m)
Spread: 2¹/₂ft (75cm)
Hardiness: Zones 4-8
Cultivation: Any good garden soil and an open, sunny position suit this plant.
Propagation: Seeds can be sown in a seed starting mix during spring and placed in a cold frame. But the easiest method of propagation is to lift and divide overgrown clumps in spring.

Right: **Phlomis russeliana** *The distinctive whorls of hooded yellow flowers appear in tiers up the stout stems. The attractive seedheads are useful for flower arrangements and can be used green or dried.*

Left: Oenothera missouriensis
This eye-catching, spreading herbaceous perennial from the Midwest has bright canary-yellow flowers, 2¹/₂-3in (6.5-7.5cm) wide. These are produced during early and midsummer.

Oenothera missouriensis

Evening Primose · Sundrop

A superb, mat-forming, low-growing herbaceous perennial with lance-shaped midgreen leaves and bright canary-yellow flowers, 2¹/₂-3in (6.5-7.5cm) wide. It has reddish stems and blooms during early and midsummer. The flower buds often have red spots on their undersides. Unlike many evening primroses, it opens its flowers during the day as well as in the evening.
Height: 5-7in (13-18cm)
Spread: 1¹/₂-2ft (45-60cm)
Hardiness: Zones 4-8

Cultivation: Sundrops are tolerant of a wide range of soil, except for those that become water logged. They become leggy in the shade, preferring full sun or at least a few hours of sun. Cut down foliage in early winter to reveal fresh rosettes.
Propagation: Seeds can be sown in spring, and the containers put in a cold frame. When they are large enough to handle, set the seedlings in a nursery bed until autumn. They can then be planted into the garden. Alternatively, divide established clumps in spring. This is the best method for named varieties of many oenotheras, as they do not breed true from seed.

Above: Phlomis fruticosa *is the Jerusalem sage, with whorls of yellow flowers in midsummer.*

Oenothera missouriensis is best seen in a raised bed. This ensures good drainage and brings the beautiful flowers nearer eye-level. Its spreading nature allows it to be blended with other plants including *Lysimachia nummularia*, creeping Jenny.

Phlomis fruticosa, the Jerusalem sage, has woolly gray-green foliage with whorls of yellow flowers, 1-1¹/₄in (2.5-3cm) long. It is evergreen in the South and dies to the ground in harsher climates.

Above: **Rudbeckia fulgida 'Goldsturm'** *This superb bright-colored form has flowers up to 5in (13cm) across. 'Deamii' is another good form, with flowers 3-4in (7.5-10cm) wide, borne in abundance.*

Rudbeckia fulgida

(*Rudbeckia speciosa· Rudbeckia newmanii*)

Coneflower

This well-known herbaceous perennial has midgreen, lance-shaped leaves and yellow to orange flowers, 2¹/₂in (6.5cm) wide, from mid- to late summer. The flowers have distinctive purple-brown cones at their centers – hence the common name.
Height: 2-3ft (60-90cm)
Spread: 1¹/₂-2ft (45-60cm)
Hardiness: Zones 3-9
Cultivation: Coneflowers need well-drained but moisture-retentive, fertile soil in an open and sunny position. They are long-blooming, low-maintenance plants that tolerate light shade. Allow flower heads to remain for winter interest.
Propagation: Seeds can be sown in spring or late summer, but for home gardeners the easiest way to increase this plant is by lifting and dividing established clumps in autumn or spring. Replant only the young parts from around the edges of the clump.

Rudbeckia fulgida blends well with ornamental grasses and white flowering varieties of *Astilbe*. It is equally at home in a perennial border, annual bed, or naturalized meadow planting.

THE FLOWER BORDER

Right: Rudbeckia hirta
'Marmalade' *This is a beautiful border plant creating a bold splash of golden-yellow, peppered with black cones. The flowers give the impression of peering upwards. They are excellent cut flowers.*

Rudbeckia hirta

Black-eyed Susan · Coneflower

This short-lived Midwestern perennial is grown as a hardy annual. It has green, lance-shaped leaves on bristly stems. During midsummer and into early autumn it bears golden-yellow flowers, 3in (7.5cm) wide, with brown-purple cones at their centers. Many forms are available. 'Marmalade' has brilliant yellow flowers with black centers, and 'Rustic Dwarfs' boasts shades of chestnut, bronze and yellow.
Height: 1-3ft (30-90cm)
Spread: 1-1½ft (30-45cm)
Cultivation: These plants need a well drained, preferably deeply-cultivated, soil in an open and sunny position. Remove dead flowers during the summer to encourage further flowers, and cut dead stems down to soil level in early winter. In exposed and windy regions tall forms will need supporting with twiggy sticks. Put these in early so that the plants can grow up and through them. If you put them in too late, the sticks will not become covered with leaves and flowers and detract from the appearance of the display.
Propagation: During late winter and early spring, sow seeds ⅛in (3mm) deep in a seed starting mix kept at 61°F (16°C). When the seedlings are large enough to handle, prick them out into flats of potting soil and harden them off in a cold frame. Plant them out into the garden when all risk of frost has passed. Alternatively, sow seeds ¼in (6mm) deep during spring where the plants are to flower, thinning them to 1-1½ft (30-45cm) apart.

Sanvitalia procumbens

Creeping Zinnia

This is a beautiful, low-growing hardy annual, with miniature, single, rudbeckia-like yellow flowers with black centers (1in/2.5cm wide) during midsummer. The form 'Flore Pleno' has double flowers. The flowers appear slightly above the pointed, oval, midgreen leaves, borne on trailing stems. Their dwarf habit makes the plants

Left: Sanvitalia procumbens
This hardy Mexican annual has miniature rudbeckia-like flowers during midsummer. Like many other Mexican plants, it needs a position in full sun.

ideal for the edges of borders, in beds of annuals, rock gardens, and even in containers where they can trail over the side.
Height: 5-6in (13-15cm)
Spread: 6-8in (15-20cm)
Cultivation: Light but moisture-retentive soil in full sun suits sanvitalias best.
Propagation: During spring, sow seeds thinly and shallowly where the plants are to flower. When the seedlings are large enough to handle, thin them to 3-4in (7.5-10cm) apart. Seeds can also be sown in late summer in the open soil, but the seedlings need cold frame protection during winter. Thin them out in spring rather than autumn. Sanvitalias can be grown to flower in hanging baskets. In such circumstances plants will be needed for setting in the container early in the year. Sow seeds at 55°F (13°C) during early spring and prick off the seedlings into pots. Harden off the plants and set them out in the container as soon as all risk of frost has passed.

Rudbeckia hirta is ideal for providing late color in the garden, at a time when many border plants are past their best and the garden generally looks bare and colorless.

Sanvitalia procumbens is superb in the garden, but equally eye-catching as a pot plant indoors or in a greenhouse. Sow seeds in late winter or early spring in 55°F (13°C), pricking out the seedlings three to a 6in (15cm) pot.

Left: **Solidago x 'Goldenmosa'**
This superb goldenrod, with frothy flowers in 6-9in (15-23cm) long heads during mid- to late summer, gains its varietal name from mimosa, which it resembles. It is ideal in flower arrangements.

Solidago x 'Goldenmosa'

Goldenrod

Goldenrod, a hardy herbaceous perennial prized in Europe, has only recently been grown in American gardens. The narrow, lance-shaped, yellow-green leaves rise from soil level to the dazzling display of flowers. Its strong stem makes it an excellent cut plant.
Height: 2$\frac{1}{2}$-3ft (75-90cm)
Spread: 2-2$\frac{1}{2}$ft (60-75cm)
Hardiness: Zones 3-9
Cultivation: Any good, fertile, well-drained garden soil in full sun or light shade is suitable. Support is necessary only in windy and exposed areas. In early spring cut the stems down to soil level.
Propagation: During autumn or spring, lift old overgrown clumps and divide them. Replant the young parts from outside the clump.

Above: **Solidago 'Crown of Rays'** *is a welcome sight in summer with its cheerful golden-yellow flowers.*

Solidago x 'Goldenmosa' blends with pink and white flowers. For example, you could try the pink-eyed white *Phlox maculata* 'Omega' and the white flowers of the obedient plant, *Physostegia virginiana* 'Summer Snow'.

THE FLOWER BORDER

Tagetes erecta

African Marigold · Aztec Marigold

A well-known, half-hardy, much-branched annual from Mexico. Its lemon-yellow, daisy-like flowers are about 2in (5cm) wide, and last from midsummer to autumn. The glossy, dark green leaves, deeply and finely-divided, are strongly scented. There are many types, including single and double-flowered forms, with flower colors from yellow to orange. They also range in height from semi-dwarf (1-1¼ ft/30-38cm) to normal types (2-3ft/60-90cm). It is an excellent cut flower.
Cultivation: Most moderately-rich soils are suitable, and an open position in full sun.
Propagation: During late winter and early spring, sow seeds ¼in (6mm) deep in a seed starting mix kept at 64°F (18°C). When the seedlings are large enough to handle, prick them out and harden them off slowly in a cold frame. Plant them out as soon as all risk of frost has passed.

Thalictrum speciosissimum

Meadow Rue

For distinction and elegance, few plants surpass this hardy herbaceous perennial, with its heads of frothy yellow flowers 6-9in (15-23cm) long, during mid- to late summer. The blue-gray leaves are long-lasting and deeply-divided and are borne dramatically on upright, stiff stems.
Height: 3½-5ft (1-1.5m)
Spread: 2-3ft (60-90cm)
Hardiness: Zones 5-8
Cultivation: Thalictrum prefers a good, well-cultivated fertile, moist soil and a position in full sun or light shade. In exposed areas it will require support from stakes or stout twiggy sticks. In spring give a top-dressing of peat or well-decomposed compost, and in early winter cut the stems down to soil level. When staking the plants, do not leave it until late in the season as they grow quickly and may be blown over easily.
Propagation: Seeds can be sown in spring, and the container placed in a cold frame, but the easiest way to propagate is to lift and divide overgrown clumps in spring and replant them firmly.

Tagetes erecta can often be a difficult neighbor for other bedding plants because of its dominant size and color, but it is useful for bringing bold color splashes to mixed borders. You could also have a border full of these plants.

Thalictrum speciosissimum, like most yellow-flowered plants, associates well with blue flowers. Michaelmas daisies and delphiniums with strong blue-colored flowers are excellent companions for it.

Trollius x cultorum

Globeflower

This is a delightful hardy herbaceous perennial, with large, globe-shaped pale yellow to orange flowers during late spring and early summer. The deeply-cleft and toothed midgreen leaves are a perfect foil for the buttercup-like flowers. Several superb varieties are available, including 'Fire Globe' (deep orange), 'Goldquelle' (golden-yellow), 'Salamander' (fiery orange), 'Canary Bird' (pale yellow) and 'Orange Princess' (orange-yellow).

Height: 2-2¹/₂ft (60-75cm)
Spread: 1¹/₂-2ft (45-60cm)
Hardiness: Zones 3-8
Cultivation: Globeflowers flourish near ponds, in bogs, and in any rich, moisture-retentive soil. Full sun or light shade will do. For more flowers, cut mature flower stems at the base.
Propagation: Lift and divide established clumps. Replant the young pieces from around the outside of the clump.

Below: **Trollius x cultorum 'Fire Globe'** *A beautiful hardy herbaceous plant for fertile, moist areas in the garden. It does well in damp areas around a garden pond. This variety flowers in spring at a height of 1¹/₂ft (75cm).*

Above right: **Thalictrum speciosissimum** *This eye-catching plant is much prized by flower arrangers. Its delicate, long-lasting foliage, closely resembling that of the maidenhair fern, is very attractive.*

Far left: Tagetes patula 'Queen Bee' *This yellow and red double crested French marigold rises to about 10in (25cm) and flowers throughout summer. Its compact but well-branched growth makes it a superb choice for any flower border, where it can be used as dominant edging.*

Trollius flowers look good mixed with blue-flowered plants, but it is essential that the blue is strong enough not to be dominated by the yellow. *Iris latifolia* (*Iris xiphioides*) is the right blue and, like *Trollius*, likes damp soil.

THE FLOWER BORDER

Tulipa

Tulips

The range of these much-loved spring bulbs is extensive. They can be used to flower in spring in bedding schemes, mixed borders, rock gardens and pots, or indoors for winter and early spring flowers. There is a wide range of species, and botanists have also classified those created by bulb experts. There are fifteen different divisions, encompassing the wide range of flower sizes, shapes and heights. These are:

DIVISION 1 – SINGLE EARLY (6-15in/15-38cm): The single flowers appear in spring when grown out-of-doors, or during winter indoors. Each flower is 3-5in (7.5-13cm) wide and sometimes opens flat when in direct and full sun. Many yellow varieties are available, as well as white, pink, red, orange and purple.

DIVISION 2 – DOUBLE EARLY (12-15in/30-38cm): The double flowers appear in spring when grown out-of-doors in bedding schemes, or earlier when forced indoors. Each flower is 4in (10cm) wide and rather like a double peony. The color range is wide, including some fine yellows.

DIVISION 3 – MENDEL (15-20in/38-50cm): These flower later than the previous types, with rounded 4-5in (10-13cm) wide flowers on quite slender stems. Colors include white and red, as well as yellow. They look like a cross between single early types and Darwins.

DIVISION 4 – TRIUMPH (up to 20in/50cm): These bear angular-looking 4-5in (10-13cm) wide flowers on strong stems in mid-spring. Colors include pink, red and lilac, as well as yellow.

DIVISION 5 – DARWIN HYBRIDS (2-2¼ft/60-65cm): These are among the largest-flowered and most brilliant of all tulips, with flowers up to 7in (18cm) across during mid-spring. There are multi-colored forms, as well as yellow, orange, red and purple varieties.

DIVISION 6 – DARWIN (2-2 ½ft/60-75cm): Widely used in bedding schemes, these produce rounded flowers up to 5in (13cm) wide in late spring. Varieties are available in white, pink, red, purple and multi-colors, as well as the yellow ones.

DIVISION 7 – LILY-FLOWERED (1½-2ft/45-60cm): These are characterized by the narrow waists of the flowers, also by the pointed petals which curl outwards, reaching 8in (20cm) during mid-spring. They look distinctive when massed in a bedding scheme. Colors include white, orange, red and multi-colored forms, as well as yellow.

DIVISION 8 – COTTAGE (up to 3ft/90cm): This old group has oval or rounded flowers, 4-5in (10-13cm) wide, in midspring. The petals sometimes have a hint of fringing, and are looser than in other forms. Colors include white, pink, red, lilac, green, and yellow.

DIVISION 9 – REMBRANDT (2½ft/75cm): These are tulips with "broken" colors. The rounded flowers, 5in (13cm) wide, have vivid splashes of color on the petals during midspring. As well as yellow, base colors include white, orange, red, pink, violet and brown.

Above: Tulip 'Golden Apeldoorn'
These Darwin Hybrids from **Division 5** *are superb in formal bedding displays, with flowers up to 7in (18cm) wide during midspring. These are borne on tall stems.*

DIVISION 10—PARROT (1 ½-2ft/45-60cm): These have flowers appearing in midspring, up to 8in (20cm) wide, easily recognizable by their feather-like and heavily-fringed petals. The color range includes brilliant white, pink, orange, red and purple, as well as yellow.

DIVISION 11—DOUBLE LATE (1½-2ft/45-60cm): These have very large and showy double flowers, somewhat resembling peonies and up to 8in (20cm) wide. They remain in flower for a long period during midspring. Colors include white, orange, pink, red and violet, as well as yellow. Some are multi-colored, with stripes and edgings.

DIVISION 12— KAUFMANNIANA VARIETIES (4-10in/10-25cm): These have been developed from *Tulipa kaufmanniana*, and have fine-pointed flowers which open nearly flat, giving the appearance of a

---

Vividly colored **Darwin Tulips,** such as the dark red 'Scarlett O'Hara', combine well with white pansies. The tulip flowers stand above the pansies, allowing their heads to be seen through the tulip stems.

Tulips blend with a carpet planting of daisies (*Bellis perennis*). Blue parrot types make an eye-catching arrangement. Even two blues together – forget-me-nots and blue parrot tulips – are attractive.

Right: Tulipa marjoletti
This is a species, and there are more than thirty different types widely available. It grows to 2ft (60cm) and bears 2in (5cm) long blooms with pointed petals during late spring.

Below: **Tulip 'Gold Medal'** *Large and showy double flowers from* **Division 11**, *these resemble peonies and are up to 8in (20cm) wide. They remain in flower for a long period. However, in areas of high rainfall they can be weighed down by water.*

Tulips are the traditional companions of forget-me-nots and wallflowers. Cottage-type tulips, with their large egg-shaped heads on stout stems, stand proudly above these underplantings.

Tulipa greigii hybrids can be mixed with grape hyacinths and *Alyssum saxatile* in beds with dry stone walls on one side, or in large containers. The alyssum helps to soften the container's edges.

water-lily. They open in spring on sturdy stems, and are ideal for fronts of borders, rock gardens and containers. Most have two-colored flowers.

DIVISION 13—FOSTERIANA VARIETIES (1½ft/45cm): These are derived from *Tulipa fosteriana* and have large blunt-ended flowers in yellows and reds in midspring.

DIVISION 14—GREIGII VARIETIES (10in/25cm): These are mainly derived from *Tulipa greigii*, and have brilliant long-lasting yellow, red and near-white flowers. The petals reach 3in (7.5cm) long in midspring, when the flowers are fully open.

Cultivation: Select well-drained soil, preferably facing south and in a sheltered position. Set the bulbs 6in (15cm) deep during early winter. Space them 4-6in (10-15cm) apart. Remove dead flowers and dig up the bulbs when the leaves turn yellow. However, if the bed is needed earlier, dig up the bulbs as soon as flowering is over and heel them into a trench until the foliage has yellowed and died down.

Propagation: The easiest way is to remove the offsets clustered at the bases of the bulbs. These can be planted in a nursery bed to develop into flowering-sized bulbs.

Above: Tulip 'Yellow Empress'
*This beautiful and distinctive **Division 13** tulip has long-lasting flowers of medium size in mid-spring. The flowers grow best in full sun.*

Below: Tulip 'Giuseppe Verdi'
*These small **Division 12** flowers open like water-lilies in full sun. They are ideal for the front of borders as well as rock gardens and containers.*

Verbascum bombyciferum

Mullein

This is a distinctive biennial mullein (some are perennial) with attractive oval and pointed silvery leaves. The silvery, woolly stems are erect, and during summer their tops are clothed with sulphur-yellow, saucer-shaped flowers, 2in (5cm) wide, with pronounced stamens.

Height: 4-6ft (1.2-1.8m)
Spread: 2-2½ft (60-75cm)
Hardiness: Zones 5-10
Cultivation: Mulleins prefer a well-drained soil in full sun. Stake the plants in exposed areas and where the soil is rich and moist.
Propagation: Sow seeds thinly in late spring in boxes of loam-based potting soil, placing them in a cold frame. As soon as the seedlings are growing strongly, plant them out into a nursery bed. In autumn, place into their flowering positions.

Right: Verbascum bombyciferum
This is a bold architectural biennial raising spires of sulphur-yellow, saucer-shaped flowers with prominent stamens during early to midsummer. The silvery leaves, covered with hairs, are a further delight.

Red tulips set in a sea of yellow primroses look superb, or try an underplanting of gold *Cheiranthus x allionii* (Siberian wallflower) and blue forget-me-nots, with cottage tulips 'President Hoover' (orange-red) and 'Mrs. John T. Scheepers' (yellow).

Yellow backgrounds are very striking: you could try an underplanting of a yellow viola, with the single early tulip 'Keizerskroon' (with yellow and red flowers) above it.

Further plants to consider

Buphthalmum salicifolium
Willow-leaf Ox-eye
Height: 1¹/₂-2ft (45-60cm)   Spread: 2-2¹/₂ft (60-75cm)
Hardiness: Zones 3-7
A hardy herbaceous perennial which spreads by underground
runners. It is ideal for moist soils. During early to midsummer it
bears bright, golden-yellow, daisy-like flowers.

Digitalis grandiflora
Yellow Foxglove
Height: 2-3ft (60-90cm)   Spread: 1¹/₄-1¹/₂ft (38-45cm)
Hardiness: Zones 3-8
A perennial with pale creamy-yellow, foxglove-like flowers, 2in
(5cm) long, during mid- to late summer. The flowers are borne on
spikes up to 2ft (60cm).

Euphorbia epithymoides
Cushion Spurge
Height: 1-1¹/₂ft (30-45cm)   Spread: 1¹/₂-2ft (45-60cm)
Hardiness: Zones 4-8
A hardy herbaceous perennial provides a spectacular display of
brilliant yellow bracts in the early spring.

Helenium autumnale 'Golden Youth'
Common Sneezeweed
Height: 2¹/₂ft (75cm)   Spread: 1¹/₄-1¹/₂ft (38-45cm)
A beautiful free-flowering, hardy herbaceous perennial with large
yellow, daisy-like flowers during late summer and into autumn.
There are several other good yellow-flowering cultivars, such as
'Butterpat' and 'Wyndley' (yellow and copper).

Heliopsis helianthoides scabra
Orange Sunflower
Height: 2-4ft (60cm-1.2m)   Spread: 2-3ft (60-90cm)
Hardiness: Zones 3-9
A beautiful hardy herbaceous perennial, ideal for brightening up a
border during mid- to late summer, with large, daisy-like yellow
flowers. Varieties to consider include 'Golden Plume' (double,
yellow), 'Goldgreenheart' (double chrome yellow).

Hunnemannia fumariifolia
Mexican Tulip Poppy · Golden Cup
Height: 1¹/₂-2ft (45-60cm)   Spread: 1¹/₄-1¹/₂ft (38-45cm)
A beautiful poppy-like hardy annual with finely-cut, blue-green
foliage and cup-shaped yellow flowers during late summer.

Verbascum thapsus, the great mullein from Europe,
has yellow flowers and thick woolly leaves and was
called Bullock's lungwort. It was also associated with
witches and earned the name hag-taper.

Abutilon pictum 'Thompsonii'

Flowering Maple

Also known as *Abutilon thompsonii*, this foliage plant is often grown in a greenhouse or conservatory as well as a "dot" plant in a summer bedding display. This plant is grown with a single upright stem from which arise maple-like, midgreen leaves heavily mottled and splashed with creamy-yellow. When grown with summer bedding plants, it is planted amid a sea of color-contrasting annuals.
Height: 3-4ft (0.9-1.2m)
Spread: 15-24in (38-60cm)
Hardiness: Zones 8-10
Cultivation: Plant in fertile, moisture-retentive soil, as soon as all risk of frost has passed. Invariably, the planting is carried out in combination with summer-bedding displays.
Propagation: During midsummer take 3-4in (7.5-10cm) long cuttings from stock plants (taking cuttings from those plants in summer-

Above: Abutilon pictum 'Thompsonii' *brings height and distinction to summer-bedding displays. Its variegated leaves create color and interest throughout summer.*

bedding schemes would ruin their appearance). Insert them in equal parts moist peat and sharp sand, and place in 61°F (16°C). When rooted, pot up into a loam-based compost and overwinter in a frost-proof glasshouse or conservatory.

Amaranthus caudatus 'Green Form'

Love-Lies-Bleeding

This attractive form of the crimson-flowered love-lies-bleeding creates a superb background for other hardy annuals. Often sold as 'Viridis', it has light green leaves and long tassel-like, pale green flowers from mid- to late summer.
Height: 3-4ft (0.9-1.2m)
Spread: 15-18in (38-45cm)

Abutilon pictum 'Thompsonii' is excellent as a "dot" plant in a sea of summer-bedding plants. Its height and color bring an attractive contrast to the red-flowered *Salvia splendens.*

Amaranthus caudatus 'Green Form' with its beautiful green leaves and tassel-like flowers, creates a superb background for other annuals, such as nasturtiums, marigolds and salvia.

Cultivation: Grow in fertile, deeply-cultivated, moisture-retentive soil. However, it also tolerates poor soil. This plant prefers warm weather.

Propagation: Where the season is long and soil warms early, direct sow seeds in drills ⅛in (3mm) deep and 12in (30cm) apart in spring. When the seedlings are large enough to handle, thin 12-15in (30-38cm) apart. Alternatively, sow seeds ⅛in (3mm) deep in seed starting mix in early spring and place in 75°F (24°C). When large enough to handle, prick out seedlings into flats. Plant into the garden as soon as all risk of frost has passed.

Left: Amaranthus caudatus 'Green Form' *This beautiful green-flowered form of love-lies-bleeding is eye-catching in a sea of low-growing hardy annuals, especially those with yellow or white flowers.*

Above: Euphorbia wulfenii *When planted at the top of a flight of stairs, so that it is a dramatic focal point, this bushy, shrubby perennial has few equals.*

Euphorbia wulfenii

This 'architectural' shrubby perennial creates a bushy shape formed of bluish-green leaves massed on stiffish stems. During midsummer, the stems are headed by 8-9in (20-23cm) of bright, eye-catching, yellowish-green bracts.

Height: 3-4ft (0.9-1.2m)
Spread: 3-4ft (0.9-1.2m)
Hardiness: Zones 8-10
Cultivation: Plant in well-drained soil in a sunny position. It dislikes disturbance. Small plants establish themselves more rapidly than large ones.

Propagation: During late spring, take 3-4in (7.5-10cm) long basal cuttings and insert in equal parts moist peat and sharp sand.

Euphorbia wulfenii creates a dominant splash of color, contrasting well with silver-leaved plants, such as artemesias and *Santolina chamaecyparissus* (lavender cotton) both with feathery and finely-dissected leaves.

THE FLOWER BORDER

Miscanthus sinensis 'Silver Feather'

A superb perennial grass, ideal for
creating a screen of narrow, blue-
green leaves, or as a specimen in a
border. In addition to the attractive
leaves, during autumn it bears
plumes of silvery flower heads.

Hakonechloa macra 'Aureola'

This beautiful, variegated perennial
grass creates a dramatic feature,
with narrow, long, green leaves
almost entirely striped in bright
yellow. It is ideal for softening the
edges of borders. It is also ideal in
raised borders.
Height: 10-12in (25-30cm)
Spread: 3-4ft (0.9-1.2m)
Hardiness: Zones 6-10
Cultivation: Plant in any fertile,
well-drained soil, in full sun or
partial shade.
Propagation: Lift and divide
overgrown plants in spring.

Hakonechloa macra 'Aureola' harmonizes with
Hosta ventricosa 'Aureo-marginata'. The narrow
leaves of this grass create eye-catching contrasts
with many hostas.

Miscanthus sinensis is the parent of several superb
varieties, including 'Silver Feather' with large plume-like
flower heads, and 'Zebrinus' which reveals foliage with
longitudinal white stripes.

Height: 5-6ft (1.5-1.8m)
Spread: 5-6ft (1.5-1.8m)
Hardiness: Zones 5-9
Cultivation: Plant in moisture-retentive, fertile soil, preferably in full sun.
Propagation: Lift and divide overgrown clumps in early spring.

Below: Miscanthus sinensis 'Silver Feather' *This large member of the grass family creates a dramatic feature in a mixed border. During autumn it develops large, silvery flower heads.*

Phormium tenax 'Variegatum'

New Zealand Flax

This superb architectural half-hardy evergreen perennial from New Zealand develops tall, sword-like, stiff and leathery leaves striped with green and yellow. From mid- to late summer plants develop dull-red flowers on tall branching stems. However, these plants are mainly grown for their attractive foliage. Other attractive varieties of this species include 'Sundowner' with wide leaves which reveal a grayish-purple midriff and creamy-pink outer band, and 'Yellow Wave' with golden-yellow leaves with green outer edges. *Phormium colensoi* is another attractive species. 'Cream Delight' has leaves with green edges and a broad creamy band

Above: Phormium tenax 'Variegatum' *creates color throughout summer, displaying long sword-like leaves, striped yellow and green.*

---

in the center, while 'Tricolor' has bright green leaves edged in red and striped with white.
Height: 6ft (1.8m)
Spread: 4-5ft (1.2-1.5m)
Hardiness: Zones 8-10
Cultivation: Plant in fertile moisture-retentive soil in full sun. These plants are not fully hardy, and benefit from a mulch over their crowns in winter. As soon as the flowers fade, cut off the main stem close to its base.
Propagation: Lift and divide overgrown plants in spring, replanting the young parts from around the outside. Ensure that each new part has three or four leaves.

Phormium tenax 'Variegatum' creates a distinctive splash of color. It can be used effectively with other bold plants.

THE FLOWER BORDER

Yucca filamentosa 'Variegata'

Adam's Needle

A variegated variety that creates an eye-catching feature in a border. This upright hardy evergreen shrub develops stiffly erect, sword-like green leaves with broad cream and yellow edges. An additional attraction is the creamy-white, bell-shaped flowers which are borne on long upright stems during mid-summer. Young plants do not develop flowers.
Height: 3-3½ft (0.9-1m)

Above: Salvia officinalis 'Icterina' *The brightly-variegated leaves of this sage are highlighted by planting the normal gray-green, wrinkled-leaved type around it. Avoid planting other variegated plants close to it, as they visually compete with each other.*

Salvia officinalis 'Aurea'

Garden Sage

This variegated form of the common sage creates a wealth of green and gold leaves. Sages are hardy, semi-evergreen plants. They are ideal for creating color alongside paths, and especially at the junctions. Other colorful varieties include 'Tricolor', with gray-green leaves splashed creamy-white and suffused pink. For young leaves suffused soft purple grow 'Purpurascens', widely known as the 'purple-leaved sage'.
Height: 1½-2ft (45-60cm)
Spread: 1½-2ft (45-60cm)
Hardiness: Zones 5-9
Cultivation: Plant in well-drained soil in full sun. If groups of three or five plants are planted together, spaced about 15-18in (38-45cm) apart, a large mound of foliage is created. Pinch off flowers, which appear during summer.
Propagation: During late summer take 3in (7.5cm) long heel-cuttings and insert in equal parts moist peat and sharp sand. When rooted, pot up into small pots, planting into the garden in spring.

Salvia officinalius 'Aurea' develops into a low-growing mound. Regular clipping will help to keep the plant tidy.

Spread: 2½-3½ft (0.75-1m)
Hardiness: Zones 4-10
Cultivation: Plant in well-drained soil in full sun.
Propagation: In spring, remove sucker-like shoots from around the plant's base and plant in a nursery bed for about three years.

Below: **Yucca filamentosa** 'Variegata' *This variegated evergreen plant has such eye-appeal that it readily captures attention. Creamy-white flowers are borne in midsummer.*

Further plants to consider

Astrantia major 'Variegata'
Great Masterwort
Height: 2-2½ft (60-75cm)   Spread: 15-18in (38-45cm)
Hardiness: Zones 4-8
This variegated variety of the herbaceous perennial masterwort is especially attractive in spring and early summer when the foliage is relatively young. The midgreen, lobed leaves are striped and splashed with yellow. It is also often known and sold as 'Sunningdale Variegated'.

Brunnera macrophylla 'Variegata'
Height: 12-18in (30-45cm)   Spread: 18-20in (45-50cm)
Hardiness: Zones 3-7
This large-leaved herbaceous perennial has matt-green, heart-shaped leaves edged with cream. Sky-blue, forget-me-not-like flowers appear during early and midsummer. It requires moist, shady conditions.

Kochia scoparia
Burning Bush · Summer Cypress
Height: 2-3ft (60-90cm)   Spread: 2ft (60cm)
A bushy, fast-growing annual with fine green leaves that turn purplish-red in fall. It is wonderful as an accent plant or a temporary hedge.

Lysimachia nummularia
Creeping Jenny
Height: 2in (5cm)   Spread: 24in (60cm)
Hardiness: Zones 3-8
A low trailing plant with rounded green leaves and bright yellow flowers. It is a good groundcover in moist, shady areas.

Miscanthus sacchariflorus
Silver Banner Grass
Height: 7-10ft (2.1-3m)   Spread: 2-3ft (60-90cm)
Hardiness: Zones 5-9
This tall, hardy, herbaceous perennial grass is ideal for creating a high screen of narrow, arching, midgreen leaves with pale mid-ribs. When grown as a screen, space the plants 2ft (60cm) apart in a single row.

Sedum spectabile 'Variegatum'
Showy Stonecrop
Height: 15-20in (38-50cm)   Spread: 15-18in (38-45cm)
Hardiness: Zones 4-10
A beautiful variegated variety of a well-known herbaceous perennial widely-grown in borders. The glaucous-green leaves are variegated buff-yellow. During late summer and autumn it bears heads of pink-tinged flowers.

Yucca filamentosa 'Variegata' creates such a dramatic color display that it captures attention from surrounding plants. Plant it in a sea of visually non-competing, low-growing, all-green plants.

Anaphalis cinnamomea

Pearly Everlasting

Hardy herbaceous perennial with
"everlasting flowers" formed of
inconspicuous flowers surrounded
by papery, modified leaves called
bracts. These are long-lived and do
not fade quickly. The white flowers
can be dried, surviving almost
indefinitely. These appear from
midsummer to early autumn in
3-4in (7.5-10cm) wide heads above
narrow, lance-shaped, stem-
clasping, gray-green leaves.
Height: 2ft (60cm)
Spread: 15-18in (38-45cm)
Hardiness: Zones 3-8
Cultivation: Well-drained soil and
a sunny position are needed,
although it tolerates slight shade.
Do not plant it under trees. During
late autumn cut back plants to soil-
level. Fresh plants can be planted
in autumn or spring.
Propagation: The easiest way to
increase it is by lifting and dividing
old and overgrown plants in
autumn or spring. Replant only
young parts from around the
outside of the clump. Alternatively,
sow seeds in loam-based seed
starting mix in flats in spring and
place in a cold frame. When
established, transplant the young
plants to a nursery bed until they
are large enough to be planted into
the garden, in autumn or spring.

Anaphalis triplinervis

Pearly Everlasting

An attractive hardy herbaceous
perennial with silvery-gray, lance-
shaped and stem-clasping leaves.
During midsummer bunched heads
of white flowers are borne in 3-4in
(7.5-10cm) wide heads.
Height: 12in (30cm)
Spread: 15in (38cm)
Hardiness: Zones 3-8
Cultivation: Well-drained soil and
a position in full sun suit it, although
slight shade is acceptable as long
as it is not under trees. Water
dripping on the leaves soon spoils
them. Set new plants in position in
autumn or spring.
Propagation: During autumn or
spring, lift and divide established
plants. Replant only the younger
parts from around the outside of the
clump. Alternatively, in spring sow
seeds in loam-based seed starting
mix in flats. Place in a cold frame.

Anaphalis margaritacea, common pearly everlasting,
is native to North America. It may grow as tall as 4ft
(1.2m) and also has gray-green leaves and pearly-white
flowers in mid-summer.

Anaphalis cinnamomea, like other species in this
genus, has "everlasting" flowers which are popular for
winter arrangements. The flowers are inconspicuous,
and it is the papery bracts that create the display.

Artemisia absinthium 'Lambrook Silver'

A hardy shrubby deciduous border plant with beautiful silvery-gray, finely-divided leaves. During mid- and late summer it develops small, round, yellow flowers.
Height: 2½-3ft (75-90cm)
Spread: 3ft (90cm)
Hardiness: Zones 3-9
Cultivation: Ordinary well-drained soil and a position in full sun suit it. Artemisia, like many gray plants, prefer hot, dry conditions.
Propagation: In late summer take 3-4in (7.5-10cm) long semi-hardwood cuttings and insert in equal parts moist peat and sharp sand. Place in a cold frame and pot up the cuttings individually when rooted.

Right: Artemisia absinthium 'Lambrook Silver' *This shrubby artemisia creates a stunningly attractive beacon of silver-colored foliage throughout summer. It is further enhanced during summer with yellow flowers.*

Artemisia ludoviciana

A bold clump of this hardy herbaceous perennial seldom fails to capture attention. The deeply divided leaves are woolly and white, with silvery-white flowers during late summer and early autumn.
Height: 4-5ft (1.2-1.5m)
Spread: 15-18in (38-45cm)
Hardiness: Zones 4-9
Cultivation: Light, well-drained soil in full sun suits it, avoid cold and wet positions.
Propagation: In autumn or spring, lift and divide overgrown clumps. Replant young pieces from around the outside.

Left: Artemisia ludoviciana *An herbaceous artemisia with deeply-divided lower leaves. It is best when planted in a large, bold clump. The variety 'Silver King' has compact growth and deep silver foliage.*

Artemisia absinthium 'Lambrook Silver' creates a superb light-colored background for dark-leaved plants such as *Sedum maximum* 'Atropurpureum', with broad, purple leaves and dark purple stems.

Artemisia ludoviciana is enhanced by a background of yellow flowers, such as those of achilleas and rudbeckias. A foreground of sedums creates additional color in autumn.

Above: Aruncus dioicus *A hardy and reliable herbaceous perennial. It yearly creates a wealth of creamy-white, tassel-like flower heads above masses of light and somewhat fern-like light green leaves.*

Aruncus dioicus

(*Aruncus sylvester/Spiraea aruncus*)
Goat's Beard

This hardy herbaceous perennial is native to a wide area of the northern hemisphere. During summer it develops flower heads formed of creamy-white, tail-like plumes. These appear above the light green, somewhat fern-like leaves which are borne on stiff, wiry stems. Male and female flowers develop on different plants, with the male flowers being more feathery than the female ones.
Height: 4-5ft (1.2-1.5m)
Spread: 2-3ft (60-90cm)
Hardiness: Zones 3-7
Cultivation: Moisture-retentive, rich, light soil in slight shade suits it best. During autumn, cut down all stems to soil-level. New plants are best set in position in autumn or early spring.

Propagation: It is easily increased by lifting and dividing overgrown plants in spring. Replant only the young parts from around the outside of the clump. The center parts are old and woody.

Chrysanthemum superbum

Shasta Daisy

This well-known and widely-grown hardy herbaceous perennial creates an eye-catching display of single white flowers, 2½-3in (6.5-7.5cm) wide, from mid- to late summer. Each flower has a golden eye. The range of varieties is wide, including single, semi-double and double types. Ones to look for include 'Snowcap' (intensely white flowers on dwarf plants about 20in/50cm high), 'Alaska' (single, pure white, cold hardy to Zone 3) and 'Wirral Supreme' (double, white flowers on plants 3ft/90cm high).
Height: 2½-3ft (75-90cm)
Spread: 18-20in (45-50cm)
Hardiness: Zones 4-9
Cultivation: Well-drained, fertile, slightly alkaline soil is best, preferably in full sun. In late autumn, after plants have started to die back, cut down the stems to soil-level.
Propagation: Lift and divide plants every three years, replanting young parts from around the outside. Do not let plants form large, woody clumps that become full of old stems at their centers.

Right: Chrysanthemum superbum *This variety of the shasta daisy has white flowers which are especially attractive when seen against a blue sky. Divide clumps every few years, before they become full of old woody stems.*

Cimicifuga racemosa

Black Snake Root · Bugbane · Black Cohosh

This North American hardy herbaceous perennial creates a mass of tall, branching stems which bear feathery spires of creamy-white flowers during late summer. Fluffy flowers are borne above somewhat fern-like, mid-green leaves. Other species include *Cimicifuga americana* (American bugbane) which grows 2-4ft (0.6-1.2m) high and with creamy-white flowers, and *Cimicifuga simplex* (Kamchatke bugbane) at 3-4ft (0.9-1.2m) high and with snow-white flowers.
Height: 4-6ft (1.2-1.8m)
Spread: 2-2½ft (60-75cm)
Hardiness: Zones 3-8
Cultivation: Plant in light, rich, deeply-cultivated and moisture-retentive soil. Once established, plants do not like to be disturbed. It looks good planted in a large

group at the back of the border. Cut down the stems to soil-level in late autumn or early winter.
Propagation: Increase this plant by lifting and dividing established clumps in autumn or spring.

Aruncus dioicus is ideal for planting in boggy areas around ponds, especially where naturalized areas merge with pools. Its height creates a natural looking backdrop for other plants around the pond.

Chrysanthemum x superbum is further enhanced when yellow flowered plants such as the herbaceous perennial *Coreopsis verticillata* is set in front of it. A border edging of *Lamium maculatum* 'Beacon Silver' completes the scene.

Left: Cortaderia selloana *The feathery plumes of this member of the grass family are especially attractive when highlighted by the sun. Don't crowd other plants in front of it.*

of long, stiff, upright but arching stems. The flower heads usually remain throughout winter and are especially decorative when covered by frost or snow. There are several varieties, including 'Pumila' at 4-6ft (1.2-1.8m) high. Pampas grass is drought and heat resistant and tolerant of air pollution.

Height: 6-8ft (1.8-2.4m)
Spread: 5-7ft (1.5-2.1m)
Hardiness: Zones 7-10
Cultivation: Plant in light, fertile, well-drained soil, during midspring. Prune established plants in early spring. Wear stout gloves to remove old stems that will have started to die down. Do not cut down the stems - just pull them.
Propagation: In spring, lift and divide established clumps that have become too large. However, take care not to spoil the shape of the clump. Usually, clumps are not disturbed until they are too large, when the whole clump is lifted - not an easy task - and young parts from around the outside replanted.

Cortaderia selloana

Pampas Grass

An eye-catching and distinctive hardy perennial from the pampas of Argentina that seldom fails to create interest in a garden. It is ideal for planting by the side of an informal garden pond or as a specimen plant in a well-manicured lawn. Silky, plume-like, silvery flower heads, sometimes 18in (45cm) long, are borne from late summer to late autumn at the tops

Right: Cimicifuga racemosa *This cimicifuga creates a bold display of midsummer, snow-white flowers at the tops of long stems. Plant it in a large group, at the back of a border, where it creates an eye-catching feature.*

Cimicifuga racemosa has a blackish, stout, rhizome with a bitter, slightly disagreeable flavor. The roots have been used in the treatment of snake bites, as well as a sedative and improving the appetite.

Cortaderia selloana is native to the vast plains of South America. The dramatic plumes may be cut and dried for use in dried arrangements.

THE FLOWER BORDER

Propagation: During late spring and early summer take 3in (7.5cm) long cuttings from basal shoots and insert them in equal parts moist, peat and sharp sand. Place in a cold frame. Pot up when rooted and during summer plant into a nursery bed until large enough to be set in the garden, preferably in spring when the soil is starting to become warm.

Left: Gypsophila paniculata *The misty, delicately presented, white flowers of this border plant are aptly described by its common name - baby's breath. If the spent blooms are removed, the plant will re-bloom in late summer.*

Onopordum acanthium

Scotch Thistle · Cotton Thistle · Silver Thistle · Oat Thistle

A distinctive hardy biennial that seldom fails to attract attention. Its densely branched and erect gray stems bear broad, jaggedly-lobed and spined, silvery-gray leaves. From mid- to late summer it bears purplish-mauve to pale lilac, thistle-like flowers up to 2in (5cm) wide, at the tops of stems. To prolong the drama of the foliage, remove flower buds. After blooming the foliage deteriorates.
Height: 5-7ft (1.5-2.1m)
Spread: 2½-3ft (75-90cm)
Hardiness: Zones 5-9
Cultivation: Fertile, moisture-retentive soil in full sun or light shade suits it. Poor soil does not encourage the development of strong stems and large plants. To prevent plants seeding themselves, cut off flower-heads immediately after flowering finishes.
Propagation: During early summer sow seeds ¼in (6mm) deep in a well-prepared seedbed outdoors. The seeds take up to five weeks to germinate. When the seedlings are large enough to handle, thin them to 12in (30cm) apart. In autumn, transplant them to their permanent positions, 2½ft (75cm) apart.

Gypsophila paniculata

Baby's Breath

A well-known and widely-grown border plant with grass-like, stiffish, gray-green leaves and clouds of white flowers from early to late summer.

Height: 2-2½ft (60-75cm)
Spread: 2½-3ft (75-90cm)
Hardiness: Zones 3-9
Cultivation: Well-drained, slightly alkaline soil suits it, but avoid those which are heavy. Plants respond to deeply-cultivated soil to which has been added compost or manure. When plants are young, insert twiggy sticks around them for support.

Gypsophila paniculata is ideal for creating a large froth of white at the front of a border. It blends well with yellow-flowered herbaceous plants like *Coreopsis lanceolata* with its midsummer flowers.

Onopordum acanthium is generally considered by Scottish antiquarians to be the thistle depicted in the badge of the House of Stuarts. Later it came to be regarded as the national emblem of Scotland.

Romneya coulteri

Californian Tree Poppy ·
Matilija Poppy

This shrubby, herbaceous perennial, native to southern California and the Baja Penninsula, produces eye-catching, 4-5in (10-13cm) wide, white flowers with bright golden globes of stamens at their centers from midsummer to autumn. It grows best in warm areas. The plant has underground runners which can often be very invasive. Therefore, reserve it for planting alongside a path or for setting in a shrub border. In an herbaceous border it sometimes becomes too vigorous. The variety 'White Cloud' has even better blooms than the species.

Height: 4-6ft (1.2-1.8m)
Spread: 4-5ft (1.2-1.5m)
Hardiness: Zones 6-10
Cultivation: Deeply-cultivated, well-drained fertile soil and a sunny and southerly position suit it best. It dislikes root disturbance and therefore is best planted from pots in late spring or early summer. In autumn, cut down the stems to just above soil-level. In colder areas, plant in a sheltered site and mulch well.
Propagation: Seeds are difficult to germinate. However, Californian tree poppy may be easily propagated from root cuttings in the autumn.

Left: Romneya coulteri *Large white flowers with bright, golden centers are borne amid bluish-green, deeply-lobed leaves from midsummer to autumn. Its beautiful flowers compensate for its invasive and spreading nature.*

Romneya coulteri looks superb when planted at the bottom of a flight of garden steps. Its shrubby and spreading nature softens the sides of the steps with foliage and white flowers.

THE FLOWER BORDER

Above: Santolina chamaecyparissus *This hardy evergreen shrub is superb in hot, sunny borders. It is mainly grown for its attractive leaves.*

Santolina chamaecyparissus

(*Santolina incana*)
Lavender Cotton

A beautiful aromatic, evergreen shrub with finely-divided, silvery, woolly leaves. In midsummer it bears bright lemon-yellow, button-like flowers. *S. virens* is a narrow-leaved green form.
Height: 1½-2ft (45-60cm)
Spread: 1½-2ft (45-60cm)
Hardiness: Zones 6-8
Cultivation: Well-drained soil in full sun assures success with this warmth-loving plant. If the plant becomes straggly, lightly trim back in spring or after the flowers fade.
Propagation: From mid- to late summer take 2-3in (5-7.5cm) long half-ripe cuttings from sideshoots. Insert them in equal parts moist peat and sharp sand. Overwinter in a cold frame.

Senecio cineraria

(*Cineraria bicolor/Cineraria maritima*)
Dusty Miller

This half-hardy perennial from Mediterranean regions is usually grown as a half-hardy annual for summer-bedding schemes. In warm, southerly areas it will survive outdoors most winters and can be seen in many gardens as a left-over from summer bedding arrangements. However, it looks best when combined with other plants, so that its attractive silvery appearance acts as a color and texture contrast. The leaves are covered with white, woolly hairs which give this plant its distinctive appearance.
From midsummer to autumn it has 1in (2.5cm) wide flowers, but these are not as attractive as the foliage and are best removed. Several attractive varieties are available, such as 'Silver Lace' with more deeply-divided leaves than most varieties, and 'Silver Dust' with fern-like, deeply-dissected and intensely silvery-white foliage. These are small and lower-growing

than the normal type.
Height: 1½-2ft (45-60cm)
Spread: 12-15in (30-38cm)
Cultivation: Any ordinary garden soil and a sunny position suit it. Set new plants in the garden in late spring.
Propagation: From late winter to midspring sow seeds ⅛in (3mm) deep in loam-based seed starting mix. Place in 59°F (15°C). Germination takes about ten days. When the seedlings are large enough to handle, prick them off into flats of loam-based potting soil. Slowly accustom the young plants to outdoor life and plant into the garden when all risk of frost has passed.

Below: Stachys byzantina *A beautiful ground covering plant that forms a sea of leaves densely covered with silvery hairs, creating a soft and woolly texture.*

Santolina chamaecyparissus creates a superb backdrop for many border plants, but they should not be strongly colored. Instead, choose those with flowers that reveal delicate and demure pastel shades.

Dusty Miller harmonizes with many other plants, including *Salvia farinacea* 'Victoria' (blue salvia), the brightly and dominantly-flowered *Salvia splendens* (red salvia), and China asters.

Above: Senecio cineraria 'Silver Dust' *The silvery, fern-like carpet created by this summer-bedding plant is ideal for highlighting other plants. It is often better known by its earlier name* – Cineraria maritima 'Silver Dust'.

Stachys byzantina

(*Stachys lanata · Stachys olympicum*)
Woolly Betony · Lamb's Ears

This herbaceous perennial is grown for its beautiful, oval, mid-green leaves which are so densely covered with white, silvery hairs that they assume a woolly appearance. The stems spread and root freely, creating a superb ground cover plant. Upright stems develop small, purple flowers during midsummer. The form 'Silver Carpet' is excellent for covering the soil with silvery leaves, and is a non-flowering type. It less half-hardy and in severe winters can be damaged, especially by a combination of water and frost.
Height: 1-1½ft (30-45cm)
Spread: 1-1½ft (30-45cm)
Hardiness: Zones 4-8
Cultivation: Well-drained soil in light shade or full sun suits it. In autumn, cut down to soil-level those long stems that have borne flowers.
Propagation: It is easily increased by lifting and dividing overgrown plants in spring. Replant the young parts from around the outside of the clump. The species will self seed if allowed to bloom.

Further plants to consider

Colchicum speciosum 'Album'
Height: 4-6in (10-15cm)   Spread: 6in (15cm)
Hardiness: Zones 5-9
Hardy bulb with glistening white, goblet-shaped flowers during late summer and into early autumn. The leaves, which grow 12-15in (30-38cm) long, appear in spring.

Dictamnus albus
Gas Plant · Dittany · Fraxinella
Height: 2ft (60cm)   Spread: 1½ft (45cm)
Hardiness: Zones 3-8
A hardy herbaceous perennial with white, spider-like flowers borne in spikes up to 12in (30cm) long during midsummer. Plants should not be moved or divided once established. Some people have an allergic reaction to the foliage.

Euphorbia marginata
Snow on the Mountain
Height: 2ft (60cm)   Spread: 12-15in (30-38cm)
A bushy annual grown for its soft green leaves which become veined and widely edged in white as the plant matures.

Lilium candidum
Madonna Lily
Height: 4-5ft (1.2-1.5m)   Spread: 10-15in (25-38cm)
Hardiness: Zones 4-9
Well-known hardy basal-rooting lily which during midsummer bears white trumpet-shaped fragrant flowers about 3in (7.5cm) long.

Narcissus 'Actaea'
Actaea Daffodil
Height: 15in (38cm)   Spread: 4-6in (10-15cm)
Hardiness: Zones 4-9
A hardy spring-flowering bulbous plant, belonging to the *Poeticus* group, with white petals and a red-rimmed yellow cup.

Phlox paniculata 'Mt. Fuji'
Border Phlox · Summer Phlox
Height: 2½ft (75cm)   Spread: 12-15in (30-38cm)
Hardiness: Zones 2-8
Hardy herbaceous perennial with upright stems bearing pure-white flowers in cylindrical heads from mid- to late summer.

Tiarella cordifolia
Foam Flower
Height: 6-12in (15-30cm)   Spread: 12in (30cm)
Hardiness: Zones 3-8
Hardy herbaceous ground covering plant with midgreen, maple-like leaves and creamy-white spires of flowers.

Stachys byzantina is superb when grown with blue flowered plants such as cat mint (*Nepeta x faassenii*), purple-leaved sage (*Salvia officinalis* 'Purpurascens') *Salvia x superba* or *Ruta graveolens* 'Jackman's blue'.

CHAPTER TWO

ROCK AND NATURALIZED GARDENS

Rock gardens usually receive more love and attention than any other part of the garden of equal size. The plants are diminutive, often early-flowering and frequently fussy about drainage. Though they need a certain amount of special care and attention, yard-for-yard rock gardens can support a greater range of plants than other sites.

Many people consider alpine and rock garden plants to be tender and fussy plants, but this is not necessarily correct. They are normally very hardy and will tolerate low temperatures, but are susceptible to a combination of excessively wet and freezing conditions. These conditions are made worse by poor drainage and leaves which fall on and around the plants in autumn.

An ideal location for a rock garden would be a raised site either on a slope or a well drained artificial mound where the plants get plenty of light. However, if this is not available, cracks in dry stone walls, gaps in natural paving or even stone sinks provide attractive homes for rock garden plants. Hybrids of *Lewisia cotyledon* are superb candidates for sink gardens, while the cobweb houseleek, *Sempervivum arachnoideum*, with an attractive globular rosette of leaves and bright rose-red flowers, is another delight. There are many other suitable plants to be found in this chapter.

Naturalized gardens – perhaps helping a garden pond fuse into the overall garden scene, or on a warm grassy bank at the side of a rock garden, or perhaps a sheltered and lightly-shaded spot beneath a canopy of deciduous trees – can feature beautiful plants. In addition to cultivated plants, many native species are available and can be easily raised from seeds. If you have a small area which can be devoted to native plants you will be surprised by their rich colors.

Left: Grape Hyacinths (Muscari armeniacum) *with their tightly-clustered azure-blue flower heads, create a strong color contrast with a mixed assortment of yellow, pink and red polyanthus.*

Above: **Androsace primuloides 'Chumbyi'** *This is a delightful rock garden plant with beautiful clear pink flowers during midspring to midsummer. It is essential that the rosettes are kept relatively dry during winter.*

Androsace primuloides

(*Androsace sarmentosa*)
Rock Jasmine

A hardy rock garden perennial with silky white, woolly, narrow, lance-shaped, midgreen leaves. The rosettes of rose-pink flowers are borne on 2-4in (5-10cm) stems from midspring to midsummer. The form 'Chumbyi' has clear pink flowers.
Height: 4-5in (10-13cm)
Spread: 15-24in (38-60cm)
Hardiness: Zones 5-8
Cultivation: Good drainage and a sunny position are essential. Preferably, the soil should contain coarse sand or limestone grit. Set the plants in position during spring. Wet soil encourages the leaves to rot, and in very wet areas protection with cloches may be necessary during winter.
Propagation: This is quite easily achieved by potting up rooted rosettes at the edges of the main clump in early autumn. Stand the pots in an open but sheltered part of the garden during winter. Protect them from excessive rain as necessary and plant out into the garden during spring.

Below: **Anthyllis montana** *This European alpine needs full sun and a well-drained gritty soil. Once established, it is best left alone, as its tap-root system resents any disturbance.*

Androsace lanuginosa, from the Himalayas, is a delightful trailing and mat-forming rock jasmine, with silver-green leaves and pinkish flowers in midsummer and autumn. It is ideal for dry stone walls.

Armeria juniperifolia

(*Armeria caespitosa*)
Pyrenees Thrift

This hardy evergreen perennial from Spain is one of the best known rock garden plants, producing stiff grass-like, gray-green leaves in tufted clumps. The ½-¾in (12-18mm) wide, tightly packed, pink flowerheads are borne singly at the tops of 2-3in (5-7.5cm) long stems during late spring and early summer. The variety 'Splendens' displays bright pink flowers.
Height: 2-3in (5-7.5cm)
Spread: 8-10in (20-25cm)
Hardiness: Zones 4-8
Cultivation: Any good well-drained garden soil suits thrift, and it likes a position in full sun. Set the plants in position during spring or autumn. As soon as the flowers fade, clip them off to make the plants neat for the rest of the year.
Propagation: This is easily done by lifting and dividing large clumps in spring. Replant them immediately. Alternatively, 2in (5cm) basal cuttings can be taken in late summer and inserted in equal parts peat and sharp sand.

Anthyllis montana

Mountain Kidney Vetch

An unusual rock garden plant that forms a low woody bush with hairy foliage, giving it a silvery appearance. During midsummer it bears red or red-purple flowers at the stem ends.
Height: 8-12in (20-30cm)
Spread: 15-18in (38-45cm)
Hardiness: Zones 5-8
Cultivation: Anthyllis prefers a well-drained gritty soil and full sun.
Propagation: During summer, take 2-3in (5-7.5cm) long cuttings with heels. Insert them in pots containing a sandy potting soil and put them in a cold frame. It is difficult to raise from seeds, but these can be sown in early spring and placed in a cold frame. Once planted, it is best left alone as it resents disturbance.

Above: **Armeria juniperifolia 'Bevan's Variety'** *A reliable and neat tufted rock garden plant that flowers in early summer, armeria also grows well in a stone sink. The flowers and foliage can be enhanced by covering the soil with clean shingle.*

Below: **Armeria maritima 'Bloodstone'** *This species is related to the slightly smaller* Armeria juniperifolia *and rises to 6-10in (15-25cm). Again it is a reliable rock garden plant, and is also ideal for setting at the edges of a border.*

There are more than 50 species of **Armeria**; most are suitable for the rock garden or the front of a border. Thrifts form neat, grasslike tufts and are useful for seaside and poor soil plantings.

Astilbe x arendsii

False Spirea

This beautiful hardy herbaceous hybrid perennial comes in a color range from purple-red to nearly white. Many pink and red forms are available, flowering from mid- to late summer. Varieties to look for include 'Bressingham Beauty' (rich pink and free-flowering), 'Fanal' (intense deep red), 'Peach Blossom' (light pink), 'Ostrich Plume' (bright pink), 'Red Sentinel' (intense brick red), 'Rheinland' (rich pink) and 'Federsee' (rose-red).
Height: 2-3ft (60-90cm)

Spread: 15-20in (38-50cm)
Hardiness: Zones 4-9
Cultivation: Astilbes prefer fertile, moisture-retentive soil in full sun or light shade. In dry seasons it may be necessary to water the plants. Applying a mulch helps to conserve moisture in the soil. In spring, cut the foliage down to soil-level. The seed heads provide winter interest.
Propagation: Lifting and dividing established clumps every three or four years in spring is the easiest method. Replant them immediately so that the roots do not dry out.

Above left: Astilbe x arendsii
This beautiful hardy herbaceous plant has feathery spires of flowers from mid- to late summer. It is ideal for a moist area in the garden. It is best planted in large drifts where it creates a strong display for much of the summer.

Above: Astilbe chinensis 'Pumila' *Most astilbes prefer moist soils, but this diminutive form does well in drier conditions. During summer it develops fluffy pink spires that display themselves above the foliage, never failing to produce an exciting spectacle.*

Astilbes are an ideal choice for the moist surrounds of informal garden pools. The red and pink forms blend well with yellow hemerocallis and the large blue heads of *Hydrangea macrophylla*.

Astilbe chinensis 'Pumila'

Without a doubt, this miniature astilbe is a treasure in a rock garden. Its herbaceous perennial nature ensures fresh, midgreen, fern-like foliage each year, with 9in (23cm) long spires of fluffy pink flowers flushed purple appearing from midsummer to autumn.

Height: 9-12in (23-30cm)
Spread: 12-15in (30-38cm)
Hardiness: Zones 3-8
Cultivation: Relatively moist and fertile soil in full sun or light shade suit this plant. The roots like a cool position, for example by the side of a rock that affords a shady and cool root run.
Propagation: It is most easily increased by lifting and dividing clumps every three or four years and replanting them 10-12in (25-30cm) apart. Do this in midspring and water well until the plants are established.

Cornus alba

Tatarian Dogwood

This hardy, vigorous, wide-spreading, deciduous shrub belongs to the dogwood family and is native to Eastern and North Central North America. This particular species has a suckering habit and produces masses of upright stems. The current year's stems are bright red in winter. All are suitable for naturalizing in a garden or for creating a light screen.

Height: 7-9ft (2.1-2.7m)
Spread: 6-10ft (1.8-3m)
Hardiness: Zones 3-8
Cultivation: Rich, moist soil and full sun suit these shrubs best. In early spring, cut down the stems to within a few inches of the soil to encourage the development of shoots that will display good rich color in late summer and winter.
Propagation: It is easily increased by layering long shoots in autumn. Alternatively, take hardwood cuttings in autumn, inserting them in trenches with sand along their bases to prevent waterlogging.

Above: **Cornus alba 'Sibirica'** *This distinctively bright-stemmed shrub makes an impressive picture during winter. To obtain highly-colored shoots, the previous season's growth must be cut down nearly to soil level in spring. 'Sibirica' is more brightly colored than the species.*

Astilbe chinensis 'Pumila' with its upright spires can create the effect of sudden height in a rock garden. It often looks good by a dry stone wall, whose color and texture complement the flowers.

Cornus alba looks best in a site where low-angled winter sun will catch the stems. It makes an ideal companion for daffodils, which will provide color to hide its stems when cut down in spring.

Daphne cneorum

Rose Daphne

This is a beautiful and highly scented ground-hugging and spreading evergreen shrub from Central and Southern Europe, ideal for a rock garden. The wiry stems are well clothed with narrow, deep green leaves, and the ½in (12mm) wide rose-pink flowers appear during early summer. The variety 'Eximia' boasts deeper pink flowers and is slightly larger.
Height: 6in (16cm)
Spread: 2½-4½ft (75cm-1.3m)
Hardiness: Zones 4-7
Cultivation: Daphnes like a well-drained but moisture-retentive garden soil in full sun or slight shade. They tolerate lime in the soil. As the roots need to be kept cool, mulch with well-rotted compost in spring. If the plants spread too much, prune them back carefully after flowering.
Propagation: The easiest way for a home gardener to increase this plant is by layering shoots in autumn. Alternatively, take 2-4in (5-10cm) long heel cuttings in mid- to late summer and insert them in pots containing equal parts peat and sharp sand, placed in a cold frame. When the plants are rooted, pot them up into loam-based potting soil, setting them out in the garden about eighteen months later into their final positions.

Left: **Daphne cneorum** *One of the most beautiful and pleasantly-scented of all garden plants, this daphne will spread up to 4½ft (1.3m) wide. The four-petalled rose-pink flowers appear during early summer.*

Dianthus pavonius

(*Dianthus neglectus*)

This attractive but variable hardy rock garden plant forms neat hummocks of narrow gray-green leaves. During mid- to late summer these are smothered with pale pink to deep crimson 1¼in (3cm) wide flowers on short stems 1in (2.5cm) long.
Height: 4-8in (10-20cm)
Spread: 6-8in (15-20cm)
Hardiness: Zones 3-7
Cultivation: Ordinary well-drained garden soil and a sunny position assure success. Sprinkling stone chips over the surface helps to prevent heavy rain from splashing soil on to the plants. The chips also improve surface drainage.
Propagation: During mid-summer take 3-4in (7.5-10cm) long cuttings and insert them in pots containing equal parts peat and sharp sand. Place these in a cold frame. When rooted, pot the plants up into loam-based potting soil in small pots and replace in the frame. When established, plant out into the garden.

Below: **Dianthus pavonius** *This dainty rock garden plant is often better known as* Dianthus neglectus. *During summer it displays fringed pale pink to deep crimson flowers.*

Daphne cneorum is very adaptable and mixes well with many other plants. The flowers have a sweet fragrance and often re-bloom in late summer.

Left: Erinus alpinus
This beautiful and highly adaptable plant lives happily in a rock garden or on a dry stone wall. It seeds itself readily, rapidly producing a supply of fresh plants.

Right: Fritillaria imperialis
This distinctive and eye-catching spring-flowering bulb produces an impressive stem bearing bell-shaped flowers. The tuft of leaves at the top of the stem creates the impression of a crown.

Fritillaria imperialis

Crown Imperial

This vigorous and distinctive plant from the Himalayas produces stiff, upright stems with wavy lance-shaped glossy green leaves partly clasping them. During spring, it bears dense clusters of bell-shaped 2in (5cm) long flowers at the tops of the stems. These range from yellow to rich red. Above the flowers is a cluster of partially erect leaves, resembling a crown. It is just as attractive in large drifts in a woodland garden as in a formal setting, perhaps alongside a path.
Height: 2-3ft (60-90cm)
Spread: 12-15in (30-38cm)
Hardiness: Zones 5-9
Cultivation: Fritillarias require fertile, well-drained soil in full or light shade. As the fleshy bulbs are easily damaged, they are best planted 8in (20cm) deep during autumn and left in one position for several years. Setting the bulbs on their sides prevents water rotting their tops. In heavy soils, put a handful of sharp sand under each bulb. During autumn, cut down the stems to soil level.
Propagation: Fritillarias can be grown from seed, but this method takes up to six years to produce flowering-sized bulbs, so it is better to propagate from offsets taken from the parent bulb in late summer. Plant them in a nursery bed for two years before transferring them to their final flowering positions.

Erinus alpinus

A hardy though relatively short-lived dwarf evergreen perennial for rock gardens or dry stone walls. It also does well between natural paving stones. The spoon-shaped, midgreen leaves are deeply toothed and borne in low, tufted mounds with bright pink ¼in (6mm) wide, star-shaped flowers from early spring to late summer. A plant for the rock garden aficionado, it is available from speciality nurseries.
Height: 3in (7.5cm)
Spread: 6-8in (15-20cm)
Hardiness: Zones 5-8
Cultivation: Well-drained soil is essential, as is a sunny position.
Propagation: Erinus seeds itself quite readily, and even the cultivated varieties come true when grown from seed.

Erinus alpinus is a delight when allowed to fill the gaps in natural stone paths, or used to tumble down a dry stone wall. Be sure to grow in well-drained soil.

Fritillaria imperialis is ideal for naturalizing with other plants, like miniature tulips and violas, in a wild garden. However, it also does well in narrow beds in small, more formal gardens.

Geranium dalmaticum

This neat Yugoslavian and Albanian cranesbill is a densely foliaged herbaceous perennial with deeply-lobed, rather palm-like, midgreen, flossy leaves that take on red to orange tints in autumn. During mid- to late summer it bears 1in (2.5cm) wide, demure pink, five-petalled, saucer-shaped flowers on stems 4-5in (10-13cm) long.

Height: 6in (15cm)
Spread: 10-12in (25-30cm)
Hardiness: Zones 4-8
Cultivation: Any well-drained garden soil in full sun or partial shade is suitable.
Propagation: It is easily increased by lifting and dividing clumps in spring or autumn. It is quite easy to split up the plants. If some of them are rather small, pot them up into small pots and allow them to establish themselves properly before setting them out in the rock garden in their permanent positions.

Left: Geranium dalmaticum
A dainty cranesbill for a rock garden, this species has midgreen leaves that take on lovely red and orange tints in autumn. These form a bonus to the soft pink flowers.

Gypsophila repens

Creeping Baby's Breath

This pretty mat-forming, wiry-stemmed, trailing alpine gypsophila with narrow gray-green leaves looks superb when clothed with $\frac{1}{3}$in (9mm) wide pink or white flowers throughout the summer. Varieties include 'Bodgeri' (double, light pink), 'Fratensis' (rich pink) and 'Rosea' (pale pink).

Height: 4-6in (10-15cm)
Spread: 1½-2ft (45-60cm)
Hardiness: Zones 3-8
Cultivation: Well-drained, slightly alkaline soil is best, although gypsophilas also do well in acid conditions. They are best positioned to trail over the top of a dry stone wall or large rocks.

Geranium dalmaticum has a flattened-dome shape, making it an ideal choice for the junction of two paths in a rock garden. It is also superb for a terrace or dry stone wall where it can spill over.

Gypsophila repens is spectacular in a rock garden trailing over rocks and walls. It is also effective in containers, blooming throughout the summer.

Propagation: During spring, take 2in (5cm) long cuttings and insert them in pots containing equal parts of peat and sharp sand. Place these in a cold frame. When rooted, pot up the plants into 3in (7.5cm) pots of loam-based potting soil. They can be planted out in autumn or spring.

Right: Helianthemum nummularium 'Ben Dearg'
Few midsummer-flowering rock plants are as impressive as this low-growing, somewhat sprawling perennial. And even if it does exceed its position, it can easily be trimmed back after flowering.

Below: Gypsophila repens *This distinctive pink-flowered alpine gypsophila produces a frothy mass of flowers well suited for tumbling over walls and large rocks. Its loose and lax nature when trailing over walls allows the attractive nature of the stone to be seen.*

Helianthemum nummularium

(Helianthemum chamaecistus H. vulgare)
Sun Rose

This shrubby, low-growing and spreading plant is invaluable in a rock garden. The deep green, narrow, elliptical leaves are borne sparsely on trailing stems, with 1/2in-1in (12-25mm) wide, saucer-shaped flowers appearing during midsummer. The color range is wide, including 'Beech Park Scarlet' (crimson-scarlet), 'Wisley Pink' (pink), 'The Bride' (white) and 'Cerise Queen' (rosy-red).
Height: 4-6in (10-15cm)
Spread: 1 1/2-2ft (45-60cm)
Hardiness: Zones 5-7
Cultivation: Well-drained garden soil and a sunny position assure success. They prefer cool summers and mild winters. They will withstand quite severe pruning after flowering.
Propagation: During mid- to late summer take 2-3in (5-7.5cm) long cuttings with "heels". Insert them in pots of equal parts peat and sharp sand and place these in a cold frame. Pot up the plants when rooted into small pots of loam-based potting soil and replace in a cold frame. Plant out in spring.

Helianthemum nummularium is extremely impressive when trailing over a low wall, so the plant can be seen from above as well as the sides. It is useful for breaking up the stark outline of a wall.

Oxalis adenophylla

Sorrel

This unusual, delightful, dainty, low-growing hardy perennial has a fiber-coated bulb-like rootstock, grayish leaves and long-stemmed, solitary, cup-shaped, satiny-pink flowers in early summer. It requires very well-drained soil and is best grown in the rock garden. The blossoms close on cloudy days.
Height: 2½-3in (6.5-7.5cm)
Spread: 6in (15cm)
Hardiness: Zones 6-9
Cultivation: A well-drained, light soil and a sunny position are essential. A light soil covering of well-washed shale helps to ensure good drainage and an attractive background for the flowers and foliage. The foliage dies down during winter. It may also be forced indoors for winter bloom.
Propagation: This can be easily done by separating the bulb offsets in early spring. These can be replanted directly into the rock garden or potted into a gritty potting soil until healthy young plants become properly established.

Below: Oxalis adenophylla
The delicate appearance of this Chilean hardy perennial never fails to add an element of interest to rock gardens.

Parahebe catarractae

This unusual and tender dainty-flowered sub-shrub delights in cascading over and between rocks, displaying its massed terminal heads of flowers, featuring rose-purple lines set on a background of white, during summer. The mid- to dark green leaves are an attractive bonus.
Height: 10-12in (25-30cm)
Spread: 15-18in (38-45cm)
Hardiness: Zones 8-9
Cultivation: Parahebes delight in a well-drained neutral soil, preferably covered with well-washed shale and in a sunny position. Set them at the top of the rock garden so

Oxalis adenophylla has delicate coloring, and needs subtly colored neighbors if it is not to be dominated. It looks at its best when given plenty of space, rather than being hemmed in.

Left: **Penstemon newberryi**
This sprawling and scrambling penstemon produces pink to rose-pink flowers, and there are many other superb penstemons suitable for rock gardens.

Penstemon newberryi

This is a useful bushy semi-evergreen sub-shrub for trailing over rocks and dry stone walls, where its sprawling nature helps to merge the structural elements. The species is native to northern California and Nevada. Its elongated, $1\frac{1}{4}$-$1\frac{1}{2}$in (3-4cm) long, snapdragon-like, pink to rose-pink flowers appear against a carpet of small, midgreen leaves.

Height: 8in (20cm)
Spread: 12-15in (30-38cm)
Hardiness: Zones 5-10
Cultivation: A well-drained soil is essential. Penstemons flourish in full sun, though a sheltered site on a north slope may be needed, as the plants will suffer during exceptionally cold winters. Poorly drained soils contribute to failure during cold spells.
Propagation: Although they can be increased from seed sown during early spring in boxes of loam-based seed starting mix, the resulting seedlings can be variable. Instead, take 2-3in (5-7.5cm) long cuttings from non-flowering shoots during late summer or early autumn. Insert them in pots containing equal parts peat and sharp sand and put these in a cold frame. When the young plants are rooted, pot them up into loam-based potting soil and place in a cold frame during winter. Plant out into the garden in late spring. Another attractive alpine species is *P. davidsonii*, a low sub-shrub which grows up to 4in (10cm) high and produces ruby-red flowers in midsummer.

they can tumble between rocks and benefit from better drainage at the top of a slope.
Propagation: It is easily increased by taking soft cuttings 2-3in (5-7.5cm) long, from mid- to late summer. Insert them in pots of sandy potting soil and place these in a cold frame. When the plants are properly rooted, nip out their growing tips to encourage dense bushy growth. This species is related to the hebes and veronicas, and very frequently there is some confusion about the identity of plants. To ensure you have the right plants buy only those listed as *Parahebe catarractae*, not *Hebe catarractae*.

Left: **Parahebe catarractae**
This beautiful shrubby plant delights in well-drained soil and a sunny position.

Parahebe catarractae blends well with dainty bright yellow flowers, but beware of overdoing such a combination as the contrast can be overpowering. A good companion is *Sedum acre* 'Aureum'.

Penstemon barbatus, which grows to 3ft (90cm) is a penstemon that is suitable for the border. It is available with flowers that range from soft pink to deep red.

Saponaria ocymoides

Rock Soapwort

This delightful, vigorous, trailing rock-garden perennial is invaluable for creating prostrate mats of color flowing over rocks or cascading from dry stone walls. It produces long, lance-shaped, mid-green leaves, with five-petalled, $^1/_2$in (12mm) wide, bright rose-pink flowers from mid- to late summer. Several excellent varieties are available, such as 'Rubra Compact' (rich carmine), 'Splendens' (dark pink) and 'Floribunda' which has more flowers than normal and is soft pink.

Height: 3in (7.5cm)
Spread: 1ft (30cm)
Hardiness: Zones 2-7
Cultivation: Soapworts appreciate a well-drained fertile garden soil in full sun or light shade.
Propagation: Plants can be lifted and divided in autumn or spring. Alternatively, soft stem cuttings can be taken in summer from non-flowering shoots and inserted in pots of sandy potting soil. Pot plants up into loam-based potting soil when rooted.

Above: Saponaria ocymoides
This delightful rock garden plant cascades in a spectacular manner over stone walls and rocks. In such positions the bright rose-pink flowers are a delight, appearing from mid- to late summer.

Below: Saponaria officinalis
This is the original single-flowered form, with fragrant rose-pink flowers borne on erect stems. A superb double-flowered pink form is now available, too. It is best positioned in a wild garden where its invasive nature does not interfere with neighboring plants.

Saponaria officinalis

Soapwort · Bouncing Bet

This hardy herbaceous perennial is a native of Europe and parts of Asia, and is often found naturalized in areas that are or have been inhabited by humans. The common name soapwort refers to the leaves which, when bruised in water, create a lather. At one time, soapwort was known as fuller's herb; a fuller was a person whose trade was to cleanse cloth. In the past it was used to clean old curtains, although why it was relegated to such a job is not clear when it was perfectly efficient on other cloths. The 1-1$^1/_2$in (2.5-4cm) wide flowers are pink and single and borne in mid- to late summer in terminal clusters on stiff, upright stems, clasped by pale-green leaves. Several attractive forms are available, such as 'Roseoplena' (double pink flowers) and 'Rubra-plena' (double red flowers).
Height: 1$^1/_2$-2ft (45-90cm)
Spread: 2ft (60cm)
Hardiness: Zones 2-8
Cultivation: Soapwort prefers a well-drained fertile soil and a position in full sun or light shade. In exposed areas it will require support from twiggy sticks that the foliage can grow through and hide. In autumn, cut down the stems to soil level.
Propagation: You can take cuttings in summer, but it is much easier to increase by lifting and dividing established clumps in autumn or spring.

Saponaria ocymoides is such a spectacular plant when in bloom that the pink flowers can be dominated by stronger colored plants nearby, so take care when planting it in a group.

Saponaria officinalis is also known as bouncing Bet. In this context, 'bouncing' refers to the good health and vitality this medicinal herb may bring; 'Bet' is an abbreviation for Elizabeth.

Above: **Thymus praecox arcticus**
This groundcover thyme is a delight with its fragrant summer flowers, and is invaluable for covering bare soil with color.

Thymus praecox arcticus

(*Thymus serpyllum, T. drucei*)
Mother-of-Thyme

This prostrate thyme has narrow, rather spoon-shaped gray-green leaves. The variably colored flowers – from red to pink and white – appear in small clustered heads from mid- to late summer. Several varieties are available, including 'Annie Hall' (pale pink) and 'Coccineus' (rich crimson).
Height: 1¹/₂-3in (4-7.5cm)
Spread: 2-3ft (60-90cm)
Hardiness: Zones 4-9
Cultivation: Any good, well-drained garden soil in a sunny position suits thyme. To keep the plants neat, use a pair of garden shears to clip off dead flower heads.
Propagation: The easiest way to increase this plant is by lifting and dividing overgrown clumps in spring or early autumn.

Further plants to consider

Antennaria dioica
Common Pussytoes
Height: 2-12in (5-30cm)   Spread: 1-1¹/₂ft (30-45cm)
Hardiness: Zones 3-8
A hardy evergreen perennial with a creeping habit and white, pink-tipped flowers during early summer. The variety 'Rosea' has deep pink blooms.

Dianthus deltoides 'Flashing Light'
Maiden Pink
Height: 6-9in (15-23cm)   Spread: 6in (15cm)
Hardiness: Zones 3-9
A beautiful rock-garden plant for crevices and between natural paving stones. From midsummer to autumn it reveals bright crimson flowers. Other forms include 'Rosea' (shades of pink) and 'Brilliant' (bright rose-pink).

Epimedium x rubrum
Height: 8-12in (20-30cm)   Spread: 10-12in (25-30cm)
Hardiness: Zones 4-8
An evergreen groundcover for woodland or dry areas. The delicate heart-shaped leaves are edged with red in autumn. The airy sprays of spring blooms are deep red.

Helleborus orientalis
Hellebore · Lenten Rose
Height: 15-18in (38-45cm)   Spread: 12-15in (30-38cm)
Hardiness: Zones 4-9
An evergreen woodland plant with deep green, leathery leaves that stand above the blooms. The subtle, pink-tinged, cup-shaped flowers appear from late winter through spring.

Sempervivum arachnoideum
Cobweb Houseleek
Height: 4in (10cm)   Spread: 9-12in (23-30cm)
Hardiness: Zones 3-8
An unusual succulent plant with rosettes of green leaves, often flushed with red, and bright red, ³/₄in (18mm) wide flowers during midsummer. Available from speciality nurseries.

Phlox subulata
Moss Pink · Moss Phlox
Height: 2-4in (5-10cm)   Spread: 1-1¹/₂ft (30-45cm)
Hardiness: Zones 2-9
A beautiful sub-shrub forming a mat of midgreen, narrow leaves with pink or purple flowers in spring. Varieties to look for include 'Crimson Beauty' (red), 'Cushion Pink' (pink) and 'Scarlet Flame' (brilliant scarlet).

Thymus vulgaris, common thyme, is a small perennial with tiny lavender-white flowers. Many hybrids of this plant exist, including *Thymus x citriodorus* 'Aureus' (with yellow leaves) and 'Silver Queen' (with variegated leaves).

Anemone blanda

Windflower

This welcome and reliable spring-flowering plant has rather fern-like deeply-cut dark green leaves and 1-1½in (2.5-4cm) wide daisy-like flowers in pale blue, pink, lavender or white.

Height: 5-6in (13-15cm)
Spread: 4-5in (10-13cm)
Hardiness: Zones 6-9
Cultivation: Well-drained fertile soil neutral or slighty acid, in light dappled shade, suits it best. The corms are best planted in autumn 2in (5cm) deep and 5-6in (13-15cm) apart.
Propagation: Lift and divide crowded clumps in late summer. Alternatively, sow seeds when ripe in pots or flats of potting soil, placing them in a cold frame. Prick off the seedlings into flats when they are large enough to handle.

Right: **Anemone blanda 'Blue Pearl'** *Anemones are always welcome in spring, with their neat, daisy-like flowers with bright centers. There is a range of colors, including this striking blue variety. They can be naturalized beneath trees or set in clumps in a rock garden.*

Aubrieta deltoidea

Rock Cress

This is one of the best-known rock garden plants, well suited for covering large areas and for trailing over walls. It is also useful as an edging to paths and for combining with herbaceous plants. There are many varieties, originated from selected seedlings of this hardy, spreading and low-growing evergreen perennial. These include 'Barker's Double' (rose-purple), 'Dr. Mules' (violet-purple), and 'Royal Blue' (dark blue).

Height: 3-4in (7.5-10cm)
Spread: 1½-2ft (45-60cm)
Hardiness: Zones 4-8
Cultivation: Well-drained garden soil and a sunny position suit it best.

Keep the plants neat by trimming them after flowering.
Propagation: The plants can be easily increased by lifting and dividing in early autumn.

Far right: **Aubrieta deltoidea** *growing with a white Iberis sempervirens. This handsome, spreading and trailing evergreen perennial is ideal for cascading over walls, as an edging to paths and even for growing with herbaceous plants. There are many varieties to choose from in a variety of colors.*

Right: **Anemone coronaria** *This is the well-known florist's anemone, popular in both borders and in rock gardens, as well as being extensively grown for cut-flowers.*

Anemone blanda is striking when naturalized among the dappled light filtering through silver-barked trees. Also, try a mixture of anemones, grape hyacinths, scillas and species tulips.

Aubrietia deltoidea harmonizes with many others including the hardy pink or white perennial *Arabis caucasica,* the yellow-flowered bulb *Tulipa tarda,* and the hardy perennial yellow *Alyssum saxatile.*

Above: **Campanula cochleariifolia**
This hardy small perennial with its nodding thimble-like flowers is a delight in a rock garden. It is one of the most amenable and rewarding of all campanulas.

Campanula cochleariifolia

(*Campanula pusilla*)
Spiral Bellflower

A dainty, easily-grown hardy perennial, ideal for a rock garden. It displays midgreen, shallow-toothed leaves and $\frac{1}{2}$in (12mm) long, nodding, bell-shaped, sky-blue flowers during mid- to late summer. A white form is also available.

Height: 4-6in (10-15cm)
Spread: 12-15in (30-38cm)
Hardiness: Zones 6-10
Cultivation: Well-drained soil and full sun suit it. Set the plants in position in autumn or spring.
Propagation: It is easily increased by lifting and dividing large clumps in autumn or spring. Alternatively, take soft cuttings 2in (5cm) long in spring, insert them in pots of equal parts peat and sharp sand and place these in a cold frame. When the cuttings are rooted, pot them up into small pots until they are large enough to be planted in the garden. When given well-drained soil, it soon spreads to form large mats of flowers and foliage.

Campanula cochleariifolia is ideal for trailing and cascading over rocks. It also delights in growing between the cracks in stone pavers, and is superb for planting at the sides of paths in large rock gardens.

129

Above: **Chionodoxa luciliae gigantea** *The dominant color of these delicate flowers will brighten any garden in late winter. It is not a fussy plant, and grows well in any well-drained soil in full sun. All chionodoxas are superb for bringing color during late winter.*

Chionodoxa luciliae

Glory of the Snow

This bright hardy bulb from Asia Minor produces brilliant sky-blue, 1in (2.5cm) wide flowers during late winter and early spring. Each flower has a white center. The form *Chionodoxa luciliae gigantea,* often called *C. gigantea,* is larger, and has pale violet-blue 1½in (4cm) wide flowers with small white centers. Chionodoxas are ideal for rock gardens, woodland gardens and for placing at the front of borders.
Height: 7-8in (18-20cm)
Spread: 3-4in (7.5-10cm)
Hardiness: Zones 4-9
Cultivation: Ordinary well-drained garden soil and full sun assure success. Plant the bulbs 2½in (6.5cm) deep.
Propagation: Lift and divide large clumps as soon as the leaves have died down. Replant the bulbs immediately.

Colchicum autumnale

Autumn Crocus ·
Meadow Saffron

This hardy corm-bearing plant bears large mid to dark green leaves up to 10in (25cm) long in spring and early summer, which later die back. In autumn, it produces 6in (15cm) high, goblet-shaped, rosy-lilac flowers. It looks best when planted to grow through the foliage of a ground cover such as myrtle (*Vinca minor*), or plumbago (*Ceratostigma plumbaginoides*).
Height: 10-12in (25-30cm)
Spread: 8-10in (20-25cm)
Hardiness: Zones 4-9
Cultivation: It delights in well-drained soil in full sun or light shade. Plant the corms during autumn, 3in (7.5cm) deep in small groups or drifts.
Propagation: It can be raised from seed, but the production of flowering-sized corms takes up to seven years.

Above: Colchicum speciosum
This unusual corm-bearing plant flowers in autumn after its foliage has died down. It thrives in sun or partial shade and is superb for bringing color to the fall garden.

It is easier to lift overgrown clumps when the leaves have died down and remove the offsets. Plant them out in a nursery bed for a couple of years until ready for their final positions, and replant the parent corms, too.

Colchicum speciosum

Autumn Crocus

Similar to *C. autumnale*, this corm-bearing plant displays 1ft (30cm) long, 4in (10cm) wide leaves in spring and early summer. In autumn, when the leaves have died back, its 6in (15cm) high stems bear flowers in a wide range of colors, from white to pinkish-lilac

---

Chionodoxa luciliae is superb for planting under the golden-yellow flowers of the Chinese witch hazel (*Hamamelis mollis*). It also blends perfectly with *Narcissus cyclamineus* 'February Gold'.

Colchicum autumnale, the autumn crocus or meadow saffron, has nothing to do with crocuses or with saffron which comes from *Crocus sativus*. However, its dried corms are a valuable ingredient of medicines.

Right: **Colchicum autumnale**
Autumn crocus produces leaves in spring that die back in the summer. Its crocus-like flowers provide welcome fall color.

and reddish-purple. It has been crossed with other species to create many superb hybrids.
Height: 12-15in (30-38cm)
Spread: 10-12in (25-30cm)
Hardiness: Zones 4-9
Cultivation: Well-drained soil in full sun or light shade suits it. During autumn, plant the corms 3-4in (7.5-10cm) deep in small clumps.
Propagation: It can be raised from seed, but will take up to seven years to bloom. It is easier to lift overgrown clumps when the leaves have died down and remove the offsets, planting them out in a nursery bed for a couple of years until ready for their final positions. Replant the large, parent corms, too.

Colchicum speciosum is useful for planting under shrubs and trees, where its spring and early summer leaves cannot swamp nearby plants. It is superb for planting under species roses.

Convolvulus mauritanicus

This handsome North African trailing and mat-forming perennial is not fully hardy, so it is ideal for warm, sunny rock gardens or even in hanging-baskets in very mild climates. The 1-1½in (2.5-4cm) long, almost round, midgreen leaves are surmounted by 1in (2.5cm) wide, purple-blue trumpet-shaped flowers with small white throats borne singly from mid- to late summer.

Height: 2-3in (5-7.5cm)
Spread: 1½-2ft (45-60cm)
Hardiness: Zones 8-10
Cultivation: Light, well-drained sandy soil in a warm area and a sheltered position suit it best. It is only really successful in warmer areas.
Propagation: During midsummer, take 2in (5cm) long cuttings, inserting them in pots of equal parts peat and sharp sand, placing these in a cold frame. When the cuttings are rooted, pot them up singly into small pots of potting soil and over-winter them in a frost-proof green-house. Wait until late spring before planting them out into the garden or in containers.

Below: Convolvulus mauritanicus
This delightful member of the bindweed family is not fully hardy but well worth growing for its beautiful blue flowers.

Above: Crocus tomasinianus
This is one of the earliest crocuses to flower, in late winter. It needs protection from cold winds but, once established, it will thrive in most gardens.

Crocus tomasinianus

An attractive late-winter flowering bulb, this crocus displays narrow dark green leaves with pronounced white midribs. The lilac-mauve flowers are borne during late winter and into early spring. They close-up in the shade, but open with the first sign of sun.

Convolvulus mauritanicus can be used in a rock garden to cover large, bare areas or to trail over rocks where it helps to fuse the various elements of the rock garden together.

Crocus tomasinianus mixes well with many other late-winter flowering bulbs, such as snowdrops *(Galanthus nivalis)* and the winter aconite *(Eranthis hyemalis)*.

Crocus vernus

Dutch Crocus

The species is the parent of the many varieties of Dutch crocus with large goblet-shaped flowers in a range of colors including lilac, purple and white, often with striking veining. Flowering is during early spring. There are many varieties to choose from and blue or purple ones include 'Pickwick' (silvery-white with lilac stripes and a deep purple base), 'Remembrance' (silvery-purple), 'Vanguard' (violet-blue) and 'Purpureus Grandiflorus' (purple-blue).

Height: 3-5in (7.5-13cm)
Spread: 1½-2in (4-5cm)
Hardiness: Zones 3-9
Cultivation: Well-drained soil and a sheltered and sunny position suit it. It can be grown in rock gardens or naturalized in a meadow.
Propagation: Lift and divide the corms when the foliage has died down after flowering. Remove the small cormlets and replant them.

Below: **Crocus vernus 'Striped Beauty'** *This Dutch crocus has delicate veining on its large goblet-shaped flowers. The bulbs increase naturally until large drifts are formed if given well-drained soil and a position where they get plenty of sun.*

Height: 3-4in (7.5-10cm)
Spread: 2-2½in (5-6.5cm)
Hardiness: Zones 3-9
Cultivation: Ordinary well-drained soil and a sunny, sheltered place free from cold winds are suitable. It is often recommended for naturalizing in short grass, but is best planted in the bare soil of a garden or under deciduous trees and shrubs. Plant 2½-3in (6.5-7.5cm) deep.
Propagation: It will seed and naturalize itself quite readily, especially in bare soil. Alternatively, remove cormlets from around the corms. When replanted, these take two or three years to produce good plants.

Crocus vernus is the large flowered spring crocus that is well-loved by many. The bulb is easy to grow and multiplies quickly.

Left: **Cyclamen hederifolium**
This is one of the hardiest and most free-flowering of all cyclamens. The flowers appear from late summer to early winter, growing best under trees where the plant gains shelter and shade.

Edraianthus pumilio

Grassy Bells

This unusual hardy herbaceous perennial from Yugoslavia is an excellent rock garden plant. It produces clumps of narrow gray-green leaves, and clusters of upturned lavender-blue funnel-shaped flowers during early summer. It is ideal for planting in troughs.
Height 2-3in (5-7.5cm)
Spread: 6-10in (15-25cm)

Hardiness: Zones 6-9
Cultivation: Well-drained deep soil and a sunny position suit it best.
Propagation: During late winter, sow seeds in small pots of sterile potting soil and place them in a cold frame. Prick out the seedlings into bigger pots when they are large enough to handle. Alternatively, in late summer, take 2in (5cm) long cuttings and insert them in pots of equal parts peat and sharp sand, placing them in a cold frame. When they are rooted, pot up the cuttings. Plant them in the garden in spring.

Below: **Edraianthus pumilio**
This is an excellent choice for a well-drained scree bed in a rock garden, or for a trough. The lavender-blue, funnel-shaped flowers appear in early summer.

Cyclamen hederifolium

(*Cyclamen neapolitanum*)
Hardy Cyclamen

A hardy corm-bearing plant, this cyclamen has deep green leaves, red beneath and with silvery markings above. The variable, mauve to pink, 1in (2.5cm) long flowers appear from late summer to early winter. The foliage persists through the winter before going dormant in the spring. There is also a white form.
Height: 4in (10cm)
Spread: 4-6in (10-15cm)
Hardiness: Zones 5-9
Cultivation: Humus-rich, well-drained soil in light, dappled shade suits it best. Plant the corms in late summer, where they can be left undisturbed for many years. It is a long-lived plant and even old corms produce flowers. Do not overwater in summer, when the dormant corms are resting.
Propagation: The corms may be propagated from offsets or seed. Sow seeds in late summer in pots of sterile potting soil. Place the pots in a cold frame. When the seedlings are large enough to handle, prick them off into pots of potting soil. When they are strong, plant them into their final positions.

Cyclamen hederifolium is ideal for naturalizing in bare soil beneath trees, planting on banks, or in a rock garden. If left undisturbed, the plants eventually create large drifts of color.

Edraianthus pumilio is ideal for a scree bed, where its foliage blends with small stone chips. Even when grown in a stone sink, it can be given a similar background.

Endymion hispanicus

(*Hyacinthoides hispanica · Scilla campanulata · Scilla hispanica*) Spanish Bluebell

A dramatic plant, this bluebell has broad strap-like leaves and blue, pink or white bell-shaped flowers, suspended from upright stems, which appear from spring to mid-summer. Several varieties are available, including 'Excelsior' (deep blue) and 'Myosotis' (clear blue).
Height: 1ft (30cm)
Spread: 6-8in (15-30cm)
Hardiness: Zones 4-9
Cultivation: Fertile, moist but not boggy soil and an open or slightly shaded position are best. It is most suited to a moist wild garden.
Propagation: Self-sown seedlings appear if the seeds are allowed to fall on surrounding soil. Alternatively, lift and divide clumps annually, replanting them immediately as the bulbs do not have outer skins and soon become dry and damaged. The bulbs do not store well, shrivelling if kept too dry.

Right: Erythronium dens-canis *This is a beautiful corm-bearing plant for a moist naturalized garden or the side of an informal pool. It needs shade and a north-facing slope, which help to prevent the soil drying out during summer.*

Below: Endymion hispanicus *This striking bluebell forms large clumps in moist soil under light shade. When set in light woodland in a wild garden, it creates a carpet of color from spring to midsummer.*

Erythronium dens-canis

Dog's-tooth Violet

This hardy corm-bearing plant for woodland gardens has broad lance-shaped leaves blotched with brown or gray. During spring, it displays pink-purple nodding six-petalled 2-3in (5-7.5cm) wide flowers with reflexed petals, resembling those of the Turk's cap lily, *Lilium martagon*. Several varieties are available, including 'Lilac Wonder' (pale purple). Be sure you buy only bulbs that have been nursery grown rather than wild collected to avoid endangering native populations.
Height: 6in (15cm)
Spread: 4-6in (10-15cm)
Hardiness: Zones 4-9
Cultivation: Moisture-retentive but not totally saturated soil is needed. Semi-shade and a north-facing slope are desirable.
Propagation: The quickest way to increase this plant is by removing offsets in late summer, when the leaves have died down. Place them in a nursery bed for three or four years to develop into plants large enough to be set in the garden. Growing from seed takes five or more years to produce sizeable plants. During this period, keep the nursery bed free from weeds and well watered.

Endymion hispanicus can be planted with a wide range of plants, such as primulas, or underneath *Magnolia x soulangiana* (saucer magnolia) with its white chalice-shaped flowers in spring.

Erythroniums are a delight in a moist, naturalized area. Other species useful for creating color contrast are the fawn lily (*E. revolutum*), with pink flowers, and trout lily *(E. americanum),* with bright yellow flowers.

Gentiana acaulis

Stemless Gentian

This is a beautiful hardy perennial for a rock garden, creating early summer color. The brilliant blue, 2-3in (5.5cm) long, trumpet-shaped flowers are near stemless and borne amid mats of glossy, midgreen leaves.

Height: 3in (7.5cm)
Spread: 15-18in (38-45cm)
Hardiness: Zones 3-8
Cultivation: Rich, moisture retentive but well-drained loam and a sunny position with light shade. They are easy to grow, but sometimes cantankerous to flower. Rich soil will help. Do not allow to dry out.
Propagation: It is easily increased by division of the plants in late spring or early summer. Alternatively, take 2in (5cm) long cuttings from basal shoots in mid- to late spring. Insert them in pots of equal parts peat and sharp sand and place these in a cold frame. Pot up the cuttings, when rooted, into small pots of potting soil and replace in the cold frame. Plant out into the garden during spring of the following year.

Right: **Gentiana acaulis**
A beautiful but often variable plant for a rock garden, this gentian displays its brilliant blue trumpets in early summer. It often spreads to form a large clump only a few inches high.

Gentiana septemfida

Crested Gentian

This hardy, reliable and undemanding gentian from Iran and Asia Minor has lance-shaped, midgreen leaves and a profusion of terminal, deep blue flowers from mid- to late summer. Each flower is about 1½in (4cm) long and resembles an upturned trumpet.

Height: 8-12in (20-30cm)
Spread: 10-12in (25-30cm)
Hardiness: Zones 3-9
Cultivation: Any good, rich, moisture-retentive garden soil suits it. Grow in full sun or light shade.

Propagation: Good forms are best raised from 2in (5cm) long cuttings taken in spring and inserted in pots of equal parts peat and sharp sand, placed in a cold frame. When the cuttings are rooted, pot them up into small pots and replace in the cold frame until spring of the following year. It can also be increased by sowing seeds in autumn and placing them in a cold frame.

Right: **Gentiana septemfida**
This is one of the easiest gentians to grow, with an abundance of deep blue upturned trumpet-like flowers from mid- to late summer.

Gentians are interesting plants for the woodland and rock garden. Not commonly available, seek them out from speciality nurseries.

Gentiana septemfida is superb on its own in a rock-garden pocket, but also combines well with alpine species of gypsophila, such as *Gypsophila repens,* with white or pink flowers.

Gentiana sino-ornata

This is an outstanding autumn-flowering gentian with 2in (5cm) long, brilliant blue, trumpet-shaped flowers. These are striped with a deeper blue, as well as greenish-yellow. The leaves are narrow, midgreen and rather grass-like, producing a pleasant background for the flowers. This gentian was discovered by the plant hunter George Forrest (1873-1932) in 1910-11 in South-west China. On the same expedition Forrest collected seeds of the shrub *Pieris formosa forrestii,* which was named in his honor.
Height: 6in (15cm)
Spread: 12-18in (30-34cm)
Hardiness: Zones 3-9
Cultivation: Fertile, deep, moist acid soil and a shaded position suit it best. Take care that the soil does not dry out during hot summers. Set the plants out in the garden during spring when the soil is warm.
Propagation: The easiest way to increase this plant is by lifting and dividing large clumps in spring.

Ipheion uniflorum

(*Brodiaea uniflora · Milla uniflora*)
Spring Starflower

This beautiful and reliable bulbous plant forms a hummock of grass-like leaves and 2in (5cm) wide, six-petalled, star-shaped, scented flowers during spring. They range from white to deep lavender-blue in color. There are several good varieties, including 'Caeruleum' (pale-blue), 'Wisley Blue' (violet-blue) and 'Violaceum' (violet).
Height: 6-8in (15-20cm)
Spread: 3-4in (7.5-10cm), but plants grow together to form a large clump.
Hardiness: Zones 5-10
Cultivation: Ordinary well-drained garden soil in full sun suits it and a sheltered position. Plant the bulbs 2in (5cm) deep in autumn.
Propagation: During autumn, lift and divide large clumps, replanting the bulbs immediately so that they do not dry out. You can also do this immediately after flowering.

Right: **Gentiana sino-ornata**
This beautiful Chinese and Tibetan gentian is a true delight in autumn, and when seen in a large drift is highly memorable. It needs a soil rich in leaf mold and a shady site. The midgreen leaves provide a perfect foil for the brilliant blue, trumpet-shaped flowers.

Below: **Ipheion uniflorum**
'Violaceum' *This beautiful variety of the spring starflower bears lovely six-petalled flowers during spring. It is native to Peru and Argentina. It is ideal for creating low hummocks of color alongside paths, and looks especially attractive at the sides of flagstone and gravel paths.*

Gentiana sino-ornata is often difficult to combine with other plants and is therefore best seen on its own, planted as a large, bold splash of color against a wall or foliage plants.

Ipheion uniflorum makes a welcome early splash of color in rock gardens or as an edging to paths. In borders it can be combined with deciduous azaleas and *Rhododendron.*

Iris cristata

Crested Dwarf Iris

Native to the Southeast, this iris is suited for a rock or woodland garden. During late spring, it bears 2-2½in (5-6.5cm) wide, lilac-purple flowers, whose white crests are tipped with orange.
Height: 6in (15cm)
Spread: 6-8in (15-20cm)
Hardiness: Zones 3-9
Cultivation: Slightly moist, fertile soil enriched with leaf mold, either slightly acid or neutral. A sheltered position in light shade is desirable.
Propagation: After flowering, lift and divide the plants, replanting the rhizomes immediately.

Below: **Iris cristata** *This dwarf crested iris needs slightly acid or neutral soil in light shade. It also comes in a white flowering variety, 'Alba'.*

Iris gracilipes

This unusual crested iris belongs to the group of irises which have orchid-like flowers with cock's-comb crests instead of beards. This species is hardy, with slender, dark green leaves, and 1-2in (2.5-5cm) wide, lavender-pink flowers.
Height: 8-10in (20-25cm)
Spread: 8-10in (20-25cm)
Hardiness: Zones 4-9
Cultivation: Fertile, moisture-retentive acid soil, in a sheltered

and slightly shaded position. To ensure that the soil is rich in humus, top-dress it with compost in spring. Plant the rhizomes in late spring, just below the surface.
Propagation: It is easily increased by lifting and dividing the rhizomes in late spring. Other crested irises are best lifted, divided and replanted immediately after the flowers have faded, but this beautiful species is the exception to the rule.

Below: **Iris gracilipes**
This small crested iris displays pretty flowers in spring. It is ideal for planting in moist, acid soil, in a sheltered, slightly shaded position.

Iris ensata

(Iris kaempferi)
Japanese Iris

This beardless iris belongs to a group that delights in moist soil. It displays deeply ribbed, deciduous, deep green leaves, and 4-8in (10-20cm) wide flowers in early summer. Many varieties have been developed, with colors including blue, reddish-purple, pink and white. Some are completely one color, while others have a mixture.
Height: 2-3ft (60-90cm)
Spread: 1½-2ft (45-60cm)
Hardiness: Zones 4-9
Cultivation: Moist soil at the edge of an informal pool is best, but the roots

---

Iris cristata, crested dwarf iris is an attractive groundcover plant on rich, woodland slopes. Though blooming for only several weeks the spiky, light green foliage provides interest.

Iris ensata forms a bold display at the side of a pool, ideal as a backdrop for the pool itself and for bringing height to the pool surroundings. The large, bright flowers are best grown on their own.

should not be set in the water. Rich soil and an annual mulch of well-rotted compost are aids to success. Plant the rhizomes just below the surface during the spring or autumn.

Propagation: It is easily increased by lifting and dividing the rhizomes immediately after flowering is over. At this time the plants can be easily lifted, even from very boggy soil. They must be replanted immediately.

Below: **Iris kaempferi** *This handsome beardless iris for moist soil at the edges of a pond has been bred in Japan to produce a wide range of flower forms and colors.*

Above: **Iris reticulata** *This is a reliable bulbous iris for a rock garden or front of a border, flowering in late winter and early spring.*

Iris reticulata

This well-known, small, bulbous iris is ideal for a rock garden or the front of a border. It is now available in a range of colors, but the true species is blue and violet, with or without orange blazes on the falls (the lower, drooping petals). Flowers appear during late winter and early summer. Good forms include 'Cantab' (light blue), 'Clairette' (sky-blue) and 'Harmony' (royal blue).

Height: 4-6in (10-15cm)
Spread: 4-6in (10-15cm)
Hardiness: Zones 5-9
Cultivation: Light, well-drained soil in full sun or light shade suits it. Plant fresh bulbs in autumn, covering them with a 2-3in (5-7.5cm) layer of soil. This attractive bulb can also be forced indoors, but they are better grown in a cold greenhouse or conservatory.

Propagation: It is easily increased by lifting and dividing large clumps in late summer or early autumn. Large bulbs can be replanted, while smaller ones should be planted in a nursery bed and grown on for a few years until large enough to set out in their final, flowering positions.

Iris reticulata blends with many early spring-flowering plants, such as the snowdrop (*Galanthus nivalis*), the yellow-flowered shrub *Hamamelis mollis* and the Corsican hellebore (*Helleborus lividus corsicus*).

Above: Lithodora diffusa 'Grace Ward' *This is a beautiful prostrate plant for a rock garden, cascading over rocks to form a large mat of color. This variety produces intense blue flowers from midsummer to early autumn.*

Lithodora diffusa

(*Lithospermum diffusum*)

This superb hardy, spreading, mat-forming perennial for a rock garden, is often better known by its previous botanical name, even though this has been superseded. The creeping stems are covered with small, oval dark green leaves, and the five-lobed, ½in (12mm) wide, deep-blue flowers appear from midsummer to early autumn. Two varieties are widely available: 'Heavenly Blue' (deep blue) and 'Grace Ward' (a beautiful intense blue).
Height: 3-4in (7.5-10cm)
Spread: 1½-2ft (45-60cm)
Hardiness: Zones 6-8
Cultivation: Light, well-drained, acid soil rich in leaf mold, and a position in full sun will ensure success.
Propagation: It is not easy to increase, the exact time for taking the cuttings being critical. Take 1½-2½in (4-6.5cm) long heel cuttings after the first week in mid-summer. Insert them in flats of equal parts peat and sharp sand and place in a cold frame. Ensure that the flats do not dry out.

Right: Muscari armeniacum *This stunningly attractive blue bulbous plant for spring color, ideal for naturalizing under deciduous shrubs or as a path edging, is a native of Turkey and the Caucasus.*

Below: Pontederia cordata *This eye-catching North American water plant brings height and color late in summer. Eventually it forms a large clump, with purple-blue flowers.*

Lithodora diffusa can be used with other prostrate plants, such as *Helianthemum nummularium* and the blue-purple *Campanula portenschlagiana*.

Muscari armeniacum

Grape Hyacinth

In spring, this well-known hardy bulb has the heads of its stems tightly clustered with bell-like, azure-blue to deep purple-blue flowers, which have whitish rims to their mouths. The narrow dark green leaves tend to spread and separate as the flowers appear. Several forms are available, such as 'Cantab' (pale sky blue), 'Heavenly Blue' (bright blue) and 'Blue Spike' (double and mid-blue). It is ideal for naturalizing in large drifts. When planted in a rock garden, it needs careful watching as it can soon spread and dominate choice plants.

Height: 7-9in (18-23cm)
Spread: 4-5in (10-13cm)
Hardiness: Zones 4-8
Cultivation: Any well-drained garden soil in full sun suits it. During late summer or early autumn, plant new bulbs 3in (7.5cm) deep.
Propagation: It often spreads quite easily by self-sown seedlings. Alternatively, large clumps can be lifted and divided when the leaves are yellowing. Replant them immediately.

Pontederia cordata

Pickerel Weed

This is a hardy and vigorous herbaceous perennial for the edge of a garden pool, in water up to 9in (23cm) deep. The glossy, deep green heart-shaped leaves are borne on stiff, long, upright stems, with 2-4in (5-10cm) long heads of purple-blue flowers during late summer and into early autumn.

Height: 1¹/₂-2¹/₂ft (45-75cm)
Spread: 1-1¹/₂ft (30-45cm)
Hardiness: Zones 3-9
Cultivation: Rich, fibrous loam and a sunny position are needed, with the rhizomes covered by several inches of water. Planting in late spring or early summer.
Propagation: It is best increased by lifting and dividing the rhizomes in late spring. Take care that they do not dry out. Also, make sure that the roots are submerged deeply until the plants are established.

Muscari armeniacum is a superb early spring bulb, blooming for more than a month. After blooming the foliage dies down only to reappear in the late fall.

Pontederia cordata is ideal for the side of a formal pool, where its foliage spills out over the edges, softening and blending the structured elements with the pool and creating a bright splash of color.

Primula vialii

A short lived primrose, this species has a rosette of large pale green narrow lance-shaped leaves and 3-5in (7.5-1.3cm) long, poker-like, dense spikes of slightly scented lavender-blue flowers during mid-summer.

Height: 8-12in (20-30cm)
Spread: 9-12in (23-30cm)
Hardiness: Zones 5-9
Cultivation: Moisture-retentive fertile soil and light shade suit it. The soil must not dry out during summer, but at the same time should never be waterlogged.
Propagation: Established plants can be divided and replanted directly after the flowers have faded. However it is often better to sow seeds and place them in a cold frame. Shade the flats and subsequent seedlings from strong sunlight. When they are large enough to handle, prick off the seedlings into flats and replace them in the cold frame. Plant them out into the garden in spring.

Right: Primula vialii This beautiful Chinese primrose bears poker-like spikes of slightly-scented lavender-blue flowers in midsummer. When planted in a large drift, perhaps at the side of an informal garden pool, it is a stunning sight in flower.

Primula denticulata

Drumstick Primrose

This hardy primrose produces a dramatic garden display. The pale-green lance-shaped leaves form a compact rosette at its base while during spring and into early summer the stems bear 2-3in (5-7.5cm) wide globular flower heads in colors ranging from deep purple to deep lilac and carmine. A white variety 'Alba' is available.

Height: 9-12in (23-30cm)
Spread: 8-10in (20-25cm)
Hardiness: Zones 4-8
Cultivation: Moisture-retentive loam, enriched with leaf mold, and

Above: Primula denticulata This is the well-known drumstick primose, with globular heads of flowers during spring and into early summer. It is an excellent and reliable plant for beginners to gardening and seldom fails to attract attention.

a lightly shaded site are ideal.
Propagation: Sow seeds in mid-summer in pots of sterile potting soil and place them in a cold frame. When they are large enough to handle, prick out the seedlings into flats of potting soil and plant them out into the garden in autumn.

Puschkinia scilloides

(*Puschkinia libanotica*)
Striped Squill

This attractive small hardy bulb suits many sites in the garden, from naturalizing at the woodland edge to planting in rock gardens or alongside narrow borders at the base of walls. The midgreen, strap-like leaves are surmounted by arching stems, bearing up to six, silvery-blue, bell-shaped, 1/2in (12mm) long flowers in spring.

Height: 5-8in (13-20cm)
Spread: 3-4in (7.5-10cm)
Hardiness: Zones 4-9
Cultivation: Any light garden soil and a position in sun or partial shade

Primula denticulata is an amenable plant that mingles happily with many other spring-flowering types, such as *Anemone blanda*, the grape hyacinth (*Muscari armeniacum*), daffodils and primroses.

Primula vialii needs careful positioning in a garden, as its distinctive flowers are best not forced to compete with other low-growing plants. It is best given a bed or corner to itself.

Above: Ramonda myconi *A distinctive alpine plant that prefers not to have moisture covering its leaves, Ramonda is therefore often happier planted at a slight angle on a slope or between rocks. It will not tolerate freezing temperatures.*

Ramonda myconi

(*Ramonda pyrenaica*)

An unusual, dainty-flowered, rosette-forming rock-garden plant with evergreen, deep green, crinkled leaves. The 1-1½in (2.5-4cm) wide, lavender-blue flowers are borne in late spring, several to a stem.
Height: 4-6in (10-15cm)
Spread: 8-10in (20-25cm)
Hardiness: Zones 9-10
Cultivation: Well-drained leaf mold enriched garden soil and a cool position on the north side of a slope suit it best. It will not tolerate frost conditions or extreme heat and humidity. Do not allow the soil to dry out.
Propagation: During autumn or early spring, sow seeds in a tray of sterile potting soil and place it in a cold frame. When they are large enough to handle, prick out the seedlings into small pots and replace them in the frame. Plant them out into the garden when they are well established. Alternatively, take leaf-cuttings in mid-summer. They take about six weeks to produce roots. Pot up immediately.

assure success. Plant the bulbs in autumn, 2in (5cm) deep, and leave them where they are for many years.
Propagation: After flowering and when the foliage has died down, lift and divide overgrown clumps. Remove and dry the bulbs, replanting them in autumn.

Right: Puschkinia scilloides *This attractive bulbous plant produces silvery-blue flowers in spring on arching stems. It tolerates sun or partial shade, and, once planted, can be left undisturbed for many years.*

Puschkinia scilloides displays such soft-colored flowers that they can be blended with many other rock garden plants. The vivid mauve flowers of *Viola labradorica* are highlighted by puschkinia's flowers.

Ramonda myconi, with its wrinkled rusty-colored leaves and blue flowers, is so distinctive that it is best given plenty of space to reveal itself. A background of gray rock helps to show it off even better.

Above: Rhododendron 'Blue Tit'
This dwarf dome-shaped evergreen shrub has funnel-shaped lavender-blue flowers that darken with age. It is ideal for a rock garden, creating height and dramatic color in late spring and early summer.

Rhododendron 'Blue Tit'

A hardy and unusual small-leaved evergreen dwarf rhododendron for a rock garden. It forms a dense, rounded shrub with small funnel-shaped lavender-blue flowers at the tips of the branches during late spring and into early summer. As the flowers age, they become dark blue.
Height: 3ft (90cm)
Spread: 3-4ft (90cm-1.2m)
Hardiness: Zones 5-7
Cultivation: Moisture-retentive acid soil in light shade under trees is best. To keep the soil moist, mulch the surface with well-decomposed compost in spring.
Propagation: After flowering, take cuttings of young shoots with heels and insert them in pots of compost. Place them in a cold frame and grow on until ready for planting out in the garden.

Scilla sibirica

Siberian Squill

This popular, hardy, spring-flowering bulbous plant has wide, dark green, strap-shaped leaves, which appear in spring. These are followed by

Above: Scilla sibirica 'Spring Beauty' *These vivid-blue flowers appear in spring, delighting in moist but well-drained soil in a wild garden or boggy area around a pond.*

several stems, each bearing two to five brilliant blue, nodding, bell-shaped flowers. 'Spring Beauty' (often known as 'Atrocaerulea'), with deep blue flowers, is most frequently seen. There is also a white form 'Alba'.
Height: 5-6in (13-15cm)
Spread: 3-4in (7 5-10cm)
Hardiness: Zones 4-8
Cultivation: Well-drained but moist soil in full sun or slight shade suits it. Set the bulbs 2-3in (5-7.5cm) deep in late summer.
Propagation: Established clumps can be lifted and divided in autumn; otherwise they are best left alone.

Right: Rhododendron 'Blue Star' *This dominantly colored dwarf rhododendron creates a bold display. Several other varieties are noted for their flowers, too, including 'Blue Diamond', with clusters of rich lavender-purple flowers in spring. It is slow-growing and only 3-2ft [1m] high.*

Right: Scilla tubergeniana *Although its coloring is not so striking as Scilla sibirica it does form a soil-covering mass of color and is ideal for planting in rock gardens or under deciduous shrubs, where it brings early color.*

Other **blue-flowered rhododendrons** can be used in small gardens, such as 'Blue Diamond' (lavender-blue) suitable for the Northwest and 'Blue Peter' (rich blue), New England coast and Southeast.

Scilla sibirica is a delicately-flowered bulb that naturalizes well in a woodland setting. It can also be used in combination with early daffodils.

Above: **Sisyrinchium bermudianum** *This is a beautiful tender blue-eyed grass (Zones 8-10) for a rock garden, where it readily increases itself by self-sown seedlings which grow in the gaps between paving stones.*

Scilla tubergeniana

Tubergen Squill

This attractive hardy bulbous plant from North-west Iran displays its pale blue or white flowers in early spring. At first, the flowers are bell-like, but later they flatten amid wide strap-like glossy bright green leaves. The flower has a deep blue stripe running down each petal. The species blooms even earlier than *S. sibirica.*
Height: 3-4in (7.5-10cm)
Spread: 3-4in (7.5-10cm)
Hardiness: Zones 4-8
Cultivation: Moist but well-drained soil in full sun or light shade suits it best. Plant the bulbs 3in (7.5cm) deep in late summer.
Propagation: Overgrown clumps can be lifted and divided in autumn. Alternatively, it can be raised from seed, but this takes up to five years to produce flowering-sized plants.

Sisyrinchium augustifolium

Blue-eyed Grass

A hardy member of the iris family, with stiff and erect narrow light green leaves and branched stems. At their tips, the stems bear ¹⁄₂in (12mm) wide, star-shaped, light blue flowers in the spring. It will naturalize well in meadows or the edge of moist woods.
Height: 1-¹⁄₂ft (30-45cm)
Spread: 9-12in (23-30cm)
Hardiness: Zones 2-9
Cultivation: Well-drained, humus enriched, moist garden soil and a sunny position ensure success. In autumn, cut off dead leaves and flowered stems.
Propagation: It tends to readily increase itself by seed. Bring them on in a cold frame and set them out in the garden when they are growing strongly. It also propagates easily by division. Early spring is the best time to divide. Include 3 or 4 small crowns in each division.

Scilla tubergiana has subtly colored flowers, and can be mixed with other small bulbs, like the winter aconite (*Eranthis hyemalis*) and snowdrop (*Galanthus nivalis*), without being dominated by or overwhelming them.

Sisyrinchium striatum is another delightful species, with ³⁄₄in (18mm) wide, star-shaped, yellow flowers, borne from early summer onwards on 12in (30cm) plants. Hardy from Zones 4-8.

Tecophilaea cyanocrocus

Chilean Crocus

This unusual, crocus-like, South American bulbous plant is not fully hardy in temperate regions, but is well worth growing for its gorgeous 1½in (4cm) long flowers, with deep blue to purple petals and white throats, which appear in spring.
Height: 4-5in (10-13cm)
Spread: 5-6in (13-15cm)
Hardiness: Zones 9-10
Cultivation: In its native Chile, it grows on stony, well-drained slopes. In the garden, therefore, it needs well-drained sandy soil, and a warm and sunny position. It grows outdoors only in mild areas, free from severe frost. In wet climates it needs protection with cloches during winter.
Propagation: It is not easily increased and usually the plants produce few cormlets. When grown in a cool greenhouse, the plants can be removed from the pots in autumn and the cormlets potted up.

Above: Tecophilaea cyanocrocus
A low-growing rock garden plant that thrives in a well-drained sheltered and warm position. Excessive moisture in winter will harm it. The richly-colored, crocus like flowers appear in spring.

Below: Veronica teucrium 'Trehane'
This beautiful rock garden plant has golden-yellow leaves, and bears spires of pale blue flowers during most of summer. Its foliage blends well with rocks, harmonizing with the color of the stone.

Veronica teucrium

Hungarian Speedwell

This hardy alpine veronica forms a clump of upright stems bearing mid- to dark green, toothed lance-shaped leaves, with 2-3in (5-7.5cm) long spikes of sky blue flowers during most of summer. Several varieties are available, which are lower growing than the original species: these include 'Trehane' (golden-yellow leaves and pale blue flowers) and 'Shirley Blue' (deep blue flowers).
Height: 9-15in (23-38cm)
Spread: 1½-2ft (45-60cm)
Hardiness: Zones 3-8
Cultivation: Ordinary well-drained garden soil and a sunny position are essential for continued success.
Propagation: During spring, lift and divide large clumps. Alternatively, take cuttings from mid- to late summer and insert them in pots of equal parts peat and sharp sand. When rooted, pot up the cuttings and overwinter them in a cold frame.

Tecophilaea cyanocrocus is a warmth-loving bulb that does well in situations similar to those needed by the tender South African nerines and the beautiful Algerian iris *(Iris unguicularis)*, also known as *Iris stylosa*.

Veronica teucrium is ideal for planting at the front of borders as well as rock gardens, especially mixed with yellow and white flowers. In a rock garden it blends well with the lemon-yellow *Hypericum olympicum* 'Citrinum'.

Above: **Viola cornuta** *This beautiful hardy viola is ideal for well-drained but moist and fertile soils in sun or slight shade. It is perfect for bringing color to path edges or in rock gardens. There is also a white-flowered variety.*

Viola cornuta

Horned Violet

A reliable and robust violet from the Pyrenees, the horned violet bears lavender or violet-colored flowers that provide early or midsummer color. The 1in (2.5cm) wide, spurred flowers are borne above the mid-green, oval leaves, which have rounded teeth. Several cultivars are available, including 'Blue Perfection' (sky-blue), 'Jersey Gem' (blue-purple) and 'Alba' (white).
Height: 4-12in (10-30cm)
Spread: 12-15in (30-38cm)
Hardiness: Zones 6-9
Cultivation: Fertile, well-drained but moist soil in full sun or slight shade suits it best. Pick off dead flowers to encourage further blooms.
Propagation: During spring or summer, sow seeds ¼in (6mm) deep in a prepared seedbed outdoors. When they are large enough to handle, thin the seedlings to 10-12in (25-30cm) apart. In autumn, transfer them to their flowering positions.

Further plants to consider

Brunnera macrophylla
Height: 1-1½ft (30-45cm)   Spread: 15-20in (38-50cm)
Hardiness: Zones 3-7
A hardy, herbaceous perennial for a moist, shaded site. Dark green, heart-shaped leaves with azure blue spring bloom.

Meconopsis betonicifolia
Himalayan Blue Poppy
Height: 3-5ft (90cm-1.5m)   Spread: 1½ft (45cm)
Hardiness: Zones 7-9
A short-lived herbaceous perennial for a moist, shaded area, producing 2½-3in (6.5-7.5cm) wide, sky blue flowers during mid-summer.

Mertensia virginica
Virginia Bluebell · Virginia Cowslip
Height: 1-2ft (30-60cm)   Spread: 1½ft (45cm)
Hardiness: Zones 3-9
A hardy herbaceous perennial with light green, lance-shaped leaves and pendulous clusters of purple-blue flowers in early summer. The plants go dormant by midsummer.

Omphalodes verna
Blue-eyed Mary
Height: 5-6in (13-15cm)   Spread: 12-15in (30-38cm)
Hardiness: Zones 6-9
A spreading herbaceous perennial for a rock garden or woodland. From early spring to early summer, it bears white-throated, bright blue flowers, ½in (12mm) wide.

Pulmonaria saccharata 'Mrs. Moon'
Lungwort
Height: 9-18in (23-45cm)   Spread: 20-24in (50-60cm)
Hardiness: Zones 3-8
A hardy, herbaceous perennial for a moist shaded site. The broad, oval leaves are white spotted – brightening a dull corner. The early spring blooms are pink in bud turning blue.

Pulsatilla vulgaris
(*Anemone pulsatilla*)
Pasque Flower
Height: 10-12in (25-30cm)   Spread: 12-15in (30-38cm)
Hardiness: Zones 5-8
A beautiful and highly memorable hardy herbaceous perennial with midgreen, fern-like leaves and 2-3in (5-7 5cm) wide, cup-shaped, purple flowers with bright centers during spring and early summer.

Viola labradorica
Labrador Violet
Height: 1-4in (2.5-10cm)   Spread: 8-10in (20-25cm)
Hardiness: Zones 3-8
A woodland violet native to Northeastern U.S. Dark violet ¾in (18mm) bloom with dark green to purple leaves.

Viola cornuta is robust enough to be set at the front of a border with a backing of white flowers. Alternatively, position it in a rock garden, where it can trail over the rocks and merge with other plants.

ROCK AND NATURALIZED GARDENS

Right: **Achillea tomentosa**
This delightful herbaceous perennial has mats of fern-like leaves and tightly-packed flower heads during mid- to late summer. It needs well-drained soil and a sunny position.

Achillea tomentosa

Woolly Yarrow

This is a bright, dwarf herbaceous perennial for the rock garden, crevices between natural stone paths and in dry stone walls. It displays long, softly hairy and fern-like gray-green leaves which form prostrate mats. Densely-packed heads of bright yellow flowers, 3in (7.5cm) wide, appear on 6in (15cm) long stems during mid- to late summer.
Height: 6-7in (15-18cm)
Spread: 10-12in (25-30cm)
Hardiness: Zones 3-7
Cultivation: Achilleas need a well-drained soil and a sunny position. Avoid damp conditions, which encourage slugs.
Propagation: The easiest way to increase this plant is by division of the roots in autumn or spring. Spring is the best time, as autumn-divided plants need to be overwintered in a cold frame. Alternatively, take soft cuttings in midsummer and place in sandy compost in pots in a cold frame.

Aurinia saxatilis

Basket-of-Gold

This well-known shrubby evergreen perennial has a tumbling and cascading growth habit, making it ideal for covering dry stone walls. Its gray-green leaves are lance-shaped, with 4-6in (10-15cm) wide heads of golden-yellow flowers in early summer. Several superb cultivars are widely available, including 'Tom Thumb', only 6-8in (15-20cm) tall, and 'Citrinum', with lemon-yellow flowers.
Height: 9-12in (23-30cm)
Spread: 1-1½ft (30-45cm)
Hardiness: Zones 3-7
Cultivation: Ordinary garden soil,

Achillea tomentosa is ideal for planting between flagstone or in crevices at the top of dry stone walls. In a rock garden, sprinkle stone chips around the plant for an attractive background and good drainage.

Aurinia saxatilis can be used in combination with many other plants, including the biennial forget-me-not, primroses, the bulbs *Chionodoxa luciliae* and grape hyacinth or the rock-garden aubrietia.

well-drained, and a position in full sun are needed. After flowering, cut the plants back to encourage the development of young growths.

Propagation: Named types do not come true from seed and are therefore best raised by taking 2-3in (5-7.5cm) long cuttings in summer. Insert them into equal parts peat and sharp sand. When the plants are rooted, pot them up into potting soil and place in a cold frame. Plant in the garden in spring. The young plants are best set out in their new positions in spring, though this can be done in late summer in mild areas.

Left: **Aurinia saxatilis 'Dudley Neville'** *This beautiful shrubby perennial has soft-yellow flowers which cascade down walls in early summer like a colored waterfall. Other forms are brighter.*

Cedrus deodara 'Golden Horizon'

Deodar Cedar

This semi-prostrate slow-growing evergreen conifer is often twice as wide as it is high. It has graceful, pendulous, golden-leaved branches, resembling a golden cascade as it matures.

Height: 2-2½ft (60-75cm)
Spread: 2½-4ft (75cm-1.2m)
Hardiness: Zones 7-9
Cultivation: Well-drained garden soil suits it – it will do well even in coastal areas.
Propagation: It is a grafted form, best propagated by nurseries.

Below: **Cedrus deodara 'Golden Horizon'** *This beautiful slow-growing evergreen conifer produces a cascading array of golden foliage. Its spread is frequently up to twice its height.*

Above: **Chamaecyparis lawsoniana 'Aurea Densa'** *This dense, slow-growing dwarf conifer is ideal for rock gardens, containers and troughs.*

Chamaecyparis lawsoniana 'Aurea Densa'

Lawson Falsecypress

A densely-foliaged slow-growing dwarf evergreen conifer, this tree is ideal for rock gardens and containers. It has a dome-shaped habit, with bright golden-yellow foliage. After ten years, it reaches about 12-20in (30-50cm) high and 10-15in (25-38cm) wide.
Height: 3-3½ft (90cm-1m)
Spread: 2½-3ft (75-90cm)
Hardiness: Zones 5-7
Cultivation: Well-drained garden soil is essential for success, and a position in full sun to help maintain the golden-yellow foliage.
Propagation: Take 4in (10cm) long heel cuttings in spring, inserting them into equal parts peat and sharp sand. Place them in a cold frame and, when rooted, pot up into small pots. In the autumn, plant them out into a sheltered bed for a few years.

Cedrus deodara 'Golden Horizon' is ideal in a heather garden, surrounded by prostrate color-contrasting conifers. Alternatively, place it between blue-foliaged upright conifers, such as *Picea pungens* 'Hoopsii' or *Picea pungens* 'Koster'.

Chamaecyparis lawsoniana 'Aurea Densa' is ideal for a small collection of dwarf and slow-growing conifers, and looks attractive when positioned among prostrate blue-foliaged junipers such as *Juniperus horizontalis* 'Blue Moon'.

and plunge these into soil in a nursery bed. During autumn, put the young plants into a nursery bed for three or four years before setting them out in their permanent positions. It is often confused with *C.l.* 'Aurea Densa', which has a compact habit and golden-yellow foliage arranged in short, densely-packed and flattened sprays. In *C.l.* 'Minima Aurea' the sprays of foliage are mainly arranged vertically. Both, however, are ideal and distinctive conifers for a rock garden.

Left: **Chamaecyparis lawsoniana 'Minima Aurea'** *A beautifully-foliaged dwarf conifer, it also has an attractive shape. The golden-yellow foliage remains bright throughout the year and grows in a distinctive vertical pattern.*

Below: **Chamaecyparis pisifera 'Filifera Aurea'** *A slow-growing conifer, this variety is prized for its thread-like golden foliage which droops at its tips and gives a weeping appearance. Eventually, it will develop into a pretty large tree.*

Chamaecyparis lawsoniana 'Minima Aurea'

Lawson Falsecypress

An attractive, slow-growing, evergreen conifer with a rounded form and vertically-arranged, scale-like, golden-yellow leaves, it reaches 20in (50cm) high and 16in (40cm) wide.
Height: 3½ft (1m)
Spread: 32in (80cm)
Hardiness: Zones 5-7
Cultivation: This conifer needs ordinary well-drained garden soil. It does best in full sun, which helps to maintain the golden foliage.
Propagation: During spring, take 4in (10cm) long heel cuttings, inserting them into equal parts peat and sharp sand and placing them in a cold frame. When rooted, pot them up into small pots

Chamaecyparis lawsoniana 'Minima Aurea' looks superb on its own in a rock garden, or in a heather garden where it can be set in threes in a sea of white-flowered ericas. Set them several feet apart so that their shapes are not impaired.

Chamaecyparis pisifera 'Filifera Aurea'

Japanese Falsecypress

This distinctive slow-growing evergreen conifer has thread-like golden foliage which trails at its tips, giving it a weeping appearance. It has a mop-head, somewhat conical shape. It is ideal for planting in a large rock garden. After ten years it will reach 3½ft (1m) high, with a spread of 4ft (1.2m). Several other cultivars of this species are a delight in the rock garden. These include the conical *C.p.* 'Plumosa Aurea Nana' with a height of 3ft (90cm) and a 2ft (60cm) spread. It retains its golden color throughout the year. Other golden forms include *C.p.* 'Squarrosa Sulphurea' with a rounded form and bright sulphur-yellow foliage, and *C.p.* 'Gold Spangle' with an open but rounded form and bright golden foliage. It is especially attractive in winter.
Height: 15ft (4.5m)
Spread: 15-18ft (4.5-5.4m)
Hardiness: Zones 3-8

Cultivation: Well-drained garden soil, and a position in full sun are needed.
Propagation: During spring, take 3-4in (7.5-10cm) long cuttings from side-shoots, insert them into pots of equal parts of peat and sharp sand and place these in a cold frame. Pot up the cuttings when rooted, and eventually set them in a nursery bed for three or four years, until they are large enough to be planted in the garden.

Above: Cytisus x beanii
This dwarf broom is ideal where it can tumble over rocks or dry stone walls and display its pea-shaped yellow flowers in late spring and early summer. It delights in a sunny position and well-drained but not very rich soil.

Cytisus x beanii

Broom

A beautiful hard to find hybrid broom, this is a semi-prostrate deciduous shrub. During late spring and early summer, its yellow pea-like flowers are produced in ones, twos or threes on the previous year's shoots. The leaves are narrow, hairy and mid-green.
Height: 1½-2ft (45-60cm)
Spread: 2½-3ft (75-90cm)
Hardiness: Zones 6-9
Cultivation: Well-drained garden soil in full sun is best. Do not plant this broom in rich soil. Always use container-grown plants, because it dislikes root disturbance. No regular pruning is needed.
Propagation: During late summer, take 2-3½in (5-9cm) long heel cuttings, inserting them into equal parts peat and sharp sand. Place the pots in a cold frame and, when the cuttings are rooted, pot them up. Plunge the pots into a sheltered part of the garden and plant them out either in late spring or early autumn.

Chamaecyparis pisifera 'Filifera Aurea' is suitable for a prime position in a rock garden. Its strong color, attractive foliage shape and eventual size make it an ideal focal point.

Cytisus x beanii is ideal for bringing color and height to a rock garden. When trailing over a drystone wall, it relieves the flatness of its top. Retaining walls alongside paths often present the best sites.

Eranthis hyemalis

Winter Aconite

This distinctively-flowered, tuberous-rooted plant blooms late in winter, often amid snow. The 1in (2.5cm) wide, buttercup-like, lemon-yellow flowers appear with a ruff of pale green leaves. They are borne on stiff, near upright stems which rise from pale green and deeply-cut leaves.
Height: 4in (10cm)
Spread: 3-4in (7.5-10cm)
Hardiness: Zones 4-8
Cultivatlon: Winter aconite needs a well-drained but moisture-retentive soil in full sun or partial shade. Set the tubers 1in (2.5cm) deep in late summer.
Propagation: Lift the tubers as soon as the plant dies down and cut them into sections. Replant 3in (7.5cm) apart. Alternatively, sow fresh seed in sterile potting soil. It also produces self-sown seedlings that can be replanted.

Erythronium americanum

Trout Lily

This beautiful corm-bearing plant has nodding, pale yellow, turk's-cap flowers during early spring. Each flower has six-pointed petals. The mottled, glossy, spatula-shaped leaves arise from soil level, and provide a superb background for the yellow flowers.
Height: 6-9in (15-23cm)
Spread: 6-9in (15-23cm)
Hardiness: Zones 3-8
Cultivation: Fertile, moisture-retentive soil with light shade is best. Plant the corms in late summer. It is essential that the soil does not dry out. To ensure this, add peat, leaf mold or compost before planting.
Propagation: It can be raised from seed, but this method often takes several years to produce flowering plants. The best way for home gardeners to increase this plant is by removing offsets in summer as the leaves die down.

Eranthis hyemalis is ideal for a corner in the rock garden or woodland garden. It blooms very early, often through the last of winter's snow in northern climates. Eranthis mixes well with snowdrops (*Galanthus hyemalis*).

Erythronium americanum is a wild garden plant, blending well with wake robin (*Trillium grandiflorum*), Virginia bluebells (*Mertensia virginica*) and woodland shrubs such as rhododendron and azaleas.

Left: **Eranthis hyemalis**
This ground-hugging tuberous plant has distinctive large, buttercup-like flowers with ruffs of pale green leaves. It grows best in organic soils which do not dry out in spring or summer.

Euryops acraeus

A beautiful miniature evergreen shrub from the Drakensberg Mountains in Lesotho, southern Africa, euryops is an upright plant, densely clothed in summer in bright silver leaves and pure gold daisy-like flowers on short gray stems. It is often wrongly called *Euryops evansii*. Although suitable for a mild climate rock garden, it won't tolerate high heat and humidity. It is an unusual plant that is difficult to find.

Height: 10-12in (25-30cm)
Spread: 1¹/₂-2ft (45-60cm)
Hardiness: Zones 8-10
Cultivation: Euryops likes ordinary well-drained garden soil and a position in full sun.
Propagation: Cuttings of non-flowering shoots can be taken in summer and inserted in sandy soil. However, it is easier and quicker to detach suckers from around the base of the plant. Pot them up in a well-drained sandy soil and place the pots in a cold frame until the plants are large enough to be set out in the garden.

Far-left: **Erythronium americanum** *This California native delights in moist soil and shade, producing yellow flowers in late spring. It likes to be left undisturbed, so a wild garden setting is best. It can be planted in an informal group with other erythroniums.*

Left: **Euryops acraeus**
This beautiful low-growing evergreen shrub for the mild climate rock garden has silvery foliage. The large, pure-gold, daisy-like flowers appear during summer, forming a handsome combination with the striking leaves.

Euryops acraeus grows well in hot places in mild climates: a scree-bed on a hot, dry slope suits it well, and its silvery foliage is highlighted by the stone chip. The foliage is also attractive when set with dark-green-leaved plants.

Genista tinctoria

Dyer's Greenweed · Woadwaxen

A low deciduous shrub with green twiggy branches. In the early to late summer, it has bright golden-yellow, pea-shaped flowers on glabrous green shoots. The gray-green leaves are very narrow. It is ideal for a large rock garden, or for groundcover in poor soils.

Height: 2-3ft (60-90cm)
Spread: 2-3ft (60-90cm)
Hardiness: Zones 3-8
Cultivation: Genista does well in well-drained light soil in full sun, but it even succeeds in poor soils.
Propagation: During late summer, take 2-3in (5-7.5cm) long heel cuttings and insert them into pots of equal parts peat and sharp sand. Place these in a cold frame. When the plants are rooted, pot them up into free-draining sandy soil and plunge the pot in soil in a well-drained corner of the garden. Plant into the garden in autumn or spring.

Right: Genista lydia
The golden-yellow flowers appear in late spring and early summer on this low-growing deciduous shrub. It is commonly grown in Europe and prized for its hummock form.

Left: Genista pilosa prostrata
This useful prostrate deciduous shrub has ground-hugging shoots, and small broom-like yellow flowers in late spring and early summer. It is essential to provide free-draining soil and a sunny position.

Genista pilosa

Silkyleaf Woadwaxen

This distinguished, ground-hugging, deciduous shrub has procumbent shoots when young, later becoming an attractive tangled mass of slender twiggy shoots. During late spring and early summer, it reveals small pea-shaped yellow flowers. A prostrate form is also available

Genista tinctoria is a good low-growing shrub for areas with poor soil. It can be grown as a specimen in a rock garden providing a bright burst of yellow in early summer.

Genista pilosa is a delight when set at the top of a low wall where its shoots can trail over the top. Plant small dry-wall plants below it to continue the interest and color for a longer period.

Genista sagittalis

Winged Broom

This curious and unusual hardy shrub acquires the character of an evergreen plant from its unusual winged branches. The leaves themselves are scattered and few. Small, yellow, pea-like flowers appear in summer. It is an excellent groundcover plant.

Height: 4-6in (10-15cm)
Spread: 1½-2ft (45-60cm)
Hardiness: Zones 3-8
Cultivation: Most garden soils suit it, as long as they are well-drained, light and in a sunny position, but it will even grow in poor soils. It requires little pruning.
Propagation: During summer, take soft cuttings, inserting them around the edge of a 5-6in (13-15cm) clay pot containing a mixture of four parts sharp sand and one part peat. Next spring, when they are rooted, pot them up and plant out the following autumn.

Below: **Genista sagittalis**
This excellent prostrate shrub produces pea-like yellow flowers in summer. Its winged shoots are an attractive bonus, with the true leaves scattered and few, and small and hairy when young.

which grows no more than 3in (7.5cm) high, and 3-4ft (90cm-1.2m) wide.

Height: 15-18in (38-45cm)
Spread: 2-3ft (60-90cm)
Hardiness: Zones 5-9
Cultivation: Any ordinary garden soil that is not too rich and has good drainage is suitable. Choose a sunny position.
Propagation: During late summer take 2-3in (5-7.5cm) long heel cuttings and insert them into pots of equal parts peat and sharp sand. Place these in a cold frame. When the cuttings are rooted, pot them up into free-draining sandy potting soil and plunge the pots in soil in a well-drained corner of the garden. During autumn or spring, set the plants in the garden.

Genista sagittalis is ideal as a groundcover shrub filling large spaces between rocks. Another ground-hugging shrub is *Genista delphinensis*, the most prostrate of all brooms, only 1-2in (2.5-5cm) high, with bright yellow flowers in midsummer.

Juniperus communis 'Depressa Aurea'

Common Juniper

This is a dwarf, wide-spreading and prostrate evergreen conifer with needle-like foliage. In spring, the leaves are butter-yellow, remaining golden throughout summer and dulling to bronze in autumn.
Height: 1-1½ft (30-45cm)
Spread: 8-10ft (2.4-3m)
Hardiness: Zones 3-8
Cultivation: This juniper needs good, well-drained soil in full sun. Like all golden-leaved conifers, it requires good light to ensure that the foliage remains bright.
Propagation: During late summer, take heel cuttings 2-4in (5-10cm)

Above: **Iris innominata**
This is another yellow-blooming iris, this one from the Pacific Northwest. It comes in a range of colors, has evergreen foliage and is only 6-10in (15-25cm) tall.

Iris pseudacorus

Yellow Flag

This rhizome-bearing iris comes originally from Europe and has been in cultivation for centuries. Its bold, upright, sword-shaped leaves provide an architectural form. The lemon-yellow bloom appears in early spring. If the plants are grown along a stream or pond they may reach 5ft (1.5m).However, they will perform well in a standard garden site.
Height: 2½-5ft (75cm-1.5m)
Spread: 1½-2ft (45-60cm)
Hardiness: Zones 4-9
Cultivation: This plants delights in neutral or slightly acid soil. It also grows well in a pocket of fertile and humus-rich soil in a rock garden. It will do well in full sun or light shade.
Propagation: Sow seeds in autumn or spring in a seed starting mix, keeping them at 45°F (7°C). Prick out the seedlings into small pots. Use small plants, because large ones do not transplant easily. Particularly good forms can be increased by detaching pieces of the rhizomes in autumn.

Iris pseudacorus excels as a streamside planting, obtaining a height of 5ft (1.5m). It's considered to be the "Fleur de lis" of the French royalty. It makes a long-lasting cut flower.

Juniperus communis 'Depressa Aurea' is well suited to a rock garden. If positioned at the bottom of a slight slope, its beautiful foliage can be admired from above; planted by the side of a pond, it is a delight.

long, inserting them into pots of equal parts peat and sharp sand. Place these in a cold frame until the plants are rooted, then set them out in a nursery bed for a couple of years before planting them in the garden. When setting them out, remember that ultimately they will have a wide spread. Do not position them where they will eventually have to be pruned severely and their shape ruined.

Below: Juniperus communis 'Depressa Aurea' *A prostrate juniper with golden foliage, its shoots spread out just above soil level, forming a dense shrub. In time it forms a golden carpet up to 10ft (3m) wide.*

Above: Juniperus x media 'Old Gold' *A well-known, wide-spreading slow-growing conifer, this variety retains its golden foliage throughout the year. Its ascending branches give it the appearance of a golden explosion.*

Juniperus x media 'Old Gold'

This is an old and trusted semi-prostrate compact evergreen conifer. It has golden scale-like leaves which remain bright throughout the year. In ten years, it should reach 28in (70cm) high and 5ft (1.5m) wide.
Height: 6ft (1.8m)
Spread: 8ft (2.4m)
Hardiness: Zones 3-9
Cultivation: Well-drained garden soil and a position in full sun or light shade are required. Good light ensures continuity of golden foliage throughout the year. It is a distinctive conifer and should not be cramped by other plants.
Propagation: During late summer, take heel cuttings 2-4in (5-10cm) long, inserting them into pots of equal parts peat and sharp sand. Place in a cold frame until rooted, then set them out in nursery beds for a couple of years before planting in their final positions.

Juniperus x media 'Old Gold' is superb for a junction between two paths or for creating a focal point. Its foliage also contrasts handsomely with a stone or brick patio.

Narcissus bulbocodium

Hoop Petticoat Daffodil

This is a delicate bulbous plant with funnel-shaped, crinoline-like yellow flower trumpets, 1in (2.5cm) wide. These have tapering and slightly spiky petals, appearing during late winter and early spring. It is especially useful for naturalizing among fine grasses. Alternatively, it can be grown in soil pockets in a rock garden.
Height: 4-6in (10-15cm)
Spread: 4-5in (10-13cm)
Hardiness: to Zone 6
Cultivation: Free-draining but moisture-retentive soil and light shade are needed. Avoid soils which dry out in spring. Set the bulbs in holes three times their own depth in late summer. If setting them in grass, first spread out the bulbs irregularly on the grass and plant them where they lie. This helps to create a natural arrangement.
Propagation: Overgrown clumps can be lifted and replanted every three or four years.

Narcissus cyclamineus

This eye-catching miniature narcissus has bright, rich-yellow, tube-like trumpets, and petals completely swept back. It flowers in late winter and early spring. Like *Narcissus bulbocodium*, it can be naturalized in short, fine grass, or planted in sheltered corners in a rock garden.
Height: 6-8in (15-20cm)
Spread: 4in (10cm)
Hardiness: to Zone 6
Cultivation: This narcissus prefers a moist, but not waterlogged, soil in light shade. Plant the bulbs in late summer, setting them in holes three times their own depth.
Propagation: Lift and divide overgrown clumps in summer, but do not thin out the bulbs too much; generous clumps look best.

Narcissus bulbocodium can be harmonized with other spring-flowering plants, such as the winter-flowering jasmine (*Jasminium nudiflorum*) and the early spring purplish-pink *Rhododendron* 'Tessa'.

Narcissus cyclamineus is attractive when planted in short grass, with random clumps of a pink winter-flowering heather set behind it. Varieties of *Erica herbacea* (*E. carnea*) are ideal choices for this purpose.

Left: **Narcissus bulbocodium**
This is the hoop petticoat daffodil, a small, delicate bulb with late winter and early spring flowers which resemble crinolines. It is excellent for naturalizing in areas covered by short, fine grass.

Right: **Portulaca grandiflora**
This beautiful rock garden or border flower is ideal for poor, dry soils. During summer, it displays saucer-shaped flowers in a range of colors, including yellow.

Below: **Narcissus cyclamineus**
A distinctive early, spring-flowering dwarf narcissus, ideal for naturalizing in short grass. It also does well alongside streams.

Portulaca grandiflora

Rose Moss · Sun Plant

An unusual, half-hardy succulent annual, the sun plant has narrow, fleshy, cylindrical bright green leaves and semi-prostrate, sprawling reddish stems. From early to late summer, it bears 1in (2.5cm) wide saucer-shaped red, purple or yellow flowers with bright yellow stamens. There are several varieties, extending the color range to pink, crimson orange and white. The F1 forms display double, rose-like flowers. It is ideal for a rock garden or border, and is also useful for filling gaps in any sunny site.
Height: 6-9in (15-23cm)
Spread: 6-8in (6-20cm)
Cultivation: Well-drained – even poor – soil and a sunny position are essential.
Propagation: During late winter and early spring, sow seeds ⅛in (3mm) deep in pots of seed starting mix, keeping them at 61°F (16°C). When the seedlings are large enough to handle, prick them out into flats of potting soil and slowly harden them off in a cold frame. Set the plants in the garden in late spring, when all risk of frost has passed. Alternatively, sow seeds ¼in

Above: **Solidago virgaurea** *This unusual miniature goldenrod, rarely exceeds 6in (15cm) high, with golden-yellow flowers held in clusters during late summer and early autumn.*

(6mm) deep in late spring where the plants are to flower. Thin out the seedlings to 6in (15cm) apart.

Solidago virgaurea

Dwarf European Goldenrod

This unusual and difficult to find hardy herbaceous goldenrod has midgreen, lance-shaped leaves and golden-yellow flowers borne in clusters during late summer and into early autumn. Its low, slightly sprawling nature makes it ideal for a rock garden.
Height: 6in (15cm)
Spread: 12-15in (30-38cm)
Hardiness: Zone 4-9
Cultivation: Plant in any good, well-drained garden soil in sun or light shade.
Propagation: During spring lift and divide established clumps. Replant the young pieces from around the outside, discarding old parts. They will produce self-sown seedlings, but avoid growing these as they do not resemble the parents.

Portulaca grandiflora is superb as a ground-cover plant. The flowers have particular interest to children as they close at night. Remove spent blooms to encourage new flowers.

Goldenrods are seldom grown in the United States because they are mistakenly thought to be the cause of hay fever; the inconspicuous ragweed is the true culprit.

Sternbergia lutea

Winter Daffodil

This delicate bulb-bearing rock garden plant bears goblet-shaped, shining waxy-yellow flowers up to 2in (5cm) long, in late summer and into early autumn. The strap-shaped, deep green leaves remain small and immature until the following spring.
Height: 4-6in (10-15cm)
Spread: 4-5in (10-13cm)
Hardiness: to Zone 7
Cultivation: Well-drained soil and a sunny position are needed. Leave the bulbs undisturbed for as long as possible. Set new bulbs 4-6in (10-15cm) deep in late summer.
Propagation: Lift overgrown clumps in late summer, dividing and replanting them as soon as possible. Offset bulbs often take two years before producing flowers.

Taxus baccata 'Repens Aurea'

Spreading English Yew

This is a low, prostrate, slow-growing evergreen conifer with dense foliage. Each leaf is green, with gold edges. The gold is pale in spring, gradually deepening during summer. The spreading branches have attractive drooping tips. In ten years, it will have grown about 4ft (35cm) high and 3½ft (1m) wide.
Height: 3ft (90cm)
Spread: 10ft (3m)
Hardiness: Zones 5-7
Cultivation: Well-drained soil in full sun suits it best. Indeed, if grown in shade, it soon loses its beautiful color, so ensure it gets plenty of light.
Propagation: During late summer or early autumn, take 3-4in (7.5-10cm) long heel cuttings. Insert them into equal parts peat and sharp sand and place these in a cold frame. When the cuttings are rooted, plant them out in a nursery bed for a couple of years before setting them in the garden.

Above: **Sternbergia lutea**
A distinctive late-flowering bulb which looks like a crocus and produces a welcome display of brilliant yellow flowers, it is ideal for bringing late color to the corner of a rock garden.

Below: **Taxus baccata 'Repens Aurea'** *It is essential that this attractive prostrate yew with bright green and gold foliage is planted in full sun if it is to keep its bright variegated coloring.*

Sternbergia lutea, with its dominantly-colored flowers, needs to be set in a passive, non-conflicting setting. A background of green or gray foliage will provide the right setting.

Taxus baccata 'Repens Aurea' needs a neighbor of contrasting color and shape. Blue or dark-green foliaged conifers are best; if you want this golden yew to have a domed appearance, trim it with shears.

Thuja orientalis 'Aurea Nana'

Dwarf Oriental Arborvitae

This attractively rounded, slow-growing, evergreen dwarf conifer has vertical plates of yellow-green, scale-like leaves which turn gold in winter. In ten years it will reach 2ft (60cm) high, with a spread of 20in (50cm).

Height: 3½ft (1m)
Spread: 2½-3ft (75-90cm)
Hardiness: Zones 6-9
Cultivation: Deep, moist but not continually saturated garden soil, and a position in full sun assure success.
Propagation: During late summer or early autumn, take 2-4in (5-10cm) long cuttings, inserting them into pots of equal parts peat and sharp sand. Place these in a cold frame and, when the cuttings are rooted, plant them out in a nursery bed for a couple of years before transferring them to the garden.

Above: Thuja orientalis 'Aurea Nana' *This beautifully-shaped, slow-growing compact conifer has yellow-green scale-like leaves which turn gold in winter. It needs full sun in order to keep its attractive coloring.*

Below: Thuja plicata 'Rogersii' *This beautiful evergreen dwarf conifer has dense foliage, green with golden edges. In winter, the leaves turn bronze and remain attractive throughout that too often dull period.*

Thuja plicata 'Rogersii'

Dwarf Western Arborvitae

This dwarf slow-growing conical evergreen conifer has a lovely yellow glow. The fine foliage is packed in tight green clusters, with the edges of the scale-like leaves a rich golden-yellow. In winter the leaves become bronze. It is ideal for rock gardens. In ten years it will reach only 28in (70cm) high and 16in (40cm) wide.

Height: 3½ft (1m)
Spread: 3ft (90cm)
Hardiness: Zones 5-7
Cultivation: Ordinary garden soil is suitable, but it must not become dry during summer. A sheltered position in full sun also suits it.
Propagation: During late summer or early autumn, take 2-4in (5-10cm) long cuttings and put them into pots of equal parts peat and sharp sand. Place these in a cold frame and, when the cuttings are rooted, plant them out into a nursery bed for a couple of years before you set them in the garden.

Thuja orientalis 'Aurea Nana' is excellent for a rock garden. Prostrate conifers with contrasting colors can be set near it. In a rock garden, small spring bulbs give added interest.

Thuja plicata 'Rogersii' looks especially good when set with stone chips around it. The changing light patterns of the chips pick up the colors in the thuja. This is especially effective in full sun.

ROCK AND NATURALIZED GARDENS

Above: **Tropaeolum polyphyllum**
This spectacular, tuberous-rooted rock garden plant from South America has long stems clothed in gray leaves and yellow flowers during midsummer. It tends to die down when flowering is over.

Tropaeolum polyphyllum

This distinctive, difficult to find, tuberous-rooted, ground-hugging herbaceous perennial has lobed gray-green leaves on arching stems. The large, rich yellow flowers, 1/2in (12mm) wide, appear on stems arising from the leaf joints during early and midsummer. The whole plant often dies down after flowering.
Height: 3-4in (7.5-10cm)
Spread: 3-4ft (90cm-1.2m)
Hardiness: Grow as an annual
Cultivation: Plant the tubers during spring, in friable soil, at a depth of 10-12in (25-30cm). Position them so that the plants will trail naturally, preferably over a large rock. It delights in a warm and sunny position, but it also grows in light shade.
Propagation: Once established, propagation is very easy. Just dig up the tubers in spring, replanting them before they dry out.

Tulipa sylvestris

This bulbous, easily grown tulip species has narrow gray-green leaves and scented yellow flowers, 2in (5cm) wide. The reflexed petals make the flowers appear even larger than they are. Flowering is during midspring. These tulips are suitable for rock gardens, borders, and naturalizing.
Height: 12-15in (30-38cm)
Spread: 4-6in (10-15cm)
Hardiness: to Zone 4
Cultivation: Well-drained soil, a sheltered site and a sunny south-facing position are ideal. Plant the bulbs in late summer or early autumn.
Propagation: You can raise plants from seed, but it is easier to increase from offsets.

Tulipa tarda

This eye-catching species tulip has narrow midgreen leaves, developing in a rosette from soil level. It bears up to five flowers on each stem. They have star-shaped, pointed yellow petals with white edges, up to 1 1/2in (4cm) long. This tulip is ideal at the front of a border or in a rock garden.
Height: 6in (15cm)
Spread: 7.5cm (3in)
Hardiness: to Zone 4
Cultivation: Well-drained soil and a sheltered position, preferably in good light and facing south, are most suitable. The bulbs can be left in the soil, but remember to remove the leaves as soon as they have died down.
Propagation: Overgrown clumps can be lifted and divided in autumn, replanting the bulbs 6in (15cm) deep and 3-4in (7.5-10cm) apart.

Left: **Tulipa sylvestris** *An easily-grown species with beautiful scented yellow flowers, this tulip is ideal for rock gardens and borders as well as for naturalizing in woodland and grass.*

Below: **Tulipa tarda** *This small tulip is ideal for a rock garden. It needs an open and sunny position, where the flowers will open wide in good light. Up to five are produced on each stem.*

Tropaeolum polyphyllum, a spectacular plant, is difficult to locate. It is probably best grown as an annual.

Tulipa tarda associates well with many plants: in the rock garden with the pasque flower (*Pulsatilla vulgaris*), and in the border with crown imperial (*Fritillaria imperialis*) and mauve-flowered violas.

Above: **Verbascum x 'Letitia'**
This beautiful hybrid bears little resemblance to its coarse cousin, the roadside weed, common mullein. The clear yellow flowers appear from midsummer onwards.

Verbascum x 'Letitia'

Mullein

A pretty hybrid between *V. dumulosum* and *V. spinosum*, with a twiggy but compact habit, it has velvety, gray-green lance-shaped leaves and numerous clear yellow flowers, 1in (2.5cm) wide, from midsummer onwards.
Height: 10-15in (25-38cm)
Spread: 15-18in (38-45cm)
Hardiness: Zones 8-10
Cultivation: This lovely plant needs a sandy, well-drained soil in full sun. It dislikes continual dampness during winter and may require protection with panes of glass. It is ideal for dry stone walls.
Propagation: The easiest way to increase it is by taking 2in (5cm) long heel cuttings during early summer, inserting them in pots of equal parts peat and sharp sand. Place them in a cold frame.

Further plants to consider

Corydalis lutea
Yellow Corydalis
Height: 9-12in (23-30cm)   Spread: 9-12in (23-30cm)
Hardiness: Zones 5-7
A mounded woodland plant with blue-green lace-like foliage. Prefers well-drained soil, sun to partial shade. Soft yellow blooms in summer.

Draba densiflora
Rock Cress Draba
Height: 2-2½in (5-6.5cm)   Spread: 1½-2in (4-5cm)
Hardiness: Zones 4-7
An attractive, compact, hardy herbaceous perennial for the rock garden, with small cross-shaped golden-yellow flowers in spring.

Fritillaria pallidiflora
Height: 10-12in (25-30cm)   Spread: 4-6in (10-15cm)
Hardiness: to Zone 4
An unusual fritillaria, with 1½in (4cm) long bell-shaped yellow flowers during spring.

Hypericum polyphyllum
St. John's-wort
Height: 6in (15cm)   Spread: 10-30in (25-30cm)
Hardiness: Zones 6-8
A low-growing shrubby perennial, with 1½in (4cm) wide golden flowers from mid- to late summer. The cultivar 'Sulphureum' bears pale yellow flowers.

Roscoea cautleoides
Height: 12-15in (30-38cm)   Spread: 10-12in (25-30cm)
Hardiness: Zones 8-9
A hardy herbaceous perennial, with pale yellow, orchid-like flowers, 1½-2in (4-5cm) long, in midsummer.

Uvularia perfoliata
Bellwort
Height: 8-10in (20-25cm)   Spread: 6-8in (15-20cm)
Hardiness: Zones 3-9
A pretty rhizome-bearing perennial for a rock garden or woodland garden. In late spring it produces many bell-shaped, pendant, pale-yellow flowers, singly or in pairs.

Waldsteinia fragarioides
Barren Strawberry
Height: 5-8in (13-20cm)   Spread: 10-12in (25-30cm)
Hardiness: Zones 4-7
A strawberry-like plant, ideal for a large rock garden. During early summer it bears small, five-petalled, golden-yellow flowers above three-lobed, strawberry-like leaves.

Verbascum x 'Letitia' delights in a sunny position, especially one with good drainage such as the top of a dry stone wall. Its compact nature helps to interrupt the flatness of many such walls, and provides color.

Above: **Arabis ferdinandi-coburgi 'Variegata'** *has a low, somewhat sprawling nature. It is blessed with white flowers as well as variegated leaves.*

Arabis ferdinandi-coburgi 'Variegata'

This unusual very attractive evergreen rock garden plant has gray-green leaves with whitish edges, and a mat-forming habit. It is ideal for planting between rocks. During spring it develops white, cross-shaped flowers.
Height: 3½-4in (8-10cm)
Spread: 12-18in (30-45cm)
Hardiness: Zones 4-8
Cultivation: Plant in well-drained soil in light shade.
Propagation: Lift and divide overgrown plants in spring or autumn.

Arundinaria japonica

(*Pseudosasa japonlca*)
Arrow Bamboo

This tender bamboo is vigorous and superb for creating a screen or hedge. It develops upright, olive-green canes, later arching slightly under the weight of foliage, which matures to a dull matt-green. The dark, glossy-green leaves are 6-12in (15-30cm) long and 1-2in (2.5-5cm) wide. It is a bamboo that does not become too invasive, seldom spreading rapidly.
Height: 10-15ft (3-4.5m)
Spread: Forms a large, dense clump.
Hardiness: Zones 7-10
Cultivation: Set new clumps in position only when the soil has warmed up. The best time to

transplant or plant the canes is when the young, underground buds are just becoming active. Keep the young plants well-watered. No pruning is needed or desirable, just let the canes develop naturally.
Propagation: In late spring or early summer, as soon as the soil has warmed up, lift and divide large clumps. Keep the

---

Arabis ferdinandi-coburgi 'Variegata' harmonizes well with dwarf conifers and spring-blooming plants, such as *Aurinia saxatilis*, basket-of-gold. *Arabis caucasîca* is a related species with gray-green foliage and fragrant white flowers.

Arundinaria japonica, a member of the grass family, flowers sporadically but not frequently. Suggestions that clumps die after flowering are untrue, most continue to grow normally.

Epimedium perralderanum

Barrenwort

An attractive low-growing and ground-covering evergreen perennial, ideal for a naturalized garden in light shade. When young the leaves are bright green with bronze-red tints. In autumn these assume rich coppery hues. During early to midsummer, plants bear bright yellow flowers.

Height: 9-12in (23-30cm)

Spread: 12-15in (30-38cm)
Hardiness: Zones 5-8
Cultivation: Plant in light, sandy, well-drained soil in light shade.
Propagation: In spring, lift and divide overgrown plants.

Below: Epimedium perralderanum *This ground-covering evergreen plant has bright green leaves that assume rich tints in autumn. The bright yellow flowers are borne on arching stems during early and midsummer.*

Above: Arundinaria japonica *This handsome bamboo forms a wonderful screen or hedge. It can also develop into a beautiful clump in an ornamental grass border.*

clumps well-watered until established, especially if the weather is dry and the soil is sandy.

Epimedium x rubrum is a hybrid, widely grown as ground-cover. When young the midgreen leaves are tinted red, becoming first orange and later yellow in autumn. In addition, crimson flowers are borne in early summer.

Glyceria maxima 'Variegata'

Manna Grass

This perennial grass delights in having its roots in water or the moist soil around a pond. In spring, the young green shoots have pinkish-white stripes, but as the season progresses the pink fades. It is a strong-growing plant, and may become too invasive for small ponds.

Height: 3-4ft (0.9-1.2m)
Spread: 3-4ft (0.9-1.2m)
Hardiness: Zones 5-10
Cultivation: If grown in a pond, plant it in a container so that its top is 2-3in (5-7.5cm) below the surface of the water. Do not plant directly into the soil in a pond, as the roots can be invasive and pierce plastic lining materials. If planted in surrounding moist soil, again set in a container. In autumn the leaves die down and these need to be removed.
Propagation: Divide overgrown plants in spring.

Above: Glyceria maxima 'Variegata' *When planted in a garden pond surrounded by concrete it helps to soften the harsh edges. Ensure that it is planted in a container, as the roots can damage plastic pool liners.*

Below: Gunnera manicata *A gravel-surfaced path near a large clump of this giant-leaved plant creates an harmonious association, as well as allowing the leaves to be seen close-up. They are most attractive in spring.*

Glyceria maxima 'Variegata', manna grass, is eye-catching and creates a dramatic feature in the soil around a pond or in the shallow edges. Do not crowd other variegated plants around it, as they will fight for attention.

Gunnera manicata

This distinctive, large-leaved, herbaceous perennial is superb in a naturalized garden. It forms a large clump of thick, prickly, upright stems with large, dark green, kidney-shaped leaves. Leaves up to 6ft (1.8m) wide are frequently seen. Green flowers are borne in cone-shaped heads up to 12in (30cm) wide and 2ft (60cm) high.

This eye-catching plant is not suitable for small gardens, but where it can be accommodated it is certain to attract attention – garden visitors will want to be photographed next to it!

Height: 5-9ft (1.5-2.7m)
Spread: 10-15ft (3-4.5m)
Hardiness: Zones 7-10
Cultivation: Plant in moisture-retentive peaty soil in full sun or light shade. Shelter from hot, summer winds is beneficial. The crown of the plant can be protected from severe frost by allowing the leaves, as they die down in autumn, to rest on the plant's center. A thin layer of soil over the leaves adds further protection. In spring, draw the old leaves and soil away from the plant's center.
Propagation: Plants can be raised from seeds sown in spring and placed in 61°F (16°C), but division is quicker and easier. In late spring, remove small clumps from around the edge of the main plant. Transfer into pots and place in a frost-free place until established.

Hosta fortunei 'Albopicta'

Plantain Lily

Hostas are widely-grown hardy, herbaceous, perennials. Many species have leaves totally of one color, but many are variegated and bring additional color to gardens. *Hosta fortunei* 'Albopicta', often sold as 'Picta', is superb when planted in a wild garden, alongside an informal garden pond or near to small pools in a series of waterfalls. The young leaves are pale green, broadly variegated with buff-yellow. As a bonus, mauve flowers are borne in midsummer on stiff, upright stems. Another attractive variegated hosta variety of the species is 'Aureomarginata', displaying leaves edged with light yellow.

Height: 1½-2ft (45-60cm)
Spread: 20-24in (50-60cm)
Hardiness: Zones 3-9
Cultivation: Plant in well-drained but moisture-retentive fertile soil in light, dappled shade. Variegated hostas retain their variegations best in light shade, but not in dark and gloomy positions.
Propagation: Divide and replant overgrown plants in spring.

Left: Hosta fortunei 'Albopicta'
This attractively foliaged plant is superb when planted around the edges of a water garden. It likes moisture-retentive soil.

Gunnera manicata provides a focal point in a water or bog garden. Its large rhubarb-like leaves create a superb contrast with spiky, upright plants such as moisture-loving irises.

Hosta fortunei 'Albopicta' is such a handsome and distinctive plant that its shape and color impact are spoiled if it is crowded.

Hosta rectifolia 'Tall Boy'

Plantain Lily

In addition to the many variegated leaved hostas there are some superb single-color types. The above variety is tall, with beautiful green leaves and high spires of violet-mauve flowers in mid-summer. Other single-colored species include *Hosta sieboldiana* 'Elegans', *Hosta* 'Halcyon' which forms a mound of bright silvery-gray leaves and *Hosta* 'Blue Skies' with vivid-blue foliage. The leaves of hostas help to soften the edges of borders, in flower borders as well as wild and naturalized gardens.

Height: $3\frac{1}{2}$-$4\frac{1}{2}$ft (1-1.3m)
Spread: $2\frac{1}{2}$-3ft (75-90cm)
Hardiness: Zones 3-9
Cultivation: Plant in well-drained but moisture-retentive soil in light, dappled shade.
Propagation: Divide and replant overgrown plants in spring.

Right: Hosta rectifolia 'Tall Boy' *is a dominant plant creating a backdrop for other plants as well as producing its own flowers in eye-catching spires in midsummer.*

Iris pseudacorus 'Variegatus'

Yellow Flag Iris

This water-loving tall iris is ideal for planting alongside the margins of ponds where its upright, sword-like, bluish-green leaves with yellow stripes create a distinctive feature. It has the bonus of producing yellow flowers during early summer.

Height: $2\frac{1}{2}$-3ft (75-90cm)
Spread: $1\frac{1}{2}$ft (45cm)
Hardiness: Zones 5-9
Cultivation: Plants may be grown at the water's edge or in moist soil.
Propagation: Every three or four years lift and divide overgrown clumps after flowering.

Hosta rectifolia 'Tall Boy', as well as other hostas, harmonize well in a naturalized garden with azaleas. They provide interesting shapes and colors when the azaleas are not in flower.

Above: **Iris pseudacorus 'Variegatus'** *This water-loving plant is ideal for planting alongside paths surrounding ponds. It is equally at home in fertile, moist soil in a border or naturalized garden.*

Lamiastrum galeobdolon 'Variegatum'

Variegated Yellow Archangel

A superb groundcover hardy perennial with upright stems bearing silvery-flushed evergreen leaves that assume bronze tints in autumn and winter. It has the bonus of developing whorls of yellow, nettle-like flowers during early and midsummer. 'Herman's Pride' has smaller flowers and deeper markings.
Height: 6-12in (15-30cm)
Spread: 1-1½ft (30-45cm)
Hardiness: Zones 4-9
Cultivation: Grow in moist, well-drained soil in light to medium shade. To encourage the development of thick growth, use garden shears to cut back the spent flower stalks as soon as the blooms fade.
Propagation: Lift and divide overgrown plants in autumn or spring.

Above: **Lamiastrum galeobdolon 'Variegatum'** *has attractive leaves that create a superb foil for other plants, as well as preventing the growth of weeds. It has the bonus of bearing yellow nettle-like flowers during early and midsummer.*

Iris pseudacorus 'Variegatus' harmonizes with the well-known double marsh marigold *(Caltha palustris* 'Flore Pleno'), with golden-yellow flowers in late spring and early summer. They like the same water depth, 6in (15cm).

Lamiastrum galeobdolon 'Variegatum' is a striking plant both when in flower, during early and midsummer, and just when the variegated leaves are present. They create a superb background for other plants.

Above: **Lamium maculatum** *is ideal for planting as a groundcover, where it soon carpets the soil with attractive foliage.*

Lamium maculatum

Spotted Nettle

An excellent hardy perennial with midgreen leaves displaying central silver stripes. It has the bonus of developing pinkish-purple flowers during early summer. It is ideal for creating contrast in a woodland garden or in an herbaceous border.
Height: 10-12in (25-30cm)
Spread: 1-1½ft (30-45cm)
Hardiness: Zones 3-8
Cultivation: Plant in moisture-retentive, fertile soil in full sun or light to medium shade.
Propagation: Lift and divide overgrown plants in autumn or spring.

Right: **Osmunda regalis** *In late summer and autumn, when the sun's rays are low, the russet-tinted foliage looks especially eye-catching. The colors are clearly reflected in the surface of still water.*

Lamium maculatum creates a superb weed-smothering background for other plants, especially all-green leaved ones. These range from large-leaved hostas to phormiums and ferns.

Osmunda regalis

Royal Fern

This superb, large, hardy fern is ideal for planting around the edge of an informal pond. Large clumps of it often grow 8-10ft (2.4-3m) high, but in gardens it is less vigorous and therefore more manageable. The fresh-green fronds assume rich tints in autumn. As plants grow they develop a mass of black roots at their bases, occasionally 2-2½ft (60-75cm) high in old plants.The variety 'Purpurescens' is attractive, with bright coppery-pink fronds in spring, becoming glaucous-green as the season progresses and assuming rich tints in autumn.
Height: 4-5ft (1.2-1.5m)
Spread: 6-8ft (1.8-2.4m)
Hardiness: Zones 3-10
Cultivation: Plant in moisture-retentive, fertile soil in full sun or light shade. Position at the edge of an informal pond, where some roots can grow into the water or in a moist woodland garden.
Propagation: In spring divide overgrown plants.

Above: Pachysandra terminalis 'Variegata' *This variegated groundcover, with white-edged green leaves, creates a complete carpet of weed-smothering leaves.*

Pachysandra terminalis 'Variegata'

A variegated variety of the well-known hardy, evergreen, low-growing groundcover has mid- to deep-green leaves with white edges. During late winter and spring it bears greenish-white flowers.
Height: 9-12in (23-30cm)
Spread: 15-18in (38-45cm)
Hardiness: Zones 4-9
Cultivation: Plant in any good soil, preferably moisture-retentive, in light shade. It is an ideal plant for creating attractive groundcover under trees. If the shade is dense however, the ordinary all-green form is best.
Propagation: In spring lift and divide overgrown plants. Keep them well watered until established in their new positions.

Osmunda regalis creates a striking arching form around ponds. It also harmonizes well with other moisture-loving plants such as the yellow flag iris, *Iris pseudacorus*, and the large-leaved umbrella plant, *Peltiphyllum peltatum.*

Pachysandra terminalis 'Variegata' creates an attractive groundcovering in a naturalized setting. It is especially suitable for creating groundcover around deciduous, summer-flowering shrubs.

Sasa veitchii

Kuma Bamboo Grass

This eye-catching tender bamboo develops large thickets of deep purplish-green stems later becoming dull purple. These are headed by oblong dark green leaves up to 8in (20cm) long and about 2in (5cm) wide. The purple foliage becomes pale straw or whitish along their edges in autumn, providing winter interest.

Height: 3-4ft (0.9-1.2m)
Spread: Eventually forms a large clump.
Hardiness: Zones 8-10
Cultivation: Plant in moisture-retentive but not waterlogged soil, in full sun or light shade. Avoid positions exposed to cold, drying winds. No pruning is needed.
Propagation: Lift and divide overgrown plants in early summer.

Do not divide bamboos early in the year, before the soil has become warm. Keep new plants moist until established.

Below: Sasa veitchii *This thicket-forming bamboo develops very attractive leaves. It does not grow excessively high and therefore can be planted in moderately-sized gardens. It is a trouble-free plant.*

Sasa veitchii is ideal for planting on a bank alongside streams and paths. It is a tender bamboo suitable for warmer climates.

Above: Vinca major 'Variegata'
This sprawling ground-hugging plant is very tolerant and amenable, creating color in poor soil as well as diffused shade. It flowers in late spring and summer.

Vinca major 'Variegata'

Variegated Periwinkle

This well-known and widely-grown evergreen groundcover is normally grown in its all-green form. However, for extra color and interest, the variegated type with pale green and white leaves is worth growing. Also known as 'Elegantissima', it has pale purple-blue flowers during late spring and early summer, and often re-blooms in late summer and into autumn. It is ideal for creating color under trees and around shrubs in a woodland.
Height: 6-15in (15-38cm)
Spread: 3-4ft (0.9-1.2m)
Hardiness: Zones 7-9
Cultivation: Well-drained, but not parched soil, in light shade.
Propagation: Divide overgrown plants in late summer or spring, replanting healthy young parts.

Further plants to consider

Juniperus
Juniper
The junipers are among the most popular evergreen landscape plants. They vary widely in growth habit, from tall and narrow to short and spreading; colors include green, blue and yellow. Junipers can be used as accent plants, hedges, and groundcovers. *J. chinensis* 'Pyramidalis' is a tall (30ft/10m) dense columnar plant, with bluish-green needles. *J. communis* 'Compressa' is a dence upright dwarf (2-3ft/60-90cm) cultivar. *J. horizontalis* 'Bar Harbor' makes a good groundcover, growing less than 12in (30cm) tall. *J. squamata* 'Blue Star' is a rounded, low-growing (20in/50cm) plant; 'Meyeri' is a bushy blue cultivar, reaching about 6ft (1.8m)

Picea pungens 'Globosa'
Colorado Spruce
Height: 3ft (90cm)   Spread: 3-3¹⁄₂ft (90cm-1.05m)
Hardiness: Zones 2-7
Picea pungens 'Globosa' is a rounded dwarf shrub with blue foliage. It may also be sold as *P. pungens* 'Glauca Globosa'.

Sedum ternatum
Whorled Stonecrop
Height: 2-6in (5-15cm)   Spread: 18in (45cm)
Hardiness: Zones 4-8
Small rounded leaves are borne at the end of the stems, which spread by rooting at the nodes. Starry white flowers appear in spring.

Sempervivum tectorum
Hens-and-Chicks, Common Houseleek
Height: 6-10in (15-25cm)   Spread: 8in (20cm)
Hardiness: Zones 3-8
Popular and easy to grow, this plant forms tight rosettes of evergreen foliage. Offsets are produced around the parent plant during the growing season. Purplish red flowers are produced in summer.

Thuja occidentalis
American Arborvitae
Height: varies by cultivar   Spread: varies by cultivar
Hardiness: Zones 2-8
This is a popular conifer with a dense upright growth habit and aromatic foliage. 'Holmstrup' is a compact pyramidal green cultivar. 'Lutea' grows to about 30ft (9m) high and has golden-yellow foliage. 'Rheingold' reaches about 5ft (1.5m), with pinkish-yellow needles.

Tsuga canadensis 'Pendula'
Weeping Eastern Hemlock
Height: 10ft (3m)   Spread: 15ft (4.5m)
Hardiness: Zones 4-8
An outstanding small tree for the rock garden or water feature. The branches weep gracefully, forming a spreading mound of foliage.

Vinca major 'Variegata' is ideal in a wild naturalized garden, creating color around the bases of shrubs, smothering weeds and softening the edges of paths.

Aponogeton distachyos

Water Hawthorn · Cape Pondweed · Cape Asparagus

A beautiful warm climate, aquatic plant with light green, elongated leaves and heavily-scented, pure white flowers with black anthers from mid- to late summer, and often into autumn.
Height: Surface of water
Spread: 1½-2ft (45-60cm) or more
Hardiness: Zones 9-10

Cultivation: It is a true aquatic and needs a water depth of 9-24in (23-60cm). Plant in neutral or slightly acid soil at pond bottom or in a submerged container. Full sun is needed, although it will flower in slight shade. New plants are best set in position in late spring or early summer.
Propagation: New plants can be raised from seed, but for home gardeners it is easier to lift and divide overgrown plants with several crowns in late spring or early summer. Young plants are slow to become established.

Above: Aponogeton distachyos
The pure-white flowers with black anthers are borne in forked clusters just above the surface of the water.

Galanthus nivalis

Common Snowdrop

Snowdrops are frequently confused with snowflakes (*Leucojum*), but can be easily identified. Snowdrops have three short inner petals and three long outer petals, whereas snowflakes have six petals all the same size. The common snowdrop

Aponogeton distachyos is outstandingly eye-catching, especially in full sun. It may be grown as an annual for a small pond in cool climates.

flowers during late winter and into spring, with nodding heads of white flowers amid glaucous, strap-like leaves. There are several superb varieties, such as 'Flore-plena' with double flowers, and 'S. Arnott' with larger flowers, up to 1½in (36mm) long. The giant snowdrop, *Galanthus elwesii*, is nearly 1ft (30cm) tall.

Height: 3-8in (7.5-20cm)
Spread: 3-5in (7.5-13cm)
Hardiness: Zones 3-7
Cultivation: Moisture-retentive, slightly heavy soil suits it best, although this bulb will survive in most soils. Good light is needed, so avoid heavily shaded sites. If the soil is rich and moist, plants grow much larger than when in poor, slightly drier positions.
Propagation: Lift and divide large clusters just after the flowers fade. Do not allow the bulbs to dry out, replanting them immediately into new positions and setting them 4-5in (10-15cm) deep.

Below: Galanthus nivalis
Snowdrops are particularly welcome in late winter, with their bright, white flowers. They are superb in a rock garden when clustered around rocks, which create an attractive background for the flowers.

Above: Houttuynia cordata *A moisture-loving hardy herbaceous perennial, ideal for planting around an informal pond. It also grows well in shallow water. However, it spreads rapidly and can become too invasive for small gardens.*

Houttuynia cordata

Chameleon Plant

A hardy herbaceous perennial from China and Japan that thrives in moist soil in a cool, shaded position. It also grows well in shallow water, up to 2in (5cm) deep. Unfortunately, it can be invasive, spreading by underground stems. These grow direct from soil-level and bear near heart-shaped blue-green leaves with a metallic sheen. During midsummer it displays terminal heads of pure white flowers. The best variety is 'Flora Pleno', with double flowers.

Height: 1-1½ft (30-45cm)
Spread: 12-15in (30-38cm) or more
Hardiness: Zones 3-8
Cultivation: Moisture-retentive soil and light shade suit it best. Do not allow dry out.
Propagation: During autumn or spring lift and divide overgrown clumps.

Galanthus nivalis can be left to form large clusters in the woodland or rock garden. It harmonizes superbly with color and shape-contrasting bulbous plants such as purple and blue varieties of *Iris reticulata*, which flower in late winter and early spring.

Houttuynia cordata 'Chameleon' has leaves variegated with white, pink and red. It is slightly less invasive than the species. In Vietnam the species is cultivated as a salad plant, while in Nepal the leaves are eaten in soups.

Left: Iberis sempervirens *This neat, small plant is ideal for planting in a rock garden, where it develops masses of white flowers during early to midsummer. The variety 'Little Gem' is slightly smaller.*

Iberis sempervirens

Evergreen Candytuft

A reliable hardy evergreen perennial with narrow, dark green leaves. From early to midsummer it creates a wealth of clear white flowers in heads 1½in (4cm) wide. There are several superb forms, such as 'Little Gem' at 4in (10cm) high and spreading to 9in (23cm), and 'Snowflake' at 6-9in (15-23cm) high and spreading to form a mat of foliage and pure-white flowers. The ordinary form of this plant is best for border edges but 'Little Gem' is ideal for rock gardens.
Height: 8-10in (20-25cm)
Spread: 1½-2ft (45-60cm)
Hardiness: Zones 3-9
Cultivation: Well-drained soil and full sun suit it. Remove dead flower heads to extend the flower period – after they fade use shears to lightly cut off the old heads.
Propagation: It is easily increased during mid- and late summer by taking 2in (5cm) long softwood cuttings from non-flowering shoots. Insert them in a mixture of equal parts moist peat and sharp sand. Place in a cold frame. When rooted, pot individually into small pots and overwinter in a cold frame.

Ipheion uniflorum

Spring Starflower

A dainty, hardy bulbous plant, ideal for planting alongside a path in a naturalized area or in a rock garden. The long, narrow, pale green leaves have a slightly garlic-like aroma. However, the star-like white flowers, which appear from mid- to late spring, are sweetly scented. Flower color is variable, ranging from white to violet-blue.
Height: 6-8in (15-20cm)
Spread: Forms a clump
Hardiness: Zones 5-9
Cultivation: Plant in well-drained soil in full sun or light shade. Plant the bulbs 2in (5cm) deep in late summer or early autumn. Remove dead leaves and old flower stems in late summer.
Propagation: Lift and divide overgrown plants, every two or three years, in autumn.

Iberis saxatilis, rock candytuft, is ideal for growing on rocks. Its compact, evergreen growth creates a 3-6in (7.5-15cm) mound. The white blooms appear in spring. Rock candytuft is hardy in Zones 2 to 7.

Juniperus virginiana 'Grey Owl'

Grey Owl · Eastern Red Cedar

This vigorous, spreading conifer is too large for small rock gardens, but it can create a superb background in large ones or even form a break between a wild area and a rock garden. It is an elegant, spreading conifer, with slender sprays of soft, silvery-gray foliage.
Height: 3-4ft (0.9-1.2m)
Spread: 5-6ft (1.5-1.8m)
Hardiness: Zones 2-9
Cultivation: Ordinary well-drained soil and a position in light shade or

Above: Juniperus 'Grey Owl' *The elegant, silvery-gray foliage has slightly cascading tips, which enhance the plant. The yellowish stems create an additional feature. Plants which intrude on their neighbors can be pruned in spring. It cohabits well with callunas and ericas.*

full sun suits it.
Propagation: During late summer and into early autumn take 3-4in (7.5-10cm) long heel-cuttings from lateral shoots. Insert them in equal parts moist peat and sharp sand. Place in a cold frame.

Ipheion uniflorum is often seen in its blue varieties, such as 'Caeruleum' and 'Wisely Blue', but the white form is just as attractive. It is ideal as an edging to a path.

Juniperus virginiana 'Grey Owl' is superb for covering the soil with silvery-gray foliage. It is almost identical in appearance to *Juniperus chinensis* 'Hetzii' and 'Pfitzerana Glauca'.

Polygonatum x hybridum

Solomon's Seal

A hardy herbaceous perennial, it is a cross between *Polygonatum multiflorum* and *P. odoratum*. Each year the fat, rhizomatous roots develop long, upright but arching stems clothed with lance-shaped midgreen and ribbed leaves that clasp the stems. The slightly waisted, white, midsummer flowers, up to 1in (2.5cm) long, hang in clusters of two to five from the leaf-joints during midsummer. When cut, and while still in bud and taken indoors, the flowers soon fill

Leucojum aestivum 'Gravetye Giant'

Giant Snowflake · Summer Snowflake

This small, late spring-flowering bulbous plant develops nodding, cup-shaped, white flowers. The tips of the petals are delicately lined in green. Unlike snowdrops, all of its six petals are the same size.
Height: 20in (50cm)
Spread: 6-8in (15-20cm)
Hardiness: Zones 4-9
Cultivation: Moisture-retentive soil

Above: Leucojum aestivum 'Gravetye Giant' *The late spring flowers create an attractive feature in a rock garden, lightly shaded wild garden or around the bases of deciduous shrubs. Once established it needs little attention and is quite hardy.*

and light shade are needed. Plant the bulbs 3-4in (7.5-10cm) deep during late summer and early autumn.
Propagation: Divide overgrown clumps as the leaves die down.

Leucojum aestivum 'Gravetye Giant', summer snowflake, is ideal in a woodland garden, where it co-habits well with late blooming daffodils.

Polygonatum x hybridum, with its arching stems of white flowers, harmonizes with variegated hostas. A backdrop of the *rhododendron* or mountain laurel creates extra color and interest.

a room with a delicious scent. *Polygonatum odoratum* 'Variegatum', a variegated variety of Solomon's seal, has beautiful white edged leaves that are dramatic in light shade.
Height: 2-3¹/₂ft (0.6-1m)
Spread: 15-18in (38-45cm)
Hardiness: Zones 4-10
Cultivation: It is so successful that it grows in most soils, but is happiest in moisture-retentive rich soil in light shade under trees. It delights in leafmold and welcomes an annual mulch of leafmold or compost in late spring. This prevents the roots becoming dry during hot summers. During late autumn, cut down stems to soil level.
Propagation: During autumn or spring lift and divide overgrown clumps. Take care not to damage the roots or to allow them to become dry. Replant them just below the surface.

Below: Polygonatum x hybridum *This easily-grown and undemanding herbaceous perennial is superb at the fringe of a wild garden, or perhaps planted near the edge of a patio. It has the bonus of bearing sweetly-scented flowers.*

Sanguinaria canadensis 'Flore Pleno'

Bloodroot

This hardy herbaceous perennial from Eastern North America is ideal for a rock garden or woodland planting. During spring and early summer it produces white flowers that open to about 1¹/₂in (4cm) wide. These are followed by grayish-green, hand-like and lobed leaves that die down by late summer.
Height: 5-6in (13-15cm)
Spread: 12-15in (30-38cm)
Hardiness: Zones 3-9
Cultivation: Well-drained but moisture-retentive soil is needed, in full sun or slight shade. Once established plants are best left undisturbed. Set new plants in position in autumn or spring, or immediately after the flowers fade.
Propagation: Lift and divide overgrown plants immediately after flowering.

Above: Sanguinaria canadensis 'Flore Pleno' *The pure white double flowers are highlighted by the grayish-green, lobed leaves. It is ideal in a rock garden. Once established leave undisturbed.*

Sanguinaria canadensis 'Flore Pleno' gains its common name from the red sap that exudes from the thick, fleshy roots. North American Indians used the juices to color their bodies and to stain domestic articles.

Saxifraga cotyledon

Jungfrau Saxifrage

This graceful, hardy evergreen rock garden plant seldom fails to create interest with its mid- to late summer plume-like sprays of pure white, ½in (12mm) wide flowers. The sprays can be up to 2ft (60cm) long.
Height: 1½-2ft (45-60cm)
Spread: 12-15in (30-38cm)
Hardiness: Zones 4-7
Cultivation: Good drainage is essential. Plant in lime-free soil in partial shade.
Propagation: After the flowers

white, frothy-looking flowers at the tops of arching stems. These are clothed with glossy, lance-shaped, light green leaves.
Height: 2½-3ft (75-90cm)
Spread: 3-4ft (0.9-1.2m)
Hardiness: Zones 3-7

Right: Smilacina racemosa
During late spring and early summer, fluffy, white flowers appear at the tops of arching stems. Eventually, this North American hardy herbaceous plant forms a dominant feature in a woodland or naturalized setting.

fade in late summer, lift and divide overgrown clumps. Large pieces can be planted straight into a rock garden, but small pieces are best potted-up and placed in a cold frame during winter to give them protection.

Smilacina racemosa

False Solomon's Seal · False Spikenard · Treacleberry

This North American hardy herbaceous perennial is superb when naturalized in a woodland garden. During late spring and early summer it develops 4in (10cm) long heads of creamy-

Above: Saxifraga cotyledon 'Southside Seedling' *This superb plant never fails to capture attention. It is an excellent crevice plant, creating a display of color from quite small plantings.*

Cultivation: Deeply cultivated, rich, moisture-retentive slightly acid soil in light shade is needed. Eventually, it spreads to form a large clump. In early winter, cut the stems down to soil level. It prefers cool weather.
Propagation: Lift and divide large clumps of plants in the autumn, replanting the young parts from around the outside of the clump.

Zantedeschia aethiopica

Florist's Calla · Garden Calla · Calla Lily · Pig Lily · Trumpet Lily

This unusual South African, rhizomatous and deciduous perennial is not hardy outside in most areas. During spring and early summer it displays 5-9in (13-23cm) long, white, fleshy, flower heads that resemble those of arum lilies. Botanically, these are spathes (modified leaves), and are borne at the tops of long, fleshy, stiff stems. The proper flowers are yellow and borne in the insides of the white spathes. The hardiest variety is 'Crowborough', and this is the one mainly grown outdoors. 'Little Gem' is a dwarf variety.
Height: 1½-3ft (45-90cm)
Spread: 2-3ft (60-90cm)
Hardiness: Zones 9-10
Cultivation: Because this plant is not fully hardy, select a warm, sheltered, south-facing position, in the lee of a wall or where it can gain protection from other plants. Moisture-retentive soil is best, although 'Crowborough', once established, grows well in dry soils. Set the plants in position in late spring, covering them with 4in (10cm) of soil. In areas with very cold winters, lift the roots in autumn and overwinter them in large pots in a greenhouse.

Saxifraga cotyledon 'Southside Seedling' has long stems of cascading flowers which look at their best when highlighted against large rocks. Don't cramp them with other plants - it spoils their display.

Smilacina racemosa is ideal in a lightly-shaded woodland setting, but take care not to crowd it with large plants. A backdrop of the yellow-flowered *Enkianthus campanulatus*, redreined enkianthus creates a pleasing combination.

Alternatively, cover the roots in winter with a thick mulch of leafmold or compost.

Propagation: During spring, lift plants and remove offsets from around their bases. Divide large plants at the same time.

Above: Zantedeschia aethiopica 'Crowborough' *A fairly hardy calla lily, with beautiful heads of white flowers during summer. It harmonizes superbly with astilbes and moisture-loving primulas.*

Further plants to consider

Anacyclus depressus
Mt. Atlas Daisy
Height: 2-3in (5-7.5cm)   Spread: 4in (10cm)
Hardiness: Zones 6-8
A low-growing perennial that bears white daisy-like flowers in summer. It needs a loose, well-drained alkaline soil in full sun.

Anemone blanda 'White Splendor'
Windflower
Height: 6-8in (15-20cm)   Spread: 6-8in (15-20cm)
Hardiness: Zones 4-8
An early spring tuber with low, daisy-like flowers and delicate airy foliage.

Anemone nemorosa
Wood Anemone
Height: 6-8in (15-20cm)   Spread: 6in (15cm)
Hardiness: Zones 4-8
This hardy herbaceous perennial is ideal for naturalizing in a lightly shaded woodland garden. The 1in (2.5cm) wide white flowers are borne in mid- to late spring.

Cimicifuga simplex
Kamchatka Bugbane
Height: 3-4ft (0.9-1.2m)   Spread: 3-4ft (0.9-1.2m)
Hardiness: Zones 3-8
A fern-like perennial with white flower spikes in late summer. Prefers moist soil and light shade.

Convallaria majalis
Lily of the Valley
Height: 6-8in (15-20cm)   Spread: 12-18in (30-45cm)
Hardiness: Zones 2-9
A hardy, invasive, herbaceous perennial with elliptic, midgreen leaves and white, waxy flowers during late spring and into early summer.

Echinacea pallida
Pale Coneflower
Height: 3-4ft (0.9-1.2m)   Spread: 1-2ft (0.3-0.6m)
Hardiness: Zones 4-8
A hardy perennial, native to the meadows of south central United States. The creamy-white, daisy-like blooms have a dark center and appear in summer.

Phlox stolonifera 'Bruce's white'
Creeping Phlox
Height: 6-12in (15-30cm)   Spread: 9-12in (23-30cm)
Hardiness: Zones 2-8
This white-flowered, shade-tolerant hardy phlox is ideal for the edge of woodlands or under trees.

Zantedeschia aethiopica 'Crowborough' is attractive when planted within the protection of a small hedge formed of box (*Buxus sempervirens* 'Suffruticosa'). The small, pale green leaves of the box harmonize with the white spathes.

CHAPTER THREE

CONTAINER GARDENING

Houses and patios with flowers growing in windowboxes, in tubs, hanging baskets and other containers are rather like cakes with large glossy cherries on top; they are the first features to capture attention. They sparkle and show off their colors. Few containers are successfully planted solely with single-color flowers; usually, a colorful, bright mixture looks best and creates color over a longer period. However, some colors can be the key to an impressive display and benefit from being displayed against certain background colors. For instance, strong yellows look extra bright and distinguished against white backgrounds. Zinnias and marigolds interplanted with red geraniums are a delight against white walls. Dark backgrounds also show off yellow flowers to advantage, but the containers are best painted white to give extra contrast. Red-flowered plants look vibrant against a white wall – scarlet flowers in particular can look very dramatic. Pink-flowered container plants look superb against a gray background and in such a position, plants with deep red flowers can also be used to effect.

White walls provide color-contrasts for blue flowers. Try a mixed planting of deep blue grape hyacinths and yellow-flowered primroses in a large tub positioned against a white wall. White-flowered plants are not candidates for display against a white wall. Instead, red walls offer the greatest color-contrast, but can be too dominant.

A wall-basket is similar in appearance to a hanging basket which has been cut vertically in half and secured to a wall. Position the basket so that its top is about 3ft (90cm) above the ground. These baskets are admirable for displaying plants, but remember that they need regular watering during summer and that some water will trickle down the wall. On brick-surfaced walls this is not a problem, but if it is a painted wall then the water may eventually create stains. However, this can be prevented by lining the basket with heavy plastic and piercing holes in its base and towards the front.

Left: Flowers *in tubs and hanging baskets are especially welcome on patios and terraces. They are a delight in small gardens.*

Above: **Amaranthus caudatus** *This tender annual is worthy of a place in any garden. The long tassels of crimson flowers are borne from mid-summer to autumn. It looks superb when planted in large containers.*

Amaranthus caudatus

Love-lies-bleeding · Tassel Flower

A beautiful tropical tender annual with large light green leaves and drooping 15-18in (38-45cm) long tassels of crimson flowers from midsummer to autumn. In late summer and autumn the leaves and stems take on a bronze or crimson appearance. It is ideal for mixed borders and beds of annuals, or for planting in large containers such as tubs. The dramatic tassels last for weeks.
Height: 3-4ft (90cm-1.2m)
Spread: 15-18in (38-45cm)
Cultivation: Fertile, moisture-retentive and well-cultivated soil in a sunny position assures success. When grown in containers, use loam-based potting soil.
Propagation: During midspring, sow seeds ⅛in (3mm) deep in loam-based seed starting mix in 59°F (15°C). When they are large enough to handle, prick off the seedlings into pots or flats of loam-based potting soil and place them in a cold frame to harden off. Plant them out in the garden or in containers when all risk of frost has passed. When grown in a bed of annuals, the seeds can be sown in place during late spring. Thin the seedlings to 15-18in (38-45cm) apart when big enough to handle.

Camellia japonica

Of all tub-grown plants this hardy evergreen shrub is one of the most spectacular. The dark green, leathery leaves taper to a point, while the 3-6in (7.5-15cm) wide flowers appear from late winter to late spring, in a color range from white to pink, red and purple. At one time this plant was thought to be quite tender, but it has since proved to be relatively hardy, although the flowers are easily damaged by early-morning sun glancing on those covered with a layer of frost.
Height: 6-8ft (1.8-2.4m) in tubs

Camellia japonica varieties are numerous and there is often confusion about the correct name. It is best to see the plant in bloom before buying.

Above: **Camellia japonica** *This distinctive shrub with early season flowers is a delight on a sheltered patio or terrace. It also does well in a city garden where outdoor space is limited. Camellias provide year-round beauty, with both evergreen foliage and flowers.*

Spread: 4-6in (10-15cm)
Hardiness: Zones 5-9
Cultivation: Light, well-drained but moisture-retentive soil suits it. When grown in the garden, the bulbs should be set in position, 5-6in (13-15cm) deep, in autumn. This is usually best done after summer-flowering plants have been removed. Set the bulbs about 6in (15cm) apart. Leave them in position until after they flower, then lift and replant them in an out-of-the-way position where they can be left undisturbed to bloom during the following and successive years in a naturalized display. When grown in containers, use loam-based potting soil, setting the bulbs 5-6in (13-15cm) deep and the same distance apart. Plant the bulbs during autumn. When grown in small-area containers take care to ensure that the soil does not alternately freeze and thaw during the winter. After flowering, replant among shrubs.
Propagation: Buy fresh, healthy bulbs each year for replanting.

Spread: 5-6ft (1.5-1.8m) in tubs.
Hardiness: Zones 7-9
Cultivation: Camellias in containers need to be planted in large tubs. Use a well-drained compost, such as three parts peat, two of loam and one of sharp sand. Ensure the base of the tub is pierced with several holes and a thick layer of coarse drainage material placed over them. Position the tub out of cold winds and direct early morning sunshine. They may be grown in the North but must be brought indoors during winter, preferably into a cool greenhouse.
Propagation: During mid- to late summer, take 3-4in (7.5-10cm) long cuttings, inserting them in pots containing equal parts peat and sharp sand. Keep at 15°F (13°C). When the cuttings are rooted, pot them up into lime-free compost. Although it is normally easier to increase this plant by layering low shoots, this is nearly impossible when it is grown in a tub.

Hyacinthus orientalis

Hyacinth · Dutch Hyacinth · Common Hyacinth

Most gardeners and houseplant enthusiasts are familiar with these beautifully-scented bulbs that are equally at home in raised beds, tubs and windowboxes, as well as in spring-bedding schemes in borders. They can also be forced to flower during winter and early spring indoors, but specially prepared bulbs are needed. The true species is no longer generally grown and it is the larger-flowered Dutch hyacinths that are commonly seen. These have elegant, scented, 4-6in (10-15cm) high spires of wax-like flowers in a wide color range. Pink and red varieties include 'Amsterdam' (salmon-pink), 'Anne Marie' (clear pink), 'Jan Bois' (cerise-pink), 'Pink Pearl' (pink) and 'Princess Margaret' (pale pink).
Height: 6-9in (15-23cm)

Below: **Hyacinthus orientalis**
Many of these bulbs are suitable for growing indoors, while some are ideal for planting in containers on patios and terraces, or for using in formal spring-bedding displays.

Hyacinthus orientalis does well in a large tub, in combination with other spring-flowering bulbs. Pink hyacinths mix well in tubs and window-boxes with red species tulips, grape hyacinths and yellow crocuses.

Petunia x hybrida

Common Garden Petunia

A half-hardy annual that can be used in containers as well as for bedding schemes in the garden. The large trumpet-shaped flowers appear from mid- to late summer and often into autumn, and are available in a wide color range, including bicolors. They also come in singles and doubles, plain and frilled, and cascading varieties. These include 'White Cascade' (ideal for hanging baskets), 'Peppermint Daddy' (apple blossom pink) and 'Appleblossom' (an All-American winner with coral blooms).
Height: 6-12in (15-30cm)
Spread: 9-15in (23-38cm)
Cultivation: Light, well-drained and moderately-rich potting soil is best for containers. Excessively rich potting mixture encourages lush growth at the expense of flowers.
Propagation: During late winter and early spring, sow seeds lightly and thinly in loam-based seed starting mix in 59°F (15°C). After germination, and when large enough to handle, prick off the seedlings into flats or pots of loam-based potting soil. Set into the garden when all risk of frost has passed.

Top: Petunia x hybrida
The large trumpet-shaped heads of this Argentinean half-hardy annual are a delight in all types of containers, from windowboxes and tubs to hanging baskets.

Above: Zinnia eiegans
Large-flowered and tall varieties can be grown in big tubs, but it is the small types that are better for windowboxes. Also, these smaller types are easier to blend with other container plants.

Left: Salvia splendens
The bright scarlet flower spikes of this tender annual contrast well with its dark foliage. It is ideal for summer-bedding schemes, as well as for planting in containers and windowboxes.

Salvia splendens

Scarlet Salvia

A well-known Mexican tender annual for use in summer-bedding schemes and containers, from tubs to windowboxes. It is a plant with bright-green tooth-edged foliage and 1½-2in (4-5cm) long scarlet flowers which are themselves surrounded by scarlet bracts. Flowering is over a long period, from midsummer to the frosts of autumn. Varieties include white, scarlet, purple, and salmon flowers, such as 'Hall of Fame' (brilliant scarlet with white streaks), 'Flamenco' (deep red), 'Pirate' (fiery red), 'Blaze of Fire' (bright scarlet) and 'Carabiniere' (intense scarlet).
Height: 12-15in (30-38cm)
Spread: 12-15in (30-38cm)

The name **petunia** is derived from the Brazilian *petun*, meaning tobacco, and refers to the petunia's connection with the tobacco plant. Both belong to the same plant family, the Solanaceae.

Salvia splendens, with its scarlet flowers, is an obvious color-contrasting candidate for summer-bedding schemes. Whites, light blues and silver-leaved plants are excellent companions.

Cultivation: Ordinary well-drained garden soil and a sunny position assure success. Pinching out the tips of the growing shoots when the plants are 3in (7.5cm) high encourages bushiness.

Propagation: During late winter and early spring sow seeds ¼in (6mm) deep in loam-based seed starting mix at 68°F (20°C). When they are large enough to handle, prick out the seedlings into flats of loam-based potting soil and slowly harden off in a cold frame. Plant out into the garden after all risk of frost has passed.

Zinnia elegans

Common Zinnia · Youth-and-old-Age

This well known tender Mexican annual normally grows to 2-2½ft (60-75cm). It is therefore the lower growing types, at 6-15in (15-38cm) high, that are better for window-boxes. The taller types can also be grown, but are best reserved for large tubs, and then in a massed display. The lower forms are often in mixed colors as well as single types. Those in pink and red include 'Peter Pan Red' (red) and 'Rose Starlight' (rich salmon rose).

Height: 6in-2½ft (15-75cm)
Spread: 9-12in (23-30cm)
Cultivation: Well-drained loam-based soil is needed. To ensure that the soil in tubs and window-boxes does not dry out during summer, water your zinnias regularly. A sunny and sheltered position suits them, and pinching out the tips of young plants encourages bushiness. Remove dead flowers to encourage the development of further ones.

Propagation: During early spring sow seeds ¼in (6mm) deep in trays of loam-based seed starting mix, kept at 59°F (15°C). When they are large enough to handle, prick out the seedlings into flats or pots and slowly harden them off in a cold frame. Plant them out into containers as soon as all risk of frost has passed.

Further plants to consider

Begonia semperflorens
Wax Begonia
Height: 6-9in (15-23cm)   Spread: 6-9in (15-23cm)
This well-known summer-bedding begonia is really a greenhouse perennial, but is usually grown as a tender annual. It can also be used in containers on patios and terraces. It is a bushy, much-branched plant with glossy bright-green or bronze leaves and pink, red or white flowers from mid- to late summer and often into autumn. Red and pink varieties include 'Brandy' (clear pink with bronze foliage), 'Gin' (rose pink with bronze leaves), 'Vodka' (scarlet with bronze foliage), 'Linda' (deep rose with green leaves) and 'Thousand Wonders' (scarlet with green foliage).

Impatiens: Hybrid Varieties
Height: 6-18in (15-45cm)   Spread: 6-15in (15-38cm)
These abundantly flowering half-hardy perennials are often treated as tender annuals for bedding schemes and for growing in tubs and windowboxes. Grow in moist, shady areas. In mild climates they may be grown as a perennial. Shear regularly to avoid leggy growth. Varieties include 'Blitz' (12in/30cm tall) in red and rose selections, and 'Accent' (6in/15cm tall) available in deep pink, red, rose, and scarlet.

Pelargonium peltatum
Ivy-leaf Geranium
Trailing stems up to 3ft (90cm) long.
A superb pelargonium for hanging baskets or the fronts of window-boxes or tubs. Red and pink forms include 'Mexican Beauty' (semi-double crimson), 'Barbary Coast' (semi-double, pinkish-white), 'Desrumeaux' (brilliant pink), 'Sugar Baby' (soft pink), and 'Summer Showers' (shades of rose, red, lavender, plum, and white).

Pelargonium x hortorum
Zonal Geranium
Height 1-3ft (30-90cm)   Spread: 1½-2½ft (45-75cm)
This tender perennial is usually grown as an annual for tubs and window boxes. Grow from seeds or over-winter cuttings indoors. The showy clusters of flowers are available in colors ranging from pink and rose to scarlet.

Roses – Miniature Types
These are just like normal roses, but a great deal smaller. The almost thornless branches bear double or semi-double flowers ¾-1½in (18-40mm) wide in clusters during midsummer. Many continue to flower intermittently for much of summer. These miniatures are suitable for deep windowboxes or tubs. Even within this group there is a wide range of sizes, from those at 9in (23cm) to varieties at 12-15in (30-38cm). The color range is wide and includes white, yellow, orange and purple. Pink and red forms include 'cup cake' (12-15in/30-38cm, double, soft pink), 'Red Cascade' (9-12in/23-30cm, double, cascading, scarlet), and 'Minnie Pearl' (18-24in/45-60cm, double, pearl pink, good for cutting).

Zinnias are named after the German botanist Johann Gotfried Zinn (1727-1759). *Zinnia elegans,* originally native to Mexico, comes in a wide color range, including striking red and pink forms.

Cultivation: Well-drained, fertile soil and a sheltered sunny position suit it. Spring is the best time to set the plants out in the open soil. You should cover the crowns with 2in (5cm) of soil. In containers, use a free-draining, soil-based potting mix. After flowering, cut the stems down to soil level and cover the base of the plant with straw or light mulch. Plants in containers are best placed in a cold, frost-free greenhouse during winter, both to protect the crowns from frost and to prevent the soil from becoming too wet.

Propagation: The easiest method is to lift and divide overgrown clumps in mid- to late spring. Take care not to damage the roots.

Convolvulus tricolor

Dwarf Morning Glory

This beautiful hardy bushy annual from Southern Europe has dark green wide lance-shaped leaves and rich blue trumpet-shaped 1½in (4cm) wide flowers with yellow or white throats from mid- to late summer. The dwarf morning glory is an old-fashioned plant that deserves a comeback. Several superb varieties are available, 'Blue Ensign' with a trailing habit and deep blue flowers displaying yellow and white centers. The shorter varieties include 'Rainbow Flash' at 6in (15cm) high. This is a new dwarf hybrid in a wide range of colors including blue, purple, pink and rose.

Height: 12-15in (30-38cm)
Spread: 8-10in (20-25cm)
Cultivation: Ordinary well-drained fertile garden soil and a sunny position suits them. Select a sheltered position, and the taller-growing types may require support from twiggy sticks. These delightful plants make a colorful splash in windowboxes and containers, or at the fronts of borders. And of course they can also be grown in annual borders.

Propagation: When growing for window-boxes or the fronts of borders, sow seeds in early spring in pots of sterile potting soil at

Above: Agapanthus campanulatus
This is a beautiful plant for the garden as well as in large containers, where it quickly forms a strongly colored focal point.

Agapanthus campanulatus

African Lily

This fleshy-rooted nearly hardy herbaceous plant from Natal has midgreen, sword-like leaves that arise from its base. During late summer, it reveals pale blue flowers in crowded, rounded heads, borne at the tops of long, stiff stems above the foliage. Several varieties extend the color range from white to amethyst. Most gardeners will need to treat *Agapanthus* as a pot plant, moving it to a frost-free location during the winter.

Height: 2-2½ft (60-75cm)
Spread: 15-18in (38-45cm)
Hardiness: Zones 8-10

Agapanthus campanulatus needs a large container all to itself – do not try mixing it with bulbous plants. These are best planted in separate containers and stood around the *Agapanthus*.

Convolvulus tricolor brings a distinctive brightness to borders, happily blending with many annuals such as marigolds (*Tagetes erecta* and *T. patula*).

59°F (15°C). When they are large enough to handle, prick out the seedlings into flats of potting soil and harden them off in a cold frame. Plant them out when all risk of frost has passed. Alternatively, sow seeds in late spring where the plants are to flower, ½in (12mm) deep. When large enough to handle, thin the seedlings to 9in (23cm) apart. For larger plants, sow seeds indoors in early winter.

Right: Convolvulus tricolor 'Rainbow Flash' *This dwarf hybrid produces bright new flowers each morning, and is ideal for window-boxes and containers. Other varieties are a good choice for annual and mixed borders.*

Felicia bergeriana

Kingfisher Daisy

This stunningly attractive half-hardy annual has a mat-forming habit and gray, hairy, lance-shaped leaves. The ¾in (18mm) wide, steel-blue flowers with gold centers appear from mid- to late summer. It is ideal for growing in containers, such as tubs and window-boxes, as well as for positioning as an edging to paths or in a rock garden.
Height: 6in (15cm)
Spread: 6-8in (15-20cm)
Cultivation: Well-drained garden soil and a sheltered position in full sun suits it. When grown in containers use a well-drained potting soil.
Propagation: From early to mid-spring sow seeds thinly in pots of sterile potting soil at 59°F (15°C). Prick out the seedlings into flats of potting soil and harden them off in a cold frame. Set the plants out in the garden or in containers during late spring, after all risk of frost has passed.

Right: Felicia bergeriana *This is an eye-catching half-hardy annual ideal for growing in containers, as a path edging or in a rock garden. It is a South African plant that requires a sheltered and warm position.*

Felicia bergeriana is neat and dwarf, making it suitable for inclusion in a potpourri of bright annuals in containers. These plants look best when viewed from above, so do not plant them in high window-boxes.

Hyacinthus orientalis

Hyacinth · Dutch Hyacinth

These beautifully-scented bulbs are equally at home whether in spring-bedding schemes or in raised beds, tubs and window-boxes. The true species is no longer generally grown and therefore it is the larger-flowered Dutch hyacinths that are commonly seen. These have elegant, scented, 4-6in (10-15cm) high spires of wax-like flowers in a wide range of colors, including blue.

Height: 6-9in (15-23cm)
Spread: 4-6in (10-15cm)
Hardiness: Zones 3-7, may be grown as annual in Zones 8-10.
Cultivation: Light, well-drained but moisture-retentive soil suits it, and when grown in a garden the bulbs can be set in position, 5-6in (13-15cm) deep, in autumn. This is usually done after summer-flowering plants have been removed from the border or container. The bulbs are left in position until after they flower, then lifted and re-planted in an out-of-the-way position where they can be left undisturbed to flower during the following and successive years. When grown in containers, use a soil-based potting mix, setting the bulbs 5-6in (13-15cm) deep and the same distance apart. Plant the bulbs during autumn. When grown in small-volume containers, take care to ensure that the potting mix does not become totally saturated with water and then freeze for long periods during winter. Large containers usually need less care and attention. After flowering, the bulbs can be lifted and planted among shrubs.
Propagation: Although hyacinths can be raised from seeds, they take up to six years to produce flowering-sized bulbs by this method and even then large-flowered types do not always come true. It is therefore much easier to buy flowering-sized bulbs each year. Make sure you buy your bulbs from a reputable supplier who can guarantee their quality.

Above: **Hyacinthus orientalis** *The fragrance and colors of these flowers can be better appreciated when they are grown in containers or raised beds. Such beds are easily maintained by gardeners who are in wheelchairs or have infirmities that prevent them from bending. But take care not to make the beds too wide or the wrong height.*

Left: **Hyacinthus orientalis** **'Ostara'** *This is a deep purple-blue hyacinth that produces a dense sea of color in borders or containers. It also gives off a wonderful scent.*

Hyacinthus orientalis can be mixed with many bulbs, such as grape hyacinths, species tulips and yellow crocuses. Another combination is blue crocuses, grape hyacinths, species tulips and *Narcissus cyclamineus* 'February Gold'.

Lobelia erinus

Edging Lobelia

This well-known reliable border edging and container plant is a half-hardy perennial invariably grown as a half-hardy annual. It has light green leaves, with masses of ¼in (6mm) wide blue or white flowers from early summer to the frosts of autumn. There are both trailing and compact border edging varieties, in a range of colors. The border-edging compact types include 'Cambridge Blue' (pale blue), 'Crystal Palace' (dark blue) and ' Mrs. Clibran' (brilliant blue). Trailing types include

'Blue Cascade' (Cambridge blue) and 'Sapphire' (brilliant blue). Some varieties, such as 'Color Cascade Mix', reveal flowers in shades of blue, mauve, red and rose.

Height: 4-9in (10-23cm)
Spread: 4-6in (10-15cm)
Cultivation: Fertile, moist garden soil in a sheltered and sunny position in light shade suits it. In containers use well-drained soil-based mix.

Propagation: During late winter and early spring, sow seeds thinly and shallowly in pots of sterile seed starting mix at 59°F (15°C). As soon as the seedlings can be handled,

Above: **Lobelia erinus** *These are indispensable half-hardy annuals for both containers and the garden. When growing them in containers, take care that the potting soil does not dry out during summer, especially when in shallow urns that hold relatively small amounts of soil.*

prick them out into flats of potting soil and harden them off in a cold frame. Move the plants to the garden when all risk of frost is over. To create an instant display of color, plant lobelias in pots in a greenhouse.

Lobelia erinus blends with a wealth of other plants. A happy combination for containers is the pink-flowered fibrous-rooted *Begonia semperflorens* and *Lobelia erinus* 'Cambridge Blue'.

Lobelia erinus is a good companion for geraniums in both containers and borders. Try pink pelargoniums with dark blue lobelia, or light or dark blue lobelia with French marigolds (*Tagetes patula*) that display strong, rich colors.

Above: **Myosotis alpestris** *The deep blue flowers of this forget-me-not form a dense, low carpet. It is ideal for bringing color to a rock garden or for planting in combination with spring-flowering yellow or orange bulbs. It is traditionally used as an underplanting for tulips.*

Myosotis alpestris

(*Myosotis rupicola/Myosotis sylvatica*)
Forget-me-not

This well-known hardy perennial, best treated as a hardy biennial, is ideal for planting in a container, a rock garden or a bed with spring-flowering bulbs where it forms a dense blanket of fragrant azure-blue flowers from late spring to midsummer. Several exciting forms are available, including 'Victoria' (gentian blue) and 'Blue Ball' (rich indigo-blue).
Height: 4-8in (10-20cm)
Spread: 6-9in (15-23cm)
Hardiness: Zones 3-8
Cultivation: Moderately fertile well-drained but moisture-retentive soil in light shade is best.
Propagation: During midsummer sow seeds ¼in (6mm) deep in a well-prepared seedbed. When they are large enough to handle, plant out the seedlings 6in (15cm) apart in nursery rows. If originally sown thinly they can just be thinned to 6in (15cm) apart. Keep the rows weeded and in autumn plant out into their flowering positions.

Right: **Myosotis alpestris**
This half-hardy perennial is just as good in containers as in a border perhaps as an edging. Even on its own it creates a dense splash of color early in the year.

Myosotis alpestris is a short-lived perennial, but it self-sows. These plants will tolerate full sun in the North if provided with plenty of moisture.

Further plants to consider

Browallia speciosa
Height: 8-12in (20-30cm)   Spread: 12-16in (30-40cm)
A long-blooming tender annual for shady borders or hanging baskets. Will tolerate sun in mild climates. Covered with 1½ (3.5cm) wide star-shaped blue flowers. Varieties include 'Blue Bells' (violet-blue) and 'Major' (dark blue).

Campanula isophylla
Italian Bellflower · Star of Bethlehem
Height: 6in (15cm)   Spread: 1½-2ft (45-60cm)
A tender trailing dwarf perennial, most often used indoors as a house plant or outside in hanging baskets. The heart-shaped midgreen leaves are borne amid a mass of tangled trailing stems, with 1in (2.5cm) wide star-shaped blue flowers appearing in late summer and into autumn; overwinter indoors.

Crocus chrysanthus
Golden Crocus
Height: 3in (7.5cm)   Spread: 2½in (6.5cm)
Hardiness: Zones 4-9
This delightful spring-flowering bulb brings color to containers as well as to rock gardens. The species type is golden-yellow, but there are several blue or mauve forms, such as 'Blue Pearl' (pale blue on the outside, white within) and 'Lady Killer' (purple-blue, edged white).

Crocus vernus
Dutch Crocus
Height: 4-5in (10-13cm)   Spread: 3in (7.5cm)
Hardiness: Zones 3-9
This spring-flowering bulb is the parent of the large Dutch crocuses widely seen in gardens and containers. Blue, mauve and purple forms include 'Remembrance' (silvery-purple), 'Vanguard' (soft violet-blue) and 'Purpureus Grandiflorus' (purplish-blue).

Petunia x hybrida
Common Garden Petunia
Height: 10-15in (25-38cm)   Spread: 12-15in (30-38cm)
A half-hardy annual, used in containers as well as for bedding schemes in the garden. Grandiflora Types have large, showy blossoms. Smaller blooms but better disease resistant are exhibited in the Multiflora varieties. The large trumpet-shaped flowers from mid- to late summer and often into autumn, are available in a wide color range, including mauve and blue. Among these are 'Blue Frost' (deep violet-blue with a pure white edge) and 'Blue Filaire' (blue). There are also many varieties with mixed colours including blue, violet and mauve.

Viola x wittrockiana
Pansy
Height: 6-9in (15-23cm)   Spread: 9-12in (23-30cm)
Perennial grown as hardy annual. Blooms, 2-5in (5-12.5cm) wide from early spring to summer. Many blue varieties available.

Myosotis alpestris also looks splendid when planted in a spring-flowering bedding display with creamy-yellow tulips and an occasional edging tuft of the lemon-gold *Aurinia saxatilis* 'Citrinum'.

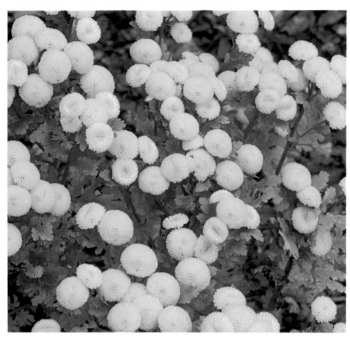

Chrysanthemum parthenium

Feverfew

This hardy herbaceous perennial is grown as an annual, with pungent light green leaves and small white flowers, ³⁄₄in (18mm) wide, from mid- to late summer. Several old and trusted varieties are available, such as 'Golden Ball' which grows to 10in (25cm) and has golden-yellow double flowers on compact plants. 'Snow Ball' is another good variety, up to 1ft (30cm) high, with masses of ivory-white double flowers. 'Gold Star' at 8in (20cm) has yellow-centered flowers, surrounded by white petals. Other varieties reach 2¹⁄₂ft (75cm), but it is the low-growing types that are best for border edging and containers such as tubs, troughs and windowboxes.
Height: 9in-2¹⁄₂ft (23-75cm)
Spread: 9in-2ft (23-60cm)
Hardiness: Zones 6-8
Cultivation: Feverfew likes well drained, fertile, light soil in full sun or light shade. In containers, use

Above: Chrysanthemum parthenium 'Golden Ball'
This is a useful compact annual for the edges of borders and tubs, as well as windowboxes and troughs. The bright button-like flowers bring life to the garden.

a good potting soil and, to encourage bushiness, nip out the initial flower buds.
Propagation: To produce plants for growing in containers, sow seeds ¹⁄₈in (3mm) deep in flats of seed starting mix in late winter or early spring. Keep the trays at 59°F (15°C). As soon as the seedlings are large enough to handle, prick them off into flats of potting soil and harden them off in a cold frame. Plant them out into the garden in late spring. Alternatively, sow seeds directly into the border where the plants are to flower. Make shallow drills in the soil during late spring, lightly covering the seeds. When large enough to handle, thin the seedlings to 10in (25cm) apart.

Coreopsis tinctoria

Golden Coreopsis

This is one of the best known hardy annuals, bringing a profusion of color to the garden from mid- to late summer. The 2in (5cm) wide, daisy-shaped, bright yellow flowers are borne on stiff stems. The plant is just as good in containers on a patio as in the garden with other annuals. However, the dwarf varieties, at 9-12in (23-30cm), are better in containers than the taller types, at 2-3ft (60-90cm). 'Dwarf Dazzler' at 1ft (30cm) and 'Dwarf Mixed' at 9in (23cm) are best in containers, while 'All Double Mixed' and 'Single Mixed' at 2¹⁄₂-3ft (75-90cm) are best in a border. The lower ones can be used in borders, but towards the front.
Height: 9in-3ft (23-90cm) range
Spread: 6-10in (15-25cm) range
Cultivation: Well-drained fertile soil in a sunny position ensures success.
Propagation: When grown in a hardy annual border, sow seeds thinly in drills during spring and early summer in the positions where the plants are to flower. When they are large enough to handle, thin out the seedlings. However, when grown for use in containers, sow seeds in early

---

Chrysanthemum parthenium 'Golden Ball' suits formal bedding schemes, set as an edging to *Pelargonium* 'Masterpiece', with its double orange flowers and tricolored foliage. For added height use *Senecio maritima* as a "dot" plant.

Coreopsis tinctoria is available in a wide range of heights, suitable for a variety of positions: front and middle of borders, edging to paths and borders, and in containers. For a quick display, rapidly covering the soil, set the plants closer together.

spring in seed starting mix kept at 61°F (16°C). When the seedlings are large enough to handle, prick them out into pots, five to a 6in (15cm) container, and harden them off in a cold frame. Plant them into containers in the garden during late spring and early summer.

Left: **Coreopsis tinctoria 'Dwarf Dazzler'** *A beautiful and reliable dwarf form with golden and crimson flowers through much of summer, this is a useful plant for towns and cities with pollution problems.*

Hypericum olympicum 'Citrinum'

Olympic St. John's-wort

This low-growing, deciduous, mound-like St. John's wort develops 9-12in (23-30cm) high stems clothed with small, gray-green, narrowly oval or oblong stalkless leaves. The bright lemon-yellow five-petalled summer flowers, 2in (5cm) wide, have long, spiky stamens. It is ideal for container culture, as well as the corner of a rock garden or front of a mixed border. It is often wider-spreading than the figures given below; instead of being 1½ft (45cm) in breadth, it may after several years reach 3ft (90cm) wide. At the same time it forms a slightly higher mound.
Height: 9-12in (23-30cm)
Spread: 1-1½ft (30-45cm)
Hardiness: Zones 6-8
Cultivation: Well-drained fertile soil and a sunny position suit this plant.
Propagation: During early and mid-summer, take 2in (5cm) long cuttings, inserting them into pots of equal parts peat and sharp sand. Place these in a cold frame. Pot up the cuttings when rooted into potting soil and overwinter in a cold frame. Transplant them into the garden during spring.

Above: **Hypericum olympicum 'Citrinum'** *The bright lemon-yellow flowers, 2in (5cm) wide, with large central bosses of spiky stamens, are a delight in summer. The flowers appear at the tops of leaf-clad stems.*

Hypericum olympicum 'Citrinum' with its strong yellow flowers, blends with the blue-flowered *Veronica prostrata*. Position it so that the blue flowers are next to the yellow ones of the hypericum.

Mesembryanthemum oculatus 'Lunette'

Fig Marigold

This beautiful early-flowering, low-growing, half-hardy annual boasts bright yellow daisy-like flowers with darker centers. It is ideal for the front of windowboxes and in hanging baskets.

Height: 3-4in (7.5-10cm)
Spread: 6-10in (15-25cm)
Cultivation: It performs best in dry, sandy soils and arid Western climates. It requires full sun and will tolerate cooler climates if grown in poor soil.
Propagation: During spring, sow seeds in trays of seed starting mix

Above: **Mesembryanthemum oculatus 'Lunette'** *A new, early-flowering, half-hardy annual, this variety is ideal for the edge of windowboxes and hanging baskets. It is a bright and reliable plant.*

kept at 65°F (18°C). After germination, prick off the seedlings into boxes or pots, and harden them off in a cold frame. Set the plants 8-9in (20-23cm) apart in the containers. Alternatively, if no heat is available, sow seeds in the open soil where they are to flower during late spring, thinning the seedlings later. However, germination may not be rapid.

Mesembryanthemum oculatus 'Lunette' is ideal for filling bare patches in rock gardens in arid climates, creating color before the permanent plants are fully established. It provides good groundcover, and brings color right up to the edges of rocks and paths.

Sedum spathulifolium

Stonecrop

This Northwest American perennial succulent plant will soon form a dense mat of foliage. The gray-green leaves, borne in fleshy rosettes, are covered during midsummer with 2in (5cm) wide heads of bright yellow flowers on 4in (10cm) stems. The variety 'Cape Blanco' displays silvery-gray foliage. It will not tolerate hot, humid conditions. These plants can be used in containers as well as rock gardens. For a stonecrop more tolerant of humidity, grow *Sedum acre* 'Aureum', a form of the biting stonecrop, native to Western Europe. It is an invasive and mat-forming plant and is best grown in crevices in dry stone walls, where it produces a mass of small mid- to yellow-green leaves. During midsummer, it bears flattened 1-1$\frac{1}{2}$in (2.5-4cm) wide heads of golden-yellow star-like flowers. Its spreading and mat-forming growth habit can be used to create an attractive feature by planting it where it can spread – away from choice rock garden subjects – and underplanting it with miniature bulbs. *Sedum acre* is also known as the wall-pepper, an indication of its natural home.

Height: 2-4in (5-10cm)
Spread: 9-12in (23-30cm)
Hardiness: Zones 4-10
Cultivation: Well-drained garden soil in full sun is best, and although all sedums are relatively drought-resistant, do not allow the soil to become rock hard.
Propagation: The easiest way to increase this plant is to divide overgrown clumps. Plant at almost any time, but spring is best. Alternatively, small pieces which break off soon produce roots when pushed into compost.

Left: **Sedum spathulifollum 'Cape Blanco'** *A distinctive stone-crop, this has silvery-gray leaves and bright yellow flowers during midsummer. It does well in rock gardens and containers, but will not tolerate hot, humid summers.*

Sedum 'Ruby Glow' is just one of many sedums suited to containers. Others include *Sedum cauticolum* with rosy-blush blooms, and *Sedum* 'Vera Jameson'.

Ursinia anethoides

This half-hardy perennial is usually grown as a half-hardy annual. It has daisy-like, brilliant orange-yellow flowers, 2in (5cm) wide, with central purple discs from early to late summer. Several superb varieties are available, including 'Sunstar' with deep orange flowers and dark red central discs, and 'Sunshine', with bright golden-yellow flowers and maroon discs. It does well in borders and containers.

Height: 15-18in (38-45cm)
Spread: 10-12in (25-30cm)
Cultivation: Light, relatively poor soil suits it best, and a position in full sun. It prefers a long, cool growing season.
Propagation: During early spring, sow seeds ⅛in (3mm) deep in trays of seed starting mix kept at 59°C (15°C). When the seedlings are large enough to handle, prick them out into boxes and place them in a cold frame to harden off. In late spring, after all risk of frost has passed, plant them out into a container.

Above: **Ursinia anethoides** *This bright, half-hardy annual with golden-yellow flowers needs plenty of sunshine and a cool growing season. It is admirable for bringing color to hot, sunny patios and terraces, where its flowers create interest over a long period.*

Venidium fastuosum

Cape Daisy

This superb half-hardy annual from South Africa brings color to all gardens, whether in containers or in a border. It has deeply-lobed leaves and stems with a silvery-white texture, and large, rich orange daisy-like flowers, 4in (10cm) wide, from early to late summer. The inner edges of the petals are banded purple-brown, with a central black cone. They are ideal as cut flowers. Another species, *Venidium decurrens*, also native to South Africa, boasts beautiful, large-faced, daisy-like, dark-centered, golden-yellow flowers up to 2½in (6.5cm) wide. It is really a half-hardy perennial but is invariably grown as an annual. Its flowers appear from midsummer to early autumn on plants 10-12in (25-30cm) high and with a similar spread, with deeply-lobed grayish-

Ursinia anethoides is worth planting on its own in a large tub or low urn: its boldly-colored and long-lasting flowers would dominate and subjugate plants set with it. However, in a border it can be planted in small groupings, with bold blues around it.

Above: Tagetes patula *Popularly known as French marigolds, these favorite border flowers make a bold display of bright yellow.*

green leaves. Like *Venidium fastuosum*, it is ideal as a cut-flower for home decoration.
Height: 20-24in (50-60cm)
Spread: 12-15in (30-38cm)
Cultivation: Well-drained, fertile, light soil in containers or borders is essential, and a sunny position.
Propagation: Sow seeds thinly in flats of seed starting mix during early spring. Keep them at 16°C (61°F). When the seedlings are large enough to handle, prick them out into flats or pots of potting soil and harden them off in a cold frame before planting them in containers or a border in late spring, after all risk of frost damage has passed.

Left: Venidium fastuosum
The stunningly attractive 4in (10cm) wide flowers make an ideal feature for a container on a sunny patio or for a border.

Further plants to consider

Calceolaria 'Fothergillii'
Slipperwort · Slipper Flower · Pocketbook Flower
Height: 6in (15cm)   Spread: 6-8in (15-20cm)
Hardiness: Zones 7-9
A hardy perennial, well suited to rock gardens or windowboxes, with yellow pouch-shaped flowers revealing purple-flecked throats. Two other low-growing cultivars are available: 'Golden Bunch' at 8in (20cm) with yellow flowers, and 'Midas' at 8in (20cm) with pure yellow flowers.

Cheiranthus alpinus
(*Erysimum alpinum*)
Alpine Wallflower
Height: 6in (15cm)   Spread: 4-6in (10-15cm)
Hardiness: Zones 3-10
A beautiful, diminutive hardy biennial that can be set at the edge of a container to create extra 'instant' color during early summer. The sulphur-yellow 1/2in (12mm) wide flowers are beautifully fragrant.

Petunia 'Summer Sun'
Height: 12-15in (30-38cm)   Spread: 12-15in (30-38cm)
Ideal for flowering in large containers on patios. Other good yellows include: 'California Girl' and 'Yellow Magic'.

Tagetes erecta
African Marigold · American Marigold
Height: 16-18in (40-45cm)   Spread: 16-18in (40-45cm)
A half-hardy annual, with flowers in shades of hot yellow, orange, and gold from early summer onwards.

Tagetes patula
French Marigold
Height: 10-18in (25-45cm)   Spread: 10-12in (25-30cm)
A smaller marigold than *Tagetes erecta*, also creating a brilliant display. Many cultivars are available in yellows, golds, oranges and bi-colors. A long-lasting cut flower.

Tagetes tenuifolia 'Lemon Gem'
Lemon Gem Marigold
Height: 9in (23cm)   Spread: 9-12in (23-30cm)
A beautiful, small, half-hardy annual with a neat, mound-like habit, clothed with lemon-yellow flowers from early summer onwards. 'Golden Gem', 6in (15cm) has golden flowers.

Zinnia 'Short Stuff'
Height: 6-7in (15-18cm)   Spread: 6-8in (15-20cm)
This hybrid is available in six different colors, including yellow. Its blooms are double, disease-resistant and ideal for containers.

Venidium fastuosum needs white or blue color around it to show off its beautiful flowers. But remember to choose flowers that do not rise above and hide the rich orange blooms.

CONTAINER GARDENING

Above: Arundinaria viridistriata
With its tufted nature and green leaves striped rich yellow, this dwarf bamboo has plenty of eye-appeal. It can be used on even the smallest of patios.

Arundinaria viridistriata

This superb bamboo, often sold as *Arundinaria auricoma* or *Pleioblastus viridistriatus*, is ideal for growing in a container on a patio. It is a hardy, erect, tufted plant with purplish-green stems and green leaves striped rich yellow. Usually, the whole plant assumes a yellowish and light green nature in the spring.
Height: 3-4ft (0.9-1.2m)
Spread: 15-24in (38-60cm)
Hardiness: Zones 8-10
Cultivation: Plant in moisture-retentive soil in a large pot, or eventually, a tub. It requires partial to full shade and a winter mulch in cool climates. Cut out the old canes in autumn to encourage new growth.
Propagation: Divide overgrown plants in early summer, but never when the soil is cold.

Above: Arundinaria nitida *This superb bamboo is eye-catching when planted in either a garden or a tub on a patio. Large wooden tubs are the best containers. Ensure that the soil is well-watered in summer.*

Arundinaria nitida

(*Sinoarundinaria nitida*)

A graceful, fast-growing, hardy bamboo that creates a thicket of greenish-purple canes that mature-to deep purple. The evergreen leaves, about 3½in (8cm) long and ½in (12mm) wide, are hairy on their undersides, with finely-bristled edges. Appropriate to the garden, it also makes an excellent plant for a large tub on a patio.
Height: 8-12ft (2.4-3.6m)

Spread: Forms a large clump
Hardiness: Zones 5-10
Cultivation: Plant in moisture-retentive soil in full sun or light shade. It requires well-drained fertile soil. It may also be used as a screen or specimen or planted by the edge of a pond.
Set new clumps in position only when the soil has warmed up in spring, which may be as late as early summer in cold regions. Keep the young canes well-watered. If they are allowed to become dry they soon suffer. No pruning is needed or even desirable, just allow them to grow naturally.
Propagation: In late spring or early summer, as soon as the soil is warm, lift and divide large clumps. Keep them well-watered until established.

Arundinaria nitida is such a graceful plant that it is known as queen of the arundinaria. As well as being attractive, it produces a gentle rustling sound even in the slightest breeze.

Arundinaria viridistriata is one of the most attractive bamboos. It is eye-catching when planted in a white container and positioned on a patio. Select a shady position and keep the soil moist in summer.

Aucuba japonica 'Variegata'

Japanese Aucuba · Japanese Laurel · Gold Dust Plant

This well-known evergreen shrub (sometimes known as 'Maculata') has an attractive dome-shaped outline, with leathery, somewhat oval, shiny green leaves spotted yellow. During spring it bears insignificant purple flowers, followed in autumn and through to the following spring with clusters of bright red berries.

Height: 4-5ft (1.2-1.5m) in a tub
Spread: 3½-4ft (1-1.2m) in a tub

Hardiness: Zones 7-9
Cultivation: When grown in a border it often reaches 6-10ft (1.8-3m) high and 6-8ft (1.8-2.4m) wide, but in a tub on a patio is reserved in growth. It is such a useful shrub that when young and very small it is grown in cool rooms indoors. Outdoors it thrives in coastal areas, surviving salt spray. No regular pruning is needed, although occasionally a misplaced shoot may need to be removed in spring.
Propagation: In late summer and early autumn take 4-5in (10-13cm) long cuttings. Insert them in equal parts moist peat and sharp sand, and place in a cold frame. When rooted, during the following spring, plant into a nursery bed until well established and large enough to be planted into a tub on a patio. Keep the compost evenly moist to enable the plant to become established in the container.

Below: Aucuba japonica 'Variegata' *The leathery, shiny green leaves, attractively spotted in yellow, seldom fail to attract attention. It is undemanding and can be grown with little trouble - a very 'gardenworthy' shrub.*

Aucuba japonica 'Variegata' is an evergreen shrub that brings color to patios and gardens throughout the year. In spring place pots of bright yellow daffodils around it.

Buxus sempervirens

Common Box

This slow-growing evergreen shrub is popular in its normal form. It is also available in less vigorous, lower-growing forms, such as 'Elegantissima' (densely clothed in small, dark green leaves with irregular creamy-white edges) and 'Suffruticosa' (known as the edging box and widely planted alongside beds, as well as in tubs).
Height: 6-8ft (1.8-2.4m)
Spread: 4-6ft (1.2-1.8m)
Hardiness: Zones 6-9
Cultivation: Plant in any good soil, in full sun or light shade. No regular pruning is needed for the species other than occasionally cutting out misplaced shoots. However, the dwarf types grown as dwarf hedges or in containers need trimming with shears in late summer.
Propagation: During late summer, take 3in (7.5cm) long cuttings. Insert them in equal parts moist peat and sharp sand, and place in

Below: Buxus sempervirens 'Suffruticosa' *This evergreen shrub creates a superb background for other plants on a patio, in particular light-colored variegated plants. It is slightly less hardy than species.*

a cold frame. When rooted, plant into a nursery bed for two or three years before setting in the garden or a tub.

Euonymus fortunei 'Emerald and Gold'

Emerald and Gold Wintercreeper

This evergreen, dwarf and bushy shrub is superb for creating year-round color in a tub, as well as softening the edges of a patio. The small, oval, midgreen leaves are variegated in bright gold and in winter become tinged bronzy-pink. Other beautiful evergreen varieties, differing in height slightly from the above variety, include 'Emerald Cushion' with deep green leaves; 'Silver Queen' with green leaves variegated creamy-white; 'Emerald Gaiety' with a spreading and upright habit and green leaves edged in white; 'Golden Prince' (sometimes known as 'Gold Tip') with new foliage tipped in bright gold; and 'Sunspot' with dark green leaves splashed at their centers with golden-yellow.
Height: 1ft (30cm)
Spread: 15-24in (38-60cm)
Hardiness: Zones 5-9
Cultivation: Well-drained soil and a slightly sheltered position suit this evergreen shrub. A position in full sun or heavy shade. No regular pruning is needed.
Propagation: In late summer take 3-4in (7.5-10cm) long heel-cuttings, inserting them in equal parts moist peat and sharp sand. Place in a cold frame. In sprlng, pot up the rooted cuttings and when established plant into a tub or into the garden.

Left: Euonymus fortunei 'Emerald and Gold' *This hardy, bushy, variegated shrub creates color throughout the year. The small, midgreen leaves are variegated in bright gold.It is at its best when positioned to brighten a shady spot, preferably where the stems can sprawl.*

Buxus sempervirens is the parent of more than fifteen attractive forms, including variegated, pendulous and prostrate types. The dwarf type 'Suffruticosa' has been grown as a border edging for several centuries.

Fatsia japonica

Japanese Fatsia · Paper Plant

This slightly tender evergreen shrub (often grown as a houseplant) benefits from the protection of a south or west-facing wall or fence. The leathery, glossy-green leaves, up to 15in (38cm) wide, have seven to nine large lobes with coarsely-toothed edges. During autumn, milky-white flowers are borne in large, branching heads. The variety 'Moseri' has more compact growth while 'Variegata' has creamy-yellow variegations at the leaf tips.

Height: 6-15ft (1.8-4.5m)
Spread: 6-12ft (1.8-3.6m)
Hardiness: Zones 8-10
Cultivation: Plant in well-drained but moisture-retentive soil in a sheltered position. No regular pruning is needed, other than cutting out misplaced and straggly shoots in spring.
Propagation: Although plants can be raised by sowing seeds in

Above: Fatsia japonica *This distinctive slightly tender evergreen shrub has large leaves that create dignity and quiet in a garden. For success it needs a slightly sheltered position and moisture retentive soil.*

potting soil in spring and placing them in 50-55°F (10-13°C), it is easier to detach sucker-like shoots in spring and to pot them into a loam-based potting soil. Place them in a cold frame. When established plant into the garden.

Euonymus fortunei 'Emerald and Gold' is a sprawling, evergreen, variegated shrub that is ideal for planting in a tub or in a border around a patio. Its spreading nature helps to soften the edges of patios.

Fatsia japonica can be grown outdoors in cool climates if brought in during the winter and treated as a houseplant.

Hebe x andersonii 'Variegata'

This tender, evergreen shrub has soft, light-green leaves edged in cream. It has the bonus of developing 3-5in (7.5-13cm) long, stiffish, tassel-like heads of lavender flowers from mid- to late summer, and even into early autumn. It grows well in a sheltered corner on a patio.
Height: 2-3ft (60-90cm)
Spread: 2-2½ft (60-75cm)
Hardiness: Zones 9-10
Cultivation: Plant in well-drained alkaline, potting soil in a large pot or small tub, and place in a sheltered, sunny position. No regular pruning is needed, other than cutting out misplaced shoots in spring. In cold areas it needs the protection of a conservatory or greenhouse in winter, as it will not withstand severe frosts.
Propagation: In late summer take 3-4in (7.5-10cm) long cuttings from non-flowering shoots. Insert them in equal parts moist peat and sharp sand, and place in a cold frame until rooted.

___

Below: Hebe x andersonii 'Variegata' *Either displayed on its own in a pot on a patio, or in a low grouping with other plants, this tender variegated evergreen plant is well worth growing for its year-round color.*

___

Pieris japonica 'Variegata'

Variegated Japanese Andromeda

A beautiful slow-growing, bushy, evergreen shrub with midgreen leaves, attractively edged yellowish-white. When young they are tinged pink. It has the bonus of developing terminal clusters of drooping lily-of-the-valley-like, white waxy flowers during spring.
Height: 2-2½ft (60-75cm)
Spread: 2½-3ft (75-90cm)
Hardiness: Zones 5-10
Cultivation: Plant in moisture-retentive, acid soil in a medium to

Hebe x andersonii 'Variegata' is superb in a container on a patio, as well as in a small border perhaps alongside a paved area. Choose a pot that harmonizes with the plant.

Above: Pieris japonica 'Variegata'
This slow-growing, variegated, evergreen shrub has midgreen leaves with attractive yellow-white edges. When in a tub do not allow the soil to dry out, especially in summer.

large-sized tub. Position in light shade, with protection from cold winds. No regular pruning is needed.
Propagation: In late summer take 3-4in (7.5-10cm) long cuttings and insert in pots of sandy potting soil. Place in a cold frame. In spring, pot up the rooted cuttings singly into small pots.

Further plants to consider

Hedera helix
English Ivy
Height: Varies with variety   Spread: 2-3ft (0.8-1.2m) in containers
Hardiness: Varies with variety
This well-known ivy has many varieties that are ideal as climbers, but others, especially when young, are superb for planting in windowboxes to create color during summer. When planted at the edges of containers they help to soften sharp outlines, as well as providing color from late spring to the frosts of autumn. Many of these variegated varieties are hardy, but are best placed in a frost-proof conservatory or greenhouse during winter.

Laurus nobilis
Bay Laurel · Sweet Bay
Height: 40ft (12m) in ground   Spread: 30ft (9m) in ground
Hardiness: Zones 8-10
An evergreen shrub whose aromatic, dark green leaves are often used for culinary purposes. If left unpruned, it will form a conical bush. In the North, it should be planted in a container and overwintered outdoors.

Salvia officinalis 'Tricolor'
Tricolor Sage
Height: 15-18in (38-45cm)   Spread: 15-18in (38-45cm)
Hardiness: Zones 5-9
When in a tub, this hardy aromatic shrub reaches the above size, but in a border is slightly larger. This variegated plant, related to the common sage, has grayish-green leaves splashed creamy-white and suffused pink. There are many other forms of *Salvia officinalis* – both ornamental and culinary, such as the common sage, that can be planted in containers on patios.

Vinca major
Periwinkle · Greater Periwinkle
Height: 6-15in (15-38cm)   Spread: 3-4ft (0.9-1.2m)
Hardiness: Zones 7-9
This well-known trailing and sprawling plant can be planted around edges of large tubs, helping to soften their often harsh sides, as well as creating a background of shiny, mid- to dark green leaves. From spring to midsummer, and sometimes continuously throughout summer, it bears blue flowers about 1in (2.5cm) wide.

Pieris japonica 'Variegata' is ideal in a woodland setting or in a large tub on a sheltered, lightly-shaded patio. It is best on its own, or combined with all-green plants.

Alyssum maritimum

(*Lobularia maritima*)
Sweet Alyssum

This popular annual is widely grown as a border edging, as well as for use in containers. It creates a mass of white, lilac or purple flowers from early to late summer. For white flowers, select varieties such as 'Snow Crystals', 'Carpet of Snow' and 'Minimum'. The pink-flowered 'Wonderland' is attractive as well. Correctly, this plant is now known as *Lobularia maritima* but invariably sold as *Alyssum maritimum*.

Height: 3-6in (7.5-15cm)
Spread: 8-12in (20-30cm)
Cultivation: Ordinary well-drained soil and a position in full sun suit it.
Propagation: During late winter or early spring sow seeds ¼in (6mm) deep in seed starting mix in flats and place in 50-59°F (10-15°C). When the seedlings are large enough to handle prick them out and re-pot. Slowly harden off the young plants and set into the garden as soon as all risk of frost has passed. Alternatively, in mid-spring sow seeds ¼in (6mm) deep in the garden.

Alyssum maritimum, when grown in one of its many white forms, creates a pleasing contrast with blue lobelia. It may also be used at the edge of a perennial border.

Left: Anthemis cupaniana This bright-faced perennial creates a pleasing partnership with an old container. It is superb when positioned near a lawn, as well as on a warm sunny patio.

soil, in a bright sunny position.
Propagation: Lift and divide overgrown plants in spring. Alternatively, in midsummer take 2½-3in (6.5-7.5cm) long cuttings. Insert them in equal parts moist peat and sharp sand, and place in a cold frame.

Anthemis nobilis

(*Chamaemelum nobile*)
Chamomile · Russian Chamomile

A well-known mat-forming perennial wlth moss-like, finely-dissected, aromatic, deep green leaves that form a carpet. From mid to late summer it bears white, daisy-like flowers up to 1½in (4cm) wide, as well as creating a sea of attractive foliage. While this plant may be used for tea, the annual German chamomile (*Matricaria recutita*) is more aromatic and better for tea.
Height: 4-6in (10-15cm)
Spread: Mat-forming and spreading
Hardiness: Zones 4-10
Cultivation: Plant in well-drained soil in full sun. Plant in poor, acid soil. The plants become leggy if overly fertilized.
Propagation: If only a few plants are needed, lift and divide overgrown plants in early spring. Alternatively, take 2-3in (5-7.5cm) long basal cuttings in late spring. Insert them in a sandy compost and place in a cold frame. When rooted, pot up into a light, sandy compost.

Left: Alyssum maritimum creates a sea of white flowers throughout summer. Do not let the potting soil become dry, as this quickly reduces the display.

Anthemis cupaniana

An attractive spreading perennial that can be planted in containers as well as flower borders. It also looks good when planted to trail and tumble over a dry stone wall. The finely-dissected, aromatic, grayish leaves create a superb foil for the bright-faced white flowers which appear from mid- to late summer.
Height: 6-10in (15-25cm)
Spread: 12-15in (30-38cm)
Hardiness: Zones 5-9
Cultivation: Plant in well-drained

Left: Anthemis nobilis Ensure that the color of the container harmonizes with the deep green foliage. Terracotta containers create the most harmonious combination; avoid garish colors.

Anthemis cupaniana, when in a flower border, should not be planted close to strongly-colored flowers, as these soon distract attention. Lavender and the pinks (*Dianthus x allwoodii*) are good companions.

Anthemis nobilis, better known as chamomile, can be used to create an unusual, but not hard-wearing, lawn. For this purpose, use the variety 'Treneague', a non-flowering variety.

Dimorphotheca ecklonis 'Prostrata'

(*Osteospermum ecklonis 'Prostrata'*)

This low-growing, bushy and spreading perennial creates a display of white, 3in (7.5cm) wide flowers with mustard-yellow centers during mid- and late summer. These are borne amid midgreen, lance-shaped leaves.

Height: 6-8in (15-20cm)
Spread: 12-15in (30-38cm)
Hardiness: Zones 9-10
Cultivation: Light, well-drained potting soil and a warm, sunny position suit it best. In autumn, cut down the old stems. During winter, keep excess water off the plants by placing cloches over them.
Propagation: During midsummer, take 3in (7.5cm) long half-ripe cuttings. Insert them in equal parts

Above: Dimorphotheca ecklonis 'Prostrata' *The white, mustard-yellow centered flowers glisten and sparkle when in sunlight, creating a dramatic display. The old stone sink adds further interest to the display.*

moist peat and sharp sand. Overwinter the plants in a cold frame and plant out into containers in the garden in late spring.

Dimorphotheca ecklonis 'Prostrata' creates a stunningly attractive display for containers in mild climates. It is also available in blue and violet varieties.

Helichrysum petiolatum

Licorice Plant

An attractive, sprawling and cascading, tender perennial (often grown as annual), ideal for planting in a hanging basket or in a large pot, where it happily mingles with the other plants. The silver stems and leaves create a superb foil for plants. When planted in a border, it grows up to 15in (38cm) high and creates a mound of attractive foliage. In a container it is more reserved.

Height: 8-15in (20-38cm)
Spread: 15-24in (38-60cm)
Hardiness: Zones 9-10, though often grown as annual
Cultivation: Plant in light, well-drained potting soil and position in full sun. Occasionally, trim back long stems to encourage the development of sideshoots and a neater, less sprawling appearance.
Propagation: During midsummer, take 2in (5cm) long cuttings from sideshoots. Insert in a sandy potting soil. When rooted, pot up into small pots and overwinter in a frost-proof frame. Avoid high temperatures during winter. Plant into a container in spring.

Further plants to consider

Agapanthus 'Bressingham White'
African Lily
Height: 2½-3ft (75-90cm)   Spread: 1½-2ft (45-60cm)
Hardiness: Zones 8-10
A beautiful, fleshy-rooted plant with large, white flower heads borne at the tops of upright stems. Many African lilies are not fully hardy outside, but this superb plant is ideal for growing in tubs on a patio. It looks especially attractive when planted in a square-sided tub.

Begonia semperflorens 'Whiskey'
Wax Begonia
Height: 6in (15cm)   Spread: 6-8in (15-20cm)
A compact half-hardy annual which is planted into windowboxes and tubs in early summer, after all risk of frost has passed. It is just as attractive when planted in the garden. Pure-white flowers appear above glossy, bronze leaves during summer.

Crocus chrysanthus 'Snow Bunting'
Height: 3-5in (7.5-13cm)   Spread: 2½-3in (6.5-7.5cm)
Hardiness: Zones 4-9
This small bulbous plant has white petals and a deep yellow throat. The outsides of the petals are marked with deep purple. The flowers appear during late winter and are ideal for brightening containers, as well as the edges of patios.

Echeverias
Height: 3-6in (7.5-15cm) - wide range   Spread: 3-5in (7.5-13cm)
These are usually thought to be houseplants, but during summer they can be placed outdoors on a sunny patio. The range of echeverias is wide. Many have attractive, succulent leaves, which are borne in rosettes and have a white, waxy sheen.

Impatiens hybrids
Height: 1-1½ft (30-45cm)   Spread: 1-1½ft (30-45cm)
This well-known, shade-loving annual is useful for containers and windowboxes in shady, moist sites. The white-flowered varieties brighten dark corners.

Nicotiana alata
Flowering Tobacco
Height: 1½-2ft (45-60cm)   Spread: 1½-2ft (45-60cm)
Nicotianas are generally grown as annuals, although they may be perennial in very mild climates. *N. alata* bears fragrant star-shaped flowers in a range of colors. An unusual variety with green flowers is known as 'Lime Green'. Another species, *N. sylvestris*, has large green leaves and tall flower stalks topped with trumpet-shaped fragrant white blooms.

Helichrysum petiolatum, like many other silver-foliaged plants, thrives in sunny places and in a well-drained light soil. These plants are usually also relatively tolerant of dry soils.

CHAPTER FOUR

WALLS AND TRELLISES

There are few gardens that do not have space for several climbers. Even the most modest bungalow has growing space that is not usually exploited, and a rear garden is likely to have an area of wall or fence available to plants. If garden fencing cannot be used, pergolas, rustic poles or trellises can be erected. All too often vertical space is ignored, and the smaller the garden, the more valuable this area of space becomes.

There are climbers and wall shrubs to suit all walls, from those with a warm and southerly aspect to those which face east or north. Wall shrubs for southerly or westerly aspects include the poet's jasmine (*Jasminum officinale*), with glossy semi-evergreen foliage and fragrant, white flowers in late spring and summer, and bluecrown passionflower (*Passiflora caerulea*), with fragrant, dramatic blue, light pink and white blooms in the summer. Wall shrubs for cold walls include the firethorn (*Pyracantha* 'Watereri') with foamy-white flowers in summer, followed by bright red berries which last well into the winter months.

Several climbers and wall shrubs also bloom in winter. One of the best known of the winter-brighteners is the winter-flowering jasmine (*Jasminum nudiflorum*). It is one of nature's leaners, needing a framework to which it can be tied. From early winter and often to early spring it bears yellow, star-shaped flowers along shoots bare of leaves.

Climbers with colored foliage, such as the soft–yellow leaved *Humulus lupulus aureus* bring further vertical color to a garden, while those with leaves that become richly-colored in autumn are a further attraction. Perhaps the best known one is the Boston ivy (*Parthenocissus tricuspidata*), which has rich crimson and scarlet leaves in autumn.

Heights and spreads given for the plants in this chapter should only be taken as guides. If more space is available in one direction, the plant will adapt its growth accordingly.

Left: Wisteria sinensis 'Alba' *soon clothes a wall with large, pendulous bunches of white, pea-like and sweetly-scented flowers.*

Abutilon megapotamicum

Trailing Abutilon · Flowering Maple · Parlor Maple

A distinctive, tender wall shrub with slender stems bearing maple-like three-lobed, slender-pointed bright green leaves. During early to late summer, it reveals pendulous, bell-shaped, red and yellow flowers. There is also a variegated variety which has yellow and green foliage. *Abutilon pictum* is a taller growing species (up to 15ft/4.5m). Varieties include 'Thompsonii' with variegated foliage and 'Pleniflorum' with double blooms available in either green or variegated foliage. The hybrid abutilons are usually grown as houseplants, known as parlor maples. They make bushy houseplants for a sunny windowsill; many bloom year-round. The blossoms may also be used for cut flowers or corsages. Hybrid abutilons are available in a wide range of colors including coral pink, soft pink, rose, red and the bicolor 'Clementine' with pink and orange blooms.

Height: 5-6ft (1.5-1.8m)
Spread: 6-8ft (1.8-2.4m)
Hardiness: Zones 9-10
Cultivation: Good, well-drained garden soil in a sheltered and sunny position is essential. It is not hardy outside in most areas. In cold areas it is best grown in a greenhouse or as a houseplant where it can be expected to bloom in winter or early spring. This plant does not need regular pruning.
Propagation: During midsummer take 3-4in (7.5-10cm) long half-ripe cuttings. Insert in pots containing equal parts peat and sharp sand and keep at 58°F (15°C). When the plants are rooted, pot them up into loam-based potting soil.

Right: Abutilon megapotamicum
This tender wall shrub soon attracts attention with its red and yellow flowers, borne from early to late summer. A sunny position against a wall is essential.

Abutilon megapotamicum is an adaptable plant for warm climates. Its slender stems allow it to be trained to suit many positions – in corners, under windows or between large windows. It needs wire for support.

Above: **Camellia x williamsii 'Donation'** *This unusual Camellia is a hybrid between* C. japonica *and* C. Salvenensis. *It requires acid soil and a sheltered position, producing a wealth of semi-double orchid-pink flowers from late winter to spring.*

Camellia sasanqua

Sasanqua Camillia

This well-known evergreen shrub is popular in regions where it is hardy. The flowers, fragrant, waxy and rose-like, are either single or semi-double and range from white and pink to rose-purple, all displaying distinctive yellow stamens. They are $1^1/_2$-$2^1/_2$in (4.6cm) wide and appear in a 2 to 3 month period in autumn. There are many pink and white varieties, but availability and adaptability varies from region to region. Check with local sources.

Camellia japonica, the common camellia is a splendid shrub with larger leaves, showier flowers, and similiar hardiness. There are red, pink, and white varieties.

Height: 6-8ft (1.8-2.4m)
Spread: 4-6ft (1.2-1.8m)
Hardiness: Zones 7-9

Cultivation: Fertile, light, acid moisture-retentive soil and a position in sun or partial shade suit this beautiful shrub. Light shade from trees is ideal, giving protection from frost and strong sun in the early morning. A south-facing position should be avoided because these plants need a cool root-run. No pruning is needed, except in the initial shaping of the shrub and the annual removal of misplaced and straggling shoots.

Propagation: During midsummer, take 3-4in (7.5-10cm) long cuttings and insert them in pots containing equal parts peat and sharp sand, kept at 55°F (13°C). Pot up the rooted cuttings into an acid loam-based potting soil and slowly acclimatize them to a lower temperature. Alternatively, layer low-growing shoots in early autumn, although it takes about 18 months to produce roots.

Camellia japonica, and **Camellia sasanqua** may also be grown in a cool greenhouse or conservatory where they bloom in the winter.

Above: **Cotoneaster horizontalis** *A reliable shrub that brings color to any garden in autumn with its beautiful red berries. It is excellent for planting against walls, on banks or as groundcover.*

Cotoneaster horizontalis

Rock Cotoneaster · Rockspray Cotoneaster

This popular semi-evergreen or deciduous hardy shrub has small, dark glossy green leaves borne on stiff frameworks of branches that spread out in a herringbone fashion. The 1/3-1/2in (8-12mm) wide pink flowers appear in midsummer and are followed in autumn by round red berries borne in profusion along the branches. This is an adaptable shrub with many roles in the garden, from covering banks, where it will rise to 2ft (60cm) with a spread up to 6ft (1.8m), to sprawling over low walls or planting against a wall, where it will grow to 6-8ft (1.8-2.4m) tall with a spread of 5-7ft (1.5-2.1m). It is an ideal shrub for east and north-facing walls.
Hardiness: Zones 5-8
Cultivation: Any good garden soil and a sunny position suit it, although it is hardy enough for a cold wall.
Propagation: Although it can be increased by seeds sown in autumn or early winter in pots of loam-based potting soil, placed in a cold frame or a sheltered position in a corner of the garden, this method takes a long time to produce sizeable plants. As an alternative, take heel cuttings 3-4in (7.5-10cm) long in late summer and insert them in pots of equal parts peat and sand, placed in a cold frame. Plant out the cuttings in a nursery bed when they are rooted and established. A further method is to layer low-growing shoots in late autumn or early winter.

Parthenocissus tricuspidata

Boston Ivy · Japanese Creeper

This is a hardy and vigorous self-clinging deciduous climber from Central China to Japan. The shape of the leaves is variable, but usually toothed and trifoliate in young leaves and three-lobed in older ones. In autumn they turn a gloriously rich crimson and scarlet. The variety 'Veitchii' (previously known as *Ampelopsis veitchii*) bears small leaves tinged purple when young.
Height: 20-50ft (7.5-15m)
Spread: 15-25ft (4.5-7.5m)
Hardiness: Zones 4-8
Cultivation: Fertile soil and a large wall or tree up which it can climb are the essential elements for success with this beautiful and popular climber; given these, it flourishes with little or no assistance.
Propagation: During late summer take 4-5in (10-13cm) long cuttings. Insert them in sandy potting soil and keep at 55°F (13°C). Pot up when rooted. Alternatively, long shoots can be layered in late autumn.

Robinia hispida

Moss Locust · Rose Acacia · Bristly Locust · Mossy Locust

This is an open, rather gaunt hardy deciduous shrub from South-east United States, ideal for growing against a south or west-facing wall. The dark green leaves, up to 10in (25cm) long, are formed of seven to thirteen leaflets each 1 1/2-2 1/2in (4-6.5cm) long. The distinctive pea-like rose-pink flowers are about 1 1/4in (3cm) long and borne in drooping bunches of five to ten flowers, in early to midsummer.
Height: 6-8ft (1.8-2.4m)
Spread: 7-9ft (2.1-2.7m)
Hardiness: Zones 4-9
Cultivation: Any well-drained moderately-rich soil in a sunny position suits a robinia. Avoid excessively rich soil. No regular pruning is needed.

Cotoneaster congestus is a low, compact rounded shrub. It bears pinkish white flowers in early summer, followed by bright red fruits. This plant is a good evergreen for a rock garden or small border.

Propagation: It is best raised by grafting onto its relative *Robinia pseudoacacia,* although suckers can be detached from the bases of non-grafted plants.

Above: **Parthenocissus tricuspidata** *This hardy deciduous climber produces a generous covering of rich crimson and scarlet leaves in autumn. The only drawback is that it needs a large wall up which to climb. Alternatively, it is at home climbing a large, old tree that would be enhanced by a dash of color and glamor in autumn.*

Right: **Robinia hispida** *The pea-like rose-pink flowers of this early-summer-flowering wall shrub are especially appealing against an old brick wall. A sunny position is essential for success.*

Parthenocissus henryana, the Chinese Virginia creeper, has dramatic foliage but limited hardiness (Zones 8-9). The leaves, formed of three or five leaflets, turn shades of red in autumn.

Robinia hispida has a strong inclination to create thickets by suckering. This characteristic makes it useful for stabilizing banks.

Right: **Tropaeolum speciosum**
Bright scarlet flowers appear on the scrambling stems during summer, with a background provided by midgreen six-lobed leaves. The plant is seen at its best when it is growing through and over other shrubs.

Right: **Tropaeolum speciosum**
Bright scarlet flowers appear on the scrambling stems during summer, with a background provided by midgreen six-lobed leaves. The plant is seen at its best when it is growing through and over other shrubs.

Tropaeolum majus

Nasturtium · Indian Cress

A well-known and widely-grown climbing and trailing tender annual from South America, ideal for covering fences, trelliswork and for scrambling over banks. The highly distinctive smooth and mid-green leaves are circular, and the early to late summer 2in (5cm) wide orange or yellow flowers are faintly scented. Also, the leaves have a strong, pungent smell. The color range has been extended to include red, pink and maroon flowers. The leaves can be used as a salad green.

Height: 6-8ft (1.7-2.4m) climbing type

Spread: 2-4ft (60cm-1.2m) climbing type

Cultivation: This is an ideal plant for poor soils and a sunny position. If the soil is rich, the growth of the plants is excessive and at the expense of the flowers. Initially, the young plants need twiggy sticks up which to climb, but once established on a framework, they need no extra support.

Propagation: During spring, seeds can be sown ³/₄in (18mm) deep where the plants are to flower. If the seedlings are crowded, thin them out to 4-6in (10-15cm) apart. However, for early-flowering plants, especially those for hanging baskets, sow seeds in early spring in trays of loam-based seed starting mix at 55°F (13°C). When they are large enough to handle, put the seedlings singly in 3in (7.5cm) pots and slowly harden them off in a cold frame until they can be planted outside during late spring or early summer when they are growing strongly.

Left: **Tropaeolum majus** *The original form of this hardy trailing and climbing annual is yellow and orange, but seedsmen have extended the color range to include red, pink and maroon. It is an ideal climber for poor soil.*

Tropaeolum speciosum

Flame Creeper · Flame Nasturtium · Scotch Flame Flower

An unusual exotic-looking Chilean deciduous perennial climber, the flame creeper has a creeping rhizome-producing rootstock that dies down to soillevel in autumn. It has a sprawling growth habit, with downy and hairy stems bearing six-lobed midgreen leaves, which have downy undersides. During

Tropaeolum majus has long been used by cooks as well as gardeners. The flowers and young leaves can be added to salads, and have a warm taste not unlike that of common cress.

midsummer to autumn it reveals 1½in (4cm) wide long-stemmed trumpet-like scarlet flowers formed of five rounded and waved petals.
Height: 10-15ft (3-4.5m)
Spread: 2½-3½ft (75cm-1m)
Hardiness: Zones 6-9
Cultivation: Acid or neutral soil enriched with leaf mold and peat suits this plant. It does best when planted in association with a shrub through which its stems can climb. The flowers are then able to reach the light, while the roots remain cool.
Propagation: It is easily increased by lifting and dividing the roots in early spring, setting them 6-8in (15-20cm) deep. Take care not to damage the fleshy roots. It can also be increased by sowing seeds in a cold frame in spring.

Further plants to consider

Akebia quinta
Five-leaf Akebia
Height: 5-8ft (1.5-2.4m)   Spread: 4-5ft (1.2-1.5m)
Hardiness: Zones 4-9
A sprawling and lax semi-evergreen climber with leaves formed of five leaflets. The fragrant red-purple flowers appear in spring.

Campsis radicans
Common Trumpet Creeper · Trumpetvine
Height: 26-33ft (8-10m)   Spread: 10-20ft (3-6m)
Hardiness: Zones 4-9
A superb self-clinging hardy deciduous climber with light green leaves formed of seven to eleven leaflets. During late summer, it displays rich scarlet and orange trumpet-shaped flowers.

Clematis montana var. rubens
Anemone Clematis
Height: 25-35ft (7.5-10.5m)   Spread: 15-20ft (4.5-6m)
Hardiness: Zones 6-8
A beautiful vigorous deciduous climber with bronze-green leaves and pale pink flowers.

Clematis – Large-flowered
Hardiness: Zones 4-8
Several of these magnificent vines have red and pink forms including 'Ernest Markham' (petunia-red), 'Hagley Hybrid' (shell-pink), and 'Nelly Moser' (mauve-pink with a carmine bar). 'Henryi' is a long-blooming white-flowered cultivar.

Lonicera sempervirens
Trumpet Honeysuckle
Height: 13-20ft (4-6m)   Spread: 3-8ft (90cm-2.4m)
Hardiness: Zones 4-9
A hardy vine with bluish-green leaves and fragrant, scarlet and yellow showy blooms.

Roses-Climbing Types
Climbing roses add an elegant air to any landscape. Single or double flowers are borne alone or in clusters. Some plants bloom only in the spring, while others may continue to flower all season. Climbing roses are ideal for covering arbors, fences, and trellises. Many types are available in a range of colors. Among these are 'Etoile de Holland' (red), 'Belvedere' (pink and double) and 'Mme. Alfred Carriere' (white).

Tropaeolum speciosum is useful for growing through shrubs, but it can also be planted in conjunction with a climber, such as the variegated small-leaved ivy *Hedera helix* 'Goldheart'.

WALLS AND TRELLISES

Above: **Abutilon vitifolium** *This nearly-hardy shrub is a delight when set against a warm wall, where it will produce pale to deep mauve flowers in early and midsummer. It likes the shade and protection afforded by nearby plants.*

Abutilon vitifolium

Flowering Maple · Parlor Maple

This beautiful deciduous shrub needs the protection of a warm wall, and only grows outdoors in mild climates. It develops downy, gray, three or five-lobed, palm-like leaves, and 2in (5cm) wide, pale to deep mauve flowers that open flat during early and midsummer. Grow in containers or as houseplants in cold climates.
Height: 8-15ft (2.4-5m)
Spread: 5-7ft (1.5-2.1m)
Hardiness: Zones 9-10
Cultivation: Well-drained ordinary garden soil suits it; choose a position in slight shade and against a warm south or west-facing wall. No regular pruning is needed.
Propagation: It is best raised from seeds sown in midspring in soil-based potting mix at 61°F (16°C). When they are large enough to handle, prick out the seedlings into pots of soil-based potting mix and place them in a cold frame. Once the young plants are established, plant them out into a nursery bed for a couple of years.

Ceanothus impressus

Californian Lilac ·
Santa Barbara Ceanothus

This impressive evergreen shrub with a bushy habit is best grown against a warm wall in mild Western climates. During spring, it reveals clusters of deep blue flowers amid small deep green leaves with deeply impressed veins.
Height: 8-10ft (2.4-3m).
Spread: 6-8ft (1.8-2.4m)
Hardiness: Zones 8-10
Cultivation: Light, fertile soil and a south or west-facing wall suit it best. It tolerates lime in the soil. No regular pruning is needed, other than initially shaping it when young.
Propagation: During late summer take half-ripe cuttings 2½-3in (6.5-7.5cm) long, inserting them in pots of equal parts peat and sharp sand. Place them in a propagation frame at 61°F (16°C). When the cuttings are rooted, pot them up into small pots, setting them out in the garden when they are well grown.

Above: **Ceanothus impressus**
This beautiful evergreen Californian lilac with small deep blue flowers in spring prefers the protection of a south or west-facing wall. Ceanothus is native to North America, mostly from California where they are best grown.

Ceanothus rigidus

Californian Lilac
Monterey Ceanothus

This beautiful half-hardy evergreen wall shrub has distinctive wedge-shaped dark green leaves and ¾-1in (18-25mm) long clusters of purple-blue flowers during spring. It has a stiff, upright, compact growth habit, ideal for narrow areas in mild Western climates.
Height: 6-10ft (1.8-3m)
Spread: 4-5ft (1.2-1.5m)
Cultivation: Light, fertile soil and a warm wall facing south or west ensure success. No regular pruning is needed, other than shaping during formative years.

Abutilon vitifolium is superb with yellow-flowered shrubs and trees, such as the glorious bright yellow daisy-like flowers of *Senecio* 'Sunshine' and the sweetly-scented yellow broom *Genista cinerea*.

Ceanothus impressus is superb when positioned under a high window or at the side of a lower one. Because of its neat, tight growth small late-winter and spring-flowering bulbs can be set at its base.

Propagation: During late summer, take half-ripe cuttings 2½-3in (6.5-7.5cm) long, inserting them in pots of equal parts peat and sharp sand. Place them in a propagation frame at 61°F (16°C). When the cuttings are rooted, pot them up into small pots of soil-based potting soil, planting them out in the garden when they are well grown.

Left: Ceanothus rigidus *This half-hardy evergreen shrub is ideal for a narrow, restricted area against a wall. It is a native of California and doesn't tolerate the humidity of the Southeast.*

Ceanothus thrysiflorus repens

Californian Lilac
Creeping Blueblossom

This hardy, vigorous, mound-forming evergreen shrub is ideal for planting against a wall, where it creates a dense screen of small shiny green leaves and light blue flowers in 3in (7.5cm) long clusters during early summer. This shrub is also suitable for a large rock garden.
Height: 4-5ft (1.2-1.5m)
Spread: 5-6ft (1.5-1.8m)
Hardiness: Zones 8-10
Cultivation: Light, fertile soil and a south or west-facing position are best. No regular pruning is needed, other than an initial pruning during its formative years.
Propagation: During late summer, take half-ripe cuttings 2½-3in (6.5-7.5cm) long, inserting them in pots of equal parts peat and sharp sand. Place them in a propagation frame at 61°F (16°C). When they are rooted, pot up the cuttings into small pots of soil-based potting mix, and plant them in the garden when they are well grown. Ensure the young plants are well established.

Left: Ceanothus thrysiflorus repens *This hardy evergreen shrub is ideal for covering walls, especially under windows. It is lower growing than* Ceanothus thrysiflorus, *which often reaches 10ft (3m) or more.*

Ceanothus rigidus is an excellent partner for low growing yellow-flowered shrubs that will continue the display into summer. Potentillas, with their long flowering period, are ideal for this purpose.

Ceanothus thrysiflorus repens creates a display of flowers at an earlier stage in its life than most ceanothus species – often when only two years old – so it is useful in new gardens or re-planned ones.

Clematis – Large-flowered Types

These are some of the most spectacular and well-known of all climbers, producing a stunning display of large flowers during summer. They are derived from several forms, such as *florida, Jackmanii, lanuginosa, patens, texensis* and *viticella*. They are superb for training over pergolas, trellises or along wires strung against a wall. Most are single forms, but a few have double flowers. They include a wide range of colors, among which blue, mauve and purple can be found in the following types: 'Alice Fisk' (mauve), 'Belle of Woking' (pale mauve, and double), 'General Sikorski' (dark lavender), 'Jackmanii' (rich purple), 'Mrs. Cholmondely' (pale blue), 'Percy Picton' (intense mauve, with a pink eye), 'President' – also called 'The President' – (deep purple-blue), 'Ramona' (deep-blue), 'Vyvyan Pennell' (deep sky-blue), and 'Will Goodwin' (sky-blue). Henryi' is a long-blooming white-flowered clematis.

Height: 4-10ft (1.2-3m)
Spread: 2½-6ft (75cm-1.8m)
Hardiness: Zones 4-8
Cultivation: Slightly alkaline, fertile, well-drained soil and an open and sunny position suit it, but the roots must be shaded from strong sunlight and you must not allow the soil to become dry during summer. Low-growing plants, as well as shrubs, can be positioned to keep the roots shaded and cool.
Propagation: They root readily from 4-5in (10-13cm) long stem cuttings taken in midsummer and inserted in pots of equal parts peat and sharp sand, kept at 61°F (16°C).When the cuttings are rooted, pot them up singly into 3in (7.5cm) pots of soil-based potting soil and place them in a cold frame during winter. Transfer the cuttings to larger pots in spring or summer and plant them out into the garden in autumn. Alternatively, new plants can be obtained by layering low shoots in spring; they will root within a year or so.

Above: **Clematis 'Alice Fisk'**
This eye-catching clematis, which produces an abundance of large blooms, is a delight in a flower border when given a rustic pole for support. It does well in combination with other plants, which give its roots welcome shade.

Left: **Clematis 'Percy Picton'**
This is a relatively weak-growing type, but is ideal when planted in a small area. It is especially attractive when planted against a well-weathered wall.

Right: **Cobaea scandens**
This vigorous climber is grown as a half-hardy annual, and needs a sheltered and sunny position. The large bell-shaped purple flowers have distinctive green calyces (their outer protective parts).

Clematis are easily trained up supports, as they hang by their leaves. Each leaf is formed of several leaflets held on long stalks, and it is these that secure the shoots in position.

Clematis are exciting when planted in combination with roses, perhaps either side of an entrance. Blue clematis are eye-catching with yellow, creamy-white or pink roses, and low growing plants at the base to keep their roots cool.

Cobea scandens

Cathedral Bells · Cup and Saucer
Vine · Mexican Ivy

This spectacular Mexican half-hardy perennial climber is best grown as a half-hardy annual. Fast-growing, it is ideal for trelliswork and pergolas, displaying mid- to dark green leaves formed of three pairs of leaflets, and 2¹/₂-3in (6.5-7.5cm) long, bell-shaped, purple flowers with green, saucer-like calyces (outer, protective parts) from early to late summer. It grows best during warm weather. In a greenhouse it soon reaches 20ft (6m), but it does not grow so tall outdoors. It is also available with a white bloom.

Height: 10-15ft (3-4.5m)
Spread: 6ft (1.8m)
Cultivation: Ordinary well-drained garden soil and a sunny, sheltered position are needed. If the soil is too rich, excessive growth is produced at the expense of flowers. Pinch out the tips of young plants to encourage the development of sideshoots. Wire supports or wooden trelliswork are needed for support.
Propagation: During late winter and early spring, sow seeds singly ¹/₂in (12mm) deep in 3in (7.5cm) pots containing soil-based potting mix and kept at 61°F (16°C). When young plants are established move them to a cold frame to harden off.

Further plants to consider

Clematis alpina
Alpine Clematis
Height: 5-6ft (1.5-1.8m)   Spread: 3-4ft (90cm-1.2m)
Hardiness: Zones 6-8
An attractive, but weak-growing deciduous climber, with 1-1¹/₂in (2.5-3cm) wide, cup-shaped, violet-blue, late spring and early summer flowers that hang with their faces downwards. Not commonly available, but worth looking for.

Clematis macropetala
Height: 8-12ft (2.4-3.6m)   Spread: 4-5ft (1.2-1.5m)
Hardiness: Zones 3-7
A hardy, bushy, deciduous climber, related and quite similar to *C. alpina*. It produces 2-3in (5-7.5cm) wide, pendulous, light and dark blue flowers in early to midsummer.

Clematis viticella
Height: 8-12ft (2.4-3.5m)   Spread: 5-6ft (1.5-1.8m)
Hardiness: Zones 5-7
A slender though bushy deciduous climber, with bell-shaped 2-2¹/₂in (5-6.5 cm) wide blue, violet or reddish-purple flowers during mid to late summer and in to early autumn. 'Betty Corning' is more free-flowering than species.

Ipomea tricolor 'Heavenly Blue'
Morning Glory
Height 8-10ft (2.4-3m)   Spread: 2-3ft (0.8-1.2m)
A quick-growing hardy annual vine from South America. The showy funnel-shaped blooms open in the morning.

Passiflora caerulea
Blue Passion Flower
Height: 20-25ft (6-7.5m)   Spread: 15-20ft (4.5-6m)
Hardiness: Zones 8-10
A vigorous evergreen climber, not hardy in cold areas. During summer, it has 3in (7.5cm) wide white-petalled flowers with blue-purple centers.

Lathyrus odorata
Sweet Pea
Height: 4-6ft (1.2-1.8m)   Spread: 1-2ft (0.4-0.8m)
A hardy annual vine with fragrant pea-like flowers. Blooms early spring through summer. Prefers cool weather, though heat-resistant varieties are available.

Wisteria floribunda 'Macrobotrys'
Japanese Wisteria
Height: 25-30ft (7.5-9m)   Spread: 20-25ft (6-7.5m)
Hardiness: Zones 5-9
A spectacular hardy deciduous climber, displaying fragrant lilac-blue and purple flowers in drooping clusters up to 3ft (90cm) long in early to midsummer. Arguably, it is the last word in climbers, and is certain to catch the eye.

Annual climbers have the advantage of quickly
covering trelliswork or pergolas and of producing
variety each year – important in small gardens where
change is needed to create continuing interest.

WALLS AND TRELLISES

Above: **Cytisus battandieri** *This wall shrub is a spectacular plant from Morocco, with pineapple-scented flowers displayed in cone-like heads during midsummer. The silvery leaves are a further delight.*

Cytisus battandieri

Moroccan Broom

This startlingly attractive deciduous or semi-evergreen shrub from the Atlas Mountains in Morocco is often grown as a free-standing shrub, and is ideal for south or west-facing walls in very mild climate. The pineapple-scented, golden-yellow flowers are borne in 4in (10cm) long cone-like clusters during midsummer. The large, gray leaves are covered with silky-white hairs.
Height: 8-12ft (2.4-3.5m)
Spread: 8-10ft (2.4-3m)
Hardiness: Zones 9-10
Cultivation: Well-drained, deeply-cultivated neutral or slightly acid soil is best. Soils which are alkaline tend to make the plant short-lived. A south or west-facing wall is best. The shrub flowers on wood formed the previous season, so cut back the shoots after flowering to within a few inches of their bases. Do not cut into the old wood, as it may then not break into new growth.
Propagation: You can sow seeds in spring and raise the seedlings in a cold frame. Alternatively, take 3-4in (7.5-10cm) long heel cuttings in late summer. Insert them into pots containing equal parts of peat and sharp sand, and transfer to a cold frame. Pot up the cuttings, when rooted, into small pots of a potting soil and plant out into the garden in late summer.

Humulus lupulus aureus

Hops

This is an unusual herbaceous perennial climber with soft yellow three to five-lobed coarsely-toothed leaves, 4-6in (10-15cm) wide. It is especially useful for clothing garden features such as arches and pergolas, or perhaps trailing over a path and forming a tunnel of soft yellow leaves.
Height: 10-20ft (3-6cm)
Spread: 8-12ft (2.4-3.5m)
Hardiness: Zones 5-10
Cultivation: Fertile, moist but not waterlogged soil suits it best, and a position in full sun. In autumn, cut the stems down to soil level.

Cytisus scoparius, Scotch broom, is a good broom for cold climates. Hardy to zone 6, its yellow blooms and mounded form can be shown off against a brick wall.

Humulus lupulus aureus soon takes to a trellis or pergola, but will also trail and climb through a neglected, sparse hedge, filling the gaps with its attractive yellow leaves.

Jasminum nudiflorum

Winter Jasmine

This hardy deciduous shrub with long, whip-like stems is perhaps one of the best known winter-flowering shrubs, blooming from late winter to early spring. It has lustrous dark green leaves, each made up of three leaflets, and $^3/_4$-1in (18-25mm) wide, bright yellow, fragrant, star-shaped flowers, borne singly or in small clusters on shoots developed since the previous spring. During flowering, the shoots are bare of leaves. It is not strictly a climber, but a "leaner" that needs support.

Height: 6-10ft (1.8-3m)
Spread: 6-8ft (1.8-2.4m)
Hardiness: Zones 6-10
Cultivation: This jasmine needs moderately fertile well-drained soil, preferably against an east or north-facing wall. The dainty flowers do not appear to be damaged by frost alone, but when frost is combined with early-morning sun, it causes damage. Because the flowers are produced on shoots developed since the previous spring, it can be pruned back hard in spring. Leave all the main shoots alone and just cut back the flowered shoots to two or three buds of their origin. This pruning encourages the development of side-shoots which will bear flowers the following winter. The new shoots will need tying-in to supports throughout the summer months.

Propagation: During late summer, take 3-4in (7.5-10cm) long semi-ripe cuttings; cut the lower ends just below a leaf-joint. Insert them into pots containing equal parts of peat and sharp sand, and keep at 45°F (7°C). When the cuttings are rooted, pot them up into 3in (7.5cm) containers of potting soil and put them in a cold frame. Alternatively, layer low-growing shoots in autumn. Rooting usually takes about a year.

Above: **Humulus lupulus aureus**
The soft yellow, three to five-lobed leaves of this herbaceous perennial form a dense screen ideal for covering unsightly objects. In fertile, moist soil it soon becomes an eye-catching display.

Right: **Jasminum nudiflorum**
This winter-flowering shrub can be trained against a wall or allowed to sprawl up and over a low wall. The bright yellow, star-shaped flowers are borne singly or in small clusters along bare shoots.

Propagation: It can be increased from seed, but division of the rootstock in early autumn or spring is an easier method of propagation.

Jasminum nudiflorum is favored for its early-blooming, fragrant yellow blooms. The green twigs are attractive in the winter and can be easily forced to bloom indoors.

Right: **Lonicera nitida 'Baggesen's Gold'** *Few golden-leaved plants are as eye-catching in full sun as this small-leaved, evergreen shrub. When planted against a wall or fence, it soon becomes a handsome screen.*

Lonicera nitida 'Baggesen's Gold'

Boxleaf Honeysuckle

This densely-leaved semi-evergreen shrub sports $1/4$in (6mm) long, golden-yellow leaves. It can be grown as a specimen shrub in a border, where its foliage has year-round interest. But it is best positioned against a sunny wall or unsightly shed or garage, where it soon forms an attractive screen.
Height: 5-6ft (1.5-1.8m)
Spread: 3-5ft (90cm-1.5m)
Hardiness: Zones 6-9
Cultivation: Lonicera likes a well-drained fertile soil in full sun. Good light enhances the attractive leaves and maintains their gold coloring. No regular pruning is needed, other than trimming it in spring to fill the space allotted to it. Although, like its parent form, it can be trimmed with shears, it is far better left with a more informal shape.
Propagation: An easy way is to layer low-growing shoots in late summer or early winter. They usually take about a year to develop roots. Also, hardwood cuttings, 8-10in (20-25cm) long, can be taken in late summer and inserted in a sheltered corner. These also take about a year to produce roots. Another way is to take 4in (10cm) long cuttings during mid- to late summer, inserting them in pots containing equal parts of peat and sharp sand and placing them in a cold frame. Pot up the cuttings, when they are rooted, into a potting soil, and replace in the cold frame. Plant out in a nursery bed in spring until established, when they can be planted in their final sites in autumn or in the following spring.

Lonicera tragophylla

Chinese Woodbine

A beautiful, vigorous, deciduous climber, ideal for fences, archways, pergolas and walls, this plant was introduced into cultivation in 1900. During midsummer, it displays large terminal clusters of scentless, bright golden-yellow flowers with trumpets up to $1\frac{1}{2}$in (4cm) wide and tubes up to 3in (7.5cm) long.
Height: 15-20ft (4.5-6m)
Spread: 10-15ft (3-4.5m)
Hardiness: Zones 6-9
Cultivation: It delights in a position where the roots are shaded and the vine is in full sun. Well-drained relatively fertile soil is needed. No regular pruning is necessary, other than cutting out dead wood after flowering.
Propagation: Seeds can be sown in seed starting mix when ripe in early autumn, and placed in a cold frame. Alternatively, take 3-4in (7.5-10cm) long cuttings in mid-summer. Insert them into pots containing equal parts of peat and sharp sand and place them in a cold frame. When rooted, pot up the cuttings and replace them in the cold frame.

Lonicera nitida 'Baggesen's Gold' is ideal for covering unsightly sheds or garages. Bulbs with strong blue flowers make a superb color contrast; grape hyacinths are ideal.

Piptanthus nepalensis

Evergreen Laburnum

This is an unusual, slightly tender, almost evergreen shrub with dark green leaves formed of three lance-shaped leaflets, 3-6in (7.5-15cm) long. The pea-shaped, bright-yellow laburnum-like flowers, 1¹/₂in (4cm) long, appear in late spring and early summer. It can be grown in the open, but does better against a south or west-facing wall.
Height: 8-12ft (2.4-3.5m)
Spread: 6-10ft (1.8-3m)
Hardiness: Zones 5-10
Cultivation: Light, well-drained soil in a sheltered, warm position is essential. No regular pruning is needed, other than cutting out dead branches in spring. If the foliage has been badly damaged by frost, cut it back in spring.
Propagation: It is easily increased from seeds sown in early spring in sterile potting soil and placed in a cold frame. When large enough to handle, prick off the seedlings into small pots of potting soil. The plants can be set in a nursery bed in autumn, for a year or so. Alternatively, take 3-4in (7.5-10cm) long, half-ripe heel cuttings in late summer. When they are rooted, pot them up into small pots.

Above: Lonicera tragophylla
This vigorous climber is well suited to a large wall, in a position which gives it a cool root-run and plenty of sun for the foliage. Flowering is during midsummer. It is best positioned where its roots are in shade, perhaps from a shrub.

Right: Piptanthus nepalensis
This unusual, almost evergreen shrub bears pea-shaped, bright-yellow flowers in late summer. It can be grown as a specimen shrub, but is better against a warm wall. It will not live long in cold or very windy areas.

Lonicera tragophylla is ideal for trailing over a sparsely foliaged tree, a trellis or a pergola. The roots soon find the cool side of the tree, while the flowers climb into the sunlight.

Rosa 'Golden Showers'

'Golden Showers' is a large-flowered, hardy, deciduous climbing rose with dark, glossy foliage and fragrant daffodil-yellow flowers. The buds open to golden yellow 5in (12.5cm) flowers. It blooms freely from spring to late fall.

Height: 6-8ft (1.8-2.4m)
Spread: 4-5ft (1.2-1.5m)
Hardiness: Zones 4-7
Cultivation: Ordinary well-drained garden soil. A position in full sun is essential, facing south or west. Little pruning is needed, other than thinning out awkward branches and bare shoots during early spring – or late winter in mild areas. Makes a dramatic display on arbors, fences, pillars or walls.
Propagation: During late summer and early autumn, take 9in (23cm) long heel cuttings, or take cuttings just below a bud. Insert them in a sand-lined, straight-sided trench, so that two-thirds of each cutting is buried. Remove the lower leaves from the cuttings.

Right: Rosa 'Golden Showers'
Yellow flowering roses are especially attractive against a dark-colored wall or fence. There are many suitable cultivars from which to choose.

Left: **Thunbergia alata** *This bright half-hardy annual is ideal for a cool greenhouse but also excellent in a warm, sheltered and sunny position outdoors. The orange-yellow flowers, with dark purple-brown centers, appear from midsummer to autumn.*

Thunbergia alata

Black-eyed Susan Vine

This extremely bright-flowered, half-hardy annual climber has stems which twine around its supports. Many cultivars are available. It bears ovate light green leaves and orange-yellow flowers with dark purple-brown centers, 2in (5cm) wide, from midsummer to autumn. It is ideal for a cool greenhouse, but also thrives outdoors if given a warm position.

Height: 4-6ft (1.2-1.8m)
Spread: 2-3ft (60-90cm)
Cultivation: Ordinary well-drained soil and a sunny, sheltered position are essential.
Propagation: In spring, sow seeds 1/4in (6mm) deep, three seeds to a 3in (7.5cm) wide pot. Use seed starting mix and keep at 61°F (16°C). When the seedlings are growing well, slowly harden them off, setting the plants outside as soon as all risk of frost is over.

Rosa 'Golden Showers' can be planted with a flowering vine such as clematis. *Clematis montana* with pure white clematis flowers will mingle attractively with the yellow rose blooms.

Thunbergia alata can be grown on its own, but it is more attractive when allowed to climb among a blue-flowered clematis. If you grow it in a pot, make a tripod from bamboo canes for a support.

Above: Tropaeolum peregrinum
This beautiful half-hardy annual bears interestingly shaped canary-yellow flowers from midsummer to autumn. The light green, five-lobed leaves provide an attractive foil for the dramatic flowers.

Tropaeolum peregrinum

Canary-bird Flower

This rapid-growing, twining vine is frequently grown as a half-hardy annual. It bears five-lobed blue-green leaves and canary-yellow, elegantly-fringed flowers, ³/₄-1in (1.8-2.5cm) wide and adorned with graceful green spurs, from midsummer to autumn. It looks superb when planted in bold drifts in a border, or in hanging baskets or windowboxes, where it can trail. It is difficult to find.
Height: 8-12ft (2.4-3.5m)
Spread: 2¹/₂-3ft (75-90cm)
Cultivation: Fertile soil in a warm and sunny position is best. It needs support from trelliswork or canes. It also requires a cool climate and doesn't do well in the Southeast.
Propagation: During late winter and early spring, sow two seeds ¹/₂in (12mm) deep in a 3in (7.5cm) wide pot of seed starting mix. Keep the pot at 61°F (16°C). After germination, thin to one seedling per pot. Harden them off and plant them out into the garden in early summer, after all risk of frost damage has passed. Cuttings taken in the fall make excellent houseplants.

Further plants to consider

Campsis radicans
Trumpet Creeper · Trumpetvine
Height: 26-33ft (8-10cm)   Hardiness: Zone 4-9
A rapidly-growing, vigorous, hardy vine. Large, 2in (5cm), trumpet-shaped orange to yellow flowers in midsummer. Will rapidly cover a large area. Requires strong support.

Clematis orientalis
Orange-peel Clematis
Height: 3.5-4m (10-18ft)   Hardiness: Zones 5-9
A vigorous, deciduous climber with a mass of tangled shoots, bearing slightly fragrant, bell-shaped, nodding yellow flowers, 2in (5cm) wide, during late summer and into autumn.

Clematis tangutica
Height: 10-15ft (3-4.5m)   Hardiness: Zones 5-9
An attractive, deciduous, slender, vigorous climber. It bears lantern-shaped, rich-yellow flowers in late summer and into autumn.

Forsythis suspensa
Weeping Forsythia
Height: 8-12ft (2.4-3.5m)   Hardiness: Zones 5-8
A weeping species that is otherwise identical to the common shrub. Excellent for covering walls.

Hedera helix 'Goldheart'
Ivy
Height: 6-15ft (1.8-4.5m)   Spread: 6-8ft (1.8-2.4m)
Hardiness: Zones 4-9
A hardy, self-clinging climber with dark green leaves displaying dominant yellow central splashes. It produces its best coloring on south or west-facing walls, but will nevertheless survive the coldest of northerly aspects if required to.

Jasminum mesnyi
Primrose Jasmine
Height: 6-10ft (1.8-3m)   Hardiness: Zones 8-9
An evergreen climber, best suited to a south or west-facing wall in a warm area. During spring and into early summer, it bears 2in (5cm) wide, semi-double yellow flowers.

Pittosporum tobira
Japanese Pittosporum
Height: 8-12ft (2.4-3.5m)   Hardiness: Zones 7-9
A slow-growing evergreen for sheltered, warm areas. From spring to mid-summer, it displays orange-blossom-scented, creamy-white flowers. It needs the protection of a south or west-facing wall.

Tropaeolum peregrinum blends well in cottage-style gardens, but it also suits modern gardens, especially as a cloak for hiding ugly objects. For example, it will soon clothe a pole supporting a bird house.

Actinidia chinensis

Chinese Gooseberry · Kiwi Fruit

This hardy deciduous climber soon clothes a wall or pergola with large, heart-shaped dark green leaves up to 8in (20cm) long and 7in (18cm) wide. It also has fragrant, creamy-white flowers which turn to buff-yellow, during late summer. They are followed by edible fruits, first green then brown.

Height: 18-30ft (5.4-10.5m)
Spread: 12-25ft (3.6-7.5m)
Hardiness: Zones 7-9
Cultivation: Grow in any good soil, fertile and well-drained. Pinch out the growing tips of young plants to encourage bushiness. Preferably, plant it against a south or west-facing wall, in full sun or light shade. Male and female flowers are usually borne on separate plants. It is therefore necessary to have plants of both sexes if fruits are to be produced.
Propagation: During midsummer, take 3-4in (7.5-10cm) long half-ripe cuttings and insert in equal parts moist peat and sharp sand. Well-drained potting soil is essential. Place in a closed propagation frame with slight bottom heat.

Actinidia kolomikta

Kolomikta Vine

This superb hardy deciduous climber has heart-shaped, dark green leaves with white or pink tips. Sometimes, this variegation spreads to cover the whole lower half of the leaf. The attractive coloring is encouraged when the plant is in full sun, against a south or west-facing wall. During early summer it bears slightly fragrant white flowers.

Height: 8-12ft (2.4-3.6m)
Spread: 6-10ft (1.8-3m)
Hardiness: Zones 4-8
Cultivation: Plant in well-drained but moisture-retentive, fertile, acid soil. Full sun or light shade suits it. Thin out shoots on those plants that have filled their allotted space

Right: Actinidia chinensis *The large, heart-shaped leaves of this deciduous Chinese climber create an impressive display during summer. It is a vigorous plant and can soon swamp its supports, and other plants, with large leaves.*

and are becoming overgrown. This is best carried out in late winter or early spring.
Propagation: In mid- to late summer take 3-4in (7.5-10cm) long cuttings and insert in a sandy potting soil. Place in a frame with slight bottom heat. When rooted, transfer into small pots and place in a cold frame.

Below: Actinidia kolomikta *When planted to grow up an old house wall this superbly variegated climber is exceptionally attractive. It can be easily trained around the windows without spoiling the plant's slightly wild nature.*

Actinidia chinensis is well-known in China for its fruits, the size of a large plum, which are eaten as a dessert. Selected forms are grown in New Zealand, where they are known as kiwi fruits.

Actinidia kolomikta, the kolomikta vine, is a superb climber even when planted on its own. When combined with the orange-scarlet flowered Chilean glory flower (*Eccremocarpus scaber*) both highlight each other.

Cotoneaster horizontalis

Rock Cotoneaster · Rockspray Cotoneaster

This well known and widely grown hardy deciduous shrub is ideal for covering north and east-facing walls with small, glossy, dark-green leaves. These are borne on a low framework of shoots. It is also ideal for clothing banks or large unsightly rocks with attractive foliage. It has the bonus of producing ½ in (2.5cm) wide pink flowers during early to mid-summer, followed by round, red, shiny berries.

Height: 5-7ft (1.5-2.1m) when grown against a wall.
Spread: 5-6ft (1.5-1.8m) when grown against a wall.
Hardiness: Zones 5-8
Cultivation: When planted to cover a bank it often has a 5-7ft

Above: Cotoneaster horizontalis
A low wall can be made more attractive by planting this shrub close to it and allowing the sprays of foliage to gently spill over the top. Use pruners in spring to remove unwanted growth.

(1.5-2.1m) spread, rising 1½-2ft (45-60cm) high. Plant it in any good soil in full sun or shade. No regular pruning is needed, other than cutting out misplaced shoots in early spring.
Propagation: In midsummer, take 3-4in (7.5-10cm) long heel-cuttings, inserting them in equal parts moist peat and sharp sand. Place in a cold frame. When rooted, plant into a nursery bed for two or three years before moving into a garden. Alternatively, layer low-growing shoots in autumn. These take about a year to develop roots.

Cotoneaster horizontalis combines well with many plants, including hydrangeas, low-growing evergreen azaleas, hostas, and *Euonymus fortunei*. All grow under a light canopy of deciduous trees, such as birches.

Hedera canariensis 'Variegata'

Canary Island Ivy · Algerian Ivy

This evergreen climber is also known as *Hedera canariensis* 'Gloire de Marengo'. Although not as hardy as *Hedera colchica* 'Dentata Variegata', and frequently grown indoors as a climbing houseplant, it is well worth growing against a warm wall in areas not subject to severe frosts. The dark green leaves are broadly heart-shaped, merging to silvery-gray then whitish-yellow at their edges.
Height: 15-20ft (4.5-6m)
Spread: 6-15ft (1.8-3.6m)
Hardiness: Zones 9-10
Cultivation: It is impossible to give the exact size of this climber, as it will quickly adapt its growth if given more support in one direction than another. Plant it in any good well-drained but moisture-retentive soil, in a sunny position. Good light

is vital to encourage the attractive variegations, and therefore select a sheltered, warm, south or west-facing position. No regular pruning is needed. In spring cut back those plants that have exceeded their positions.
Propagation: In mid- to late summer take 3-5in (7.5-13cm) long cuttings from the tips of shoots, inserting them in equal parts moist peat and sharp sand. Place in a propagation frame until rooted, then pot up individually and replace in a cold frame until well established.

Below: Hedera canariensis 'Variegata' *This variegated climber is ideal for planting on the warm, sheltered sunny side of a wall. Eventually it scales the wall and looks very attractive when peeping over its top. It blends well with the bricks.*

Hedera colchica 'Dentata Variegata'

Persian Ivy · Colchis Ivy

This evergreen climber has large, broadly oval, bright green leaves conspicuously variegated with irregular creamy-yellow edges. As the leaf ages these become creamy-white.
Height: 20-30ft (6-9m)
Spread: 6-15ft (1.8-4.5m)
Hardiness: Zone 6-9
Cultivation: It is impossible to give the exact size of this vigorous climber as, if given more support in one direction, it will take advantage of it. Plant it in any good well-drained but moisture-retentive soil, in a sunny position. Good light is vital to encourage the attractive variegations, so therefore select a south or west-facing position. No regular pruning is needed, other than cutting back in spring those plants which have exceeded their positions.
Propagation: In mid- to late summer take 3-5in (7.5-13cm) long cuttings from the tips of shoots, inserting them in equal parts moist

---

Hedera canariensis 'Variegata' is not so hardy as *Hedera colchica* 'Dentata Variegata', but usually recovers after being damaged by frost in Zone 8. Preferably grow against a warm sheltered wall.

Hedera colchica 'Dentata Variegata' eventually creates a large evergreen screen of brightly variegated leaves. It can be used to cover porches, and forms an attractive combination with tubs of hydrangeas.

peat and sharp sand. Place in a propagation frame until rooted, then pot up individually and place in a cold frame until well established.

Left: Hedera colchica 'Dentata Variegata' *The variegated leaves create welcome color throughout the year. Each leaf has a drooping nature with bright, broad, yellow edges. Spray the leaves with clean water during summer. This helps to keep them clean and to prevent an infestation of red spider mites.*

Hedera helix 'Goldheart'

Goldheart English Ivy

This hardy, evergreen, variegated variety of English ivy, creates an eye-catching climber for walls. It is self-clinging (and not too vigorous for small walls) revealing bright, dark green leaves with conspicuous yellow splashes at their centers.
Height: 5-15ft (1.5-4.5m)
Spread: 5-8ft (1.5-2.4m)
Hardiness: Zones 7-9
Cultivation: It is impossible to predict the exact spread and height of this climber. Plant it in any good well-drained but moisture-retentive soil in a sunny position. Good light is vital to encourage the attractive variegations. No regular pruning is needed.
Propagation: In mid- to late summer take 3-4in (7.5-10cm) long cuttings from the tips of shoots, inserting them in equal parts moist peat and sharp sand. Place in a propagation frame until rooted, then pot up individually and place in a cold frame until well established.

Right: Hedera helix 'Goldheart' *creates a dominant eye-catching display throughout the year, but especially in spring when the new leaves appear. The center of each leaf is conspicuously splashed bright yellow.*

Hedera helix 'Goldheart' is a small-leaved, variegated climber that is ideal for growing on brick walls. *H. helix* 'Tricolor' is another attractive variety, with small leaves margined with white in summer and rose-pink in winter.

Lonicera japonica 'Aureoreticulata'

Variegated Japanese Honeysuckle

This variegated, evergreen or semi-evergreen climber is superb when climbing a trellis on a sheltered patio. Its bright green leaves, conspicuously veined in golden-yellow, always attract attention. This variety is less vigorous than the species. Dry soil also encourages the leaves to fall off.
Height: 6-10ft (1.8-3m)
Spread: 6-8ft (1.8-2.4m)

Hardiness: Zone 5-9
Cultivation: It is impossible to be precise about the height and spread of this climber. Well-drained but moisture-retentive fertile soil in full sun or light shade suits it. Preferably select a warm south or west-facing position. No regular pruning is needed, other than thinning overgrown stems in spring.
Propagation: In mid- and late summer take 3-4in (7.5-10cm) long cuttings and insert them in equal parts moist peat and sharp sand. Place in a cold frame. When rooted, pot up individually and later plant into their growing positions preferably in spring or early summer.

Below: Lonicera japonica 'Aureoreticulata' *This eye-catching climber with small, brightly variegated leaves is ideal for bringing color to a trellis in a warm part of a garden, perhaps close to a patio.*

Trachelospermum jasminoides

Star Jasmine · Confederate Jasmine

This slow-growing, evergreen climber is ideal for clothing walls with leathery, shiny, somewhat lance-shaped dark green leaves. During mid to late summer it bears fragrant, 1in (2.5cm) wide, white flowers in lax heads.
Height: 3-6ft (1.5-3m)
Spread: 3-6ft (1.5-3m)

Lonicera japonica 'Aureoreticulata' is an attractively variegated form of the Japanese honeysuckle. However, it is not so vigorous as the all-green type, and needs the protection of a warm wall.

Below: Trachelospermum jasminoides *The fragrant, 1in (2.5cm) wide white flowers appear during summer. They are highlighted by the glossy, dark-green leaves. It may also be grown as a mild climate ground-cover.*

Hardiness: Zones 8-9
Cultivation: Plant in well-drained, slightly acid, peaty soil against a warm west or south-facing wall. Remove dead flowers and thin out overgrown shoots in late spring.
Propagation: During midsummer take 3-4in (7.5-10cm) long cuttings from sideshoots. Insert them in equal parts moist peat and sharp sand and place in a propagation frame. When rooted, pot up into a loam-based potting soil and overwinter in a cold frame.

Further plants to consider

Aristolochia durior
Dutchman's Pipe
Height: 12-20ft (3.6-6m)   Spread: 8-15ft (2.4-4.5m)
Hardiness: Zones 4-8
This is a fast-growing, vigorous and twining, hardy, deciduous climber that needs support. When grown against a wall trelliswork is necessary, but occasionally it is allowed to sprawl over other plants or dead trees. It becomes clothed with broadly heart-shaped, large, midgreen leaves up to 10in (25cm) long and slightly less in width. During midsummer it bears pipe-shaped, 1-1½in (2.5-4cm) long, yellow, brown and green flowers.

Hedera helix 'Bulgaria'
Bulgaria English Ivy
Height: 5-15ft (1.5-4.5m)   Spread: 5-8ft (1.5-2.4m)
Hardiness: Zones 4-9
An extremely hardy small-leaved ivy with dark green leaves. It was developed at the Missouri Botanical Garden.

Parthenocissus henryana
Chinese Virginia Creeper
Height: 10-20ft (3-6m)   Spread: 10-15ft (3-4.5m)
Hardiness: Zones 9-10
An exceptionally beautiful deciduous branching and bushy, self-clinging climber, with dark green leaves formed of three or five leaflets. The mid-rib and main veins are attractively variegated in pink and white. Towards the end of summer, and especially in autumn, the variegations become more pronounced as the green changes to brilliant red.

Smilax lanceolata
Florida Smilax · Lanceleaf Greenbrier
Height: to 33ft (10m)   Spread: to 15ft (4.5m)
Hardiness: Zones 7-10
An evergreen woody vine with shiny, deep green lance-shaped leaves. It climbs with tendrils and provides excellent screening or wall cover. It prefers acid soil and will tolerate full sun or shade. Useful for quickly covering a wall in mild climates.

Tropaeolum peregrinum
Canary Creeper · Canary Bird Vine
Height: to 8ft (2.4m)   Spread: 2-3ft (60-90cm)
This annual climber creates a wealth of finely-cut, midgreen leaves on twining stems. It has small, 1in (2.5cm) yellow flowers that resemble birds in flight, from summer to early fall. Native to the Andes, it prefers cool growing conditions.

Trachelospermum jasminoides clothes walls throughout the year with beautiful leaves. It is a tender vine, appropriate to mild climates and sheltered positions.

Carpenteria californica

Tree Anemone

This near hardy evergreen shrub from California grows well in the shelter of a south or west-facing wall. It looks especially attractive when planted against a wall with an old and weathered appearance. It has rich, glossy-green leaves and terminal clusters of up to seven, 2-3in (5-7.5cm) wide, white flowers during midsummer.
Height: 10-12ft (3-3.6m)
Spread: 6-8ft (1.8-2.4m)
Hardiness: Zones 7-10
Cultivation: Well-drained, light soil, and the shelter of a warm wall suit it. New plants are best set in position in late spring, rather than in autumn. No regular pruning is needed, other than cutting out straggly shoots after the flowers fade.
Propagation: During late spring, sow seeds in loam-based seed starting mix in flats, and place in 61°F (16°C). When large enough to handle, prick off the seedlings into small pots and place in a cold frame.

Clematis montana

Anemone Clematis

This is an easily-grown clematis, creating a mass of pure white flowers up to 2in (5cm) wide during early summer. It is a deciduous climber, with dark green leaves. When initially planted it tends to grow straight up, but at about 10ft (3m) it branches out and forms a large, tangled head of shoots and flowers. This growth habit makes it ideal for trailing over the top of a wall, across an arch or over a porch.

Right: Carpenteria californica
This Californian evergreen shrub creates a wealth of 2-3in (5-7.5cm) wide white flowers at the tips of shoots during midsummer. These appear among a foil of rich, glossy-green leaves.

Carpenteria californica looks at its best when peeping over an old wall and highlighted by clear blue sky. Be sure soil is well-drained, as too much water in the winter can be fatal.

Left: Clematis montana *has clouds of white, four-petalled and scented blooms. It is alluring when planted to lean over the top of an old wall.*

Height: 20-30ft (6-9m)
Spread: 15-20ft (4.5-6m)
Hardiness: Zones 5-8
Cultivation: Fertile, moisture-retentive, deeply-cultivated, slightly alkaline soil suits it. It enjoys warmth and sunlight, but ensure that the roots are cool and moist. Initially it needs a cane to lead the young shoots to a supporting framework. Little pruning is needed, other than cutting back old plants in spring to fit their allotted areas.
Propagation: The easiest way for a home gardener to increase this plant is by layering low-growing shoots in early spring. Alternatively, take 4-5in (10-13cm) long cuttings during midsummer, formed of half-ripe wood. Insert in equal parts moist peat and sharp sand, and place in 61°F (16°C). When rooted, pot up individually and overwinter in a frost-proof greenhouse.

Lonicera japonica

Japanese Honeysuckle

This well-known, evergreen or semi-evergreen rampant climber creates masses of white, fragrant flowers which change to yellow with age. These are borne from early summer to early autumn. The variety 'Halliana' (Hall's honeysuckle) is especially attractive, with highly fragrant, white flowers. 'Aureoreticulata', has bright green leaves with conspicuous golden veins and is less vigorous than the species. It flowers well when grown against a warm wall.
Height: 15-25ft (4.5-7.5m)
Spread: 10-15ft (3-4.5m)
Hardiness: Zones 5-9
Cultivation: Fertile, well-drained soil in full sun or partial shade suit it. Little pruning is needed, other than cutting out straggly shoots in spring when the plant becomes overgrown.
Propagation: During mid- to late summer take 4in (10cm) long cuttings, inserting them in equal parts moist peat and sharp sand. Place in a cold frame. When rooted, plant into a nursery bed until large enough to be transferred into the garden.

Above: Lonicera japonica *Few climbers are as pleasing on the eye and the nose as this well-known and widely-grown climber. With age, the tubular, fragrant flowers, up to 1½in (4cm) long, slowly change from white to light yellow.*

Clematis montana creates a spectacular display when planted alongside a yellow-flowered climbing rose such as 'Golden Showers'.

Lonicera japonica is superb for creating a romantic arbor or screen, decked with sweetly-scented white flowers for much of summer. However, in the South it is very invasive.

WALLS AND TRELLISES

Wisteria sinensis 'Alba'

White Chinese Wisteria

The normal form of this vigorous, hardy deciduous eye-catching Chinese climber has mauve flowers, but this variety has beautiful white ones. These are pea-shaped and borne in cascading bunches up to 12in (30cm) long during early summer, often before the foliage is fully developed. After the flowers have faded, the dark to midgreen leaves, formed of up to eleven leaflets, are an attractive feature.
Height: 20-25ft (6-7.5m) or more
Spread: 25-30ft (7.5-9m) or more
Hardiness: Zones 5-9
Cultivation: Fertile, well-drained soil and a warm position in the protection of a south- or west-facing wall suit it best. Avoid poor, shallow soils. When grown against a wall a supporting framework is needed, either from tensioned

*Above: **Polygonum aubertii** The fleecy-white flowers of this rampant climber swamp it during midsummer through early fall, creating a cloud of white. When trailing over the top of a high wall it is especially attractive.*

Polygonum aubertii

China Fleecevine · Silver Fleecevine · Silver Lace Vine

This twining, deciduous, rampant climber is not a climber for small fences or walls, as it will grow up to 15ft (4.5m) a year and soon swamp a limited area. From mid to late summer it produces flowers that open greenish-white and turn white or pinkish. The leaves are reddish while young and become a bright green. It is a vigorous vine that will succeed where others fail.
Height: 25-35ft (7.5-10.5m)
Spread: 20-40ft (6-12m)
Hardiness: Zones 4-8
Cultivation: It grows well in all soils, even those on the alkaline side. Plants need a little shelter so that they become established quickly, but after then it tolerates any aspect. No pruning is needed, other than a trim when it exceeds its allotted space.
Propagation: During midsummer take 3-4in (7.5-10cm) long heel-cuttings and insert in equal parts moist peat and sharp sand. Place in a cold frame. When rooted, pot up individually.

Polygonum aubertii, silver lace vine, requires firm support, such as a wall or chain link fence, rather than rustic poles which, when old, may become strained by strong winds blowing on the foliage.

wires or a lattice-work of wood. Wisterias also grow well on pergolas, enabling bunches of flowers to hang freely. Prune established wisterias during mid-summer by cutting back the current season's young shoots to within five or six buds of its base. Those plants which are becoming too large can be pruned back in late winter to keep them within bounds.

Propagation: During mid- to late summer take 4in (10cm) long cuttings, cutting their bases just below a joint. Insert them in a heated propagation frame. Pot up when rooted and overwinter in a cold frame. Plants can also be raised by grafting.

Below: Wisteria sinensis 'Alba'
The beautiful pea-shaped flowers in long, cascading bunches, are especially attractive when grown against a dark background. It is a vigorous climber that requires plenty of room.

Further plants to consider

Abeliophyllum distichum
White Forsythia
Height: 4-6ft (1.2-1.8m)   Spread: 5-6ft (1.5-1.8m)
Hardiness: Zones 4-8
Deciduous wall shrub best grown against a south- or west-facing wall. During late winter and into spring it bears almond-scented white flowers with bright gold stamens. Sometimes, the flowers are faintly tinged pink when opening.

Clematis maximowicziana
(Clematis paniculata)
Sweet Autumn Clematis
Height: 8-10ft (2.4-3m)   Spread: 8-10ft (2.4-3m)
Hardiness: Zones 4-9
A vigorous, deciduous climber that creates a tangled mass of bright green leaves and delicate, sweetly-scented white flowers in late summer and early fall.

Clematis 'Marie Boisselot'
Height: 10-18ft (3-5.4m)   Spread: 10-12ft (3-3.6m)
Hardiness: Zones 3-8
A superb large-flowered hybrid clematis with large, pure-white flowers with cream stamens from mid- to late summer.

Ipomoea alba
Moon-Flower
Height: 8-10ft (2.4-3m)   Spread: 4-5ft (1.2-1.5m)
A tender perennial vine grown as an annual. The morning glory-like flowers are pure white, fragrant and open at night.

Jasminum officinale
Common White Jasmine · Poet's Jasmine
Height: 6-25ft (1.8-7.5m)   Spread: 10-15ft (3-4.5m)
Hardiness: Zones 7-10
Vigorous, deciduous, twining and clambering climber with fragrant, pure-white flowers from mid- to late summer.

Magnolia grandiflora
Southern Magnolia · Bull Bay Magnolia
Height: 10-15ft (3-4.5m) grown on a wall   Spread: 8-10ft (2.4-3m)
Hardiness: Zones 6-9
Slightly tender evergreen tree best grown against a west- or south-facing wall. From mid- to late summer it bears fragrant, bowl-shaped, creamy-white flowers up to 8in (20cm) wide. Grown as a tree it can reach heights of 60ft (18m) or more.

Wisteria sinensis 'Alba' looks especially attractive when clambering along the top of an old wall, with bunches of white flowers cascading from the woody stems. Ensure that the stems are trained near to the tops of walls.

CHAPTER FIVE

TREES AND SHRUBS

Trees and shrubs are the plants that provide permanency and continuity in a garden, establishing a framework around which other garden brighteners can be set. Some can also be used to form hedges, create boundaries or separate small sections and areas within the main garden.

Many trees and shrubs bear richly-colored berries in autumn and often through much of the winter season. Red-berried trees include many species of *Malus* and *Sorbus*, while sources of blue berries are harlequin glory bower (*Clerodendrum trichotomum*) and David's viburnum (*Viburnum davidii*).

Yellow and golden-leaved shrubs and trees are especially welcome in spring and early summer, when their fresh rich colors are accentuated by the increasing intensity of the sunlight. The golden-leaved Japanese maple (*Acer japonicum* 'Aureum') makes a splendid small specimen tree, with the bonus of leaves that turn reddish-crimson in autumn before falling.

As well as yellow-leaved trees and shrubs, there is a wealth of trees and shrubs that produce reds and scarlets in their leaves during autumn. These include many members of the maple family, a group seen at their best in New England during fall. Other trees and shrubs with autumn color include the sweet gum (*Liquidambar styraciflua*), Persian parrotia (*Parrotia persica*) and the paperbark maple (*Acer griseum*), with trifoliate leaves colored red and scarlet in autumn. The paperbark maple has the bonus of peeling, light orange-brown underbark.

The heights and spreads given for plants in this chapter are those twenty years after being planted in good soil. Where a plant continues to grow after this period of time, ultimate heights are also given.

Left: Genista cinerea *creates a dazzling dense splash of color. Here, this deciduous shrub is seen framed by stone walls and a gravel path, which help to soften the impact of the intense yellow flowers and allow it to blend in with its surroundings.*

TREES AND SHRUBS

Acer palmatum 'Dissectum Atropurpureum'

Japanese Maple

This hardy and reliable deciduous shrub is a delight in any garden, producing a dome-like canopy of finely cut bronze-red leaves.
Height: 4-5ft (1.2-1.5m)
Spread: 7-9ft (2.1-2.7m)
Hardiness: Zones 5-9
Cultivation: Well-drained but moisture-retentive cool soil in full sun or light shade suits this shrub.
Propagation: It is usually grafted, so its propagation is best left to expert nurserymen.

Left: Acer palmatum 'Dissectum Atropurpureum'
When set amid a light green groundcover plant, this hardy deciduous shrub is superb. It looks just as good planted in the well-manicured lawn of a formal garden.

Below: Azalea 'Kirin'
This hardy evergreen Kurume azalea, with its magnificent display of deep rose flowers in spring, is ideal for a woodland setting in light shade. Acid soil is essential.

Acer palmatum 'Dissectum' is a similarly shaped and sized form, but with finely-cut light green leaves. In a large garden, plant it to contrast with the bronze-red form, but don't crowd them together.

Azalea Kurume Hybrids

The hardy evergreen Kurume azaleas have a relatively low and spreading habit. In spring they are covered with masses of flowers. Colors include pink, magenta, scarlet, and white. Superb Kurume types include 'Blaauw's Pink' (salmon-pink), 'Hinodegiri' (bright crimson), 'Hinomayo' (clear pink), and 'Kirin' (salmon-pink).
Height: 3-4ft (90cm-1.2m)
Spread: 4-5ft (1.2-1.5m)
Hardiness: Zones 6-9
Cultivation: Well-drained light acid soil in partial shade and a sheltered position suit it best. Keep the soil well mulched. This azalea grows well in a woodland setting.
Propagation: It can be increased by cuttings, but it is easier for home gardeners to propagate it by layering low-growing shoots in spring.

Right:Crataegus laevigata 'Rosea Flore Plena'
This superb form of this deciduous tree produces double pink flowers in spring that completely cover the attractive foliage.

Crataegus laevigata

(*Crataegus oxyacantha*)
English Hawthorn

This well-known European native deciduous tree has rounded, shallowly three or five-lobed, mid-green leaves. During late spring and early summer, it reveals 2-3in (5-7.5cm) wide, highly scented, white flowers. But many forms of crataegus create pink or red displays, such as 'Paul's Scarlet' (double and scarlet), 'Rosea' (single and pink) and 'Rosea Flore Plena' (double and pink). *Crataegus laevigata* has the showiest fruit and flower of all the hawthorns, however, it is more susceptible to disease and aphids than other species. Hawthorns are susceptible to cedar apple rust and therefore should not be planted where there are many Eastern red cedars (*Juniperus virginiana*). The Eastern red cedar is an alternate host for the disease. Most hawthorns have thorns and should be avoided where children play. *Crataegus phaenopyrum*, the Washington hawthorn, is the most disease and insect resistant of the Hawthorns. It is native to the Southeastern United States and hardy in Zones 3-8. A slightly larger tree than the English hawthorn, it can reach 30ft (9m) tall. The tree has white spring blooms, orange-red autumn foliage, and showy red fruit that persists into the winter. Varieties include 'Clark' (heavy fruiting) and 'Fastigiata' (columnar form).
Height: 15-20ft (4.5-6m)
Spread: 15-18ft (4.5-5.4m)
Hardiness: Zones 4-9
Cultivation: Any good garden soil and a position in an open and sunny position suit this tree. No regular pruning is needed, other than training the plant during its formative years.
Propagatlon: Named forms are budded or grafted, and this is best left to specialist nurserymen.

Crataegus laevigata is a good specimen tree in a lawn or in a mixed border, where it creates a background of color in spring. Its strong thorns make it unsuitable for high traffic areas.

Deutzia gracilis

Slender Deutzia

A hardy, old-fashioned deciduous shrub with a mounded, graceful growth habit. The matt-green, slender-pointed, lance-shaped leaves provide an attractive foil for the sweetly-scented, star-shaped, pure white, ¾in (1.9cm) wide flowers, borne on arching branches in late spring and early summer.
Height: 2-4ft (60cm-1.2m)
Spread: 3-4ft (90cm-1.2m)
Hardiness: Zones 4-8
Cultivation: Ordinary well-drained garden soil in full sun or light shade suits it well. Deutzias will tolerate a range of soil pH. Minimal pruning suits this shrub. Every few years in the summer, after flowering, cut out old stems to soil level. This encourages the development of fresh shoots from the shrub's base.
Propagation: Although half-ripe 3-4in (7.5-10cm) long cuttings can be taken in midsummer and inserted in equal parts peat and sharp sand, it is easier for the home gardener to take 10-12in (25-30cm) long hardwood cuttings in autumn. Insert them in a trench in a nursery bed. Line the base of the trench with sand.

Embothrium coccineum

Chilean Fire Tree · Chilean Firebush

This eye-catching ornamental evergreen tree has an upright growth habit and produces suckers. The leaves, which are scattered along the branches, are leathery, lance-shaped and mid-green. During early to midsummer, it produces brilliant orange-scarlet flowers, tubular when they first appear. It is not fully hardy in all areas, and in cold places is severely damaged by frosts. The variety 'Norquinco Valley' is a hardier type.
Height: 15-20ft (4.5-6m)
Spread: 8-10ft (2.4-3m)

Hardiness: Zone 9 on West Coast
Cultivation: Well-drained but moisture-retentive neutral or acid deep woodland soil suits it best. In most gardens a position facing south or west and against a high wall is perfect. In winter, protect young plants with a covering of straw. No regular pruning is needed, other than initially removing misplaced shoots and later shortening straggly growths after flowering.
Propagation: Although seeds can be sown in spring in loam-based potting soil at 55°F (13°C), it is far easier for home gardeners to remove sucker growths from around the base of the tree and then pot them up. Plant the young trees in late spring.

Above: Deutzia x elegantissima 'Fasciculata' *This upright hybrid deutzia is only hardy in Zones 6-8, and may be difficult to find. It is worth seeking for its bright rose-pink flowers backed by a foil of matt-green leaves.*

Right: Embothrium coccineum *This is one of the most spectacular and desirable of all garden trees, although it is hardy only in mild West Coast areas. The superb fiery flowers appear in late spring.*

Top right: Gaultheria procumbens *This beautiful groundcover has glorious berries in autumn. This is the plant from which wintergreen oil is obtained, a volatile pale-green substance.*

Deutzia scabra, the fuzzy deutzia, bears clusters of white flushed pink cup-shaped flowers. It is taller (up to 10ft/3m) than *D. gracilis* and blooms several weeks later.

Embothrium coccineum does well on mild West Coast sites when set in woodland among other trees and shrubs that give it some protection. It is native to Chile and Argentina.

Gaultheria procumbens

Wintergreen · Checkerberry · Teaberry · Mountain Tea

A creeping, prostrate, hardy evergreen groundcover native to the Northeast, with shiny dark green slightly-toothed leaves. During early summer, it produces small white or pink bell-shaped flowers, followed in autumn by bright red berries. The foliage turns reddish in fall.

Height: 4-6in (10-15cm)
Spread: 2½-4ft (75cm-1.2m)
Hardiness: Zones 3-7
Cultivation: Acid, moist soil is essential, and a position in the open, or in light shade.
Propagation: During midsummer take 2-3in (5-7.5cm) long cuttings with heels and insert them in equal parts peat and sharp sand. Place them in a cold frame. When rooted, pot up the plants into small pots of acidic potting soil with a high proportion of peat, and place them outside. Preferably, plunge the pots in soil in a nursery bed, so that the soil remains cool and moist.

Gaultheria procumbens was an invaluable plant for early North American settlers. The berries provided winter food for partridge and deer, while the leaves were used as a substitute for tea.

Hibiscus syriacus

Rose-of-Sharon·Althaea· Shrub Althaea

A native of China and India, this hardy deciduous shrub provides color in mid- to late summer and even into autumn. The 3in (7.5cm) wide flowers appear in a color range from white to pink, purple and red. Superb pink and red forms include 'Red Heart' (white flowers with conspicuous red centers), 'Woodbridge' (rose-pink with a carmine eye) and 'Lady Stanley' (semi-double white blooms with red markings at eye).
Height: 6-8ft (1.8-2.4m)
Spread: 4-6ft (1.2-1.8m)
Hardiness: Zones 5-9
Cultivation: Well-drained fertile garden soil and a position in full sun but sheltered from buffeting winds suit this lovely shrub. Regular pruning is not needed, but long shoots can be cut back immediately after flowering.
Propagation: During midsummer, take 3-4in (7.5-10cm) long heel cuttings and insert them in pots of equal parts peat and sharp sand. Place them in a heated frame at 61°F (16°C) and when the plants are rooted, pot them up into loam-based potting soil and overwinter in a cold frame. When the plants fill their pots, transfer them to larger ones and place outdoors until autumn, when they can be planted in the garden.

Top left: Hibiscus syriacus 'Woodbridge' *This highly distinctive shrub has large rosepink flowers with carmine eyes. A sheltered but sunny position is essential.*

Kalmia latifolia

Mountain Laurel

This outstandingly beautiful evergreen shrub has leathery, lance-shaped, mid- to dark green leaves. During midsummer it displays 3-4in (7.5-10cm) wide clusters of bowl-shaped flowers. There are many new varieties of mountain laurel. They include 'Alba' (pure white), 'Ostbo Red' (deep red buds opening to red), 'Pink Charm' (deep pink buds opening to pink), 'Polypetala' (double blooms) and 'Myrtifolia' (a

Above: Hibiscus syriacus 'Red Heart' *This outstandingly attractive shrub has white flowers with conspicuous red centers. It grows best in a sheltered position in the garden.*

compact, smaller leaved *Kalmia*).
Height: 6-10ft (1.8-3m)
Spread: 6-8ft (1.8-2.4m)
Hardiness: Zones 4-9
Cultivation: Moist, slightly acid fertile soil in light shade suits it best. No regular pruning is needed, other than removing faded flowers.
Propagation: The easiest way for a home gardener to increase this plant is by layering low shoots in late summer. Rooting takes about a year, when the new plants can be severed from the parent and planted in a nursery bed for a year before being set in the garden.

Hibiscus rosa-sinensis, a closely-related greenhouse plant from China, was much favored by Chinese ladies. When bruised, the flowers turn black or purple and were used to dye hair and eyebrows.

Above: **Kalmia latifolia** *This beautiful evergreen midsummer flowering native North American shrub produces clusters of bowl-shaped bright pink flowers. When out of flower, the plant has the appearance of a rhododendron. Position it in acid soil and light shade.*

Below: **Kolkwitzia amabilis** *This is a real eye-catcher, with its clear pink flowers from late spring to early summer. In winter the brown peeling bark is attractive in the low rays of winter sun.*

Kolkwitzia amabilis

Beauty Bush

This hardy deciduous shrub from Western China has an upright stance and arching branches displaying dull dark green leaves. The stems have attractive peeling brown bark. During late spring to early summer, it is profusely covered with pink foxglove-like flowers with yellow throats. The best variety is 'Pink Cloud' with clear pink flowers.

Height: 6-10ft (1.8-3m)
Spread: 5-10ft (1.5-3m)
Hardiness: Zones 4-8
Cultivation: Ordinary well-drained garden soil and a position in full sun suit it best. During midsummer, after the flowers have faded, cut out a few of the older flowering stems at soil level. This will encourage the development of further shoots.
Propagation: During mid- to late summer, take 4-6in (10-15cm) long cuttings from non-flowering shoots. Insert them in pots of equal parts peat and sharp sand and place in a cold frame. When rooted, set the cuttings in a nursery bed for a year before planting out.

Kolkwitzia amabilis is ideal for a shrub or mixed border. It looks superb with foxgloves set in front of it. The thimble-like flowers arranged in long spires form an attractive shape contrast.

Leycesteria formosa

Flowering Nutmeg ·
Himalaya Honeysuckle

This handsome and unusual deciduous hardy shrub from the Himalayas has midgreen, heart-shaped leaves and, in late summer, funnel-shaped flowerheads, formed of small white flowers surrounded by highly conspicuous dark claret bracts. These are followed by round, shiny purplish-red berries in autumn.
Height: 5-7ft (1.5-2.1m)
Spread: 4-5ft (1.2-1.5m)
Hardiness: Zones 7-10
Cultivation: Any well-drained

Above: **Lavatera olbia 'Rosea'**
This shrubby tender perennial produces a wealth of leaves topped by pink-red flowers from mid- to late summer, often into early autumn. It grows well in warm, coastal areas.

Lavatera olbia 'Rosea'

Tree Mallow · Tree Lavatera

This rough-stemmed, tender perennial is native to the Western Mediterranean region. The three to five-lobed soft and woolly gray leaves provide a foil for the large pinkish-red flowers borne from mid- to late summer.
Height: 5-7ft (1.5-2.1m)
Spread: 5-6ft (1.5-1.8m)
Hardiness: Zones 9-10
Cultivation: Rich well-drained garden soil suits the tree mallow, preferably in a warm site in full sun against a wall. Keep the soil moist during summer, and in spring cut back the foliage to soil level. Leaving the foliage on the plant during winter helps to protect the roots of the plant from severe cold, as well as appearing attractive when covered with frost.
Propagation: During spring, take half-ripe cuttings.

Lavatera arborea is also known as the tree mallow, but this is a biennial with an erect growth habit, which has soft midgreen leaves and 2in (5cm) wide pale purple flowers during mid- to late summer.

garden soil, preferably in full sun, suits this shrub. It does well in coastal areas. During spring, cut out at soil level the shoots that bore flowers the previous year.
Propagation: In autumn, take 9-10in (23-25cm) long hardwood cuttings. Insert them in a nursery bed, where they will take about a year to produce roots. They should then be left for a further year.

Below: **Leycesteria formosa** *The eye-catching flowers of this hardy deciduous shrub appear during late summer. In autumn, the flowers are followed by purplish-red berries.*

Magnolia quinquepeta 'Nigra'

(*Magnolia liliiflora 'Nigra'*)
A spectacular hardy deciduous shrub with rather straggly growth, this magnolia bears mid- to dark green leaves up to 8in (20cm) long. During late spring to early summer, it produces handsome 3in (7.5cm) long deep reddish-purple flowers.
Height: 6-8ft (1.7-2.4m)
Spread: 5-7ft (1.5-2.1m)
Hardiness: Zones 5-9
Cultivation: Well-drained loamy garden soil and a sheltered site are essential. During spring, top-dress the soil with well-rotted compost. No

Above: **Magnolia quinquepeta 'Nigra'** *Few shrubs are as stunningly attractive as this hardy deciduous species with its large, upright, reddish-purple flowers. It is ideal for planting as a specimen in a large lawn.*

regular pruning is needed.
Propagation: Although cuttings 4in (10cm) long can be taken in mid-summer and inserted in pots containing a sandy potting soil and kept at 70°F (21°C), it is much easier for a home gardener to layer low shoots in spring. However, these often take up to two years to form roots.

Leycesteria formosa produces its flowers along shoots several feet above soil level, so lower growing plants such as bergenias and hellebores make good underplantings.

Magnolias stellata, star magnolia, is another shrubby magnolia. It bears fragrant, white star-shaped blooms in early spring. 'Rosea' has light pink flowers.

Pieris x 'Forest Flame', a hybrid, has
brilliant red early spring foliage. Slowly the leaves
turn pink, then creamy-white and later green. A bonus
is the clusters of drooping white flowers.

Pieris japonica

Japanese Pieris · Japanese Andromeda

An outstanding, hardy, evergreen shrub with midgreen leaves, which are coppery when young, and clustered spring heads of white flowers. There are a number of varieties with red to pink flowers. 'Christmas Cheer' is especially hardy and develops flowers flushed deep rose at their tips during winter. 'Dorothy Wycoff' is a compact variety with deep red buds opening to pink. For added interest *P. japonica* 'Variegata' has leaves edged creamy-white, as well as creamy-white flowers flushed pink when young.
Height: 9-12ft (2.7-4.8m)
Spread: 6-8ft (1.8-2.4m)
Hardiness: Zones 5-8
Cultivation: Moisture-retentive acid soil and light shade suit it well. A sheltered site is also desirable. During spring mulch the plants with well-rotted compost, and in dry summers water the soil.
Propagation: The easiest way for a home gardener to increase it is by layering low shoots in late summer. However rooting is not rapid, often taking up to two years. Alternatively, take 4in (10cm) long cuttings in mid- to late summer and insert them in pots of equal parts peat and sharp sand. Place these in a cold frame. In spring, pot up the rooted cuttings into 3in (7.5cm) pots of acid loam-based potting soil.

Left: **Pieris japonica** *The delicate pitcher-like spring flowers never fail to create interest. This shrub has a delicate appearance, like many early-season plants. It needs acid soil.*

Prunus serrulata

Japanese Flowering Cherry

This cherry, available in many varieties, is well-known for its beautiful spring and early summer flowers. Their colors range from pink to white. Pink forms include 'Amanogawa' (a small columnar tree, with erect branches bearing fragrant semi-double shell-pink flowers in mid- to late spring); 'Kwanzan' or 'Kanzan' (a well-known variety, eventually making a large tree, which is one of the finest spring-flowering trees when it displays large and showy double purplish-pink flowers in midspring); 'Fugenzo' (a spreading tree with double pink blooms); 'Shirofugen' (a fast-growing, wide-spreading tree with double blooms that are pink in bud and open white); 'Shogetsu' (a broad, flat-topped tree with very double, pale pink flowers), and 'Takasago' (with bright pink, semi-double flowers). The beauty of any of these cultivars can be enhanced by an underplanting of spring bulbs.
Height: 20-25ft (6-7.5m)
Spread: 15-20ft (4.5-6m)
Hardiness: Zones 5-9
Cultivation: Well-drained ordinary garden soil in a sunny position suit Japanese cherries best. These trees are shallow rooting, so take care not to damage them when cultivating the soil. The wide-spreading types need staking from their earliest years if they are not to fall over later. Pruning is not usually necessary, but if it is required do it in late summer.
Propagation: This involves budding or grafting, so it is best left to expert nurserymen who have the correct rootstocks.

Prunus cerasifera 'Atropurpurea' – often called 'Pissardii' – is known as the cherry plum and displays distinctive dark red leaves when young that eventually turn purple.

Above: **Prunus sargentii**
This is one of the most attractive cherries, displaying beautiful foliage when unfurling in spring and again in autumn when assuming red and orange tints. The clear pink flowers are borne in spring.

Prunus sargentii

Sargent Cherry

This is one of the most attractive and trouble-free of all cherries, forming a rounded head with bronze-red foliage when young. In autumn, the leaves take on shades of red and orange before falling. It is one of the first trees to show autumn color. During spring, it produces clusters of clear pink single flowers. The only drawback to this species is that it eventually forms a tree too large for the average small garden.
Height: 25-30ft (7.5-9m)
Spread: 18-25ft (5.4-7.5m)
Hardiness: Zones 4-7
Cultivation: Ordinary, well-drained garden soil suits the sargent cherry. It does well in smoky and polluted areas. Cherries are shallow-rooted, so take care not to damage the roots. No regular pruning is needed, but should the removal of a large branch be necessary, do this in late summer, not during winter.
Propagation: It is increased by budding or grafting, and this is best left to a nurseryman.

Prunus subhirtella 'Pendula'

Weeping Higan Cherry

This lovely hardy deciduous spring-flowering tree creates a weeping mound of pendulous shoots that bear delicate pale pink flowers during spring. There are several other exciting varieties, such as *Prunus subhirtella* 'Pendula Rosea', with pale pink flowers on a mushroom-shaped tree. The variety *P. subhirtella* 'Pendula Plena Rosea' has semi-double rose-pink spring flowers. 'Pink Cloud' is another double pink variety that is widely available.
Height: 10-15ft (3-4.5m)
Spread: 10-20ft (3-6m)
Hardiness: Zones 4-8
Cultivation: Ordinary, well-drained, fertile, neutral soil and a relatively sheltered position suit this tree. Cherry trees are not deeply rooted, so soil cultivation must be shallow. No regular pruning is needed, but any shaping or large branch removal must be done in late summer, not winter.
Propagation: This is by grafting and budding on to selected stocks and is best left to expert nurserymen.

Left: **Prunus subhirtella 'Pendula Rosea'** *This stunningly attractive spring-flowering cherry tree forms a distinctive mushroom shape covered with pale pink flowers. It is an excellent choice for small gardens.*

Ribes sanguineum

Flowering Currant

This reliable and popular deciduous garden shrub from the Northwest seldom fails to create interest. Its currant-like, mid- to deep green, three- to five-lobed leaves provide an attractive foil for the 2-4in (5-10cm) long, deep rose-pink, spring flowers. Several excellent varieties are available, including 'Atrorubens' with red flowers and 'Glutinosum' with rose blooms.

Prunus subhirtella 'Pendula Rosea' produces a screen of color right down to soil level and looks best planted as a specimen tree on a lawn. If crowded with other trees, its distinctive form is lost.

Rosa rugosa
Rugosa Rose

This hardy and sturdy deciduous shrub comes from Eastern Asia and has established itself as one of the best-known species roses. It is handsome, with hairy and prickly shoots and wrinkled dark green leaves, glossy above but downy beneath. During mid-summer it develops moderately-scented solitary flowers up to 3in (7.5cm) wide. Flowering often continues intermittently into autumn. It is then that the bright red tomato-shaped fruits, or 'hips', appear. The plants are tolerant of saltspray and useful for seashore plantings. Several red and pink-flowered forms are available, such as 'Frau Dagmar Hastrup' (single, pale rose-pink flowers, vivid pink in bud, with cream stamens); 'Rosea' (single and rose-colored); 'Roseraie de L'Hay' (often sold as 'Plena', bearing large, double, crimson-purple flowers with cream stamens); and 'Hansa' (very cold hardy with double, purplish-red flowers).

Height: 5-7ft (1.5-2.1m)
Spread: 4-4¹/₂ft (1.2-1.3m)
Hardiness: Zones 2-7
Cultivation: Ordinary well-drained garden soil is ideal, beware of limestone soils. An open position in full sun or light shade is suitable, but avoid heavily shaded areas. Very little pruning is needed. If bushes do become overcrowded, cut them back in spring.
Propagation: Detach sucker-like growths in autumn, planting in a nursery bed. Alternatively, take hardwood cuttings 9in (23cm) long in autumn and insert them in sand-lined trenches in a nursery border.

Left: Rosa rugosa 'Frau Dagmar Hastrup' *This reliable species rose develops single, pale rose-pink flowers with cream stamens during midsummer and intermittently through to autumn. These are followed by bright red, tomato-shaped fruits, commonly called 'hips'.*

Above: Ribes sanguineum
In spring this flowering currant produces a colorful display of deep rose-pink flowers. Several superb varieties are available including some with red blooms.

Currants are an alternate host for white pine blister rust. Since currant plantings are banned in some states, check with your state forestry agent before buying.
Height: 6-8ft (1.7-2.4m)
Spread: 5-7ft (1.5-2.1m)
Hardiness: Zones 6-9, does best on the West Coast.
Cultivation: Any good well-drained soil in full sun or light shade is suitable. Prune by cutting out old wood at soil level after flowering.
Propagation: During late autumn or early winter, take hardwood cuttings 10-12in (25-30cm) long and insert them in a nursery bed. They root quite easily and after only one season can be moved to the garden.

Ribes alpinum is a smaller (3-6ft/90cm-1.8m tall), shrub that is useful in the East and Midwest (Zones 3-7). It has scarlet fruits in late summer.

Rosa rugosa has large, bright red fruit, called hips. The hips are high in vitamin C. They are used for jellies and steeped for tea.

TREES AND SHRUBS

Viburnum x bodnantense

Bodnant Viburnum

An unusual, slow-growing deciduous viburnum with dull green, toothed leaves, tinged bronze when young. The sweetly-scented densely-packed, 1-2in (2.5-5cm) long clusters of rose-flushed white flowers appear on naked branches during midwinter. It is available in several forms, including 'Dawn', with large clusters of richly-scented flowers. Another winter-flowering viburnum is the deciduous, fragrant viburnum, *V. farreri,* also known as *V. fragrans.* The highly scented nature of its pink-tinged white flowers is indicated by its synonym. From late winter to early spring it reveals its flowers in pendant clusters 1-1½in (2.5-4cm) long. For midspring scented flowers *V. carlesii,* Koreanspice viburnum, with white flowers – but pink in bud – is well worth considering.
Height: 9-12ft (2.7-3.5m)
Spread: 8-10ft (2.4-3m)
Hardiness: Zones 8-9
Cultivation: Well-drained but moisture-retentive soil is best; add well-decomposed compost, leaf mold or peat if drainage is poor. A sunny position suits it best. Very little pruning is needed, other than the occasional removal of weak or old branches. Cutting back such shoots encourages the development of fresh shoots from the plant's base.
Propagation: During late summer, low-growing branches can be layered: this is the easiest method of increasing the plant for the home gardener.

Viburnum x bodnantense is best sited by a path or near the house if the highly-scented winter flowers are to be fully appreciated. Add an underplanting of spring bulbs to create extra and continuing color.

Weigela florida

Old-fashioned Weigela

An old-fashioned hardy shrub, with 1-1¼in (2.5-3cm) long, rather honeysuckle-shaped flowers during late spring and early summer. The shrub creates a mounded form with arching branches. Many of the named varieties are hybrids between *W. florida* and other Asiatic species. Red and pink flowered varieties include: 'Abel Carriere' (deep rose-carmine with a yellow throat), 'Bristol Ruby' (bright ruby-red with near black buds), 'Centennial' (extremely cold hardy, rosy red), 'Eva Rathke' (bright red), 'Newport Red' (dark red) and 'Styriaca' (red buds opening to reveal pink flowers).

Height: 6-9ft (1.8-2.7m)
Spread: 9-12ft (2.7-3.6m)
Hardiness: Zones 3-8
Cultivation: Well-drained but moisture-retentive rich soil and a position in full sun suit it best. It requires regular pruning, each year after flowering, cutting back one or two of the old stems to soil level. This will encourage the development of fresh main shoots from ground level.
Propagation: Take hardwood cuttings 10-12in (25-30cm) long in mid- to late autumn and insert them in a nursery bed. Rooting takes about a year. Alternatively, during midsummer, take 3-4in (7.5-10cm) long half-ripe cuttings from non-flowering shoots and insert them in pots of equal parts peat and sharp sand kept at 61°F (16°C). Pot up the cuttings when rooted and slowly harden them off. Place them in a cold frame during winter and plant them out into a nursery bed in spring. They will need to remain there for about a year before being set in their permanent positions.

Left: Weigela 'Bristol Ruby' *This is one of the many hybrids, with more upright growth than most weigelas. It does best when planted in rich, moist soil and given a sunny position.*

Further plants to consider

Aesculus x carnea
Red Horse Chestnut
Height: 30-40ft (9-12m)   Spread: 15-30ft (6-9m)
Hardiness: Zones 5-8
A beautiful chestnut with midgreen leaves and 6-8in (15-20cm) high candles of rose pink flowers in early to midsummer.

Calycanthus florida
Sweetshrub · Carolina Allspice
Height: 6-9ft (1.8-2.7m)   Spread: 6-12ft (1.8-3.6m)
Hardiness: Zones 4-9
A deciduous, mounded shrub with dark green leaves. The fragrant, reddish-brown blooms appear in spring.

Magnolia x soulangeana
Saucer magnolia
Height: 20-30ft (6-9m)   Spread: 20-30ft (6-9m)
Hardiness: Zones 4-9
A large-leaved, spreading deciduous tree. Dramatic saucer-like, pink flowers in early spring before the leaves.

Malus floribunda
Japanese Flowering Crabapple
Height: 15-25ft (4.5-7.5m)   Spread: 10-15ft (3-4.5m)
Hardiness: Zones 4-8
A well-known round-headed hardy deciduous tree with single bright carmine flowers fading to pink in early summer.

Spirea x bumalda
Bumalda spirea
Height: 2-3ft (60-90cm)   Spread: 3-5ft (90cm-1.5m)
Hardiness: Zones 4-9
A mounded, delicately-leaved deciduous shrub with sprays of rosy-pink flowers in early to midsummer. 'Gold Flame' is a handsome yellow-leaved cultivar.

Tamarix ramosissima
Tamarisk
Height: 10-15ft (3-4.5m)   Spread: 10-15ft (3-4.5m)
Hardiness: Zones 4-9
A large, feathery and wispy hardy deciduous flowering shrub with pale to midgreen leaves and rosy pink flowers in early summer. It is an excellent plant for coastal areas.

Weigelas suit a mixed border or one filled by shrubs and small trees with underplantings of bulbs. The variety 'Foliis Purpureis', with purple leaves and pink flowers, creates long-term interest.

Ceanothus delilianus 'Gloire de Versailles'

Gloire de Versailles Ceanothus

This hardy deciduous rather open shrub is an attractive, unusual plant for a border. The soft, fragrant, powder-blue flowers are borne in heads up to 8in (20cm) long from midsummer until early autumn. It is best planted in a mixed border, where its long stems can splay out over lower-growing plants.
Height: 6-8ft (1.8-2.4m)
Spread: 5-7ft (1.5-2.1m)
Hardiness: Zones 4-8
Cultivation: Well-drained fertile soil in good light suits it. Because the flowers are borne on the new wood, the bush must be pruned hard in spring. Cut back the previous season's shoots almost to their points of origin. Follow this with an application of fertilizer to encourage the rapid growth of new shoots.
Propagation: During summer, take 3-4in (7.5-10cm) long half-ripe cuttings of the current season's growth, inserting them in pots of equal parts peat and sharp sand. Place them in a propagation frame at a temperature of 61°F (16°C). When they are rooted, pot up the cuttings into 3in (7.5cm) pots of soil-based potting mix and over-winter them in a cold frame. Plant them out in the garden in spring.

Cercis canadensis

Eastern Redbud

A hardy, rounded, wide-spreading, deciduous tree from the Eastern and South Central U.S. It grows in the woodland understory but is also suitable as a patio or specimen tree. The eye-catching and distinctive tree bears clusters of rich purplish/pink flowers on bare branches in early summer. After the flowers have faded it develops rounded, glaucous-green leaves with heart-shaped bases. The leaves turn yellow in the autumn. It produces attractive flat, green, pea-like pods which are most noticeable after the leaves fall, providing interest during winter.

Abies concolor 'Glauca Compacta'

Dwarf White Fir

This beautiful dwarf and compact conifer (often sold as *Abies concolor* 'Compacta') has an irregular shape and grayish-blue foliage. It is so slow-growing that even after twenty five years it often reaches no more than 2¹/₂ft (75cm) high, with a 3¹/₂ft (1m) spread. It is ideal for a rock garden, or even in a large container.
Hardiness: Zones 4-8

Above: **Abies concolor 'Glauca Compacta'** *This is one of the best slow-growing dwarf conifers for a rock garden or container. Its grayish-blue foliage is very attractive and looks at its best when the tree is planted on its own or in a color-contrasting group.*

Cultivation: Deep, well-drained, slightly acid soil suits it best. It prefers a warm, dry position.
Propagation: It is raised by grafting, a technique best left to experts.

Abies concolor is an especially beautiful blue conifer. The species grows over 50ft (15.5m) tall and is a majestic tree. It is useful as a specimen or screen.

Ceanothus 'Gloire de Versailles' is a hybrid which was bred in France. The parent species are native to the Northeastern U.S. and west to Colorado.

Above: **Ceanothus 'Gloire de Versailles'** *This strikingly impressive deciduous shrub produces large heads of powdery-blue flowers on open stems from mid- to late summer. It is best grown in a mixed border.*

Height: 20-30ft (6-9.5m)
Spread: 25-35ft (8-11.5m)
Hardiness: Zones 5-9
Cultivation: Any good garden soil and a sunny position suit it. No regular pruning is needed.
Propagation: During autumn, sow seeds outdoors in soil-based mix. When they are large enough to handle, pot up the seedlings singly in soil-based potting mix and plunge the pots up to their rims in a sheltered corner. Once established, the plants can be set out into the garden.

Right: **Cercis siliquastrum**
This is the European redbud, known as Judas tree. Similar in appearance to the Eastern redbud, but hardy only to Zone 9.

Cercis canadensis is ideal for blending with late spring and early summer bulbs. It will naturalize well in a woodland garden in light shade, and is an ideal specimen tree for small yard or patio.

Corylus maxima 'Purpurea' produces its main burst of
foliage color at eye height, and is useful for bringing
focal points to a shrub or mixed border. Its vase shape
allows it to be underplanted with spring-flowering
bulbs – but not too close to its base.

Corylus maxima 'Purpurea'

Purple-leaved Filbert

This is a rich-purple-leaved form of the European filbert. It is a deciduous shrub which has large, heart-shaped leaves. The whole shrub has an open, spreading growth habit, often becoming bare at its base. The dark purple leaves fade to green in summer, although the buds and catkins remain purple. In the warmth of the South the purple color may be quite fleeting. *Corylus americana,* a green-leaved filbert, is useful as a hedge and for its nuts. *Corylus avellena* 'Contorta' (Harry Lauder's walking stick) is a small growing 6.5ft (2m) curiosity. Its twisted and curled branches make it an eye-catching accent in a small landscape.
Height: 8-12ft (2.4-3.5m)
Spread: 8-10ft (2.8-3m)
Hardiness: Zones 4-8
Cultivation: Any good well-drained garden soil and a sunny position, preferably sheltered from cold north and east winds, is suitable. During its early years, cut it back in late winter and early spring to encourage the development of shoots from around its base. Prune back by half the growth made the previous year. As the shrub develops, do not cut it back so severely. Throughout this period, cut out awkward shoots from the center of the shrub.
Propagation: Purple-leaved forms seldom come true from seeds and are therefore best increased by layering low growing shoots in autumn.

Left: Corylus maxima 'Purpurea'
This is a useful shrub for bringing color-contrasting foliage to a garden throughout summer.

Cotinus coggygria 'Notcutt's Variety'

This hardy deciduous shrub has eye-catching deep purple leaves that are semi-translucent. It bears feathery purple flowers during midsummer.
Height: 12-15ft (3.5-4.5m)
Spread: 10-12ft (3-3.5m)
Hardiness: Zones 5-8
Cultivation: Any good well-drained garden soil and a position in full sun suit it. Avoid rich soils, as it produces the best color when in poor conditions. Hard pruning in spring will encourage a dense shrub with vivid foliage color.
Propagation: During late summer, take 4-5in (10-13cm) long heel cuttings, inserting them in pots of equal parts peat and sharp sand. Place the pots in a cold frame and during spring set out the young plants into a nursery bed until they are large enough to be planted out in the garden. Keep the nursery bed free from weeds.

Cotinus coggygria 'Notcutt's Variety' will produce a large specimen shrub on a lawn or as a backdrop for color-contrasting plants. For small gardens, *C. c.* 'Royal Purple' is better, growing to 10ft (3m) in height and the same width.

Hydrangea macrophylla

Bigleaf Hydrangea

This well-known deciduous and rounded shrub from Japan and China has oval, slightly pointed, coarsely-toothed light green leaves. The flower heads appear from mid- to late summer. There are two forms: *Hortensia* types and the *Lacecaps*. The more well-known

Hortensia forms have large globose heads, while the *Lacecaps* display flat flower heads formed almost entirely of sterile flowers with a flat disc-like corymb. In the center there is an area of tiny fertile flowers, and this has a marginal ring of ray florets which are sterile. The variety 'Blue Wave' is a good example of this type.

Height: 5-6ft (1.5-1.8m)
Spread: 5-6ft (1.5-1.8m)

Hardiness: Zones 4-9
Cultivation: Slightly acid, light, well-drained but moisture-retentive soil is best. Acid soil is essential to ensure that blue varieties remain blue. Pink varieties also produce blue colors when given an acid soil.
Propagation: From late spring to mid-summer take cuttings 3in (7.5cm) long. Remove the lower leaves and cut the bases just below leaf joints. Insert them in pots of equal

Hydrangea macrophylla is ideal for forming a background to a large lawn, where it provides color over a long period. In such a position, a *Hortensia* type is best. The *Lacecaps* are better in a naturalized garden setting.

parts peat and sharp sand and place them in a cold frame. When the cuttings are rooted, pot them up into an acid potting soil and plunge the pots to their rims in a nursery bed until they are ready to plant out into the garden.

Left: Hydrangea macrophylla
Hortensia hydrangeas are reliable garden favorites, creating a dominant display of mop-like heads from mid- to late summer.

Right: Hydrangea macrophylla 'Blue Wave' *This vigorous lacecap hydrangea provides flowers in shades of blue and pink throughout the summer months.*

Lavandula stoechas

French Lavender

This tender evergreen shrub is native to the Mediterranean region. It has narrow, gray-green leaves and distinctive, deep purple, tubular flowers borne on 1-2in (2.5-5cm) long four-angled spikes during early to midsummer. It is characterized by tufted purple bracts (modified leaves) borne at the tops of the flower spikes. It can be grown in borders, rock or herb gardens.
Height: 1-1¹/₂ft (30-45cm)
Spread: 1¹/₂-2ft (45-60cm)
Hardiness: Zones 6-9
Cultivation: Light, well-drained soils and an open and sunny position suit it. It is not as hardy as the English lavender and during severe winters can be seriously damaged in exposed areas.
Propagation: During late summer, take 3in (7.5cm) long cuttings and insert them in pots of equal parts peat and sharp sand. Place them in a cold frame. Pot them up when they are rooted and plant them out into the garden in spring.

Right: Lavandula stoechas
This pretty lavender has distinctive deep purple flowers topped by purple bracts (modified leaves) that persist long after the actual flowers have faded.

Lavandula angustifolia, English lavender, is hardier than *L. stoechas* and is more commonly grown for fragrance. Popular cultivars include 'Hidcote', with deep purple flowers, and 'Jean Davis', with pinkish-white blooms.

Above: Picea pungens 'Pendula'
With careful training and pruning, this often unpredictable conifer can be persuaded to develop a superb weeping shape and to create an exciting focal point in any garden.

Left: Picea pungens 'Koster' *This is one of the best blue spruces with a neat pyramidal habit. It looks especially attractive in spring when young and fresh growths appear.*

Picea pungens 'Koster'

Koster's Blue Spruce

This distinctive form of the Colorado spruce has intensely blue foliage and a neat growth habit, forming an upright and pyramidal shape up to 7ft (2.1m) high and 3¹/₂ft (1m) wide after ten years. During spring, the new growth is pale blue.
Height: 30ft (9m)
Spread: 10ft (3m)
Hardiness: Zones 2-7
Cultivation: Deep, moist soil – acid or neutral – is needed. A position in full sun or slight shade suits it best.
Propagation: It is grafted onto stocks of Picea pungens to produce a distinctive upright form. The cost to nurserymen of this time-consuming technique accounts for the high price they will ask for young plants of this lovely variety.

Picea pungens 'Pendula'

This distinctive blue conifer – often known as Picea pungens 'Glauca Pendula' – sometimes has an erratic shape but can be recognized by its down-swept branches and glaucous-blue leaves. During spring, the young growths are tufted and pale blue. It often produces two leading shoots: one may be trained upright, while the other trails.
Height: 10-18ft (3-5.4m)
Spread: 10-18ft (3-5.4m)
Hardiness: Zones 2-7
Cultivation: Moist, deep soil – acid or neutral – is best, and a position in slight shade or full sun.
Propagation: It needs to be grafted onto a stock of Picea pungens, so the plants are often expensive to buy, as with P. pungens 'Koster'.

Picea pungens 'Thomsen'

This eye-catching blue spruce has an upright, cone-like growth habit and branches packed with silvery-blue foliage. During spring, it develops a fresh growth of very pale silver-blue that contrasts with the older and darker foliage. Eventually a small to medium-sized tree, but after ten years it reaches only 7ft (2.1m) high and 3¹/₂ft (1m) wide.
Height: 30ft (9m)
Spread: 10ft (3m)
Hardiness: Zones 2-7
Cultivation: Moist deep soil – acid or neutral – is best, and a position in slight shade or full sun.
Propagation: It is a grafted form, so raising new plants is best left to nurserymen.

Right: Picea pungens 'Thomsen'
This is a beautiful blue spruce with a cone-shaped outline. The foliage is thick and the needles long. It grows into a strong, upright shape.

Picea pungens 'Koster' brings height to a small planting or the edge of a small rock garden. Eventually it forms a large plant, but up to the age of 15-20 years, it is quite suitable for a small area.

Picea pungens 'Pendula' must be given space and an open situation where other plants do not compete for attention. For color contrast, set it in a sea of *Spirea* x *bumalda* 'Gold Flame', a yellow-leaved shrub.

Further plants to consider

Buddleia dandii
Butterfly Bush
Height: 5-10ft (1.5-3m)   Spread: 3-6ft (90cm-1.8m)
Hardiness: Zones 5-9
An upright shrub with gray-green foliage. Fragrant purple to lilac spikes of bloom appear from midsummer to early fall. Flowers attract butterflies. Winter-kills to ground in the North, so for best form and bloom cut the shrub to within 6in (15cm) of the ground in early spring.

Chamaecyparis pisifera 'Boulevard'
Sawara False Cypress
Height: 3-8ft (90cm-2.4m)   Spread: 2-4ft (60cm-1.2m)
Hardiness: Zones 5-8
A narrow, pyramidal conifer with aromatic silver-blue foliage. An excellent small ornamental tree.

Hibiscus syriacus 'Blue Bird'
Rose of Sharon
Height: 6-8ft (1.8-2.4m)   Spread: 4-6ft (1.2-1.8m)
Hardiness: Zones 5-9
A hardy deciduous shrub, with rich green leaves and mid-blue, 3in (7.5cm) wide flowers from mid- to late summer and often into autumn.

Ruta graveolens 'Jackman's Blue'
Rue
Height: 1¹/₂-2ft (45-60cm)   Spread: 1¹/₂-2ft (45-60cm)
Hardiness: Zones 4-9
An evergreen perennial sub-shrub, with deeply divided, aromatic blue-green leaves. Clusters of yellow-green flowers appear in summer.

Syringa vulgaris
Common Lilac
Height: 8-15ft (2.4-4.5m)   Spread: 6-12ft (1.8-3.6m)
Hardiness: Zones 3-7
An old-favorite deciduous shrub with bright green heart-shaped leaves. The fragrant, showy flowers appear in late spring in many shades of purple, lavender, blue, pink and white.

Vitex negundo
Chastetree
Height: 10-15ft (3-4.5m)   Spread: 6-10ft (1.8-3m)
Hardiness: Zones 6-9
A tender shrub (hardy perennial in the North) with gray-green foliage. For best performance cut to the ground in the spring. The 5-8in (13-20cm) flower spikes appear in August in shades of lavender. Ideal for the shrub or perennial border.

Picea pungens 'Thomsen' is superb when positioned several yards in front of yellow-foliaged conifers or in an open situation with clear sky behind. Take care not to cramp it with other conifers set too close, as this will spoil its shape.

Acer palmatum 'Aureum'

Golden Japanese Maple

This beautiful, slow-growing, deciduous bushy tree has bright yellow, five to nine-lobed leaves. They are displayed in irregular layers, and in autumn turn rich crimson. It is an ideal tree for a small garden.
Height: 15-20ft (4.5-6m)
Spread: 12-15ft (3.5-4.5m)
Hardiness: Zones 6-8
Cultivation: Well-drained but moist soil in slight shade suits it best, as the foliage may be scorched in strong sunlight. No regular pruning is needed, other than initial shaping.
Propagation: It needs to be budded or grafted, and this is best left to expert nurserymen.

Left: **Acer palmatum 'Aureum'** *is a superb small maple for a lawn or in a mixed border. During autumn, the bright yellow leaves become rich crimson.*

Below: Berberis darwinii *It often forms a sprawling bush, with long shoots intermingled with neighboring shrubs. When grown as a hedge, it requires regular pruning after flowering to keep it in shape. It may be difficult to locate.*

Berberis darwinii

Darwin's Berberis

This beautiful hardy evergreen shrub bears drooping bunches of flowers amid stalkless glossy, dark-green spiny leaves. From mid- to late spring, it bears deep orange-yellow flowers. During late summer and early autumn there is a profusion of purplish-blue oval berries along the shoots.
Height: 6-10ft (1.7-3m)
Spread: 6-10ft (1.7-3m)
Hardiness: Zones 5-8
Cultivation: It succeeds in any good soil and in full light or light shade. Cut back straggly shoots after flowering.
Propagation: Although it can be increased from seed sown in April in the open soil, the plants do not always produce replicas of the parent. Therefore, take 3-4in (7.5-10cm) long cuttings with heels during late summer, inserting them into pots of equal parts of peat and sharp sand and place them in a

Acer palmatum 'Aureum' looks superb in a border, with underplantings of the spring-flowering *Crocus vernus* or variegated hostas. It also does well as a specimen in a lawn, or in a large tub on a patio.

Berberis thunbergii 'Aurea' is a yellow-leaved deciduous barberry. If may be grown as a hedge specimen or in a perennial border. A slow-growing shrub that should be planted in full sun for vivid yellow foliage.

cold frame. Set the rooted plants out into a nursery bed the following spring. Alternatively, pot up the rooted plants into large pots. This makes them easier to transplant into their permanent positions at a later date. This is a shrub that can be grown to form a spring-flowering hedge. If used as such, prune the plants by a quarter immediately after planting them, to encourage bushy growth.

Calceolaria integrifolia

Pocketbook Flower

This half-hardy, upright, bushy, semi-evergreen shrub has bright yellow, pouch-like flowers, 1/2-1in (12-25mm) long, from mid- to late summer. It grows outside only in warm areas, and even then requires the protection of a south or west-facing wall. The finely wrinkled, matt, midgreen leaves are lance-shaped.
Height: 4ft (1.2m)
Spread: 4-5ft (1.2-1.5m)
Hardiness: Zones 9-10
Cultivation: Light, well-drained fertile soil – neutral to acid – is best, and a position in full sun or partial shade. Usually the plants are discarded after flowering, but occasionally in warm and frost-free areas they may become perennial. Plants that do survive winter may still be cut back by cold weather, and are therefore best pruned in late spring to encourage new growth.
Propagation: The plant is best increased from 3in (7.5cm) long heel cuttings in late summer, inserted into pots of equal parts peat and sharp sand. Keep these at 59°F (15°C) and when the cuttings have rooted, pot them up into potting soil. Plant them out into the garden in autumn.

Right: Calceolaria integrifolia
The vivid-yellow, pouch-like flowers of this half-hardy shrub are eye-catching. But grow it outside only in warm areas and with the protection of a south or west-facing wall.

Calceolaria integrifolia, with its pouch-shaped flowers, gains its generic name because the flower parts resemble a shoe. In Latin, the word for shoemaker is *calceolarius.*

TREES AND SHRUBS

Catalpa bignonioides 'Aurea'

Golden Catalpa · Golden Indian Bean Tree

This tree provides a dramatic spring display of brilliant yellow leaves. It is a neatly-shaped, hardy deciduous tree for a small garden. The heart-shaped leaves, 4-10in (10-25cm) long and 3-8in (7.5-20cm) wide, turn green in the summer. During midsummer there are purple and yellow flowers.
Height: 20-25ft (6-7.5m)
Spread: 20-25ft (6-7.5m)
Hardiness: Zones 5-9
Cultivation: Catalpas appreciate

any good garden soil and a position in full sun, slightly sheltered from cold winds. No regular pruning is needed, other than occasionally shaping the tree in early spring.
Propagation: During late summer, take 3-4in (7.5-10cm) long heel cuttings, inserting them into pots containing equal parts peat and sharp sand, and keeping them at 64°F (18°C). When the cuttings are rooted, pot them up into small pots and overwinter in a cold frame. In spring, set them out in a nursery bed for three or four years before transplanting to their final positions.

Below: **Chamaecyparls lawsoniana 'Lutea'** *A beautiful golden conifer, raised in North America more than one hundred years ago. It requires a sunny position for the golden-yellow foliage to keep its color throughout the year.*

Right: Catalpa bignonioides 'Aurea' *The beautiful, soft-textured, woolly, heart-shaped leaves of this deciduous tree are vivid yellow in the spring. The green summer foliage perfectly highlights the purple and yellow flowers.*

Chamaecyparis lawsoniana 'Lutea'

Lawson Falsecypress

This golden-yellow-foliaged cultivar of the evergreen conifer has an upward, narrow stance, with a drooping, spire-like top and flattened, somewhat feathery sprays of slightly drooping foliage.
Height: 30ft (9m)
Spread: 5-6ft (1.5-1.8m)
Hardiness: Zones 6-8
Cultivation: Well-drained garden soil and an open but sheltered position suit it best. In shady positions it tends to become green. No pruning is required, except during early years, when you should cut out second-leader shoots during spring.
Propagation: Seeds can be sown in spring, but the seedlings will not necessarily reflect the nature of the parent. Named forms are best raised in spring from heel cuttings 4in (10cm) long, inserted into pots containing equal parts of peat and sharp sand and kept at 61°F (16°C).

Catalpa bignonioides 'Aurea' is excellent for a small garden. It can be grown in a lawn, or mixed with other plants in a border. However, do not place high plants in front of it, or they spoil its shape.

Chamaecyparis lawsoniana 'Lutea' can be grown as a specimen in a grouping with other conifers, or in a mixed border where its size and color will break up visually long vistas.

Propagation: Seeds can be sown when ripe in late summer, but they take up to two years to germinate. Often the plant has low-growing roots and these can be layered in late summer and early autumn. They take about two years to produce roots. Another method is to take 3-4in (7.5-10cm) long half-ripe heel cuttings in mid- to late summer. Insert them in equal parts peat and sharp sand and place in a propagation frame at 61°F (16°C). When they are rooted, place them in a cold frame.

Below: **Cornus mas** *The clusters of small golden-yellow flowers are a delight in late winter and early spring. The fruits of this European native have been used for preserves and tarts. The Turks used the flowers to control diarrhea, as a preventative for cholera, and for flavoring sherbet. The hard wood has been used to make forks and ladder-spokes.*

When the cuttings are rooted, pot them up into small pots and plant them out into a nursery bed during the following year for three or four seasons before setting them in their final site.

Cornus mas

Cornelian Cherry

This is a distinctive late winter and early spring flowering deciduous shrub. It is somewhat twiggy and bushy, with 1/2-1in (1.2-2.5cm) long clusters of golden-yellow flowers. These are borne along naked branches and are followed by bright red, edible cherry-like fruits. The dark green leaves turn reddish-purple in autumn. The form 'Aurea' has leaves suffused yellow.
Height: 8-12ft (2.4-3.5m)
Spread: 6-10ft (1.8-3m)
Hardiness: Zones 4-8
Cultivation: Any good garden soil, including clay, suits it. Position it in full sun, if possible, although it will tolerate light shade. No regular pruning is needed, other than an initial shaping when young.

Cornus mas is a delight in late winter. Its branches often spread to soil level, making it unnecessary to set plants beneath it. Birds enjoy the cherry-like fruits in the autumn.

TREES AND SHRUBS

Cupressus macrocarpa 'Goldcrest'

Monterey Cypress

This beautiful, hardy, densely-foliaged, medium-sized evergreen conifer has rich yellow, feathery, scale-like foliage. It has a narrow, columnar outline which broadens slightly with age. It is excellent for coastal areas and can also be planted to form a hedge. In ten years, it should have grown 13ft (4m) high and 3¹/₂ft (1m) wide.
Height: 30-60ft (9-18m)
Spread: 5-6ft (1.5-1.8m)
Hardiness: Zones 8-9
Cultivation: Suitable for seaside plantings in a sunny, open

Left: **Cupressus macrocarpa 'Goldcrest'** *This is a superbly-colored form of the Monterey Cypress. It is best suited for plantings by the sea.*

Cupressus macrocarpa 'Goldcrest' a California native, makes a striking contrast with blue-colored conifers. It is not suited for East Coast climates.

position, this lovely conifer needs no regular pruning, other than removing double leader shoots in spring.

Propagation: Seeds can be sown in spring, but the seedlings will not resemble the parent. Instead, take 3-4in (7.5-10cm) long heel cuttings during autumn, inserting them into pots of equal parts peat and sharp sand and placing them in a cold frame. When the cuttings are rooted, pot them up into small pots and plunge these in a nursery bed. Set the plants out into their final positions in the garden in autumn when they are well grown and sturdy.

Below: Cupressus macrocarpa
The golden form of this magnificent conifer forms an eye-catching hedge that can be used as a backdrop for dark-leaved plants, or as an attractive feature on its own. It looks best when positioned in good sunlight.

Above: Cytisus scoparius 'Golden Sunlight' *The rich yellow, pea-shaped flowers are dominant in early summer. The plant often appears bare when flowering is over, and is therefore best positioned in a mixed border where color can be continued by other plants.*

Cytisus scoparius

Scotch Broom

This is an upright, free-flowering deciduous shrub with pea-shaped, rich-yellow flowers, 1in (2.5cm) long, borne singly or in pairs during early summer. Although deciduous, its green stems give it an evergreen appearance. There are several superb cultivars, including 'Andreanus' (yellow and chocolate flowers), 'Burkwoodii' (shades of maroon, purple and red flowers), 'Golden Sunlight' (rich yellow flowers) and 'Sulphureus' (sulphur-yellow flowers).

Height: 5-8ft (1.5-2.5m)
Spread: 5-7ft (1.5-2.1m)
Hardiness: Zones 5-9
Cultivation: Well-drained, neutral or slightly acid soils are best, and plenty of sun. After flowering, cut off about two-thirds of the previous season's shoots. It is often easier to do this with a pair of garden shears.
Propagation: It can be increased from seeds sown in spring and placed in a cold frame, but it is easier to take 3-4in (7.5-10cm) long heel cuttings during late summer. Insert them into pots containing equal parts of peat and sharp sand and place them in a cold frame. Pot them into pots of potting soil when they have rooted, and plant out into the garden in autumn.

Cytisus scoparius is an ideal plant for poor soils, and it has little or no insect or disease problems. Buy container-grown plants, as it can be difficult to transplant.

Right: Forsythia x intermedia 'Spectabilis' *This is one of the showiest of the forsythia cultivars, its rich yellow flowers appearing with the newly-emerging leaves.*

Forsythia x intermedia

Border Forsythia

Few spring-flowering plants can match the color impact of this vigorous, deciduous hardy hybrid shrub. It has golden-yellow, bell-shaped flowers, 1-1¼in (2.5-3cm) wide, in groups of up to six on the previous year's shoots. The leaves are lance-shaped, toothed and dark green. Several superb cultivars are available, including 'Spectabilis' with large rich yellow flowers, 'Lynwood' with very large golden-yellow flowers, and 'Spring Glory' with lighter yellow flowers. The cultivar 'Spectabilis' can also be used to form hedges.

Height: 8-10ft (2.4-3m)
Spread: 7-8ft (2.1-2.4m)
Hardiness: Zones 5-8
Cultivation: Most garden soils are suitable, in sun or partial shade. They are a good choice for town gardens. If you want to grow a hedge of 'Spectabilis', set the plants 1½-2ft (45-60cm) apart in late autumn, cutting the shoots back to soil level to encourage bushiness from ground level. Because flowers are borne mainly on shoots which developed during the previous season, cut out a few of the oldest shoots from the base each spring after flowering. At the same time, remove dead wood and twiggy growths from the center of the shrub. Hedges need a light clipping in spring. Do not tightly shear. Forsythias should remain open for best bloom and effect.
Propagation: Home gardeners can readily increase forsythia in autumn, by taking hardwood cuttings, 10-12in (25-30cm) long, of the current year's growth. Insert them in a nursery bed in the garden; rooting takes about a year. Then plant in their final sites.

Forsythias are, to many people the epitome of spring and the beginning of the gardener's year. The cheerful yellow flowers add to those of naturalized daffodils to paint a strongly-colored spring picture.

Height: 2-4ft (60cm-1.2m)
Spread: 5-7ft (1.5-2.1m)
Hardiness: Zones 7-9
Cultivation: Give genistas a well-drained, slightly acid or neutral soil and a position in full sun. They do not like rich soil as this encourages soft growth, quickly damaged by frost. Because plants are difficult to transplant, use only container-grown ones. No regular pruning is required, other than thinning out congested and dead shoots after flowering. However, a light clipping at this time helps the development of further shoots, as well as maintaining an attractive shape.
Propagation: It can be increased from seeds, but the easiest method is to take 3-4in (7.5-10cm) long heel cuttings during late summer, insert them into pots of equal parts peat and sharp sand and place them in a cold frame. Pot the cuttings into potting soil when they are rooted, and transplant them into the garden in late autumn.

Below: **Genista hispanica**
This early summer-flowering shrub, native of south-west Europe, grows best on poor, well-drained soils. Rich soils encourage lush growth that is vulnerable to frost damage.

Left: Forsythia *As an added dimension, a forsythia can be grown as a standard and planted as a focal point in the corner of a garden.*

Genista hispanica

Spanish Gorse · Spanish Broom

A dense, spiny and hairy deciduous shrub, best suited to warm areas. The deep green, exceptionally narrow leaves are borne on upright stems, and the golden-yellow, pea-shaped, 1in (2.5m) wide flowers appear from early to midsummer. When it is in full flower, the color is so intense that the whole shrub appears blessed with a golden glow. It is one of the showiest brooms.

Genista hispanica produces a dense, spreading display of startlingly yellow flowers. Its spreading habit makes it ideal for covering large, warm, dry areas, and its mounded shape is attractive.

Above: **Hamamelis mollis**
The spider-like fragrant, golden-yellow flowers of this small Chinese tree or large shrub have made it a firm favorite in many gardens. The branches have a zigzag spreading habit.

Hamamelis mollis

Chinese Witch Hazel

Of all winter to early-spring flowering plants, this hardy deciduous small tree or large shrub is perhaps the most memorable. The sweetly-scented, golden-yellow flowers, 1-1¼in (2.5-3cm) wide, are formed of spider-like petals clustered along the base twigs. The broad, roundish, rather pear-shaped mid-green leaves are a delight in autumn, when they turn a beautiful yellow before falling. The form 'Pallida' bears large, sulphur-yellow and sweetly-scented flowers from late winter.

Height: 6-8ft (1.8-2.4m)
Spread: 6-8ft (1.8-2.4m)
Hardiness: Zones 5-9
Cultivation: Fertile, moist, well-drained, acid soil is best. Set the plant in full sun or light shade, and shelter it from cold winds. Little pruning is required, except for the removal in spring of dead or straggly branches.
Propagation: Although it can be increased from seeds, as well as 4in (10cm) long heel cuttings in late summer, the easiest way for home gardeners is to layer low-growing shoots in early autumn. Rooting takes about two years.

Hamamelis mollis has spreading branches, allowing plenty of light to reach plants close to it during winter and spring. The winter-flowering *Rhododendron mucronulatum* with funnel-shaped, rose-purple flowers makes an attractive contrast.

Hypericum prolificum

Shrubby St. John's-wort

This is a hardy, compact shrub, with narrow, lance-shaped deep green leaves. During summer it displays ¾in (2cm) wide, saucer-shaped, golden-yellow flowers near the ends of the shoots. It is a reliable shrub, and justifiably one of the most popular. Many other hypericums can be grown in our gardens, including Aaron's-beard (*Hypericum calycinum*). With its golden-yellow flowers, up to 3in (7.5cm) wide, and its tough, durable nature, it is ideal for covering sunny, well-drained banks. Steep slopes in gardens become awash with color from its flowers from early summer to early autumn. It forms a dense mass of ground-covering, bright-green leaves by sending out spreading roots.

Height: 1-4ft (30cm-1.2m)
Spread: 1-4ft (30cm-1.2m)
Hardiness: Zones 4-8
Cultivation: Hypericum prefers a fertile, well-drained but moisture-retentive soil and a sunny or slightly shaded position. It will tolerate slightly alkaline soils. Little pruning is required, although occasionally it may be damaged by frosts. If this happens, cut back the shoots to their bases in spring, and at the same time remove weak or diseased shoots.
Propagation: Softwood cuttings can be taken in summer, but it is often easier to take 4-5in (10-13cm) long cuttings in late summer, insert them into pots containing equal parts of peat and sharp sand and place them in a cold frame. The following year, the cuttings can be set out in a nursery bed and transplanted to their permanent sites when well-grown and sturdy.

Left: **Hypericum 'Hidcote'**
This is an exceptional shrub for the garden, with large saucer-shaped, golden-yellow flowers through most of the summer. However, it is only hardy to Zone 6.

Hypericum is useful for filling large areas in shrub borders with bright color. It can also be positioned at the junction of paths, where it can be used as a focal point, however, it eventually needs plenty of space, if it is not to encroach on the path.

Juniperus chinensis 'Aurea'

Young's Golden Juniper · Golden Chinese Juniper

A distinctive slow-growing, tall, slender evergreen conifer with golden foliage, this shrub is ideal for small town gardens, reaching only 5ft (1.5m) high and 32in (80cm) wide in ten years. It has two types of foliage: needle-like young leaves, and scale-like adult ones.
Height: 20ft (6m)
Spread: 3½ft (1m)
Hardiness: Zones 4-9
Cultivation: Ordinary well-drained soil and a position in full sun are best. No regular pruning is needed.
Propagation: Seeds can be sown in late summer and autumn, but the plants do not come true from named varieties. Therefore, in late summer take 2-4in (5-10cm) long heel cuttings, inserting them into pots containing equal parts of peat and sharp sand and place them in a cold frame. When rooted, pot up the cuttings singly into small pots and plunge these into a nursery bed. Plant them out in the garden in late autumn while the soil is still warm, to encourage rooting.

Left: Juniperus chinensis 'Aurea' *This golden form of the Chinese juniper was raised at Young's Nursery in Surrey, England, thereby gaining one of its common names. It bears both juvenile and adult foliage simultaneously producing a two-tone effect.*

Kerria japonica

Japanese Kerria

This is a beautiful spring and early summer flowering deciduous shrub with arching shoots. The long apple-green stems bear bright green, toothed, lance-shaped leaves. The 1½in (4cm) wide single flowers are borne on the ends of the previous season's stems. It is the form 'Pleniflora' that is chiefly grown, with double, 2in (5cm) wide, bright orange-yellow flowers. A variegated cultivar is also available, with creamy-white edges to the leaves.
Height: 4-6ft (1.2-1.8m)
Spread: 5-6ft (1.5-1.8m)
Hardiness: Zones 4-9
Cultivation: Ordinary garden soil is

Right: Junlperus chinensis *A golden form of this spectacular evergreen forms an exciting focal point in a sea of heathers and with a background of dark-leaved conifers. The large yellow conifer at the left of the juniperus is* Chamaecyparis lawsoniana *'Winston Churchill'.*

suitable. As soon as flowering has finished, cut back the flowered shoots of 'Pleniflora' to encourage the development of strong shoots.
Propagation: It can be increased from 4in (10cm) long hardwood cuttings in autumn, inserting them into pots containing equal parts of peat and sharp sand. During the following spring, set the rooted cuttings in a nursery bed. An easier way is to dig up rooted stems during autumn or spring.

Below: **Kerria japonica 'Pleniflora'** *The deeply-toothed, bright green leaves are a perfect foil for the double orange-yellow flowers. The pale green stems are striking in the winter landscape.*

Kerria japonica 'Pleniflora' looks superb planted against a south or west-facing wall. In such a position, it is essential to encourage spring growths from soil level. Small blue-flowered bulbs, such as scilla, do well at its base.

Juniperus chinensis has many cultivars. Some spreading
yellow-foliaged selections include: 'Gold Coast', 'Pfitzeriana
Aurea' (suitable for groundcover), and 'Old Gold'
(a very compact groundcover type).

TREES AND SHRUBS

Potentilla fruticosa 'Elizabeth'

Cinquefoil

This long-blooming hardy deciduous shrub bears 1in (2.5cm) wide, canary-yellow flowers that appear from early summer to

Laburnum x watereri

Golden Chain Tree · Water Laburnum

This small deciduous tree bears golden-yellow, pea-shaped flowers in drooping sprays 6-10in (15-25cm) long, in late spring and early summer. The bright green leaves are formed of three leaflets. As the tree ages, it tends to spread. For larger flowers and fuller habit, choose the cultivar 'Vossii'. Occasionally, this laburnum is trained over a pergola to produce a tunnel of glorious color when in full flower.

Height: 10-18ft (3-5.4m)
Spread: 8-12ft (2.4-3.5m)
Hardiness: Zones 5-7
Cultivation: Laburnums like a well-drained garden soil in full sun or light shade. This tree does not do well in the heat of the deep South or Midwest. Ensure that the tree is well supported during its early years. The seedpods are poisonous to humans and to fish, so take care to prevent children from investigating them, and do not plant a laburnum tree near a fish pool. No pruning is needed, other than an initial shaping of the tree in summer.
Propagation: Seeds can be sown in autumn and placed in a cold frame. However, named forms do not come true from seed and are therefore grafted on to special rootstocks in the nursery.

Below: **Potentilla fruticosa 'Elizabeth'** *This shrubby cinquefoil is one of the gems of the garden, with bright canary-yellow flowers from early summer to autumn. It is a reliable shrub that needs little attention.*

Laburnums form a happy and colorful combination with lilacs, especially those with blue flowers. Even when planted several yards apart, the two trees create a beautiful picture.

autumn and are borne singly or in twos and threes. They stand slightly above the midgreen, deeply-cut leaves. Other superb cultivars include 'Farreri' (bright yellow) and 'Katherine Dykes' (primrose-yellow).

Height: 3-4ft (90cm-1.2m)
Spread: 4-5ft (1.2-1.5m)
Hardiness: Zones 2-7
Cultivation: Any good well-drained garden soil suits it, and a position in full sun. No regular pruning is needed, other than cutting out dead and old stems during spring.
Propagation: Take 2-3in (5-7.5cm) long cuttings in spring, set them in pots containing equal parts of peat and sharp sand and place them in a cold frame. Alternatively, lift and divide large clumps in spring.

Below: **Laburnum x watereri** *These bright-flowered trees are occasionally used as street trees. However, remember that all parts of the tree are poisonous, especially the seeds.*

Shrubby potentillas can be grown as informal hedges. Set the plants 2½-3ft (75-90cm) apart, but allow for their spread when positioning them alongside a path or boundary.

TREES AND SHRUBS

Robinia pseudoacacia 'Frisia'

Black Locust · Common Locust

This is a beautiful, small to medium-sized tree. It has deciduous golden-yellow leaves. From spring to autumn it reveals pinnate leaves formed of up to eleven pairs of leaflets, first golden-yellow, then pale greenish-yellow in mid- to late summer. The creamy white, fragrant, pendulous 4-8in (2.5-5cm) long flowers appear in late spring.
Height: 20-26ft (6-7m)
Spread: 10-12ft (3-3.5m)
Hardiness: Zones 3-9
Cultivation: Locusts thrive in any well-drained soil and a sunny position. Avoid cold and exposed areas. No regular pruning is required, but if any shaping is needed, it is best carried out during midsummer when there is less chance of the tree bleeding.
Propagation: It is best to buy plants from a reputable nurseryman, as the propagation of the tree involves grafting the cultivar on to stocks of *Robinia pseudoacacia* in spring.

Robinia pseudoacacia 'Frisia' is useful for providing color contrasts. The 6-8ft (1.8-2.4m) high *Cotinus coggygria* 'Royal Purple', with dark plum-colored foliage, makes an excellent companion.

Far left: **Robinia pseudoacacia 'Frisia'** *The golden-yellow leaves formed of many leaflets create a beautiful and graceful tree, even for small gardens. It provides continuing interest from spring to autumn.*

Left: **Senecio 'Sunshine'** *This New Zealand plant, with its daisy-like yellow flowers in early summer, is a delight in Western coastal gardens. It is also attractive during winter when the silvery-gray leaves are covered with frost.*

Right: **Taxus baccata 'Fastigiata Aurea'** *A beautiful yew with golden foliage, especially attractive when planted in full sun. Initially, it suits rock gardens, but eventually becomes too large for a restricted site.*

Senecio x 'Sunshine'

An evergreen, spreading, mound-forming – sometimes straggly – 'Sunshine' bears silver-gray leaves that turn green with age. During early summer, it produces yellow, daisy-like flowers 1in (2.5cm) across. During winter, the leaves look handsome when they are covered by frost or a light dusting of snow. Unfortunately, heavy snow falls can flatten and destroy the shrub's attractive mounded form.
Height: 3-4¹/₂ft (1-1.2m)
Spread: 4-5ft (1.2-1.5m)
Hardiness: Zones 7-9
Cultivation: Ordinary well-drained garden soil in full sun is ideal. It is best suited for Western coastal gardens. Occasionally, it is damaged by severe frosts and heavy snow falls; if this happens, cut out the dead shoots in spring. Straggly plants should also be cut back in spring.
Propagation: During late summer, take 3-4in (7.5-10cm) long half-ripe cuttings. Insert them into pots of equal parts peat and sharp sand and place them in a cold frame. When they are rooted, transplant them to the garden.

Taxus baccata 'Fastigiata Aurea'

Golden English Yew

This is a neat, upright, golden evergreen conifer, a form of the English Yew. It has a solid appearance, with tight foliage. It is slow-growing, reaching 6¹/₂ft (2m) high and about 2ft (60cm) wide after ten years.
Height: 15ft (4.5m)
Spread: 2¹/₂-3ft (75-90cm)
Hardiness: Zones 6-7
Cultivation: Well-drained soil, acid or alkaline, suits it. A position in full sun is essential to encourage good foliage color.
Propagation: It has to be increased by 3-4in (7.5-10cm) long heel cuttings in late summer and early autumn. Insert them into pots of equal parts peat and sharp sand and place them in a cold frame. Pot them on into containers of potting soil and plant them out in the garden when well-grown.

Senecio x 'Sunshine' is best positioned near the front of a border or next to a path. Its mounded form becomes completely covered with flowers. It also looks good at a junction of two paths.

Taxus canadensis, the Canadian yew, and *Taxus cuspidata*, the Japanese yew are much hardier than the English yew, and therefore more widely planted.

Taxus baccata 'Semperaurea'

This is a slow-growing, densely-packed, golden-foliaged version of the yew. The new foliage is golden on first opening in spring, and slowly becomes rusty-yellow for the rest of the year. It grows to about 3½ft (1m) high in ten years.
Height: 10ft (3m)
Spread: 5-7ft (1.5-2.1m)
Hardiness: Zones 6-7
Cultivation: Most garden soils, in full sun or shade will do. Yews will tolerate acid or alkaline soils. No regular pruning is needed, but it can be clipped to a preferred shape.
Propagation: Take 3-4in (7.5-10cm) long heel cuttings in late summer and early autumn. Insert them into pots containing equal parts of peat and sharp sand, and place them in a cold frame. Pot them on and plant out when they are well-grown and sturdy.

Ulex europaeus

Gorse

A hardy, sharply-spined, densely-branched evergreen shrub with scale-like leaves that soon fall. From spring to early summer it displays ¾-1in (1.8-2.5cm) long, pea-shaped, golden-yellow flowers. The flowers often appear intermittently until late winter. There is a double-flowered cultivar 'Plenus', with compact hummocks of flowers.
Height: 5-7ft (1.5-2.1m)
Spread: 5-7ft (1.5-2.1m)
Hardiness: Zones 5-9
Cultivation: Gorse needs a light, well-drained poor soil and a position in full sun. Little pruning is needed, but leggy shrubs can be cut back in spring to encourage

Taxus cuspidata 'Aurescens' is a hardier (Zones 4-7) yew with yellow new growth in the spring. It is a low, 1-3.5ft (30cm-1m) compact, slow-growing shrub.

new growths from the base.
Propagation: Sow seeds in spring, placing them in a cold frame. Alternatively, take 3in (7.5cm) long cuttings in late summer and insert them into pots containing equal parts of peat and sharp sand. Place these in a cold frame and pot up the plants into pots of potting soil when rooted, transplanting them into the garden in late autumn.

Below: Ulex europaeus
This densely-spined, evergreen shrub is hardy in even the most severe weather. It forms an attractive windbreak or boundary. Bright golden-yellow, pea-shaped flowers appear during spring and early summer.

Further plants to consider

Berberis thunbergii 'Aurea'
Golden Japanese Barberry
Height: 3-5ft (90cm-1.5m)   Spread: 2½-4ft (75cm-1.2m)
Hardiness: Zones 4-9
A distinctive deciduous berberis, with yellow leaves turning pale green by late autumn.

Euonymus fortunei 'Emerald and Gold'
Yellow Variegated Wintercreeper
Height: 1½-2ft (45-60cm)   Spread: 3-4ft (90cm-1.2m)
Hardiness: Zones 5-9
A hardy, evergreen groundcover shrub, the leaves are dark glossy green with yellow margins.

Gleditsia triacanthos 'Sunburst'
Sunburst Honey Locust
Height: 18-25ft (5.4-7.5m)   Spread: 10-15ft (3-4.5m)
Hardiness: Zones 4-9
A deciduous tree with bright golden-yellow young foliage, each leaf formed of up to thirty-two narrow lance-shaped leaflets. A popular tree for street tree plantings because it is salt tolerant.

Mahonia aquifolium
Oregon Grape
Height: 3-5ft (90cm-1.5m)   Spread: 5-6ft (1.5-1.8m)
Hardiness: Zones 5-9
An evergreen shrub with dark green, leathery leaves. During early spring, it bears terminal clusters of fragrant rich yellow flowers, followed by bunches of blue-black berries.

Rhododendron calendulaceum
Flame Azalea
Height: 4-8ft (1.2-2.4m)   Spread: 4-8ft (1.2-2.4m)
Hardiness: Zones 5-8
Native to the Appalachian Mountains, this deciduous shrub has vibrant yellow, orange, or scarlet flowers in late spring. It is an ideal plant for the wild garden, and does well in light shade.

Sambucus racemosa 'Plumosa Aurea'
Golden Cut-leaved Elder
Height: 7-8ft (2.1-2.4m)   Spread: 6-7ft (1.8-2.1m)
Hardiness: Zones 3-9
An eye-catching deciduous shrub with finely-cut golden leaves. During spring, it displays white flowers. It is a plant which looks good when set in front of a dark-leaved hedge, such as yew.

Ulex europaeus is native to western Europe including the British Isles, and north-west Africa. It tolerates acid or neutral soil, and requires full sun. If cut to the base it will sprout back.

Bupleurum fruticosum

An unusual, attractive, dome-shaped, evergreen or semi-evergreen shrub, ideal for creating a background of sea-green leaves. During mid- to late summer, 3-4in (7.5-10cm) wide heads of small, yellowish flowers are borne.
Height: 4-6ft (1.2-1.8m)
Spread: 5-8ft (1.5-2.4m)
Hardiness: Zones 5-9
Cultivation: Plant in good, well-drained soil, including those that are slightly alkaline. It is ideal for

Above: Bupleurum fruticosum *The sea-green leaves of this evergreen shrub create a superb background for other plants. The yellow flowers provide a bright splash of color.*

growing in coastal areas, where salt spray may be a problem.
Propagation: In mid- and late summer take 3in (7.5cm) long cuttings and insert them in equal parts moist peat and sharp sand. Place in a cold frame.

Chamaecyparis lawsoniana

Lawson False Cypress

This well-known evergreen conifer forms a large conical tree with green or glaucous-green foliage borne in broad, fan-like, slightly drooping sprays. Among the hundreds of cultivars are 'Columnaris', a narrow tree with blue-gray foliage; 'Ellwoodii', a slow-growing plant with blue-gray needles; 'Green Allar', a conical plant that has bright green foliage; 'Lanei', with beautiful golden-yellow needles; and 'Pembury Blue', which has pendulous blue-gray foliage.
Height: 25-35ft (7.5-10.5m)
Spread: 8-12ft (2.4-3.6m)
Hardiness: Zones 5-8

Cultivation: As well as being grown as a specimen plant, this versatile conifer can also be used to form a hedge or windbreak. Plant in any well-drained soil, preferably in full sun or light shade. Plant golden-leaved varieties in full sun. No regular pruning is needed for plants grown as specimen, but if young plants develop two leading shoots, one of these must be cut out – preferably in spring.
Propagation: The ordinary all-green type can be raised from seeds sown in late winter and early spring, but named forms are raised from cuttings. Take 4in (10cm) long heel-cuttings in late spring and insert in equal parts moist peat and sharp sand.

Above: Chamaecyparis lawsoniana *The green or glaucous-green fans of evergreen foliage create a contrasting background for many plants. This versatile conifer can also be used to form a hedge or windbreak.*

Cornus alba 'Spaethii'

Tartarian Dogwood · Golden-variegated Dogwood

This deciduous willowy-stemmed and suckering shrub is superb for creating a wealth of variegated light green leaves with irregular golden-splashed edges. It has the bonus of bright red stems in winter. 'Elegantissima', another variety of this versatile shrub, may be easier

---

Bupleurum fruticosum eventually creates a dramatic display, but when young, pleasingly harmonizes with *Hebe* 'Blue Gem', framed against a background of *Tamarix* and *Spartium junceum*.

Chamaecyparis lawsoniana, native to southwest Oregon and northwest California, is a hardy, evergreen conifer, the parent of many colorful varieties, both large and dwarf.

to locate in the trade. It reveals grayish-green leaves with irregular creamy-white edges.
Height: 7-8ft (2.1-2.4m)
Spread: 7-9ft (2.1-2.7m)
Hardiness: Zones 3-8
Cultivation: Plant in fertile, moisture-retentive soil in full sun or light shade. It is superb for planting around the edge of an informal garden pond or perhaps alongside a stream. Every spring, cut back all the stems to within a few inches of ground-level. This will encourage the growth of new stems, which display red bark in winter.
Propagation: In midsummer take

Below: Cornus alternifolia 'Argentea' *This superbly variegated deciduous shrub is one of the best green-foliaged border plants. Do not crowd other plants in front of it. The tiered outline of the branches is part of its appeal.*

Above: Cornus alba 'Spaethii' *The variegated leaves of the golden-variegated dogwood create welcome splashes of color throughout summer. It has the bonus of bright, shiny red stems in the winter months.*

3-4in (7.5-10cm) long heel-cuttings, inserting them in equal parts moist peat and sharp sand. Place in a propagation frame with a temperature of 61°F (16°C). When rooted, pot up and later transplant to a nursery bed until large enough to be planted in a garden.

Cornus alternifolia 'Argentea'

Pagoda Dogwood

A superbly variegated deciduous large shrub or small tree (also known as 'Variegata') with horizontally spreading branches bearing small leaves with creamy-white edges. It needs a position where the branches are not inhibited by nearby plants.
Height: 10-15ft (3-4.5m)
Spread: 10-12ft (3-3.6m)
Hardiness: Zones 4-7
Cultivation: Plant in moisture-retentive, but not waterlogged, soil in full sun or light shade. No regular pruning is required, other than occasionally cutting out a misplaced branch in spring.
Propagation: In midsummer take 3-4in (7.5-10cm) long heel-cuttings, inserting them in equal parts moist peat and sharp sand. Place in a propagation frame with a temperature of 61°F (16°C). When rooted, pot up and later transplant to a nursery bed until large enough to be planted in a garden.

Cornus alba 'Spaethii' is mainly grown for its variegated leaves during summer, but the shiny, bright red stems in winter are equally welcome. Position in front of dark-foliaged hedges.

Cornus alternifolia 'Argentea' looks superb when planted against a background of dark foliaged trees or shrubs. It is especially attractive when situated against a yew (*Taxus baccata*) hedge.

Cotoneaster lacteus

Milky Cotoneaster

An attractive semi-evergreen shrub with leathery, deep green leaves that reveal hairy, gray undersides. It is superb as a background for other plants. It has the bonus of developing creamy-white flowers in heads up to 3in (7.5cm) wide during midsummer. These are followed in autumn and until mid-winter by clusters of red berries.

Height: 10-15ft (3.4-5m)
Spread: 8-12ft (2.4-3.6m)
Hardiness: Zones 7-9
Cultivation: Plant in any good garden soil in a sunny position. No regular pruning is needed.
Propagation: It can be raised from seeds or by taking cuttings in midsummer, but for home

Above: Cotoneaster lacteus *can be grown to create an attractive hedge. Set the plants 2-2 1/2ft (60-75cm) apart in a single row. After planting, cut off the top third of the plant to encourage bushy growth.*

gardeners layering low-growing shoots in late summer is the easiest method. When rooted,the young plant can be severed from the parent.

Cotoneaster lacteus This hardy, evergreen shrub creates a wealth of deep green leaves. Additionally, during midsummer it bears creamy-white flowers, followed in autumn by clusters of red berries.

X Cupressocyparis leylandii

Leyland Cypress

A vigorous, fast-growing evergreen conifer that rapidly creates a pleasing screen of gray-green foliage. The foliage droops slightly in sprays. It is frequently recommended for use as a hedge, but because of its rapid growth and high ultimate height it is only suitable for very large gardens.
Height: 25-30ft (7.5-9m) after 15 to 20 years.
Spread: 4-6ft (1.2-1.8m) after 15 to 20 years.
Hardiness: Zones 7-9
Cultivation: It grows well in most soils and positions, and even tolerates coastal areas where salt spray may be a problem. When grown as a hedge, set the individual plants 2¹/₂-3ft (75-90cm) apart. In exposed areas, support young plants with strong stakes.
Propagation: In late summer and early autumn take 4in (10cm) long cuttings. Insert them in equal parts moist peat and sharp sand, and place in a cold frame.

Below: X Cupressocyparis leylandii *The gray-green foliage, slightly-drooping towards its tip, creates a dense screen.*

Elaeagnus pungens 'Maculata'

Thorny Elaeagnus

A beautiful slow-growing evergreen shrub with oval, leathery, glossy-green leaves irregularly marked along their centers with golden splashes. The leaves are borne on stiff, spiny stems. Other variegated forms include 'Dicksonii' (sometimes known as 'Aurea'), with irregular golden edges to the leaves, and 'Variegata' with narrow, pale yellow edges to the leaves.
Height: 7-10ft (2.1-3m)
Spread: 8-12ft (2.4-3.6m)
Hardiness: Zones 7-10
Cultivation: Ordinary well-drained soil suits it, in either full sun or light shade. Avoid poorly drained situations. No regular pruning is needed, other than occasionally cutting out misplaced shoots in spring. If all-green stems appear, cut these out immediately.
Propagation: In late summer take 4in (10cm) long cuttings. Insert them in equal parts moist peat and sharp sand, and place in a cold frame. In the following spring pot up the rooted cuttings or plant in a nursery bed until large enough to be transferred to the garden.

Above: Elaeagnus pungens 'Maculata' *looks especially good in spring with bright yellow daffodils crowded around its base. It also forms a pleasing duo with the winter-flowering* Viburnum tinus.

X Cupressocyparis leylandii forms an effective screen. Don't position other plants too close to it, as it will monopolize available soil nutrients and moisture, as well as create shade.

Elaeagnus pungens 'Maculata' The leathery, glossy-green leaves are handsome in winter when highlighted by low-angled rays of sun. It is dramatic when planted in a large tub and positioned on a patio, especially when filling a large corner.

TREES AND SHRUBS

Fagus sylvatica

European Beech

This well-known deciduous tree can be planted to form an attractive hedge. Set young plants 1½-2ft (45-60cm) apart, either in a single row or two lines spaced 1½-2ft (45-60cm) apart. The foliage is very attractive; bright green when young, slowly changing to mid-green and becoming darker as the season progresses. In autumn, the leaves assume yellow and russet tints before falling, although often they hang on the plant until spring.

Height: 5-20ft (1.5-6m), as a hedge.

Spread: 3-4ft (0.9-1.2m) as a hedge.

Hardiness: Zones 5-9

Cultivation: Plant in most soils except those that are heavy, wet and cold. Cut back newly-planted hedges by a quarter to encourage the development of shoots. If this initial pruning is neglected, the hedge becomes bare of shoots and leaves at its base. Once established, trim the hedge to shape during midsummer.

Left: Fagus sylvatica *When grown as a hedge, this deciduous tree creates a screen of bright green leaves in spring. In autumn they turn lovely yellows and russets.*

Above: Griselinia littoralis *has softly-colored foliage that creates an ideal background for pastel-colored flowered and foliaged plants. When grown as a specimen in a border it has an informal outline.*

Fagus sylvatica is the parent of several superbly colored varieties, as well as distinctive shapes. The Dawyck beech (*Fagus sylvatica* 'Fastigiata') has a tall columnar stance, broadening with age.

Griselinia littoralis This tender, slow-growing, evergreen shrub from New Zealand is ideal in coastal areas where salt spray may be a problem. Select a sheltered position for maximum protection against strong and cold winds.

Griselinia littoralis

A very tender slow-growing evergreen shrub with leathery, shiny, yellowish-green leaves. The greenish flowers, which appear in spring, are insignificant and the plant is normally grown for its attractive leaves, which create a pleasing background for other plants. As well as being grown as a specimen plant, it can form an attractive and unusual hedge if its size is controlled.
Height: 8-15ft (2.4-4.5m)
Spread: 6-10ft (1.8-3m)
Hardiness: Zone 10
Cultivation: Plant in ordinary soil, in full sun or medium shade. It is very tender, commonly grown only in California, although once established it has a hardier constitution. It is tolerant of coastal areas, where salt spray may occur. If grown as a hedge, space the plants 1½ft (45cm) apart. Nipping out the growing tips of young plants encourages bushiness.
Propagation: During late summer take 3-4in (7.5-10cm) long cuttings and insert them in equal parts moist peat and sharp sand. When rooted, pot up into small pots and place in a cold frame for a further year. Later, plant into a sheltered nursery bed for another year.

Left: **Ilex x altaclarensis 'Lawsoniana'** *is best grown as a specimen shrub, perhaps near a path so that it can be readily seen during winter. There are many other superb variegated hollies.*

Ilex x altaclarensis 'Lawsoniana'

Lawson's Altaclara Holly

An unusual variegated variety of the Altaclara holly with large, shiny, green leaves heavily splashed at their centers. It has the bonus of bearing clusters of orange-red berries during winter.
Height: 10-18ft (3-5.4m)
Spread: 8-12ft (2.4-3.6m)
Hardiness: Zones 7-9
Cultivation: Plant in good soil in full sun or shade. Avoid soils that dry out during hot summers. Shoots often revert to being all-green, and these should be completely cut out as soon as they are noticed. Although no regular pruning is required, use

pruning shears to cut out spindly or misplaced shoots in late summer.
Propagation: During midspring take 3in (7.5cm) long heel-cuttings. Insert them in equal parts moist peat and sharp sand, and place in a cold frame.

Ilex aquifolium

English Holly

This well-known, hardy, leathery-foliaged, evergreen shrub or tree has glossy, dark green leaves with wavy edges and sharp spines. Although most apparent at Christmas, when widely used in decorations, it is superb as a background for other plants. Some plants are male, others female. Female plants bear the well-known red berries in autumn and winter if a male specimen is planted near to it. In addition to the all-green type, there is a wide range of colorfully variegated types that brighten gardens throughout the year. These include 'Argenteo-marginata', 'Aureo-marginata', 'Golden Queen', 'Silver Queen', and 'Madame Briot'.
Height: 12-25ft (3.6-7.5m) all-green type.
Spread: 8-12ft (2.4-3.6m) all-green type.
Hardiness: Zones 7-10
Cultivation: Plant in any good soil, in full sun or shade. However, avoid soils that dry out during hot summers. Protect young plants from cold winds. No regular pruning is needed, other than removing spindly, misplaced shoots during mid- to late summer.
Propagation: The ordinary all-green type, as well as variegated forms, can be increased from 3in (7.5cm) long heel-cuttings taken during midsummer. Insert in equal parts moist peat and sharp sand, and place in a cold frame. Named variegated forms can also be increased by budding in mid-summer. However, plants raised from cuttings are better, as they are not prone to develop sucker-like shoots.

Left: Ilex aquifolium 'Madame Briot' *A variegated holly, ideal on its own or for forming an eye-catching hedge. The variegated leaves are borne on attractive, purple stems.*

Ilex x altaclarensis 'Lawsoniana' a hardy evergreen shrub with dominantly yellow-splashed green leaves is further enhanced in winter when seen against a background of snow.

Hollies are steeped in superstition. The normal prickly and all-green type is supposed to be lucky for men, whereas smooth-leaved and variegated forms are luckier for women, especially when combined with ivy.

TREES AND SHRUBS

Ligustrum ovalifolium

California Privet

This well-known semi-evergreen hedging plant has glossy, oval, midgreen leaves.
Ligustrum vulgare, European or common privet, is very similar to California privet but is hardy to Zone 4.
Height: 4-6ft (1.2-1.8m) as a hedge.
Spread: 2-3ft (60-90cm) as a hedge.
Hardiness: Zones 5-9
Cultivation: Plant in any good soil, in sun or shade. When planting a hedge, set the plants 1-1½ft (30-45cm) apart in a single row or staggered into two lines. In spring after being planted, cut back all hedging plants by one-third to a half. Regular clipping, in spring and autumn, is essential for established hedges.
Propagation: In autumn, take 10in (25cm) long hardwood cuttings and insert them to half their length in the soil.

Below: Ligustrum ovalifolium
The glossy, oval, green leaves create a pleasing background for other plants, but do not plant them too close as privet depletes the soil of water and plant foods.

Ligustrum ovalifolium has several yellow-leaved forms;
Ligustrum ovalifolium 'Aureo-marginatum' has green leaves with wide and irregular yellow edges, while 'Variegatum' has cream or pale yellow borders.

Liriodendron tulipifera 'Aureomarginatum'

Variegated Tulip Tree

A distinctively variegated form of a well-known deciduous tree. The light to midgreen leaves have blunt, almost square tops and are edged and blotched in yellowish-green or yellow. During autumn the leaves

---

Left: Liriodendron tulipifera 'Aureomarginatum' *This variegated form of the tulip tree has light to mid-green leaves, blotched and edged in yellowish-green or yellow.*

---

assume rich autumn colors, but these are not as noticeable as the rich autumn colors seen in the all-green form.

Height: 70-90ft (24-30m)
Spread: 35-50ft (12-15m)
Hardiness: Zones 4-9
Cultivation: Well-drained soil in light shade or full sun. No pruning is needed, other than initially shaping the tree when young.
Propagation: The easiest way for home gardeners to increase this plant is to layer low-growing branches in spring.

Lonicera nitida

Boxleaf Honeysuckle

This evergreen shrub is often grown as a hedge – the small, glossy-green leaves which crowd along the shoots create a superb background. If left unpruned, it grows up to 6ft (1.8m) high and eventually reveals a leggy, bare base. However, when grown as a hedge and clipped regularly it is much more pleasing.

Height: 3-5ft (0.9-1.5m) as a hedge.
Spread: 1-2ft (30-60cm) as a hedge.
Hardiness: Zones 6-9
Cultivation: Plant in well-drained soil, in full sun or shade. When grown as a hedge, set the plants 10-12in (25-30cm) apart, in a single row. After planting, cut back the top third of the shoots to encourage bushiness. During subsequent years, trim the plants in early and late summer.
Propagation: Take 4in (10cm) long cuttings in mid- to late summer. Insert them in equal parts moist peat and sharp sand, and place in a cold frame. When rooted, transfer to a nursery bed until large enough to be planted into a garden.

Left: Lonicera nitida *The small, glossy-green leaves create a handsome foil for variegated subjects, as well as white and yellow plants. When not clipped, this evergreen has a pleasing, informal shape.*

Liriodendron tulipifera creates a dominant feature, either when planted as a focal point in a lawn or towards the end of a flower border, harmonizing with the white-flowered *Hydrangea arborescens* 'Grandiflora'.

Lonicera nitida is frequently grown as a hedge but tall, leggy specimens become bent over by heavy falls of snow. Clipping the top to form a slope helps to prevent light snow falls damaging the hedge.

Taxus baccata

English Yew

For centuries this evergreen conifer has been used to create hedges, but even earlier it was widely planted in churchyards. Its foliage is very attractive; dark green with yellowish-green undersides.
Height: 5-7ft (1.5-1.7m) as a hedge.
Spread: 3-4ft (0.9-1.2m) as a hedge.
Hardiness: Zones 5-7
Cultivation: Plant in any soil, even alkaline soils, and in full sun or shade. However, avoid exceptionally wet and cold soils. When grown as a hedge, set the plants 1½ft (45cm) apart in a single row. At the same time, nip out the growing shoots to encourage bushiness at their bases. Established hedges need clipping with shears in late summer.
Propagation: It is often increased

Right: Viburnum davidii *As well as creating an attractive background with its green leaves, this evergreen shrub has white flowers in terminal heads during early summer, and turquoise-blue berries later in the year.*

from seeds sown in late summer and placed in a cold frame. When the seedlings are about 5cm (2in) high, plant them into a nursery bed for three to four years. Alternatively, take 7.5-10cm long heel-cuttings in autumn. Insert them in equal parts moist peat and sharp sand. When rooted, plant into a nursery bed for about three years.

Below: Taxus baccata *As well as creating eye-catching, free-standing shrubs. Yew can also be planted to form a hedge. It creates a background that highlights light-colored flowers and variegated plants.*

Viburnum davidii

David Viburnum

An attractive evergreen shrub with prominently veined dark green leaves. It has the bonus of developing white flowers in heads up to 3in (7.5cm) wide in early summer. If male and female plants are present the flowers are followed by turquoise-blue berries.
Height: 2-3ft (60-90cm)
Spread: 4-6ft (1.2-1.8m)
Hardiness: Zones 7-9
Cultivation: Plant in good, moisture-retentive soil. Avoid light soils as they dry out rapidly in summer. No regular pruning is needed.
Propagation: During late summer take 3-4in (7.5-10cm) long cuttings. Insert them in equal parts moist peat and sharp sand, and place in a cold frame. When rooted, pot up and place in a cold frame, later setting them into a nursery bed.

Taxus cuspidata, Japanese yew, and *Taxus x media*, Anglo-Japanese yew, are hardier (to Zones 4) and more widely planted than the English yew. All make excellent hedging plants.

Weigela florida 'Variegata'

This beautifully variegated deciduous shrub with a compact habit, has light green, slightly wrinkled leaves with broad, creamy-white edges. It has the bonus of bearing clusters of tubular, foxglove-like, 1in (2.5cm) wide, pale pink flowers during early and midsummer. The variety 'Foliis Purpureis' also has attractive leaves, but all the same color purplish-green, with the bonus of pink flowers in summer.

Height: 4-5ft (1.2-1.5m)
Spread: 4-5ft (1.2-1.5m)
Hardiness: Zones 4-8
Cultivation: Plant in well-drained but moisture-retentive soil, in full sun or partial shade. It is ideal for filling borders up to 5ft (1.5m) wide between walls and paths. Every year, as soon as the flowers fade, cut out to ground-level a few of the old stems.
Propagation: During midsummer take 4in (10cm) long half-ripe heel-cuttings from non-flowering shoots. Insert them in equal parts moist peat and sharp sand, and place in 61°F (16°C). When rooted, pot up and over-winter in a cold frame. Plant out into a nursery bed in spring.

Below: Weigela florida 'Variegata' *Although this variegated variety does not have the "flower-power" of the ordinary species, it more than compensates for this with colorful leaves throughout summer.*

Further plants to consider

Acer negundo 'Variegata'
Variegated Box Elder
Height: 20ft (6m)   Spread: 20ft (6m)
Hardiness: Zones 3-9
This variegated cultivar of box elder is an adaptable, fast-growing, small deciduous tree. Shoots bearing all-green leaves should be pruned out.

Acer platanoides 'Drummondii'
Drummond Norway Maple
Height: 40ft (12m)   Spread: 25ft (7.5m)
Hardiness: Zones 4-7
'Drummondii' is an attractive cultivar of the fast-growing, deciduous Norway maple. The young leaves are edged in a pale yellow, which ages to a creamy white. All-green shoots should be removed.

Daphne x burkwoodii
Burkwood Daphne
Height: 3ft (90cm)   Spread: 3ft (90cm)
Hardiness: Zone 4
The Burkwood daphne is an attractive and sweetly-scented shrub that flowers in early summer. 'Carol Mackie' is a beautiful cultivar, bearing variegated leaves and fragrant light pink flowers.

Myrica pensylvanica
Bayberry
Height: 6-10ft (1.8-3m)   Spread: 3-4ft (0.9-1.2m)
Hardiness: Zones 3-8
This deciduous or semi-evergreen shrub has leathery, fragrant leaves and gray waxy berries used to scent candles and soaps. The shrub is tolerant of poor soils and seaside conditions.

Pinus sylvestris
Scotch Pine
Height: 40-60ft (12-18m)   Spread: 25-35ft (7.5-9.5m)
Hardiness: Zones 2-7
Scotch pine, a handsome upright conifer with bluish-green needles, is one the most popular pines for Christmas trees. It is also an interesting landscape specimen plant. While the species can grow over 60ft (18m), the yellow-needled *P. sylvestris* 'Aurea' forms a more compact garden specimen.

Salix purpurea 'Pendula'
Weeping Purple Osier
Height: 10ft (3m)   Spread: 10ft (3m)
Hardiness: Zones 3-8
A small, graceful weeping tree with purple-green stems and leaves. It is ideal for planting near small water features.

Viburnum davidii, with its evergreen, glossy-green leaves is an attractive dome-shaped shrub that creates a pleasing background for many low, prettily-flowered plants.

Weigela florida 'Variegata', with superbly variegated leaves, harmonizes well with tall, blue-flowered, bearded irises and *Lunaria annua*, a white-flowered form of honesty.

Amelanchier canadensis

June Berry · Serviceberry ·
Shadblow · Shadbush · Shad ·
Sugar Plum

Few spring flowering plants surpass the beauty of this bushy, spreading, deciduous shrub or small tree. Starry, white flowers are profusely borne amid young, coppery-red, silky, oval leaves. In autumn the leaves turn orange and red. The flowers are followed by purplish-black, sweet and succulent fruits up to ½in (12mm) wide. All amelanchiers bear fruits, and these have been used by North American Cree Indians in both a fresh and dried state. They were used as a pleasant addition to pemmican, a North American Indian cake, as well as for making puddings. *Amelanchier arborea* is a very similar plant, but rather than being shrub-like its habit is that of a small tree, 15-25ft (4.5-7m) tall. The smooth, gray bark with subtle striping is extremely ornamental.

Height: 10-15ft (3-4.5m)
Spread: 10-12ft (3-3.6m)
Hardiness: Zones 3-8
Cultivation: Any good well-drained, moist, acidic soil suits it, in either light shade or full sun. No regular pruning is needed, except during its formative years to create an attractive shape.
Propagation: The easiest way to increase this shrub is by layering low-growing branches in early autumn. However, it may take up to a year before rooting occurs. Once rooted the young plant can be planted in a nursery border.

Below: Amelanchier canadensis
The starry white flowers are certain to capture attention. In autumn the leaves assume coppery tints.

Amelanchiers are useful plants for naturalistic plantings. A grove of serviceberry in full bloom is an unforgettable early spring sight. They blend well with evergreen plants such as rhododendron, mountain laurel and *Ilex glabra* (inkberry).

Above: Cornus kousa chinensis
During midsummer, four white bracts cluster around purplish green flowers. A mature tree will have spectacular mottled bark of gray, tan and rich brown.

Cornus kousa chinensis

Kousa Dogwood · Chinese Dogwood

An attractive and unusually flowered deciduous tree with spreading growth bearing mid to dark green leaves which assume rich bronze and crimson tints in autumn. During midsummer it bears purplish-green flowers surrounded by four white bracts, each up to 1½in (4cm) long. In late summer it bears strawberry-like fruits.
Height: 20-30ft (6-9m)
Spread: 20-30ft (6-9m)
Hardiness: Zones 5-8
Cultivation: Plant in acid, well-drained, soil with good organic matter.
Propagation: In late summer, take 3-4in (7.5-10cm) long cuttings. Insert them in equal parts moist peat and sharp sand, and place in 61°F (16°C). When rooted, pot up and place in a cold frame. In spring, plant into a nursery bed for two years before planting into a garden.

Eucryphia glutinosa

Spectacular, slow growing, deciduous or partially evergreen tree-like shrub with rich green leaves that turn orange-red in autumn. The 2½in (6.5cm) wide white flowers have masses of stamens that dominate them, and are further enhanced by yellow anthers. The flowers arise from leaf joints from mid- to late summer.
Height: 10-15ft (3-4.5m)
Spread: 6-8ft (1.8-2.4m)
Hardiness: Zones 9-10
Cultivation: Slightly acid or neutral, light and peaty soil and a lightly shaded and sheltered position ensure success with this slightly delicate shrub. It requires mild winters and cool, humid

Above: Eucryphia glutinosa *With white flowers, packed at their centers with stamens bearing yellow anthers, this shrub always attracts attention. Flowers are borne singly or in pairs.*

summers, and is not suitable for cold regions, as the young shoots become damaged. Young plants should have the tips of their shoots removed in spring to encourage branching.
Propagation: During late summer, take 3-4in (7.5-10cm) long heel cuttings from non-flowering shoots. Insert them in equal parts peat and sharp sand. Place in 61°F (16°C). An easier method is to layer low-growing shoots in late summer, but the development of roots takes much longer.

Cornus kousa chinensis attracts attention so easily that it seldom needs other plants to be positioned around – white bracts in midsummer, strawberry-like fruits in late summer, colored leaves in autumn.

Eucryphia glutinosa is ideal for planting in a lightly shaded woodland setting in warm areas with appropriate climates. Ensure that a path is near by, so that the flowers can be admired close-up.

Eucryphia x nymansensis

This spectacular hybrid between *E. glutinosa* and *E. cordifolia* is an erect and fast-growing evergreen tree. During late summer and into early autumn it develops 2½in (6.5cm) wide, cup-shaped, white or cream flowers. Each of these has a large central crown of stamens, headed by pink anthers.
Height: 15-20ft (4.5-6m)
Spread: 6-8ft (1.8-2.4m)

Hardiness: Zones 9-10
Cultivation: Well-drained, light and fertile soil in slight shade and a sheltered position are needed. It tolerates lime in the soil, but grows best in neutral or slightly acid conditions. It requires warm winters and cool, humid summers, and is not suitable for cold areas. Young plants can be encouraged to develop sideshoots by nipping out their growing tips in spring.
Propagation: During late summer, take 3-4in (7.5-10cm) long heel-cuttings from non-flowering shoots.

Above: Eucryphia x nymansensis
A tender shrub with eye-catching cream flowers during late summer and into early autumn. These are borne in clusters of two or three, and make a stunningly attractive picture.

Insert them in equal parts peat and sharp sand, and place in 61°F (16°C). An easier method is to layer low-growing shoots in late summer, but the development of roots takes much longer.

Eucryphia x nymansensis looks superb in mild climates when planted with blue lace-cap hydrangeas, such as 'Blue Wave'. It also harmonizes with the white-flowered, bulbous summer hyacinth *(Galtonia candicans)*.

Hydrangea arborescens

Smooth Hydrangea

This hardy deciduous shrub has a mounded habit, with bright green, slender-pointed leaves and white flowers borne in flat heads from mid- to late summer. The best variety is 'Grandiflora', with pure-white flowers in more rounded clusters. The flowers may be dried for arrangements.

Height: 4-5ft (1.2-1.5m)
Spread: 5-6ft (1.5-1.8m)
Hardiness: Zones 4-9

Cultivation: Moisture-retentive fertile soil and a sheltered position in full sun or light shade is needed. It benefits from a mulch of compost or well-decayed manure in spring. In spring, cut the previous season's shoots to the ground. It blooms on new wood.

Propagation: In late summer take 5-6in (10-15cm) long cuttings from non-flowering shoots. Insert them in equal parts moist peat and sharp sand, and place in a cold frame. When rooted, pot up and later plant into a nursery bed until large enough to be transferred into a garden.

Hydrangea paniculata 'Grandiflora'

A stunningly attractive hardy, deciduous shrub, which during late summer and into autumn develops large, pyramidal, terminal heads of creamy-white flowers. These large heads, up to 18in (45cm) long, usually weigh down the stems.

Height: 15-25ft (4.5-7.5m)
Spread: 10-20ft (3-6m)
Hardiness: Zones 3-8

Cultivation: Moisture-retentive fertile, loamy soil is required. Prune plants in spring, cutting back the previous season's shoots by about a half. If very large flower heads are desired, thin out the shoots to seven to ten on each plant. However, severe pruning and thinning decreases the shrub's life. For general garden display, just prune back the stems in spring.

Propagation: In late summer take 5-6in (13-15cm) long cuttings from non-flowering shoots. Insert them in equal parts moist peat and sharp sand, and place in a cold frame until rooted.

Hydrangea arborescens 'Grandiflora' makes a dramatic display when in flower and is especially useful for creating a sheet of white, midsummer flowers alongside a lawn. It is equally attractive when used in a mixed border.

Hydrangea paniculata 'Grandiflora' has such large flower heads that they tend to weigh down stems and cause them to spread. Therefore, do not position it too close to paths or other large shrubs.

TREES AND SHRUBS

Left: Magnolia stellata *During spring this small tree creates a mass of star-like, fragrant, white flowers borne on naked shoots.*

Magnolia stellata

Star Magnolia

A superb deciduous, slow growing tree for small gardens, where it creates a wealth of white, star-like flowers up to 4in (10cm) across during midspring. There are a number of varieties available: 'Centennial' (double, white); 'Royal Star' (larger flowers and hardier than species); 'Rosea' (buds pink, fade to white bloom) and 'Waterlily' (buds pink, fade to white, fragrant).
Height: 8-10ft (2.4-3m)
Spread: 8-12ft (2.4-3.6m)
Hardiness: Zones 5-9
Cultivation: Well-drained, moderately rich, loamy soil is best, but it grows well in most soils. However, it benefits from a sheltered position away from cold north and east winds.
Propagation: During midsummer take 4in (10cm) long heel-cuttings. Insert them in equal parts moist peat and sharp sand, and place in a warm area. When rooted, pot up the cuttings and overwinter in a cold frame. In spring, set young plants in a nursery bed and plant them into a garden about two or three years later.

Left: Prunus laurocerasus 'Otto Luyken' *This small variety of the large common cherry laurel is ideal for small gardens. It can be pruned in early summer.*

Prunus laurocerasus 'Otto Luyken'

Cherry Laurel

This hardy, evergreen low-growing variety of the common cherry laurel develops semi-erect, 3in (7.5cm) long, white candles from mid-summer onwards. The deep green, leathery leaves, 4in (10cm) long and 1in (2.5cm) wide, are tapered.
Height: 3½-4ft (1-1.2m)
Spread: 5-7ft (1.5-2.1m)

Magnolia stellata is a superb magnolia for a small garden. To brighten the soil around and under its extreme edges, plant a medley of small, spring-flowering bulbs such as crocuses and scilla.

Prunus laurocerasus 'Otto Luyken' creates superb groundcover and edging between an informal lawn and an area under tall conifers. Tolerates shade. Water plants regularly to establish them quickly.

dome-shape with silvery-gray leaves when young, later becoming green. During mid-summer it bears masses of yellow, daisy-like flowers.
Height: 5-7ft (1.5-2.1m)
Spread: 6-8ft (1.8-2.4m)
Hardiness: Zones 8-10
Cultivation: Well-drained soil and a position in slight shade to full sun suit it. It grows well in mild coastal areas.
Propagation: During late summer take 3-4in (7.5-10cm) long half-ripe cuttings. Insert them in equal parts moist peat and sharp sand and place in a cold frame. When rooted, plant into a nursery bed until large enough to be set in a garden.

Hardiness: Zones 6-9
Cultivation: Ordinary moist, well-drained soil suits it. It is ideal for creating attractive groundcover. Normally, pruning is not necessary, but large plants can be carefully cut back in early summer.
Propagation: Take 4in (10cm) long cuttings in late summer and early autumn. Insert them in equal parts moist peat and sharp sand. Place in a cold frame. When rooted, plant into a nursery bed until large enough to be set in a garden.

Pyrus salicifolius 'Pendula'

Willow-leaved Pear

An unusual, elegant, deciduous tree with a spreading crown and pendulous branches bearing narrow, lance-shaped, willow-like, silvery-gray leaves. Eventually, the branches hang down nearly to ground level and create a dome completely covered with leaves. During spring it produces clustered heads of pure-white flowers.
Height: 15-20ft (4.5-6m)
Spread: 8-15ft (2.4-4.5m)
Hardiness: Zones 4-8
Cultivation: It is a tree that is tolerant of most conditions, flourishing in poor as well as rich soils. It also grows in areas deprived of moisture, as well as

those which are relatively moist. No regular pruning is needed.
Propagation: This is best left to professional nurserymen.

Senecio compactus

(*Senecio greyi*)

This beautiful evergreen shrub is often sold as, and confused with, *Senecio laxifolius*, which is rarer and reveals a smaller stance. It also has slender, more pointed leaves. There is further confusion with the hybrid *Senecio* 'Sunshine', which is widely sold as *Senecio greyi*. This is a beautiful shrub, forming a broad,

Pyrus salicifolius 'Pendula' looks best when planted in a slightly elevated position. When young and before branches reach the ground it benefits from an underplanting of low-growing, blue-flowered spring bulbs.

Senecio compactus is ideal for planting near to the edge of a lawn or path, its dome-shape neatly but informally creating a sloping edge. It blends well with old paving slabs, but avoid new stones.

Left: Spiraea x arguta *Beautiful spring-flowering shrub, ideal for planting near gates, where it creates a wealth of eye-catching flowers amid a background of fresh-green lance-shaped leaves.*

Spiraea x arguta

Garland Spirea

A hardy deciduous shrub creating a wealth of pure-white flowers from mid- to late spring. They appear in tight, 2in (5cm) wide clusters along the slender, arching stems. It is a hybrid between the well-known Thunberg Spirea, *Spirea thunbergii,* and *S x multiflora.*
Height: 6-7ft (1.8-2.1m)
Spread: 5-7ft (1.5-2.1m)
Hardiness: Zones 3-9
Cultivation: Fertile, well-drained soil and full sun or light shade suits it best. Little pruning is needed, other than occasionally lightly thinning overgrown plants after flowering.
Propagation: Take 8-10in (20-25cm) long hardwood cuttings in autumn. Insert them in a sheltered border, where they take about a year to produce roots.

Spiraea x arguta creates a superb background for other plants, even when not bearing flowers. The small, lance-shaped, fresh-green leaves are ideal for highlighting sweet williams (*Dianthus barbatus*).

Spiraea thunbergii is ideal for planting close to paths and lawn edges, where it produces a wall of white flowers. The light green foliage can be contrasted with the deep greens of evergreens such as yews (*Taxus*) and holly (*Ilex*).

Spiraea thunbergii

Thunberg Spirea

This hardy, deciduous and twiggy shrub from China and Japan is a delight in any shrub or mixed border, creating a wealth of white flowers in dense clusters on slender branches in spring and early summer. The flowers are borne on naked branches, before the leaves appear.
Height: 5-6ft (1.5-1.8m)
Spread: 6-7ft (1.8-2.1m)
Hardiness: Zones 4-9
Cultivation: Deep, well-drained soil and either full sun or light shade suit it.
Propagation: Cuttings 3-5in (7.5-13cm) long of the current season's growth can be taken in mid-summer and inserted in equal parts moist peat and sharp sand. Place in a cold frame. However, it is easier for home gardeners to take 8-10in (20-25cm) long hardwood cuttings in autumn and to insert them in a sheltered nursery bed. They take about a year to form roots.

Styrax japonica

Japanese Snowbell

Small, graceful tree with slender, often drooping branches bearing dark, glossy-green, oval leaves and pure-white bell-shaped flowers with yellow stamens during early summer. It looks best when the flowers can be viewed from below.
Height: 20-30ft (6-12m)
Spread: 20-30ft (6-12m)
Hardiness: Zones 6-8
Cultivation: Moist, acid, well-drained loam in full sun or light shade suits it best. Late frosts can prove disastrous for the flowers. No regular pruning is needed, other than initially shaping the plant and keeping its center open.
Propagation: It can be raised from seeds or half ripe cuttings in summer, but if you already have this tree in your garden it is easier to layer a low-growing shoot in late summer or autumn.

Left: Viburnum opulus 'Roseum' *An outstandingly attractive shrub, with maple-like dark green leaves and large heads of snowy-white flowers in early and midsummer. It makes an eye-catching display.*

Above: Styrax japonica *Clusters of bell-shaped, pure-white flowers with yellow anthers create an eye-catching display during early summer. For effect, allow branches to trail over paths and lawn edges.*

Viburnum opulus 'Roseum'

European Cranberrybush · Snowball

This superb plant has maple-like, dark green leaves and large, rounded heads of snow-white flowers during early and mid-summer. Often, the flower heads are so large that they weigh down the stems. The variety is also known as 'Sterile'.
Height: 6-10ft (1.8-3m)
Spread: 6-10ft (1.8-3m)
Hardiness: Zones 3-8
Cultivation: Plant in well-drained, moisture-retentive soil. No pruning is needed, other than cutting out misplaced and straggly shoots after the flowers fade.
Propagation: Take 3-4in (7.5-10cm) long heel-cuttings in late summer. Insert in equal parts moist peat and sharp sand, and place in a cold frame. When rooted, plant into a nursery bed for two or three years. Alternatively, layer long low-growing shoots in autumn.

Styrax americanus, American snowbell, is a Southeast native shrub that grows 8ft (2.4m) tall and is hardy to Zone 5. The bloom is similar to Japanese snowbell.

Viburnum opulus is available in other varieties: 'Compactum' (only 3-4ft/0.9-1.2m tall), 'Nanum' (a dwarf form) and 'Xanthocarpum' (yellow fruited).

Viburnum plicatum 'Mariesii'

Doublefile Viburnum

During early summer this popular deciduous shrub creates a wealth of white flowers up to 1¾in (4.5cm) wide on tiered branches. The flowers sit on small, erect stalks, resulting, from a distance, in the branches appearing to be covered with snow. It is a shrub that needs space, so that the branches are unrestricted in their spread and not obscured by other plants. The variety 'Lanarth' is similar, but bears slightly larger flowers on longer stalks, with branches less horizontally tiered.

Height: 6-10ft (1.8-3m)
Spread: 6-10ft (1.8-3m)
Hardiness: Zones 5-8
Cultivation: Moisture-retentive loamy soil in full sun or light shade suits it. Avoid planting it under overhanging trees. No regular pruning is needed, other than initially shaping the plant. Cut out dead wood after flowering.
Propagation: The easiest way is to layer low-growing shoots in late summer and early autumn. When rooted, sever from the parent and plant in a nursery bed.

Left: Viburnum plicatum 'Mariesii' *This deciduous shrub seldom fails to brighten gardens in early summer. Its flowers are borne on tiered branches. The dull green, tooth-edged leaves develop beautiful wine-red tints in autumn.*

Viburnum tinus

Laurustinus Viburnum

A tender viburnum, this bushy, dense, evergreen shrub has a round form. Masses of pink-budded white flowers are borne in 2-4in (5-10cm) wide heads from early winter to late spring. The variety 'Eve Price' is compact and slow-growing, making it ideal for hedging.
Height: 6-10ft (1.8-3m)
Spread: 5-7ft (1.5-2.1m)
Hardiness: Zones 8-10
Cultivation: Plant in moisture-retentive soil in a position sheltered from cold winds. It is superb for coastal areas, surviving slight salt spray. Also, it tolerates light shade. During late spring, cut out dead or misplaced shoots.
Propagation: Sow seeds during late summer or early autumn in well-drained seed starting mix, and place in a cold frame. Alternatively, take 3-4in (7.5-10cm) long heel-cuttings during midsummer. Insert them in equal parts moist peat and sharp sand. Place in 61°F (16°C). When rooted, pot up the cuttings and place in a cold frame.

Left: Viburnum tinus *A tender evergreen shrub that brightens winter months with white flowers. These are followed by blue fruits that turn black. It is ideal for planting in coastal areas, where salt spray can be a problem.*

Viburnum plicatum 'Mariesii' should not be obstructed by tall plants. However, when planted in a sea of relatively low-growing plants such as *Pulmonaria saccharata,* lungwort, its beauty is further highlighted.

Viburnum tinus is a welcome evergreen shrub in mild climates. It blooms during winter and is therefore best planted where the flowers can be readily appreciated - by the sides of paths and at the fronts of houses.

Yucca flaccida 'Ivory' Tower

Weakleaf Yucca

Distinctive evergreen shrub native to the Southeast. It has bluish-green leaves up to about 21in (53cm) long and 1½in (4cm) wide. It is a stemless yucca, with leaves arising from soil level, and the whole plant spreads by sucker-like growths. The ends of the leaves bend down slightly, with curly, thread-like growths at their edges. From mid- to late summer it produces erect, 2-2½in (5-6.5cm) long, creamy-white flowers in heads up to 4ft (1.2m) high.
Height: 3-4ft (0.9-1.2m)
Spread: 3-3½ft (0.9-1m)
Hardiness: Zones 4-10
Cultivation: Well-drained light soil and a position in full sun suit it. It grows well in coastal areas.
Propagation: During spring, remove and replant rooted suckers.

Below: **Yucca flaccida 'Ivory Tower'** *Few plants are as distinctive as yuccas, with their tall flower spires. This variety bears creamy-white flowers from mid- to late summer, above sharply-pointed, bluish-green, sword-like leaves.*

Further plants to consider

Betula nigra 'Heritage'
Heritage Birch
Height: 40-60ft (12-18m)   Spread: 40-50ft (12-15m)
Hardiness: Zones 4-9
An adaptable native plant, with creamy-white peeling bark, that is attractive all year. This fast-growing but strong tree is resistant to bronze birch borer.

Buddleia davidii 'White Bouquet'
Butterfly Bush
Height: 7-9ft (2.1-2.7m)   Spread: 7-8ft (2.1-2.4m)
Hardiness: Zones 5-9
Well-known deciduous shrub with long, arching branches that bear large, dense, pyramidal heads of white flowers during mid- to late summer.

Clethra alnifolia
Summersweet · Sweet Pepperbush
Height: 3-8ft (0.9-2.4m)   Spread: 4-6ft (1.2-1.8m)
Hardiness: Zones 3-9
A moisture-loving, deciduous shrub. The light green foliage is a perfect backdrop for the fragrant spires of white flowers in midsummer. The variety 'Rosea' has pink buds that open pink and fade to white.

Deutzia gracilis
Slender Deutzia
Height: 2-4ft (0.6-1.2m)   Spread: 3-4ft (0.9-1.2m)
Hardiness: Zones 4-8
Widely-grown deciduous shrub with arching stems, which bear white flowers during late spring.

Philadelphus coronarius
Mock Orange
Height: 10-12ft (3-3.6m)   Spread: 10-12ft (3-3.6m)
Hardiness: Zones 4-7
Superb deciduous hardy shrub with single, fragrant, white flowers in midsummer. *P. coronarius* 'Aureus' has golden yellow leaves in spring that age to a yellowish-green color.

Roses – Floribunda Types
The floribunda roses are hardy compact plants that bear their flowers in thick clusters. The flowers, which may be single or double, are available in a range of colors, and the plants can bloom from summer to early autumn. Many outstanding cultivars are available, including 'Iceberg', with white flowers, and 'Betty Prior', with fragrant deep pink flowers.

Yucca flaccida 'Ivory Tower' creates an exotic scene in a garden, as well as having a strong 'architectural' appearance. Position at the corners of borders, where they can be seen from several directions. Do not use them excessively, because their dramatic appearance can overpower smaller plants.

GARDEN PLANS

Planning the positions and arrangements of plants is an essential part of designing a garden. The fourteen garden plans detailed on the following pages will help you create attractive color harmonies and contrasts – as well as rich fragrances – throughout your garden. There are ideas to brighten patios, courtyards and porches, as well as flower and shrub borders.

Flowers, as well as leaves and berries, create a virtually inexhaustible color palette for gardeners. In addition, plants with variegated leaves help bring further interest to borders, often throughout the year and there are many robust and hardy variegated evergreen shrubs and climbers to choose from.

The garden plans feature plants taken from a particular part of the color spectrum. The color schemes we have selected are gold and yellow, red and pink, blue and purple and green and white. There are also plans that detail the planning of scented borders.

Each plan indicates the size, color and shape of each plant. An outline drawing identifying each plant through its common and botanical names accompanies each illustration.

Key:
1 *Rosa* 'Belvedere' (pink and double)
2 *Clematis* 'Ernest 'Markham'
3 *Buxus sempervirens* 'Suffruticosa'
4 *Helianthemum nummularium* 'Wisely Pink'
5 *Begonia semperflorens* (red)
6 *Lobelia erinus*

Right: *Bright and attractive porches are essential to all homes. This pink and red theme is especially eye-catching when seen against a white background. Small, urn-like containers complete the design.*

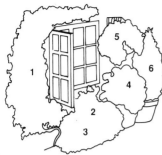

Key:
1 *Rosa* 'Etoile de Holland'
2 *Matthiola longipetala bicornis*
3 *Malcollmia maritima*
4 *Pelargonium x hortorum*
5 *Lobelia erinus, Petunia x hybrida,*
  Pelargonium x hortorum, and
  Tagetes patula
6 *Chamaecyparis pisifera* 'Boulevard'

Above: *Scented flowers planted near windows enrich rooms during the day and at night.*

Key:
1 *Lobelia erinus, Petunia x hybrida,*
  and *Begonia semperflorens*
2 *Cupressus macrocarpa* 'Goldcrest'
3 *Chamaecyparis lawsoniana*
  'Ellwoodii'
4 *Betula nigra* 'Heritage'
5 *Chamaecyparis lawsonia* 'Green
  Pillar'
6 *Chamaecyparis lawsoniana* 'Lutea'
7 *Chamaecyparis lawsoniana* 'Allumii'
8 *Juniperus squamata* 'Meyeri'
9 *Juniperus chinensis* 'Aurea'
10 *Thuja occidentalis* 'Rheingold'
11 *Begonia semperflorens* 'Gin'
12 *Tsuga canadensis* 'Pendula'
13 *Thymus drucei* 'Annie Hall'

Below: *Reds and pinks create a warm, bright and glowing garden.* *These colors contrast well with yellow and gold plants.*

GARDEN PLANS

Above: *Blue plants are eye-catching but can, if used too freely, dominate a garden. Here they contrast well with yellow plants.*

Key:
1   *Picea pungens* 'Thomsen'
2   *Pinus sylvestis* 'Aurea'
3   *Picea pungens* 'Globosa'
4   *Hydrangea macrophylla*
5   *Salix purpurea* 'Pendula'
6   *Cotinus coggygria* 'Norcutt's Variety'
7   *Robinia pseudoacacia* 'Frisia'
8   *Chamaecyparis lawsoniana* 'Columnaris'
9   *Cedrus deodara* 'Golden Horizon'
10   *Juniperus chinensis* 'Pyramidalis'

Below: *Patios steeped in scent and color throughout summer create a superb outside living area.*

Key:
1   *Wisteria floribunda* 'Macrobotrys'
2   *Nicotiana alata* 'Lime Green'
3   *Malcollmia maritima*
4   *Lobularia maritima* 'Wonderland'
5   *Petunia x hybrida*
6   *Laurus nobilis*

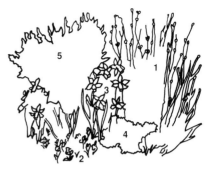

Key:
1. *Forsythia x intermedia*
2. *Crocus vernus*
3. *Narcissus cyclamineus* 'February Gold'
4. *Chionodoxa luciliae*
5. *Cornus alba* 'Siberica'

Left: *Spring is rich in fresh and pretty flowers. These bright-faced plants are especially beautiful.*

Key:
1. *Chamaecyparis lawsonia* 'Lanei'
2. *Chamaecyparis pisifera* 'Filifera Aurea'
3. *Juniperus chinensis* 'Pyramidalis'
4. *Chamaecyparis lawsoniana* 'Ellwoodii'
5. *Juniperus squamata* 'Blue Star'
6. *Spiraea x bumalda* 'Gold Flame'
7. *Chamaecyparis lawsoniana* 'Minima Aurea'
8. *Lysimachia nummularia* and *Petunia x hybrida*
9. *Pelargonium x hortorum*

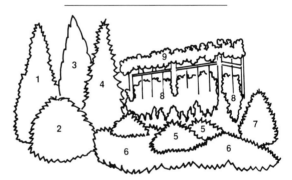

Below: *Yellow flowers and foliage always create a bright, sparkling and colorful garden.*

GARDEN PLANS

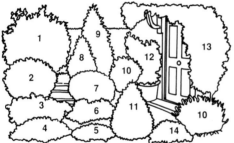

Key:
1 *Philadelphus coronarius*
2 *Lavandula stoechas*
3 *Anacyclus depressus*
4 *Thymus x citriodorus* 'Aureus'
5 *Thymus x citriodorus* 'Silver Queen'
6 *Helianthemum nummularium* 'Beech Park Scarlet'
7 *Ruta graveolens* 'Jackman's Blue'
8 *Chamaecyparis pisifera* 'Boulevard'
9 *Chamaecyparis lawsoniana* 'Lutea'
10 *Lavandula* 'Hidcote'
11 *Chamaecyparis lawsoniana* 'Minima Aurea'
12 *Tropaeolum majus*
13 *Lonicera tragophylla*
14 *Helianthemum nummularium* 'The Bride'

Right: *White borders create a cool and refreshing ambience, and look especially attractive when planted with a background of green foliage plants. Take care not to position plants too close to large hedges, as around their bases the soil may have become dry.*

Key:

1 *Chamaecyparis lawsoniana* 'Minima Aurea'
2 *Tulipa* and *Hyacinthus orientalis*
3 *Narcissus*
4 *Primula x polyantha*
5 *Crocus vernus*
6 *Muscari armeniacum*
7 *Tulipa*, *Crocus*, and *Hyacinthus*
8 *Chamaecyparis lawsoniana* 'Minima Aurea'
9 *Juniperus horizontalis* 'Bar Harbor'

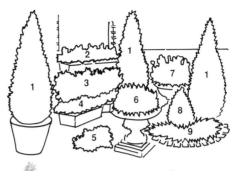

Above: *Window boxes, tubs and troughs create 'instant' color on a patio. Containers can be planted with bulbs and bedding plants, initially placed in an out-of-the way area and later, when creating a bright display, moved into position on a patio or terrace, or in a courtyard. Large, wooden tubs make ideal homes for dwarf and slow-growing conifers.*

Key:

1 *Anaphalis triplinervis*
2 *Rosa* 'Mme. Alfred Carriere'
3 *Rosa* 'Iceberg'
4 *Gypsophilia paniculata*
5 *Hosta* (variegated)
6 *Iberis sempervirens*

GARDEN PLANS

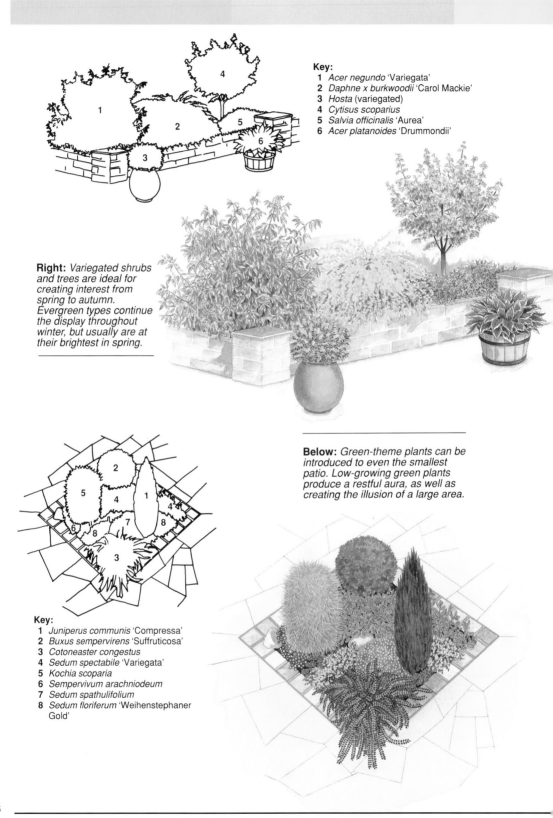

Key:
1. *Acer negundo* 'Variegata'
2. *Daphne x burkwoodii* 'Carol Mackie'
3. *Hosta* (variegated)
4. *Cytisus scoparius*
5. *Salvia officinalis* 'Aurea'
6. *Acer platanoides* 'Drummondii'

Right: *Variegated shrubs and trees are ideal for creating interest from spring to autumn. Evergreen types continue the display throughout winter, but usually are at their brightest in spring.*

Below: *Green-theme plants can be introduced to even the smallest patio. Low-growing green plants produce a restful aura, as well as creating the illusion of a large area.*

Key:
1. *Juniperus communis* 'Compressa'
2. *Buxus sempervirens* 'Suffruticosa'
3. *Cotoneaster congestus*
4. *Sedum spectabile* 'Variegata'
5. *Kochia scoparia*
6. *Sempervivum arachniodeum*
7. *Sedum spathulifolium*
8. *Sedum floriferum* 'Weihenstephaner Gold'

Key:
1 *Hedera helix* 'Tricolor'
2 *Hydrangea arborescens*
3 *Rosa* 'Mme. Alfred Carriere'
4 *Santolina chamaecyparissus*

Above: *Courtyards can be brightened with flowering climbers as well as those with variegated leaves. Tubs packed with small shrubs bring further interest and color.*

Below: *Walls and paving benefit from hanging baskets, climbers, window boxes and tubs. Also, many annuals and small shrubs can be planted into gaps left between the paving.*

Key:
1 *Clematis* 'Henryi'
2 *Arabis caucasica*
3 *Matthiola incana*
4 *Lavandula angustifolia* 'Jean Davis'
5 *Nicotiana sylvestris*
6 *Petunia x hybrida* 'White Cascade'

GLOSSARY

Acid Refers to soils with a pH below 7.0. Most plants grow best in slightly acid soil, about 6.5. However, a few such as azaleas and rhododendrons prefer acid conditions. (*see* pH)

Alkaline Refers to soils with a pH above 7.0. (*see* pH)

Alpine Correctly, a plant that grows on mountains and above the level at which trees normally grow. Usually, however, it means any small plant that can be grown in a rock garden or alpine meadow. Many delicate alpines can also be grown in an alpine house, a form of greenhouse that is unheated, which provides plentiful circulation of air around the plants and prevents their foliage being continually moist, especially in winter.

Annual A plant that grows from seed, and flowers and dies within the same year. There are two types of annual; hardy and half-hardy. The hardy ones can be sown outdoors in spring, in the position where they are to flower. The half-hardy ones are sown in seed flats or pots in the warmth of a greenhouse in late winter or early spring and subsequently planted into a garden as soon as all risk of frost has passed. However, many plants that are not strictly annuals, are treated as such. For instance, *Lobelia erinus* (edging lobelia) is a half-hardy perennial usually raised as a half-hardy annual, and *Mirabilis jalapa* (marvel of Peru) is a perennial grown as a half-hardy annual.

Aquatic Correctly, a plant that grows entirely in water. However, it is generally taken to mean any plant that grows wholly or partly submerged in water, or in wet soil at the edges of a pond.

Anther The pollen-bearing part of a flower. A small stem, known as a filament, supports an anther. Collectively, they are known as stamen. This is the male part of a flower.

Aphids These are the most common of all garden pests. They also invade houseplants. Aphids breed rapidly, sucking sap and transmitting viruses from one plant to another.

Asexual Non-sexual; usually used to refer to the propagation of plants through cuttings and other vegetative methods, rather than by seeds.

Basal The lower leaves on a plant. Sometimes these differ in size and shape from those borne higher up on the plant.

Bedding plant A plant that is raised to create a display at a specific time of year. Spring-flowering bedding plants are planted in autumn for flowering the following spring, and include such plants as wallflowers and pansies. Summer-flowering bedding plants are raised in late winter or early spring and planted into a garden to create color throughout summer.

Biennial A plant that makes its initial growth one year, flowers during the following one and then dies. However, many plants are treated as biennials, although strictly they are not. For instance, the double daisy (*Bellis perennis*) is a hardy perennial usually grown as a biennial. The sweet william (*Dianthus barbatus*) is another perennial invariably raised as a hardy biennial.

Bi-generic hybrid A plant produced by crossing two plants from different genera (plural of genus). This is indicated by placing an X before the plant's botanical name. For instance, the fast-growing *X Cupressocyparis leylandii* (Leyland cypress) has *Cupressus macrocarpa* and *Chamaecyparis nootkatensis* as its parents.

Blind A plant whose growing point has not developed properly and may be distorted.

Bloom This has two meanings; either a flower or a powdery coating, usually on the leaves and stems.

Bog plant A plant that grows in perpetually moist conditions. These are usually found around a pond or alongside a ditch.

Bottom heat The warming, from below, of potting soil or planting medium in which cuttings are inserted when encouraging them to form roots. The warmth is usually provided by electric wires buried under a layer of well-drained and aerated medium. Cuttings inserted in this root rapidly, while seeds sown in boxes and placed on top of cables are often encouraged to germinate quickly.

Bract Botanically, a modified leaf. Some plants have brightly-colored bracts that are more attractive than the proper flower. For example, the eye-catching flowers on the shrub *Cornus kouca chinensis* (Kousa dogwood) are bracts.

Budding A method of propagation, whereby a dormant bud is inserted into a T-cut in the stem of a root-stock. Roses and fruit trees, as well as some shrubs, are often increased in this way.

Bulb A storage organ with a bud-like structure. It is formed of fleshy scales attached to a flattened basal plate. Onions, daffodils and tulips are examples of bulbs. Erroneously, the term is often used to include other underground storage organs, such as corms, tubers and rhizomes, which have different structures.

Bulbil An immature and miniature bulb at the base of a mother bulb. However, some plants, such as the mother fern (*Asplenium bulbiferum*), develop plantlets on their leaves that are also known as bulbils.

Chlorophyll The green coloring material found in all plants, except a few parasites and fungi. It absorbs energy from the sun and plays a vital role in photosynthesis; the process by which plants grow.

Chlorosis A disorder, mainly seen in leaves, when parts reveal whitish areas. It is caused by viruses, mutation or by mineral deficiency in the compost or soil.

Clone A plant raised vegetatively from another, and therefore identical to its parent.

Compost The mixture of vegetable waste which is normally formed into a heap, allowed to rot down and decay, and then either dug into the soil or applied as a mulch for covering the soil around plants.

Compound leaf A leaf formed of two or more leaflets. Compound leaves are characterized by not having buds in their leaf-axils (leaf-joints). All true leaves have buds in their leaf-axils.

Conifer A cone-bearing plant usually with a tree or shrub-like stance, although some are miniature and slow-growing. Includes such plants as pines, firs and spruces. Most conifers are evergreen, but a few such as larches and *Ginkgo biloba* (maidenhair tree) are deciduous.

Cultivar A variety raised in cultivation (*see* Variety).

Container-grown plants A plant grown in a container for subsequent transplanting to its permanent position in a garden. Plants sold in containers include trees, shrubs and rock garden plants. They can be planted into a garden whenever the soil is not waterlogged, frozen or very dry. Because a plant experiences little root disturbance when being transplanted, it soon establishes itself in the soil.

Corm An underground storage organ formed from a laterally swollen stem base. A good example of a corm is a gladiolus. Young corms, cormlets, form around its base, and can be removed and grown in a nursery bed for several seasons before reaching a size when they can be planted into the garden.

Dead heading The removal of faded and dead flowers to encourage the development of further flowers. It also helps to keep plants tidy and to prevent diseases attacking dead and decaying flowers.

Deciduous A plant that loses its leaves at the beginning of its dormant season. This usually applies to trees, shrubs and some conifers. (*see* Conifers).

Division A vegetative method of increasing plants by splitting and dividing roots. It is usually done with herbaceous plants with fibrous roots.

Double flowers These have more than the normal number of petals in their formation.

Evergreen A plant that continuously sheds and grows new leaves through the year, and therefore at any time appears to be 'evergreen'.

Fertilization The sexual union of the male cell (pollen) and the female cell (ovule). Fertilization happens after pollen has alighted on the stigma (pollination), grown down the inside of the style and entered an ovule.

F1 The first filial generation; the result of a cross between two pure-bred parents. F1 hybrids are large and strong plants, but their seeds will not produce replicas of the parents.

Frond The leaf of a palm or fern.

Genus A group of plants with a similar botanical characteristic. Some genera contain many species, others just one and are known as monotypic.

Germination The process that occurs within a seed when given adequate moisture, air and warmth. The coat of the seed ruptures and the seed-leaf (or leaves) grows up towards the light. At the same time a root develops.

Glaucous Grayish-green or bluish-green in color. Usually used to describe the stems, leaves and fruits of ornamental trees and shrubs.

Groundcover A low, ground-hugging plant that forms a mat of foliage over the surface of the soil. It is useful for discouraging weeds, as well as creating a background for other plants.

Half-hardy A plant that can withstand fairly low temperatures, but needs protection from frost. For example, half-hardy annuals raised in the warmth of a greenhouse early in the year and then planted out into the garden as soon as all risk of frost has passed.

Hardening off The gradual accustoming of protected plants to outside conditions. Cold frames are usually used for this purpose.

Hardwood cuttings A vegetative method of increasing plants such as trees and shrubs, as well as some soft fruits; blackcurrants, red currants and gooseberries. A piece of ripe wood is cleanly cut from the parent plant, usually in late summer and autumn, and inserted into a nursery bed in the garden. It is an easy way for home gardeners to increase plants.

Hardy A plant that does not need to be protected from the weather and will survive outside during the cold part of the year.

Heel A hardy, corky layer of bark and stem which is torn off when a sideshoot is pulled away from the main stem while creating a heel-cutting. The heel needs to have its edges cleanly trimmed with a sharp knife before the cutting is inserted into rooting medium.

Heeling-in The temporary planting of trees, shrubs and conifers while awaiting transfer to their permanent position in the garden. Heeling-in is usually necessary when plants have arrived from a nursery at a time when the soil is too wet or too dry to enable them to be planted immediately.

Herbaceous perennial A plant that dies down to soil level in autumn. The plant remains dormant throughout winter and breaks into growth in spring, when the weather improves.

Herbicide A chemical formulation that kills plants and is generally known as a weedkiller. Some herbicides kill all plants they touch, while others are called 'selective' and kill only certain types.

Humus Microscopic, dark brown, decayed vegetable material. It is usually the product of a compost heap.

Hybrid The progeny from parents of different species or genera.

Inflorescence The part of the plant which bears the flowers.

Insecticide A chemical used to kill insects.

Layering A method of vegetatively increasing plants. It is an easy way for a home gardener to propagate plants. Low-growing shoots are lowered to ground level and slightly buried in the soil. By twisting, bending or slitting the stem at the point where it is buried, roots are encouraged to form. Rooting may take up to eighteen months, when the new plant can be severed from its parent and planted into the garden.

Lime An alkaline substance used to counteract the acidity of soil. It also has the property of improving the structure of clay soils by encouraging small particles to group together.

Loam A mixture of fertile soil, formed of sharp sand, clay, silt and organic material.

Mulch A surface dressing of organic material. It conserves moisture in the ground, smothers weeds and increases the nutrient content of the soil.

Naturalize Usually used to refer to the planting of bulbs in an informal display and allowing them to remain there undisturbed. This term can also be applied to other plants which can be left in informal groups, perhaps in a woodland setting or in a 'naturalized' garden.

Neutral Refers to soil that is neither acid nor alkaline. On the pH scale this would be 7.0. (*see* pH).

Nursery bed An area of the garden, in a sheltered and warm position, where newly-rooted and unestablished plants can be grown for several years before they are planted into the garden.

Organic The cultivation of plants without chemical fertilizers or pesticides being used.

Peat Partly decayed vegetable material, usually acid. It is frequently used as a constituent of potting soil, as well as a soil amendment for acid-loving plants.

Perennial Usually used to refer to herbaceous plants, but also to any plant that lives for several years, including trees, shrubs and climbers.

Pesticide A chemical used to kill insects and other pests.

Photosynthesis The food-building process by which chlorophyll in the leaves is activated by sunlight. It reacts with moisture absorbed by roots and carbon dioxide gained from the atmosphere to create growth.

pH A logarithmic scale used to define the acidity and alkalinity of a soil-water solution. Chemically, neutral is

7.0, with figures above indicating increasing alkalinity, and below increasing acidity. Most plants grow well in 6.5-7.0, invariably taken by gardeners to be neutral, rather than the scientific neutral at 7.0.

Pollination When pollen from the anthers falls on the stigma (female part of a flower). Not all pollen grains germinate and develop tubes which grow down the style and fertilize the ovules.

Propagation The raising of new plants.

Pruning The removal, with hand pruners or shears, of parts of woody plants. With fruit trees and bushes this is done to encourage better and more regular fruiting. With shrubs and woody climbers it is carried out to encourage better flowering, as well as to create an attractively shaped plant.

Rhizome An underground or partly buried horizontal stem.

Scree A freely-draining area of grit and small stones for alpine plants. These are plants that need very good drainage.

Shrub A woody perennial with stems growing from soil level. Unlike a tree, it does not have a trunk. However, some plants can be grown as a tree or as a shrub, depending on their initial training or propagation.

Single flowers These have the normal number of petals, arranged in a single row.

Softwood cutting A non-woody cutting with a soft texture.

Species A group of plants with the same characteristics.

Stamen The male part of a flower, formed of anthers and filaments.

Stigma Part of the female part of a flower, on which pollen alights and causes pollination.

Stoma A minute hole, usually on the undersides of leaves, enabling the exchange of gasses. During respiration a plant takes in air from the atmosphere, retaining oxygen and giving off carbon dioxide. During photosynthesis the plant absorbs air, using carbon dioxide and giving off oxygen. The plural of stomata is stoma.

Strain Seed-raised plants from a common ancestor.

Stratify A method of helping seeds with hard seed coats to germinate. The seeds are placed between layers of sand and kept cold, usually during the extent of winter.

Sucker A basal shoot arising from the rootstock of a grafted or budded plant. They should be cut out close to the roots. If necessary, remove soil from around the bases of the suckers so that they can be cut right back to the roots.

Systemic Used to refer to chemicals that are absorbed into a plant's tissue. The time they remain active within a plant depends on the chemical, type of plant and the temperature.

Tender A plant that is damaged by low temperatures.

Thinning The removal of congested seedlings to enable those that remain to grow strongly and to have more space. It can also refer to the removal of surplus shoots, again to allow more light and air to reach those that remain.

Tilth Surface soil which has been broken down, usually in preparation for sowing seeds.

Top-dress Spreading fertilizers or compost on to the surface of the soil around plants.

Top-soil The upper layer of soil, often taken to be the top 10-12in (25-30cm).

Transpiration The loss of water from a plant through stomata. The roots absorb water, which rises through the stems and passes into the atmosphere through the stomata. This is an essential process and has several purposes including helping to keep the plant cool and keeping the plant turgid.

Tuber An underground storage organ, such as a dahlia.

Variegated Multi-colored. Usually referring to the leaves.

Variety A naturally occurring variation of a species. However, the term variety is commonly used to include both true varieties, as well as cultivars. Cultivars are plants which are variations of a species and have been raised in cultivation.

Vegetative A method of propagation, including layering, grafting, budding and cuttings.

Windbreak A shrub, tree or conifer used to create a barrier that reduces the speed of wind and provides shelter for small plants.

INDEX

COMMON NAMES

INDEX

LATIN NAMES